LEFT OUT

Books by Martin Duberman

Left Out (1999)

A Queer World, ed. (1997)

Queer Representations, ed. (1997)

Midlife Queer (1996)

Stonewall (1993)

Cures: A Gay Man's Odyssey (1991)

Mother Earth: An Epic Drama of Emma Goldman's Life (1991)

Hidden from History: Reclaiming the Gay and Lesbian Past,
co-editor (1989)

Paul Robeson (1989)

About Time: Exploring the Gay Past
(first edition, 1986; second edition, 1991)

Visions of Kerouac (1977)

Male Armor: Selected Plays, 1968–1974 (1976)

Black Mountain: An Exploration in Community
(first edition, 1972; second edition, 1993)

The Memory Bank (1970)

The Uncompleted Past (1969)

James Russell Lowell (1966)

The Antislavery Vanguard, ed. (1965)

In White America (1964)

Charles Francis Adams, 1807–1886 (1961)

LEFT OUT

The Politics of Exclusion/
Essays/1964–1999

MARTIN DUBERMAN

BASIC
BOOKS

A Member of the Perseus Books Group

Designed by Rachel Hegarty

FIRST EDITION

A CIP catalog record for this book is available from the Library of
Congress

ISBN 0-465-01744-4

99 00 01 02/ 9 8 7 6 5 4 3 2 1

When we're uncommonly lucky,
family members are also friends
To Belle and Jay Zal
and
to Ron Corwin and Beth Blumenthal

If the misery of our poor be caused not by the laws of nature, but by our institutions, great is our sin.

CHARLES DARWIN
Voyage of the Beagle

CONTENTS

PART III
OLD SAWS/NEW REFRAINS

ACKNOWLEDGMENTS

For an assortment of favors, leads and correctives, my thanks to: Barry D. Adam, John Donatich, Esther Katz, Art Leonard, Stephen O. Murray, Melanie Yolles and Alan Yang. I'm especially grateful to Naomi Weisstein, whose comments on the Introduction led me to some significant reformulations. Many other people offered help of various kinds over the thirty-five-year period I wrote these essays; they are thanked in the notes attached to the individual pieces.

My dear friend and agent, Frances Goldin, was, as she has always been through the years, consistently there for me, constantly smoothing the path. My editor, Richard Fumosa, acquired this book for Basic and has seen it through all its stages; I'm grateful for his expertise and insight.

My partner, Eli Zal, remains my most astute critic. Attuned to my style and quirks, he more than anyone has been able to spot the problematic portions of the book and has helped me to solve them. For that—and for much, much more—I'm grateful. Our dog, Emma, resolutely refused the traditional role of sitting quietly at my feet (after all, she's named for Emma Goldman), thereby greatly extending the editorial process—but we love her.

Author's Note

I n the name of preserving the historical integrity of these essays, I have tried to keep them in much the form in which they were first written. In a few pieces—notably "The 'New' (1997) Scholarship on Race Relations" and "The Divided Left"—I've restored a considerable amount of material that for reasons of space had been cut at the time of their publication. In other essays, I've used postscripts to provide updated statistics and citations so that interested readers can follow a given debate down to the present day. I have also fairly often, in order to clarify a muddy phrase or to extend a thought, replaced a word or tacked on a sentence. Yet in no instance, I want to emphasize, have I tampered with my views or values as originally stated.

I have also had to resist the temptation to retroactively "clean up" some of the terminology and descriptive terms that were common usage when these essays were written but are today outmoded and even offensive. This has meant making myself live with the frustration of reprinting vocabulary—"Negro," for example, or my endemic use in the early essays of "men" (and male pronouns in general) to stand for "men and women"—that is no longer current or acceptable. Preserving the language of the essays as originally written has also meant retaining some cursory remarks (for example, the passing reference to the "Sambo" stereotype in the piece on Styron's *Nat Turner*) that if written today I would either delete or carefully elaborate.

For several essays in this volume the citations are not as full or precise as I would like; the publications in which these pieces first appeared excluded notes, and I can no longer find the manuscript drafts that did contain all the needed references. Finally, it was my initial intention when putting this collection together to avoid excerpting material from any of my books; yet in the name of providing some crucial commentary that I had not written about elsewhere, I decided to break that resolve in compiling the section "Feminism and Gay Men."

Introduction

Generalization doesn't come naturally to me—though in saying as much, I may be risking my credentials as a historian. The older I've gotten, the more wary I've become of the emphatic voice and its confident pronouncements—yes, even when sounded on the left, my home base. Tentativeness, intricacy and interpretative restraint are what now strike me as the hallmarks of a trustworthy account. Surety—confined neither to uninformed youth nor opinionated old age—seems the predictable companion to a closed mind.

I would want to distinguish pronouncements from convictions. These selected political essays of mine over some thirty-five years are full of decided convictions: the baleful influence of corporate culture, the iniquity of many aspects of American foreign policy, the tenacity of white racism, the nonpathological nature of same gender desire, the crippling falsity of the traditional male/female binary. These convictions were mostly formed in the sixties (though as regards gender and sexual orientation have evolved with the times). They remain my basic values in the late nineties.

These values inform my essays and lead me, over and over, strongly to denounce certain aspects of American life. But at the same time, I've tried not to lose sight of our country's positive attributes—of its capacity for intense (if sporadic and moralistic) self-scrutiny; its impulsive (if circumscribed and unpredictable) generosity; its dynamism, fluidity and inventiveness; its boisterously alive diversity. I've always felt myself to be a confirmed if qualified patriot—dismayed and embarrassed at our national shortcomings, but also, like most Americans, a tempered optimist about our potential. Despite my periodic skepticism, I continue, at some rock-bottom and possibly credulous level, to remain convinced that ways will yet be found to move the country in more progressive directions.

To bolster that conviction, I sometimes need to remind myself that it is here, in the land of purported conservatism that, paradoxically, we've seen develop the world's largest and most influential protest movements against institutionalized inequities based on race, gender and sexual orientation (though far less on class, about which—at least since the 1930s—we have held fast to our disingenuous blinders).

These movements have not produced the amount of change that was earlier hoped for and is still required. Disappointment has bred understandable frustration and, in growing circles, despair. Yet in partial alleviation, and in the name of sustaining the activist impulse, it might be well to remember that over the span of forty years much *has* changed.

If class distinctions, racism, sexism and homophobia are hardly dead, the evidence of heightened revulsion against these assorted inequities is, I would argue, real and must not be cynically dismissed as trivial. Likewise, there is an increased appreciation of "difference"—even if it is still more apparent in public rhetoric than in public practice.

If much remains to be done, we are more likely to summon the will to do it if we allow ourselves the comfort of knowing that time has not merely stood still.

Despite our country's bootstrap rhetoric, outsiders in this land of individualism rarely make a go of it alone. As the first essay in this collection—an analysis of the anti-slavery movement of the mid-nineteenth century—attempts to show, improving conditions for those who have been "left out" hinges on the ability of the despised and downtrodden, and their allies, to band together in collective struggle and—whether through appeals to conscience or displays of power—insist on their entitlements.

"Insisting" is no guarantee of "getting." As I argue throughout this volume, and in terms of a variety of social protest movements—the black struggle, the effort to reform the university, the confrontations over American foreign policy, the conflicts relating to gender and sexual orientation—every challenge to entrenched privilege meets with firm resistance which yields, if at all, only gradually.

In the sixties, the eagerness to confront the powers-that-be was fueled by a widespread optimism about our ability to produce social change. That optimism has largely disintegrated, crushed under the weight of accumulated disasters—endemic corruption, the globalization of greed, ethnic rape and genocide, the growing chasm between rich and poor, the indifference of elites and governments alike to the plight of the less fortunate, the ever-spreading ethic of "I'm-all-right-Jack." When optimism about human nature itself ebbs, faith in the prospects of social transformation cannot be sustained.

Such energy for protest as continues to exist in the United States is mostly found in localized settings and in regard to specific issues—police brutality, the deteriorating condition of the schools, the lack of day care facilities, welfare and workfare, toxic waste and so on. The vitality of grass-roots activism is real, even if not widely reported in the national media, and its existence is some consolation for the disintegration of mass movements for reform.

We can also take heart—if we are incorrigible optimists, as I tend to be—from the fact that our country's outsiders remain essentially untamed. They continue to articulate their grievances and to assert their demands, even if not (except, possibly, for the gay movement) with their earlier strength and volume. There is also the growing, if still insufficient, recognition that disenfranchised groups need to transcend their mutual distrust and combine forces if they are to achieve maximum impact on social policy. Additionally helpful is the subversive energy being generated through scholarly research, particularly by feminist, queer and critical race theory.

Despite these positive signs for the future of progressive politics, there is no denying the loss since the sixties of the single most important factor in nurturing and sustaining activism: namely, the conviction that nothing in "human nature" itself stands in the path of significant social transformation. That conviction is now much diluted. It has given way to the view that the evidence from history of our intrinsic wickedness—to say nothing of intrinsic disparities in individual intelligence and talent—must forever militate against attempts to create a more egalitarian world. Conservatives are quick to point with glee to the Bible—the ultimate refuge of the authoritarian mind—as confirmation that "The poor always ye have with you."

The emphasis on innate human depravity serves the privileged well. It allows them to insist that our current institutions—purportedly the wise embodiment of past experience—must be preserved intact against misguided agitators who assail them in the name of some unachievable egalitarianism. In the sixties, radicals on the left recognized this argument for what it was—a convenient cover for those intent on resisting any social rearrangements that might threaten their own hegemony.

Sixties radicals promoted a set of counter views: that so-called disparities in intelligence and talent depend on loaded definitions (and tests) that favor the already privileged; that despite periodic assertions from Social Darwinists (these days dressed up in the Emperor's newest clothes of evolutionary psychology), we in fact know almost nothing about what is "intrinsic" to human nature, or even whether *anything* is—with the exception of a few physiological constraints, like sleep, hunger and sex, which can themselves be abrogated by culture or by individual agency, dire though the survival consequences can be; that "human nature"(as Naomi Weisstein pointed out thirty-two years ago in her pioneering essay, "Kinder, Kirche, Küche as Scientific Law: Psychology Constructs the Female") is whatever a given culture at a given point in time *tells* us it is—and then socializes us to behave accordingly.

The insistence on hereditary limitations, with its emphasis on human helplessness, functions to persuade us that calls for substantive social change are a chimera peddled by fatuous left-wing romantics. Thus James Q. Wilson, the influential Harvard sociologist, can produce a book (*Crime and Human Nature*) that—despite the spectacular evidence of vastly different rates of crime in different cultures—essentially argues that criminals are born not made. Social circumstances, Wilson insists, have little or nothing to do with criminal behavior. Some people (and especially blacks) are simply born with "bad" genes. Since they cannot be changed or "reformed," the focus must be on protecting society—lock 'em up!

Inconveniently for the conservative view, a large literature has recently emerged, particularly from biology, psychology, anthropology and primate studies, to challenge the notion of "intrinsic depravity." An abundance of findings now suggests that human nature—to the extent one can responsibly say anything at all about it—is, foundationally, structured by the capacity for compassion and the need for affiliation.

The "inevitability" of male dominance? Read the new generation of primatologists on our close relatives the bonobos and lemurs, among whom male aggression toward females is low. In Frans de Waal's *Bonobo: The Forgotten Ape*, for example, we discover a matriarchal social world in which the males are relatively gentle, peaceful and ambisexual. Previously, primatology had been dominated by masculinist researchers who tended to focus on primates—chimpanzees, for example—exhibiting more pronounced (or more easily exaggerated) male aggression—thus providing reassuring confirmation of the primatologists' own starting assumptions about the "inevitability" of patriarchy.

The male sex drive is stronger than the female? Recent work by (among many others) researchers Jeanne Altmann (*Baboon Mothers and Infants*) or Patricia Adair Gowaty (*Feminism and Evolutionary Biology*) underscores the prevalence of *female* sexual adventuring and aggressiveness in the animal kingdom. It won't do to beg off with self-serving excuses about the "forbiddingly technical" nature of scientific work: we now have Natalie Angier's *Woman*, a scholarly yet accessible single-volume summary of how recent research has exploded the many long-standing myths about the presumably profound differences between males and females.

Innate human selfishness? There's a wealth of new material from a variety of disciplines and perspectives on our striking capacity for empathy: the zoologist Matt Ridley (*The Origins of Virtue*), teacher Vivian Gussin Paley (*The Kindness of Children*), philosopher Elliot Sober and biologist David Sloan Wilson's *Unto Others: The Evolution and Psychology of Unselfish Behavior*, scientists Richard Lewontin, Steven Rose and Leon Kamin (*Not in Our Genes*), primatologist Frans de Waal (*Peacekeeping Among Primates*), anthropologist Stuart Schlegel (*Wisdom from a Rainforest*)—all of whom (and many others) present persuasive evidence about the centrality to our makeup of compassion. Sympathetic feelings about the plight of others appear (contra Piaget) from infancy: newborn babies will cry in response to the cries of another infant.

Many researchers have also noted dramatic instances of altruism in animals. But here, too, we find the more markedly new interpretations forced to compete with influential commentators still devoted to older notions of patriarchal selfishness. Many psychoanalysts have remained fixated on two and only two motivational sources for altruism: masochism and the need to discharge unconscious guilt or shame. Behaviorists still see altruistic behavior as a device for allowing people to make themselves feel good by doing good. Sociobiologists describe altruism as an evolutionary survival strategy. Game theorists use the "prisoner's dilemma" model that describes human cooperation as arising from a combination of restraint and retaliation. In Robert Trivers's version (*Social Evolution*), which he calls "reciprocal altruism," we risk our lives to help strangers on the assumption that one day someone will do the same for us.

Yet even from the perspective that views cooperation as a form of self-interest, there is an implicit acknowledgment that human beings do have the capacity (however complex the origins) of reaching out to others. There seems to be agreement, moreover, despite all the explanatory variations, that one conspicuous quality of human life is the possibility of cooperation among *non*-relatives.

Some theories of altruism dispense altogether with the "selfish" component. A number of researchers have pointed to the fact that among several species of primates, members of a troop will raise an orphaned member of another troop—without thereby deriving any discernible advantage for themselves. And the sociologist Samuel Oliner, who has studied non-Jews who rescued Jews from the Nazis, has concluded that some people do good deeds because they are products of a particular family environment: of parents who are warmly nurturant but also moralizing, who passionately convey their humanitarian values to their children even as they simultaneously instill in them high self-regard and a conviction of their own competence (the latter being crucial in allowing for potentially dangerous risk-taking). The emotionally stunted do not involve themselves in good works.

Conservatives regard disobedience to authority as the telltale crime, the Original Sin, and its eternal consequence is our Fallen Nature. But if one is not a biblical fundamentalist, it is possible to note (and to find confirmation in current research for) other human attributes and capacities—curiosity, creativity, playfulness, compassion—and above all, malleability, from which it becomes possible to conclude that nothing we yet know about biology (or ever knew about Original Sin) dictates inherent obstacles to change, whether on an individual or social level, whether trivial or profound.

The past, it can be argued, needn't determine the future—unless we assume that it must. Insufficient courage, not inherent corruption, may be what places limits, narrows options. Human history may indeed be the overwhelming story of war, pillage and violence, but it hasn't been remotely proven that such behavior is genetically rather than situationally driven. What we've been taught glibly to label "instinctual" may be better seen as cultural—not given by nature but acquired through learning. We went to war in Southeast Asia because certain men with large power (given them by a social institution, the State) but limited perspective made bad decisions—not because people everywhere and always *must* seek aggrandizement through aggression and murder.

The Israeli novelist and critic Amos Oz, in analyzing the kibbutz experience, has written eloquently of the demonstrable human "yearning for fellowship."[1] Far from being one-dimensional predators, he argues, we gravitate, *under conditions that encourage us to*, toward connectedness and cooperation. As Oz puts it in regard to life on the kibbutz, there develops "a certain amount of spontaneous solidarity . . . [an openness] to voluntary sharing and . . . an ongoing sense of mutual responsibility between people who were not related by blood or marriage, and were not subordinate to any higher or external authority." What the kibbutz experience, for all of its many complicated failures, demonstrates, Oz concludes, "is a potential source of inspiration for future social reformers who can try to avoid its shortcomings."

Such potential for affiliation isn't widely advertised, or credited—most people, after all, don't read journals devoted to anthropology or primatology. Instead, many Americans, including left-wing ones, have, as balm for the failures and frustrations of the past three decades, retreated for comfort to the older, Calvinist argument from depravity—a view that has always been the pessimistic underpinning to our country's otherwise buoyant value structure.

But real comfort lies elsewhere: in a renewed emphasis—not easy in this cynical climate—on human possibilities rather than limitations. As we approach the year 2000, we need to wrest the festivities from the Christian moralists whose vocation it is to cramp our spirit and dampen down our dreams. At the risk of confirming the accusation that we are indeed naive utopians, we need to reject the popular, one-dimensional view of human beings as "killer apes" (which *is* naive) and say *something* of our unsung capacities for kindness, nurturance and harmony. It is the height of reality to emphasize the existence of what is not commonly seen, the height of unreality to deny any possibilities beyond what we can currently document within our own circles.

We must stay on the left, or move there, because it's only on the left that one hears truths not otherwise acknowledged: that human agency, not biology or the Deity, has created the structures of inequality with which we now live, structures that have long ensured that privilege, wealth and power remain the possession of the few and immiseration the lot of the many.

PART ONE

Histories of Oppression

I

Race

The Northern Response to Slavery (1964)*

The abolitionist movement never became the major channel of Northern antislavery sentiment. It remained in 1860 what it had been in 1830: the small but not still voice of radical reform. An important analytical problem thus arises: why did most Northerners who disapproved of slavery become "nonextensionists" rather than abolitionists? Why did they prefer to attack slavery indirectly, by limiting its spread, rather than directly, by seeking to destroy it wherever it existed?

On a broad level, the answer involves certain traits in our national character. Any radical attack on social problems, suggesting as it would fundamental institutional defects rather than occasional malfunctions, would compromise our engrained optimism. And so the majority has generally found it necessary to label "extreme" any measures that call for

---

* I want to re-emphasize here what I've said in my Author's Note. To preserve the integrity of the moment, I've had to bite my tongue and retain common usage at the time these essays were written. Thus I have not changed "Negro" to African American or black, nor "men" to "men and women." It is precisely the social movements I write about in this collection that brought about later changes in vocabulary—which is really to say, in consciousness. The use of "men" to cover "men and women" is especially jarring in this first essay because so many women were active in the abolitionist movement, and quite a few held leadership positions.

large-scale readjustment. Our traditional recoil from "extremism" can be defended. Complex problems, it might be said, require complex solutions, or, to be more precise, complex problems have no solutions—at best, they can be partially adjusted. If even this much is to be possible, the approach must be flexible, piecemeal, pragmatic. Clear-cut blueprints for reform, with their "utopian" demand for total solutions, intensify rather than ameliorate disorder.

There is much to be said for this defense of the American way—in the abstract. The trouble is that the theory of gradualism and the practice of it have not been the same. Too often Americans have used the gradualist argument as a technique of evasion rather than as a tool for change, not as a way of dealing with difficult problems slowly and carefully, but as an excuse for not dealing with them at all. We do not want time for working out our problems—we do not want problems, and we will use the argument of time as a way of not facing them. As a chosen people, we are meant only to have problems that are self-liquidating. All of which is symptomatic of our conviction that history is the story of inevitable progress, that every day in every way we will get better and better whether or not we make any strenuous efforts toward that end.

Before 1845, the Northern attitude toward slavery rested on this comfortable belief in the benevolence of history. Earlier, during the 1830s, the abolitionists had managed to excite a certain amount of uneasiness about the institution by invoking the authority of the Bible and the Declaration of Independence against it. Alarm spread still further when mobs began to prevent abolitionists from speaking their minds or publishing their opinions, and when the national government interfered with the mails and the right of petition. Was it possible, people began to ask, that the abolitionists were right in contending that slavery, if left alone, would not die out but expand, would become more not less vital to the country's interests? Was it possible that slavery might even end by infecting free institutions themselves?

The apathetic majority was shaken, but not yet profoundly aroused; the groundwork for widespread antislavery protest was laid, but its flowering awaited further developments. The real watershed came in 1845, when Texas was annexed to the Union, and war with Mexico followed. The prospect now loomed of a whole series of new slave states. It finally seemed clear that the mere passage of time would not bring a solution; if slavery was ever to be destroyed, more active resistance would be necessary. For the first time large numbers of white Northerners prepared to challenge the dogma that black slavery was a local matter in which the free states had no concern. A new era of widespread, positive resistance to slavery had opened.

Yet such new resolve was not channeled into a heightened demand for the abolition of the institution, but only into a demand that its further extension be prevented. By 1845 Northerners may have lost partial but not total confidence in "Natural Benevolence"; they were now wiser Americans perhaps, but Americans nonetheless. More positive action against slavery, they seemed to be saying, was indeed required, but nothing too positive. Containing the institution would, in the long run, be tantamount to destroying it; a more direct assault was unnecessary. In this sense, the doctrine of nonextension was but a more sophisticated version of the standard faith in "time."[1]

One need not question the sincerity of those who believed that nonextension would ultimately destroy slavery, in order to recognize that such a belief partook of wishful thinking. Even if slavery was contained, there remained large areas in the Southern states into which the institution could still expand; even without further expansion, there was no guarantee that slavery would cease to be profitable; and finally, even should slavery cease to be profitable, there was no certainty that the South, psychologically, would feel able to abandon it. Nonextension, in short, was far from a foolproof formula. Yet many Northerners chose to so regard it.

And thus the question remains: why did not an aroused antislavery conscience turn to more certain measures and demand more unequivocal action? To many, a direct assault on slavery meant a direct assault on private property and the Union as well. As devout Lockians, Americans did believe that the sanctity of private property constituted the essential cornerstone for all other liberties. If property could not be protected in a nation, neither could life nor liberty. And the Constitution, many felt, had upheld the legitimacy of holding property in men. True, the Constitution had not mentioned slavery by name, and had not overtly declared in its favor, but in giving the institution certain indirect guarantees (the three-fifths clause, noninterference for twenty-one years with the slave trade, the fugitive slave proviso), the Constitution had seemed to sanction it. At any rate no one could be sure. The intentions of the Founding Fathers remained uncertain, and one of the standing debates of the antebellum generation was whether the Constitution had been designed as a pro- or an antislavery document.[2] Since the issue was unresolved, Northerners remained uneasy, uncertain how far they could go in attacking slavery without at the same time attacking property.

Fear for property rights was underscored by fear for the Union. The white South had many times warned that if her rights and interests were not heeded she would leave the Union and form a separate confederation. The tocsin had been sounded with enough regularity so that some dismissed it as mere bluster. But there was always the chance that if the South felt sufficiently threatened it might yet carry out the threat.

It is difficult today fully to appreciate the horror with which most white Northerners regarded the potential breakup of the Union. Lincoln struck a deep chord for his generation when he spoke of the Union as the "last best hope of earth"; that the American experiment was thought the "best" hope may have been arrogant, a hope at all, naive, but such it was to the average American, convinced of his own superiority and the possibility of the world learning by example. Americans, enamored of their own extraordinary success story, were especially prone to look on love of country as one of the noblest of human sentiments. Even those Southerners who had ceased to love the Union had not ceased to love the idea of nationhood; they merely wished to transfer allegiance to a more worthy object.

The difficulty was compounded by the North's ambivalent attitude toward the Negro. The white Northern majority, unlike most of the abolitionists, did not believe in the equality of races. The Bible was read to mean, and the new science of anthropology was said to "confirm" the view, that the Negro had been a separate, inferior creation meant for a position of servitude.[3] Where there was doubt on the doctrine of racial equality, its advocacy by the distrusted abolitionists helped to settle the matter in the negative.

It was possible, of course, to believe in Negro inferiority, and yet disapprove of Negro slavery. Negroes were obviously men, even if an inferior sort, and as men they could not in conscience (the Christian-Democratic version) be denied the right to control their own souls and bodies. But if anti-Negro and anti-slavery sentiments were not actually incompatible, they were not mutually supportive either. Doubt of the Negro's capacity for citizenship continually blunted the edge of anti-slavery fervor. If God had intended the Negro for a subordinate role in society, perhaps a kind of benevolent slavery was, after all, the most suitable arrangement; as long as there was uncertainty, it might be better to await the slow unfolding of His intentions in His good time.

And so the average Northerner, even after he came actively to disapprove of slavery, continued to be hamstrung in his opposition to it by the competitive pull of other values. Should prime consideration be given to freeing the slaves, even though in the process the rights of property and the preservation of the Union were threatened? Should the future of the superior race be endangered in order to improve the lot of a people seemingly marked by Nature for a degraded station? Ideally, the North would have liked to satisfy its conscience about slavery and at the same time preserve the rest of its value system intact—

to free the Negro and yet do so without threatening property rights or dislocating the Union. This struggle to achieve the best of all possible worlds runs like a forlorn hope throughout the antebellum period—the sad, almost plaintive quest by the American Adam for the perfect world he considered his birthright.

The formula of nonextension did seem, for a time, the ideal formula for balancing these multiple needs. Nonextension would put slavery in the course of ultimate extinction without producing excessive dislocation; since slavery would not be attacked directly, nor its existence immediately threatened, the South would not be unduly fearful for her property rights, the Union would not be needlessly jeopardized, and a mass of free Negroes would not be precipitously thrust upon an unprepared public. Nonextension, in short, seemed a panacea: it promised in time to do everything while for the present risking nothing. But like all panaceas, it ignored certain hard realities: Would containment really lead to the extinction of slavery? Would the South accept even a gradual dissolution of her peculiar institution? Would it be right to sacrifice two or three more generations of Negroes in the name of uncertain future possibilities? Alas for the American Adam, so soon to be expelled from Eden.

The abolitionists, unlike most Northerners, were not willing to rely on future intangibles. Though often called impractical romantics, they were in some ways the most tough-minded of Americans. They had no easy faith in the benevolent workings of time or in the inevitable triumphs of gradualism. If change was to come, they argued, it would be the result of man's effort to produce it; patience and inactivity had never yet solved the world's ills. Persistently, sometimes harshly, the abolitionists denounced delay and those who advocated it; they were tired, they said, of men using the councils of moderation to perpetuate injustice.

Historians have long assumed that the abolitionists were unified in their advocacy of certain broad policies—immediate emancipation, and without compensation—and also unified in refusing to spell out "practical" details for implementation. The abolitionists did agree almost unanimously (Gerrit Smith was one of the few exceptions) that slaveholders must not be compensated. One does not pay a man, they argued, for ceasing to commit a sin. Besides, the slaveholder had already been paid many times over in labor for which he had never given wages. Though told that public opinion would never support the confiscation of property, the abolitionists stood firm. They saw themselves as prophets, not politicians; they were concerned with what was "right," not with what was possible, though they hoped that if men were once made aware of the right, they would find some practical way of implementing it.[4]

The abolitionists were far less united on the doctrine of immediate emancipation, that is, in the 1830s, before Southern intransigence and British experience in the West Indies convinced almost all of them that gradualism was hopeless. But during the 1830s, there was a considerable spectrum of opinion as to when and how to emancipate the slaves. Contrary to common myth, some of the abolitionists did advocate a period of prior education and training before the granting of full freedom. Men like Weld, Birney and the Tappans, stressing the debasing experience of slavery, insisted only that gradual emancipation be immediately begun, not that emancipation itself be at once achieved.[5] This range of opinion has never been fully appreciated. Indeed, it might be well to ask whether the abolitionists, in moving steadily toward "immediatism" were not, at least in part, driven to that position by the intransigence of their society in the preceding decade, rather than by any inherent "extremism" in their own temperaments. It has been convenient, then and now, to believe that all abolitionists always advocated instantaneous freedom, for it thus became possible to denounce any call for emancipation as "patently impractical."

By 1840, however, most abolitionists *had* become immediatists. They had come to see that not even the most gradual plan for doing away with slavery held any widespread appeal in the country, and had also come to feel the compelling moral urgency of immediatism. Men learned how to be free, the abolitionists had come to believe by 1840, only by being free; slavery, no matter how attenuated, was by its very nature incapable of preparing men for those independent decisions necessary to adult responsibility. Besides, they insisted, the Negro, though perhaps debased by slavery, was no more incapacitated for citizenship than were many poor whites, whose rights no one seriously suggested curtailing. If conditions to emancipation were once established, they could be used as a standing rationale for postponement; the Negro could be kept in a condition of semislavery by the self-perpetuating argument that he was not yet ready for his freedom.[6]

Moreover, any intermediary stage before full freedom would require the spelling out of precise "plans," and these would give the enemies of emancipation an opportunity to pick away at the "impracticality" of this or that detail. They would have an excuse for disavowing the broader policy under the guise of disagreeing with the specific means for achieving it. Better to concentrate on the larger issue and force men to take sides on that alone, the abolitionists argued, than to give them a chance to hide their opposition behind some supposed disapproval of detail. Wendell Phillips, for one, saw the abolitionists' role as exclusively that of agitating the broader question. Their primary job, Phillips insisted, was to arouse the country's conscience rather than to spell out to it precise plans and formulas. *After* that conscience had been aroused, it would be time to talk of specific proposals; let the moral urgency of the problem be recognized, let the country be brought to a determination to rid itself of slavery, and ways and means to accomplish that purpose would be readily enough found.[7]

No tactical position could really have saved the abolitionists from the denunciation of those hostile to their basic goal. If the abolitionists spelled out a program for emancipation, their enemies could nitpick it to death. If they did not spell out a program, they could then be accused of vagueness and impracticality. Hostility can always find its own justification.[8]

A second mode of attack on the abolitionists has centered on their personalities rather than their policies. The stereotype which has long had currency sees the abolitionist as a disturbed fanatic, a man self-righteous and self-deceived, motivated not by concern for the Negro, as he may have believed, but by an unconscious drive to gratify certain needs of his own. Seeking to discharge either individual anxieties or those frustrations which came from membership in a "displaced elite," his antislavery protest was, in any case, a mere disguise for "personal anguish."

Underlying this analysis is a broad assumption that has never been made explicit—namely, that strong protest by an individual against social injustice is ipso facto proof of his disturbance. Injustice itself, in this view, is apparently never sufficient to arouse unusual ire in "normal" men, for normal men, so goes the canon, are always cautious, discreet, circumspect. Those who hold to this model of human behavior seem rarely to suspect that it may tell us more about their hierarchy of values than about the reform impulse it pretends to describe. Argued in another context, the inadequacies of the stereotype become more apparent: if normal people do not protest "excessively" against injustice, then we should be forced to condemn as neurotic all those who protested with passion against Nazi genocide.

Some of the abolitionists, it is true, *were* palpable neurotics, men who were not comfortable within themselves and therefore not comfortable with others, men whose "reality-testing" was poor, whose life-styles were pronouncedly compulsive, whose relationships were unusual compounds of demand and fantasy. Such neurotics were in the abolitionist movement—the Parker Pillsburys, Stephen Fosters, Abby Folsoms. Yet even here we must be cautious, for our diagnostic accuracy can be blurred if the lifestyle under evaluation is sharply different from our own. Many of the traits of the abolitionists which today "put us off" were not peculiar to them, but rather to their age—the declamatory style, the abstraction and idealization of issues, the tone of righteous certainty, the religious context of argumentation. Thus the evangelical rhetoric of the movement, with its thunderous emphasis on sin and retribution, can sound downright "peculiar" (and thus "neurotic") to the twentieth-century skeptic, though in its day common enough to abolitionists and nonabolitionists alike.

Then, too, even when dealing with the "obvious" neurotics, we must be careful in the link we establish between their pathology and their protest activity. It is one thing to demonstrate an individual's "disturbance" and quite another then to explain all of his behavior in terms of it. Let us suppose, for example, that Mr. Jones is a reformer; he is also demonstrably "insecure." It does not necessarily follow that he is a reformer *because* he is insecure. The two may seem logically related (that is, if one's mind automatically links "protest" with "neurosis"), but we all know that many things can seem logical without being true.

Even if we establish the neurotic behavior of certain members of a group, we have not, thereby, established the neurotic behavior of all members of that group. The tendency to leap from the particular to the general is always tempting, but because one benighted monsignor has been caught with a Boy Scout does not mean we have conclusively proven that all priests are pederasts. Some members of every group are disturbed; put the local police force, the Medal of Honor winners, or the faculty of a university under the Freudian microscope, and the number of cases of "palpable disturbance" would probably be disconcertingly high. But what precisely does their disturbance tell us about the common activities of the group to which they belong—let alone about the activities of the disturbed individuals themselves?

Actually, behavioral patterns for many abolitionists do *not* seem notably eccentric. Men like Birney, Weld, Lowell, Quincy—abolitionists all—formed good relationships, saw themselves in perspective, played and worked with zest and spontaneity, developed their talents, were aware of worlds beyond their own private horizons. They all had their tics and their traumas—as who does not—but the evidence of health is abundant and predominant. Yet most historians have preferred to ignore such men when discussing the abolitionist movement. And the reason, I believe, is that such men conform less well to the assumption that those who become deeply involved in social protest are necessarily those who are deeply disturbed.

Yet recent work in psychology suggests that the very definition of maturity may be the ability to commit oneself to abstract ideals, to get beyond the selfish, egocentric world of children.[9] This does not mean that every man who reaches outward does so from mature motives; public involvement may also be a way of acting out disturbed fantasies. The point is only that "political commitment" need not be a symptom of personality disorder. It is just as likely to be a symptom of maturity and health.

It does not follow, of course, that all abolitionists protested against slavery out of "mature" motives; some may have been, indeed were, "childish neurotics." But if we agree that slavery was a fearful injustice, and if motivational theory now suggests that injustice will bring forth protest from mature men, it seems reasonable to conclude that at least some of those who protested strongly against slavery must have done so from "healthy" motives.

The hostile critic will say that the abolitionists protested too strongly to have been maturely motivated. But when is a protest too strong? For a defender of the status quo, the answer (though never stated in these terms) would be: when it succeeds. For those not dedicated to the status quo, the answer is likely to be: a protest is too strong when it is out of all proportion to the injustice it indicts. Could any non-violent protest have been too strong against holding fellow human beings as property? From a moral point of view, certainly not, though from a practical point of view, perhaps. That is, the abolitionist protest might have been too strong if it somehow jeopardized the very goal it sought to achieve—the destruction of human slavery. But no one has yet shown this to have been the case.

In this regard, there has been a persistent confusion of two separate indictments against the abolitionists: first, that they disrupted the peace, and second (in the classic formulation given by Daniel Webster), that they "bound more firmly than before" the bonds of the slave. It is undeniably true that the abolitionists contributed to the polarization of public opinion and, to that extent, to the "disturbance of the peace."

But it does not follow that because they stirred up passions, they made freeing the slaves more difficult. This would be true only if it could be shown that the slaves could have been freed without first arousing and polarizing opinion. The evidence does not support such an argument. In all the long years before the abolitionists began their campaign, the North had managed to remain indifferent to the institution, and the South had done almost nothing, even in the most gradual way, toward ameliorating it. Had the abolitionists not aroused public debate on slavery, there is no guarantee that anyone else would have; and without such a debate it is most unlikely that measures against the institution would have been taken.

The fact that the debate became heated, moreover, cannot wholly be explained by the terms in which the abolitionists raised it; what must also be taken into account is the fact that the white South, with some possible exceptions in the border area, reacted intransigently to any criticism of the institution, however mild the tone or gradual the suggestions.

At any rate, current findings in motivational theory suggest that when discussing the abolitionists we must cease dealing in blanket indictments, in simple-minded categorizing and elementary stereotyping. Such exercises may satisfy our present-day hostility to reformers, but they do not satisfy the complex demands of historical truth. We need an awareness of the wide variety of human beings who became involved in the abolitionist movement, and an awareness of the complexity of human motivation sufficient to save us from summing up men and movements in two or three unexamined adjectives.

Surely there is now evidence enough to suggest that commitment and concern need not be aberrational; they may represent the profoundest elements of our humanity. Surely there are grounds for believing that those who protested strongly against slavery were not all misguided fanatics or frustrated neurotics—though by so believing it becomes easier to ignore the injustice against which they protested. Perhaps it is time to ask whether the abolitionists, in insisting that slavery be ended, were indeed those men of their generation furthest removed from reality, or whether that description should be reserved for those Northerners who remained indifferent to the institution, and those Southerners who defended it as a "positive good." From the point of view of these men, the abolitionists were indeed mad, but it is time we questioned the sanity of the point of view.

Those Northerners who were not indifferent to slavery—a large number after 1845—were nonetheless prone to view the abolitionist protest as "excessive," for it threatened the cherished values of private property and Union. The average Northerner may have found slavery disturbing, but convinced as he was that the Negro was an inferior, he did not find slavery monstrous. Certainly he did not think it an evil sufficiently profound to risk, by "precipitous action," the nation's present wealth or its future power. The abolitionists were willing to risk both. They thought it tragic that men should weigh human lives on the same scale as material possessions and abstractions of government. It is no less tragic that we continue to do so.

—*from* The Antislavery Vanguard *(1965)*

The Latest Word on Slavery in the United States (1974)

The already famed study of slavery in the United States, *Time on the Cross*, has been hailed as the masterwork of the new (1974) "cliometric" school of history. The huge amount of attention and acclaim given the book tells us more, it seems to me, about our collective state of mind these days than about the book itself.

On one level, the acclaim is understandable enough. *Time on the Cross* comes equipped with the heavy hardware of technology: statistical tables, data banks, graphs, mathematical formulas, computer print-outs. All properly socialized Americans greet such evidence of Science with surface adulation and underlying fear.

It's important to be fair: one can't attack the arcane terminology of technology simply because it's arcane. Every unique enterprise is entitled to invent a vocabulary, and if it isn't readily comprehensible, the fault may lie with us—with *our* failure to develop the necessary skills or apply the needed concentration.

Moreover, authors Robert Fogel and Stanley Engerman themselves warn against extremists in the cliometric camp who would claim that the writing of history can be reduced to a set of equations. The "systematic component of human behavior" is limited, they admit, and the ways in which "systematic and chance factors interact with each other in political, economic, and social life" are difficult to disentangle. Indeed, in a speech delivered after the publication of *Time on the Cross,* Fogel has gone so far as to say that writing the book "has been a chastening experience"; it has made him recognize that "history is, and very likely will remain, primarily a humanistic discipline."

With the authors thus modestly narrowing the claims of quantification, and with all historians except those who still write with quill pens agreeing that the quantifiers have long since established the usefulness of their methodology in answering certain limited kinds of questions, one needn't waste time taxing Fogel and Engerman with the defense of a view they don't hold, nor in foolishly denouncing all statistical work in the social sciences as misguided. The extreme positions are not at issue.

The real question is whether in *practice* Fogel and Engerman stay within the modest parameters they have rhetorically drawn—whether they scrupulously limit their conclusions to what the nature of the evidence warrants. My overall judgment is that they do not—that they violate their own cautious guidelines, pronouncing grandly, even recklessly, from a sometimes narrow base of evidence, and that the evidence itself has often been critically influenced by their own unexamined assumptions.

The new portrait of slavery that Fogel and Engerman have drawn consists of a number of "major correctives" to the traditional view: slavery, the authors hold, was generally a profitable investment: "the slave system was not economically moribund on the eve of the Civil War" and in the decade preceding, slaveowners had been optimistic about continuing prosperity; slave labor was not inefficient—to the contrary, it was 35 percent more efficient than free labor; "the typical slave field hand was not lazy, inept, and unproductive"—even when performing industrial work, slave labor "compared favorably with free workers in diligence and efficiency"; "the belief that slave-breeding, sexual exploitation, and promiscuity destroyed the black family is a myth"; "the material (not psychological) conditions of the lives of slaves compared favorably with those of free industrial workers"; "slaves were exploited in the sense that part of the income that they produced was expropriated by their owners," but the rate of expropriation was much lower than has generally been presumed: "over the course of his lifetime the typical slave field hand received about 90 percent of the income he produced."

Fogel and Engerman credit their "discoveries" not only to cliometric techniques but also to their use of "hitherto neglected sources." Their research *has* been massive, the amount of documentation extraordinary. All the more reason why they needn't have glamorized their efforts nor disparaged those who came before. They talk of going "into the deepest recesses of the National Archives" as if that well-explored depository in Washington was Terra Incognita and they the fearless mariners of the Santa Maria.

This sits especially ill because Fogel and Engerman sometimes do *less* well than traditional historians in providing the kind of citations that would allow other scholars to recheck their data—and replication is, after all, *the* essential feature of scientific procedure. We're told at one point that 19 plantations were examined—but not which plantations. We're given conclusions based on "33 estates"—but not told where they were located. This rudimentary failure in scholarly citation is, ironically, a failure in precision, the supposed strength of the cliometric school.

Fogel and Engerman have also made some curious (to use a more benign adjective than may be warranted) choices in deciding which historians to discuss and in what tone. They begin their long historiographical essay on the literature of slavery by asking us not to attach "special significance . . . to the relative length of our comments on various works and writers." But how can one not wonder at the failure to come to grips with the writings of Eugene Genovese, one of the two or three most distinguished historians of slavery alive? They barely touch—and then with the finest of fine kid gloves—on the many trenchant arguments Genovese uses for challenging any characterization of the slave South (taking the region as a *whole*) as economically sound and buoyant; had they merely confronted Genovese's *The Political Economy of Slavery*, they may have been forced to some modification in their views that slave labor was efficient, the business habits of slaveowners effective, and Southern agricultural practices enlightened. (Genovese, unlike Fogel and Engerman, makes a needed distinction between discussions in Southern agricultural journals of improved farm techniques and actual farming practices.)

On the other hand, Fogel and Engerman pay elaborate attention to the "historians of the Negro school" (to black scholars like Carter Woodson, W. E. B. DuBois and E. Franklin Frazier)—attention clearly merited in one sense because the resourcefulness of these black historians in uncovering evidence, and the originality of their early challenge to stereotypic views of slavery, have never received adequate recognition.

But these historians are merely summarized and praised, not critically evaluated. And this is all the more bizarre because their findings often run directly counter to the views Fogel and Engerman are advocating. DuBois, for example, emphasized the ruthless, degrading aspects of slavery—"filthy hovels . . . no family life . . . an endless round of toil . . . the lack of authority in the slave father," the frequent concubinage of the slave mother. Leaving DuBois uncontradicted, they *eviscerate* the white historian Kenneth Stampp for drawing conclusions similar to those of DuBois. This is deference with a vengeance. But it won't, I think, earn the gratitude of those black historians who have long fought to have their work evaluated by the same standards applied to everyone else.

Some black historians, moreover, will surely challenge Fogel and Engerman's easy claim that their "new perspectives" are "central to the understanding of contemporary issues," that they have exposed the myths that "have served to corrode and poison relations between the races."

Apparently they've never considered the possibility that some of their "new perspectives" might heighten rather than diminish tension between the races. For example, they argue (persuasively, I think) that slaves in the United States were in closer contact with white culture and further removed from their African origins than were slaves in the Caribbean. "This is not to deny," they nervously add, "the contribution of an African heritage in shaping the culture of blacks . . . There were, of course, many ways in which the culture of whites and blacks differed in 1860."

Since the "many ways" go wholly unspecified—since, to the contrary, a central thrust of the book is to emphasize the extent to which slaves internalized the Victorian morals and Protestant work ethic of their masters—we can hardly assent to the "of course." I suspect that black historians like Vincent Harding and John Blassingham, men who *have* tried to explore the unique culture that developed in the slave quarters, are not going to find Fogel and Engerman's evasive straddle on the African heritage question very enlightening in regard to the contemporary issue of black cultural separatism, or very conducive to ending friction between the races.

Other claims in the book to having discovered "the main features of the actual operation of the slave economy" and to having exposed "poisonous myths" are subject to serious challenge. Reproaching historians Stanley Elkins and Kenneth Stampp for having stressed, respectively, the psychological and physical cruelty of the plantation regime, Fogel and Engerman conclude instead that slaves were generally well treated—whether the gauge be diet, clothing, housing, medical care, punishment, or sexual exploitation. In every instance grounds exist for doubting the certitude of those conclusions.

To start with diet: Fogel and Engerman insist that "the belief that the typical slave was poorly fed is without foundation in fact." But in computing the "average" amounts of eleven principal foods consumed by slaves, the authors rely for data on the large plantations of the cotton belt—the same bias in sampling that they criticize in the work of others. Moreover, they often employ the same impressionistic vocabulary that they're quick to denounce in noncliometric works: thus they refer to "less frequent, but not uncommon" purchases of fish, coffee, and whiskey for slaves. I'd like to see the computer readout that said "less frequent, but not uncommon." I'll bet it can also say "mesdames et messieurs, welcome to the newest game in town."

When we learn, moreover, that "diseases of the gastrointestinal tract" were (along with pneumonia) the greatest killers of slaves, we begin to wonder whether the unresponsiveness of the slave diet to *individual* needs isn't a more important factor in assessing its healthfulness than whether it was "substantial" in bulk or high in "energy value" (corn, for example, if eaten in large amounts, can wreck havoc with some people's digestive tracts). This lack of attention to individual lives is characteristic of the book: "statistical averages" cannot convey the diversity of the slave experience—for the simple reason that statistical averages never coincide with real lives.

In discussing the clothing of the slaves, Fogel and Engerman tell us that "the best information" comes—again—from the records of the large plantations: we are then treated to an impressive list of the number and type of garments issued. I think the authors had the obligation at least to suggest that "best" information may mean "most favorable" as well as "most accessible."

Their samples on housing and medical care seem equally skewed. Planters' journals and instructions to overseers are cited to prove that slave cabins were systematically cleaned and slave ailments "usually" (note, again, the scientific precision) attended by the same doctor who ministered to the planter's own family. Counterevidence from travelers like Frederick Law Olmsted, who pointed to widespread filth and disease among the slaves, is dismissed as "impressionistic"—though why it's any more so than planters' journals is not made clear. Reading about the slaves' substantial diet, clean housing, and expert medical care leaves us bewildered by Fogel and Engerman's own finding that the life expectancy of slaves in 1850 was 12 percent below the average for white Americans.

As regards the frequency of whipping, the authors admit that "reliable data" are hard to come by, that indeed the *only* "systematic record of whipping now available for an extended period" is the diary of a single planter, Bennet Barrow of Louisiana. Fogel and Engerman calculate that Barrow administered "an average of 0.7 whippings per hand per year." Are we supposed to regard that as a lot or a little? Well, the authors don't exactly say. But they do go out of their way to tell us that whipping has "always been considered" a fully acceptable form of punishment, that it was sanctified in the Bible and commonly employed in the early nineteenth century in the North (and so Barrow was justified?).

They then go on to tell us that although some masters were undoubtedly "brutal, even sadistic, most were not. . . . Most planters recognized that for whipping to be effective" it had to be administered "with restraint and in a coolly calculated manner," and therefore "many" planters forbade whipping "except by them or in their presence." Other masters limited the number of lashes that could be administered "without their permission."

Confused by all those unquantified "mosts," "manys," "somes," and "others"? Yearning for hard evidence? We get instead a summary statement: "What planters wanted was not sullen and discontented slaves . . . but devoted, hard-working, responsible" ones. And so as sensible men guided by the dictates of reason and self-interest (and apparently immune to the counterpressures of temper or the temptations of command), they wielded the whip, if at all, with calculated restraint.

Now it may well be that Fogel and Engerman, university professors weaned on the model of Rational Man, only act after a detached assessment of their self-interest, uninfluenced by rude outbursts of passion, undeflected by irrational emotional needs from their always sensible paths. But that's not proof (certainly not in the world of cliometrics) that Southern planters in the mid-nineteenth century acted similarly.

Kenneth Stampp in his book *The Peculiar Institution*—and using more than one diary—documents many incidents of *un*-restrained punishment. Fogel and Engerman patronizingly dismiss his evidence: Stampp "fell into the trap of believing that extreme observations were in fact the central tendencies." The poor man's error can be explained by his failure to employ "more elaborate statistical procedures"—why Stampp "rarely even computed means . . . relying merely on his impressions of various bodies of evidence."

Well, I don't see that as regards the question of whipping, Fogel and Engerman have done anything more with computed means or been any less impressionistic in their use of data. Where they differ from Stampp is in their total inability to communicate any sense of the *experience* of being whipped or to consider its possible effects on personality (as opposed to economic performance). The difference is not in the amount of subjectivity involved, but in the willingness to acknowledge it.

Fogel and Engerman's arrogance/innocence is at its clearest in their treatment of marriage and sexuality. Using the New Orleans slave invoices, they conclude that 84 percent of all sales over the age of fourteen involved unmarried individuals, a figure that "sharply contradicts the popular view" that slave marriages were frequently broken up. But a number of questions about the data go unanswered or poorly answered.

New Orleans *was* the largest depot in the interregional slave trade, but how can we be sure that its practices were "representative"? Fogel and Engerman themselves tell us that the New Orleans invoices "contain no direct statements regarding the marital status of slaves," that Louisiana had a law that made it illegal to sell slave children under eleven without their mothers (unless they were orphans), and that some falsification in the invoices may have occurred—that a slaveowner (or auctioneer) may have listed a slave as unmarried as a salve to conscience or a spur to price.

Even if we assume the New Orleans data are representative and accurate, we're then confronted with having to evaluate the authors' statement that "only 9.3 percent of the New Orleans slave sales were of children under 13." *Only* 9.3 percent?! The adjective is obviously designed to persuade us that the figure is low. But as compared to what? Nowhere in their reams of graphs, charts and equations do Fogel and Engerman provide the fine moral calculus that allows them to feel comfortable with such subjective (or nonexistent) reference points.

In their discussion of miscegenation, the authors begin with an admission, then qualify it out of existence. "Many planters and their overseers," they tell us, did seek sex "outside the confines of their wives' beds." But even if all reports of sexual exploitation of slave women are true, they hasten to add, the number of cases amounts to "at most a few hundred." But how do we know that for each reported case there weren't hundreds or thousands that went unreported?

One obvious gauge is the number of mulattos in the population. Fogel and Engerman come up with a figure of "just" 10.4 percent for the slave population as a whole. I don't understand what set of "objective criteria" entitles us to regard that percentage as "low" (as the use of the word "just" is designed to imply). Especially since it seems fair to assume that not every instance of miscegenation resulted in pregnancy, and not every pregnancy produced a live baby.

Given the ongoing dispute over Jefferson's paternity of Sally Hemings's children*—and Jefferson left more records, and more de-

---

*In 1998, thanks to DNA testing, the dispute has finally been resolved and Jefferson's paternity established. Until then, the large majority of mostly white male historians had continued to argue the implausibility of Jefferson ever having slept with any of his slaves; it would have been "out of character."

tailed records, than most planters—I can't see how it's possible to pin-point with mathematical precision how many slaveowners slept with how many slaves—and with what results in terms of *pregnancy,* not merely childbirth.

In lieu of precision, we can't settle for the pseudo-arguments Fogel and Engerman advance that planters would have been dissuaded from seeking sexual pleasure in the slave quarters because to do so would have produced "distraught and disgruntled" slaves and would have undermined "the air of mystery and distinction on which so much of the authority of large planters rested." Sensible men would not have run such risks, we're told, when they could easily have afforded to keep white mistresses in town.

I call these "pseudo-arguments" because they rely for their validity on certain assumptions about human nature which are themselves the product of a particular set of social values—ones that equate authority with "mystery" and promiscuity with chaos, and see the pursuit of sexual gratification as incompatible with the pursuit of economic gain. Besides, *even though* Fogel and Engerman are almost certainly correct in arguing that "Victorian attitudes" predominated in the planter class, Steven Marcus's *The Other Victorians* should alone have made them aware that Victorian rhetoric and practice often diverged sharply.

Some of the authors' other findings on sexuality suggest that their own middle-class value set may have been more important in bringing them to certain conclusions that has the logic of the evidence. Arguing sternly against the view that "wanton impregnation of very young unmarried" black women took place, they offer as proof their "discovery" that the average age at which a slave mother gave birth for the first time was 22.5 years. Apparently they equate the age at which a woman gives birth with the age at which she first has sexual intercourse.

But contrary to the stern warnings of nineteenth-century sex manuals, intercourse does not always produce babies; the age at which slave mothers had their first children tells us nothing about the incidence and frequency of their sexual experience prior to motherhood. Yet Fogel and Engerman insist that in a non-contraceptive population "only abstinence" can explain "the relative shortage of births in the late-teen ages." Apparently they've never heard of "folk" devices—from the rhythm method to herbs—for avoiding pregnancy or inducing abortion.

Apparently, too, they regard their "discovery" of slave "prudishness" (as they call it) as an encomium—and yet another contribution to the betterment of contemporary race relations. But this is to saddle blacks with those sex-negative middle-class white values for which they may have more scorn than respect, to congratulate them, with that familiar liberal pat on the back, for being just like us—just as sexually repressed, just as fearful of sensual pleasure, just as devoted to the all-American virtues of abstinence, shame, and monogamy. This is the kind of embrace you can die from—as Lorraine Hansberry and James Baldwin understood long ago when they questioned whether they wanted to be allowed to rent a room in a house that was burning down.

My guess is that at least some blacks will also receive with modulated enthusiasm Fogel and Engerman's further "discovery" that slaves worked *even more efficiently* than did white laborers, and their suggestion that this "fact" is a contribution to the saga of black "achievement." The authors berate historians Stampp and Elkins for having portrayed slaves who lied, stole, feigned illness, acted childishly and shirked their duties—as if such acts necessarily reflect badly on black people. But why should such behavior be viewed negatively? What other options existed (short of the near certain failure of violent rebellion) besides these day-to-day forms of resistance against a barbarous system? Fogel and Engerman are censorious of such behavior (and of historians who point it out) because they pass judgment from the vantage point of a Calvinist work ethic and the Boy Scout pledge to loyalty and cheerfulness.

The authors might have profited from a quick course in situational ethics: lying to avoid the lash is not the same as lying to deceive a loved one; stealing a chicken to fill a hungry belly is not the equivalent of embezzling your fellow workers' pension fund; breaking a hoe to express exhaustion or anger is not on a par with failing to take your turn behind the cash register in a cooperative food store.

Fogel and Engerman reject any suggestion that a slave's *refusal* to become an effective cog in the plantation machine can itself be seen as an achievement, a testimony to black ingenuity, resistance, pride. Indeed, they impugn "racist" motives to any historian who makes such a suggestion. But the accusation of "racist" makes at least as much sense when applied to those who would argue that blacks were so without internal resources, common sense, and self-respect that they would dutifully fulfill the role of worker heroes in a system designed to perpetuate their servitude.

The authors insist that they have no wish to "defend" slavery nor to rehabilitate its historic reputation; they reiterate over and over that no moral grounds exist for a defense of the system—regardless of how profitable, efficient and benign it may have been. I believe their protestations. I believe *they* believe them. Which makes the tone of their book all the more lamentable. When we read their learned conclusion that slave labor can be called "expropriated" labor only to the extent of 12 percent—a percentage that "falls well within the modern tax rate on workers"—and when we are told further that slaves received "services" which "offset the income expropriated" (services which, regrettably, "cannot be quantified reliably at present"), we get the strong sense that modulation and "even-handedness" are disguising the grossness of the distortion at work.

Even if one accepts Fogel and Engerman's insistence on the material well-being of most slaves and the material wretchedness of most free laborers, other distinctions remain to be made (which they do not) between the condition of slavery and the condition of freedom. There is the matter of knowing oneself to be the legal property and under the entire control of another—and the attendant psychological effects of that knowledge. By focusing exclusively on the economic aspects of slavery and omitting the *human* dimension, Fogel and Engerman have written *Hamlet* without the Prince of Denmark.

They try to anticipate and disarm this criticism simply by stating that the psychological, moral, and emotional dimensions of slavery, though important, are beyond their expertise. Tucked away in one of their footnotes to the discussion of labor expropriation is the acknowledgement that they haven't taken into account the "uncompensated 'pain and suffering' imposed on slaves for being forced to live in bondage". This aspect of slavery, they chastely tell us, is "beyond the capacity of the tools of cliometricians."

That acknowledgement, so off-handed, so antiseptic, is not merely pious but offensive. And artful, too. For in focusing on the *material* conditions of slavery, in toting up "positive" findings about diet, housing, et al., and wholly omitting the "negative" psychological costs, the net result *is* to present slavery in a favorable light. This result may be unintentional, but it is the result.

And I want to suggest that that result may be functionally connected to the mathematical techniques employed and to the habits of mind those techniques engender. Fogel and Engerman have spent eighteen years preparing this study, eighteen years of close attention to those aspects of human experience that can be measured and of careful avoidance of those that cannot. The development of one frame of reference usually entails a loss in sensitivity to others: vegetarians not only lose a taste for meat but tend to be scornful of those who retain it. My point is that the authors may have become disqualified for the task of evaluating the psychological and moral dimensions of slavery even had they wished to undertake it. The perspective on human behavior they have cultivated for so long has distorted their priorities, dimmed a certain set of discriminations.

This is a harsh judgment, but I don't know how else to account for their obtuseness when discussing those nineteenth-century Americans who strongly protested against slavery. In several gratuitous asides (for they have foresworn any direct evaluation of "moral issues"), Fogel and Engerman casually lump together the views of the pro- and antislavery forces: both camps, they tell us, held to the position "that blacks were, for racial reasons, generally inferior to whites both as laborers and as human beings."

Without a single citation (without even a graph) to back up the statement, they then further declare that the antislavery people "did as much as any other group, perhaps more, to fasten the spikes that have kept blacks in the agony of racial discrimination." To equate the views and influence of a William Lloyd Garrison and a John C. Calhoun is to expose an ethical opaqueness of stunning density—to say nothing of a total ignorance of recent scholarship. Fogel and Engerman's view of the antislavery movement went out of currency with historians in the mid-sixties, about the same time that "pragmatic" Daniel Webster ceased to be viewed as the embodiment of all the American virtues.

Ignorance of this dimension in men who pride themselves on learning cannot help but connote a psychological necessity. It's the same necessity we see everywhere around us today: the need to devalue, in the wake of the '60s, the integrity and good sense of all those who take up the cause of social reform.

I would think that men who vaunt their ability, with the help of computers and mathematical models, to transcend ideology, would be discomforted at the close approximation between what they *have* found in the past and what our society currently *wants* to have found. That the correspondences may well have been forged on an unconscious level and in response to unfelt pressures should, I think, discomfort them still more—and should put the rest of us on guard against all the swollen claims to "objective science."

—The Village Voice, *July 18, 1974*

——————— POSTSCRIPT 1999 ———————

In the Afterword to the 1989 reissue of *Time on the Cross,* (and in Fogel's own book, *Without Consent or Contract,* also 1989), Fogel and Engerman begrudgingly acknowledge the validity of *some* of the criticisms made of their 1974 volume. But they simultaneously insist that many of the findings that had "outraged some critics were subsequently confirmed"—a dubious claim. Where they do prove willing to modify some of their 1974 statements, it is usually in some twistedly reluctant form. Thus: "It now appears that children rather than adults were the principal victims of malnutrition . . . adult slaves were relatively [Relative to what? Or to whom? Their masters?] well fed, clothed, and housed."*

Fogel and Engerman do acknowledge that their 1974 book concentrated on economic issues in a way that was "almost invariably detached from their political context" (by which they seem to be conceding that their argument was detached from "the history of the ideological and political struggles against slavery"). But they then

---

*This view has been sharply challenged by two recent books: Philip D. Morgan's *Slave Counterpoint* (Univ. of North Carolina Press: 1998), and John Hope Franklin and Loren Schweninger's *Runaway Slaves* (Univ. of North Carolina Press: 1999). For more details on their findings, see the note, this volume, to "The Black Response to William Styron's *The Confessions of Nat Turner.*"

promptly proceed once again to indict the William Lloyd Garrisons who, unlike "more worldly leaders of the [antislavery] movement," mistakenly refused "to shift the basis of their assault from religious to economic grounds." Meaning: the focus of Garrison and others on the immorality of slavery was naive—"nonworldly." Is this supposed to mean that holding human beings in slavery was not *as* wrong as the Garrisons insisted, and that it would have been "worldly" of them to ignore or downplay the barbarity of the institution?

Fogel and Engerman forcefully declare their outright disagreement with those critics of the 1974 volume "who have charged that the book is 'amoral'." They claim—stretching the point more than a bit—that their "comments on moral questions are scattered throughout" the original work. At one point they suggest that *perhaps* those comments "fell short of an adequate reformulation of the moral problem of slavery." Yet in the very next sentence, they turn away from such uncharacteristic self-doubt and return to the familiar grounds of self-congratulation: "The principal contribution of *Time on the Cross* to the reformulation of the moral problem was its identification of the 'myth of black incompetence' . . . "

In the concluding section of his own book, *Without Consent or Contract* (1989), Fogel continues to excoriate Garrison and his followers for believing "that they alone knew the true road to righteousness . . ." Fogel sees their chief flaw as "impatience." They were too much "ablaze with moral fervor." They pushed, in other words, too fast and too furiously for social justice. Not too fast for the slaves, mind you—but it is not their perspective that Fogel and Engerman represent.

The insistence of economists on simplistic statistical models— which the work of Fogel and Engerman so aptly represents—is, according to the dean of contemporary economists, Robert L. Heilbroner, the bane of the field. As he has recently said, economists today "favor two-dimensional models that in trying to be scientific leave out too much and leave modern economists without a true understanding of how the system works" (*The New York Times*, Jan. 23, 1999).

Robert William Fogel won the Nobel Prize in economic sciences in 1993.

II

Gender and Sexuality

— Historical Interpretation — and the Politics of Evidence[1]

T he two manuscript letters that form this article's centerpiece have been concealed from public view for 150 years. No portion of them has been previously published, nor even obliquely paraphrased. Yet as will be seen at a glance, the content of the letters is startling, and opens up suggestive new avenues for historical interpretation.

The importance of the letters requires that they be "introduced" on several levels. To start with the simplest, we need to identify the sender ("Jeff") and the recipient ("Jim"). In 1826, when the letters were written, Jeff and Jim were inconsequential young men. Yet both were destined for distinguished careers, Jim (James H. Hammond) eventually achieving national renown. Jeff (Thomas Jefferson Withers) was also to cut a considerable, if lesser, swath—as journalist, lawyer, "nullifier," and judge of the South Carolina Court of Appeals.

In 1826, twenty-two-year-old Jeff Withers was studying law at South Carolina College. He went on, in 1828, to become editor of the Columbia Telescope, an organ of the powerful nullification movement that had arisen in South Carolina to protest and defy the recent federal tariff. For several years thereafter Withers gave full energies to the struggle, delaying the completion of his law studies until 1833 (the same year he married

Elizabeth Boykin, whose niece, Mary Boykin Chestnut, later won enduring fame for her Civil War journals, published as Diary from Dixie*). Elected a common-law judge soon after, Withers later moved up to the state Court of Appeals, where he served until his death in 1866.*[2]

As for "Jim" (James H. Hammond), he became one of the antebellum South's "great men," his career ranging from politics to agricultural reform to proslavery polemics. At various times he was governor, congressman, and senator from South Carolina, a leading exponent of southern economic diversification and a highly influential "moralist" whose theories in defense of slavery became cornerstones of the South's "proslavery argument." Hammond's name may not be well known today, but in the antebellum period he was likened in importance to John C. Calhoun—and considered his likely heir.[3]

THE DOCUMENTS

The following letter was written by Withers to Hammond, dated May 15, 1826, Columbia, South Carolina.[4]

Dear Jim:

I got your Letter this morning about 8 o'clock, from the hands of the Bearer . . . I was sick as the Devil, when the Gentleman entered the Room, and have been so during most of the day. About 1 o'clock I swallowed a huge mass of Epsom Salts—and it will not be hard to imagine that I have been at dirty work since. I feel partially relieved— enough to write a hasty dull letter.

I feel some inclination to learn whether you yet sleep in your Shirt-tail, and whether you yet have the extravagant delight of poking and punching a writhing Bedfellow with your long fleshen pole—the exquisite touches of which I have often had the honor of feeling? Let me say unto thee that unless thou changest former habits in this particular, thou wilt be represented by every future Chum as a nuisance. And, I pronounce it, with good reason too. Sir, you roughen the downy Slumbers of your Bedfellow—by such hostile—furious lunges as you are in the habit of making at him—when he is least prepared for defence against the crushing force of a Battering Ram. Without reformation my imagination depicts some awful results for which you will be held accountable—and therefore it is, that I earnestly recommend it. Indeed it is encouraging an assault and battery propensity, which needs correction—& uncorrected threatens devastation, horror & bloodshed, etc. . . .

The remaining two pages of the letter deal with unrelated matters of no special interest. But the way the letter signs off, is, however, possibly significant:

> *With great respect I am the old*
> *Stud,*
> *Jeff.*

Withers' second letter to Hammond is dated Sept. 24, 1826:

My dear Friend,

. . . Your excellent Letter of 13 June arrived[5] . . .

I fancy, Jim, that your *elongated protruberance*—your fleshen pole—your [two Latin words; indecipherable]— has captured complete mastery over you—and I really believe, that you are charging over the pine barrens of your locality, braying, like an ass, at every she-male you can discover. I am afraid that you are thus prostituting the "image of God" and suggest that if you thus blasphemously essay to put on the form of a Jack—in this stead of that noble image—you will share the fate on Nebuchadnezzer of old. I should lament to hear of you feeding upon the dross of the pasture and alarming the country with your vociferations. The day of miracles may not be past, and the flaming excess of your lustful appetite may drag down the vengeance of supernal power . . .

COMMENTARY

The portrait of young Hammond that emerges from these 1826 letters is in startling contrast with the standard view of Hammond the adult. Nineteen-year-old Jim's "flaming excess" and "lustful appetite" bear scant resemblance to James H. Hammond of the history books—conservative moralist, staid traditionalist pillar of the Old South. In an effort to reconcile this gross disparity in Hammond's image, some additional biographical details are needed.

By birth, Hammond was a "commoner"—his father a native New Englander who had gone south to teach school, his mother a native South Carolinian of undistinguished ancestry. Through his own talent and drive (he graduated near the top of his college class) and then, through what is called a "fortunate" marriage, Hammond entered the ranks of the southern planter aristocracy. His wedding to the Charleston heiress Catherine Fitzsimmons was critically important: Hammond overnight became the owner of Silver Bluff—a ten-thousand-acre plantation on the Savannah River worked by 220 slaves—and a member of the ruling elite.[6]

He used his opportunities well. Always the apt pupil, Hammond quickly acquired the cultivated externals—the manners, rituals and social preoccupations—of the master class. Just as quickly, he internalized its values. By the mid–1830s, Hammond had already won high regard as a "brilliant" advocate of "states' rights," a zealous defender of slavery and a "superb" manager of his landed estates. He had also acquired a reputation for willingness to use the lash and to send his slaves to cut fodder in malaria-infested swamps.[7] A number of Hammond's contemporaries thought his temperament more enigmatic than his social values, often describing him as mercurial and impetuous. And as well, aloof, vain, willful and proud (though to be described as having such traits was not, for that region, class and time, necessarily to be derided).

That Hammond the adult was sometimes considered "impetuous" does suggest that the tumultuous young Jim of 1826 had never been wholly superseded in later life by the Statesman and Seer. We have few details about the nature of his adult "impetuousness," but of those we do have, none suggest it ever took the form it had in his youth—of "furious lunges" at male bed partners or lusty "charges over the pine barrens" to seek out "she-males." If those youthful penchants and impulses did continue to exert some hold over Hammond in adulthood (given how pronounced they'd been in his youth, it's hard to believe they totally disappeared), if homoerotic (as we would call them) images did maintain some subterranean sway over his fantasies, there's not a scintilla of evidence that he acted them out.

But there is considerable evidence to suggest that Hammond's lusty appetite in general—however much its loci may have shifted—continued to be strong throughout his life, his public image notwithstanding. As a plantation owner, he was known for sternly enforcing puritanical sexual mores. He allowed the slaves on his plantation to marry but not to divorce unless a slave couple could convince him that "sufficient cause" existed; even then he subjected both members of the couple to a hundred lashes and forbade both the right to remarry for three years.[8]

Hammond's entrenched reputation as the guardian and exemplar of traditional morality got a sudden, nasty jolt in 1846. In that year, George McDuffie resigned his seat in the U.S. Senate and the state legislature seemed on the verge of choosing Hammond to succeed him. Hammond's brother-in-law, Wade Hampton, thwarted that result. He warned Hammond that he would publicly reveal an incident that had taken place three years earlier unless Hammond immediately removed his name from contention for the Senate seat. The nature of that incident was finally revealed twenty years ago, when the historian Clement Eaton discovered and published excerpts from Hammond's secret diary. That diary reveals that Hammond had attempted to seduce Wade Hampton's teenage daughters.[9]

Hardly a peccadillo, one might think. Yet Hammond himself apparently viewed it as no more than that. He did agree to withdraw his candidacy for the Senate; rumors of the sexual scandal had already circulated and Hammond could hardly have afforded to let Hampton confirm them. Hammond also gave up his family mansion in Columbia and retired to manage his estates—a retirement that lasted fourteen years. But he did none of this in a spirit marked by contrition or chagrin. The dominant tone he adopted (in diary entries and in letters to friends) was aggrieved petulance—*he* was the wounded party! Merely for "a little dalliance with the other sex," for an incident marked by "impulse, not design," he wrote, he had been forced into political retirement, whereas numerous other public figures, past and present, had indulged "amorous & conjugal infidelity" without incurring censure or retribution of any kind.[10]

Hammond's unapologetic tone, astonishing in itself, reveals much about his actual (as opposed to his rhetorical) sexual morality. The casual view he took of "dalliance" suggests that he had far more personal experience with it than we can currently document (indeed, aside from the 1846 run-in with Hampton, we have no documentation). But his attitude toward "dalliance" is the least of it. Hammond's truculent defense of seducing teenage girls—relatives through marriage, no less—as an event of neither great import nor cause for remorse, makes it hard to imagine what, if any, erotic expression he considered beyond the pale.

The "two" Hammonds—the youthful sexual adventurer of 1826 and the staid eminence of 1846—no longer seem unrelated. Hammond's range of sexual tastes as an older man may have narrowed—an impression based merely on the paucity of extant evidence—but his sex drive apparently remained strong, impulsive, self-justifying and defiant of the conventional mores of the day. The external circumstances of Hammond's life changed radically from youth to middle age, but his inner life apparently underwent less of a sea change.

As both a young and a middle-aged man, his lust—whether aroused by male college friends or by teenage female relatives—continued strong, arrogantly assertive, ungoverned. He never seems to have struggled very hard to control it, and certainly not as a young man. Nothing in the 1826 letters suggests that Jim Hammond saw any reason to restrain his impulses or curtail his pleasures. He may have made more of an effort as an older man, if only to protect his staid public image and safeguard his privileges.

How might we understand this uncategorizable man? Looked at from the angle of 1826, Hammond seems (by my values) admirably playful, exploratory and freewheeling, uninhibited and attractively unapologetic. Looked at from the angle of 1846, he seems merely repulsive: grossly insensitive and irresponsible, perhaps pathologically willful.

The discomforting fact is that we "understand" very little—whether about Hammond the man, or the social climate that made possible the 1826 Withers letters We can only fall back on surmise. The tone of Withers's letters—consistently ironic and playful—strongly suggests that his erotic involvement with Hammond carried no "romantic" overtones. Not that we can be sure even about that; irony, as we know, is a common device for concealing emotion. Besides, an occasional phrase in the letter—such as Withers's reference to the "exquisite touch" of Hammond's "long fleshen pole"—could be read as more than "playful." Unfortunately, no other correspondence from the period of remotely comparable content has been found to which we might turn in an attempt to draw parallels, clarify attitudes, consolidate or amplify tentative conclusions.

Given the difficulty of trying to pin down what the two letters mean, it may be foolish to move beyond the Withers/Hammond relationship itself and pose broader questions still; "foolish," because to do so invites additional futility and frustration. Yet broader questions are implicit in the material—they seem to suggest themselves—and posing them may alone be of value, though answers prove elusive.

The critical question, historically, is whether the same-gender erotic experiences suggested in the two letters should be regarded as "anomalous" or "representative." Was Withers and Hammond's behavior unique, or does it reveal and illustrate a wider pattern of male-male relationships—till now unsuspected and undocumented, yet in some sense "typical" of their time, region, race and class?

The best clues are provided by the internal evidence of the letters themselves, and especially their tone. It has a consistent ring: offhanded, flip. Jeff's bantering call to repentance is transparently mocking, his "warnings of retribution" uniformly irreverent— "campy," in the modern vernacular. The letters are *so* devoid of any serious moral entreaty or fervor, of any genuine attempt to inspire shame or reformation, as to take on negative significance. The values and vocabulary of evangelical piety had not yet, in the 1820s, come to permeate American consciousness and discourse. Even when those values carried most influence—roughly from 1830 to 1870—they seem to have held sway in the South to a lesser extent than elsewhere in the country.[11]

So the geographical locale and time period in which Jeff and Jim grew up may be important factors in explaining their freewheeling attitudes. The American South of the latter part of the eighteenth and early part of the nineteenth centuries was (for privileged, young, white males) one of those rare liberal interregnums in our history when the body could be treated as a natural source of pleasure and "wanton" sexuality viewed as the natural prerogative—the exemplification even—of Manliness.

In this sense, Jeff and Jim's relaxed attitude toward sex in general, far from being anomalous, may have been close to mainstream mores. Whether that also holds for their high-spirited, unself-conscious attitude about same-gender sexuality is more problematic. At the least, Jeff's lighthearted comedic descriptions of male bedfellows "poking and punching" each other with their "fleshen poles" seems so devoid of furtiveness or shame that it's possible to believe male-male sexual contact was not stigmatized to the degree long assumed. Withers and Hammond, after all, were ambitious aspirants to positions of leadership and power. Could Hammond have indulged so freely (and Withers described so casually) behavior widely deemed disgraceful and abhorrent, outside the range of permissible experience? If homoeroticism had been utterly taboo, wouldn't one expect Withers's tone to betray some evidence of guilt and unease? Instead, his tone is breezy and nonchalant, raising the possibility that sexual contact between males (of a certain class, region, time and place), if not commonplace, was not wholly proscribed either. Should that surmise be even marginally correct, our standard view of the history of male homosexuality in this country as an unrelieved tale of concealment and woe needs revision.[12]

The surmise, of course, is shaky, lacking any corroborating evidence, any additional documentation from the period recounting attitudes and experiences comparable to those of Jeff and Jim. That much is undeniable, but perhaps not in itself sufficient proof that same-gender sexuality never (or rarely) happened. Other corroborating records may still survive, and are only waiting to be retrieved. After all, to date we've accumulated only a tiny collection of historical materials that record the existence of *heterosexual* behavior in the past. Yet no one claims that that minuscule amount of evidence is an accurate measure of the actual amount of heterosexual activity that took place.

Just so with Jeff and Jim. What now appears unique and anomalous behavior may one day come to be seen as having been unexceptional—casually tolerated, if not actively encouraged or institutionalized. This will only happen if the new generation of scholars continues to press for access to previously suppressed materials and if the new generation of archivists continues to cultivate sympathy toward such scholarship, declassifying "sensitive" data at an accelerated pace. I myself believe that additional source material, possibly a great deal of it, relating to the history of homosexuality has survived and awaits recovery from well-guarded vaults. I base this belief on my own research experiences over the past decade. The two Withers/Hammond letters presented here are a case in point. Until they turned up, few if any scholars (myself included) would have credited the notion that "carefree" male-male eroticism ever existed in this country (let alone in the 1820s)—or that offhanded, unemphatic descriptions of it would ever be found.

In that vein, it may be worth providing some additional details about how the Withers/Hammond letters were discovered. The tale might encourage other scholars to persevere in the search for long-suppressed material; might offer tactics for extracting it; might alert them to some of the obstacles and ploys custodial guardians will use to deflect the search; and might suggest how these can be neutralized or counteracted.

Recovering the Withers/Hammond Letters

In offering this cautionary tale, the chief purpose is not to establish the villainy of archivists. As a group, they are no more the enemy of innovative scholarship nor the defenders of traditional morality than are historians as a group—most of whom scornfully dismiss the study of sexual ideology and behavior as a nonsubject. During my research travels to manuscript libraries, several individual archivists have been enormously supportive: people like Stephen T. Riley of the Massachusetts Historical Society, Sandra Taylor of the Lilly Library in Indiana, and Richard J. Wolfe of the Countway Library of Medicine in Boston. Such people (I could name others) acted from the conviction that research into the "history of intimacy" was overdue and held great potential importance for better understanding our national experience and character.

Their attitude is still a minority one within the archival profession as a whole (in the historical profession, too). Many of those who stand guard over the nation's major manuscript collections see their function as protective and preservative—of traditional moral values in general and of a given family's "good name" in particular. They tend to equate—as is true everywhere in academia (and perhaps to a greater extent than in the population at large)—the libidinous with the salacious, and to be profoundly distrustful of both. Given this discomfort, some archivists invent obstacles to put in the researcher's path or claim to be hamstrung (and to be fair, even sympathetic curators sometimes *are*) by certain access restrictions which the donor of a given manuscript collection originally appended to the deed of the gift.

The six-month tangle I had over the Withers/Hammond letters illustrates all of this. The trail began (confining myself to the main outlines) with Catherine Clinton, then a doctoral student in history at Princeton. She first brought the letters to my attention, and although she has modestly asked that her efforts not be detailed, I did at least want to acknowledge her pivotal role.[13] Once having seen the letters and realized their importance, I started in motion the standard procedures for acquiring permission to publish manuscript materials. On March 6, 1979, I sent a formal request to that effect to the South

Caroliniana Library (henceforth, SCL), where the original letters are housed.

That move, according to one of the several legal experts I later consulted, was my first, and worst, mistake. By formally requesting permission, I was (to quote the expert) being "super-dutiful" and, in the process, making life infinitely more difficult for *all* parties concerned. Technically, I had done the "correct" thing—I had gone through proper channels, adhered to the terms most manuscript libraries require regarding permission to publish manuscript material. But in real life, my chiding expert added, what is technically correct can prove functionally awkward. In practice, it seems (and after twenty years of archival research, this came as a surprise to me), some scholars publish manuscript material without making any formal request to do so. And some libraries, it seems, prefer it that way. A formal request, after all, requires a formal reply. The given library is pressured to make a clear-cut decision, one that can place it (sometimes unwillingly and unfairly) in a no-win situation: should the library grant permission, it risks the wrath of a donor or family descendant, charges of dereliction, possible loss of future acquisitions; should the library deny permission, it risks accusations of censorship from an outraged scholar.

Lacking such wisdom at the time, I sent off a formal letter requesting permission to publish. This left SCL with two choices: to act on my request (which, given the contents of the 1826 letters, almost certainly assured a negative response), or to do nothing. They opted for the latter, letting my letter go unanswered. If SCL had thereby meant to signal me to proceed (quietly) without insisting on their formal acquiescence, I misread the signal. Instead of quietly retreating, I noisily persisted. On April 15 I sent them a second letter, a near duplicate of the first. That, too, went unacknowledged.

I got angry (blame it on the zodiac: Leos can't stand being ignored). In early June, after thirteen weeks without a response, I sent—no, shot off by certified mail—a third letter, this one longer and decidedly more testy than its predecessors. SCL's obdurate silence, I wrote, could only be interpreted as "silence giving consent" or as a subtly calculated attempt at censorship. Should I opt for the first interpretation (my letter went on), I would simply publish the material without further ado—and on the assumption I had tacit approval. Should I instead opt for the second interpretation—their disapproval—I would then feel an obligation to other scholars to report the incident to the prestigious Joint Committee of Historians and Archivists, a group empowered to deal with matters of censorship. While deciding between the two courses of action, my letter concluded, "I would be glad to receive any information which might have a bearing on my pending decision." (Leos get snotty when pushed.)

Within the week, I got a reply. It came from SCL's director (Dr. Archer, I'll call him). He began by expressing regret that I had "found it necessary to write such a sharp letter"—although he acknowledged that the delayed response to my previous letters might have contributed to my ill temper. Nonetheless, he went on, I could surely understand that he had had to put my letters aside while "awaiting a convenient opportunity" to seek advice "on the status of the restrictions" attached to the Hammond Papers. Such an opportunity had finally presented itself; he was now able to report that the original donor of the Hammond Papers had "asked" (the choice of word, subsequently pointed out by several of my consultants, is significant, implying as it does a request from the donor, not a binding stipulation) that none of the manuscripts be used in a way that might "result in embarrassment to descendants." The donor was dead, but Dr. Archer considered the "restriction" to be "still in force." He was also of the view that the two Withers letters were unquestionably "embarrassing." Therefore, he had decided to deny my request to publish them.

In a curious concluding paragraph, Dr. Archer suggested he might reconsider my request if I could provide "full assurances" that the letters would be published in such a way as to disguise their provenance and prevent their identification with Hammond or Withers, if I would agree, in short, to strip the letters of all historical context—a context integral to their meaning and importance—and treat them as floating objects unanchored in time or space. That suggestion struck me as comparable to insisting a Haydn string quartet be performed solely with tambourines and vibraharp. I declined the suggestion.

I embarked instead on a double course: drafting a reply to Dr. Archer and starting up a round of consultations with various scholars, friends, and legal experts about what to include in my reply. My advisers diverged on this or that particular, but concurred on the main point: legally and morally, I was justified in proceeding straightaway to publication. In support of that conclusion they cited several arguments but put special stress on the legal doctrine of "fair usage": an author's right to quote (without permission) an appropriate amount of copyrighted material. The body of law defining what does or does not constitute a "fair" amount of unauthorized quotation has shifted over time, but in recent years (most significantly in *Nizer* v. *Rosenberg*) the courts have leaned consistently toward a permissive view.*

One of the experts I consulted in copyright law felt confident that SCL "had already fatally weakened its copyright claim to the Hammond Papers, however unintentionally." The library's long-standing practice of allowing scholars access to the papers (instead of sealing them off) was tantamount to admitting that the original deed of gift had not been encumbered by any substantive, detailed restrictions, and that aside from some vague admonitory advice, the donor had apparently left final discretionary power to the library itself. The fact that SCL had, in addition, cataloged the two Withers letters and provided photocopies of them on request had, in the view of the copyright lawyer, further weakened their position—indeed, had made my legal right to publish "unassailable." All

---

*In the years since the publication of this article, the courts have dramatically curtailed "fair usage."

this I dutifully incorporated in the ongoing draft of my letter to Dr. Archer. In the upshot, I never sent it. My Council of Experts finally persuaded me that I had nothing further to gain and might needlessly stir quiet waters. As one consultant put it, "If you formally notify SCL of your intention to publish, the library might feel obligated to bring suit, though they'd much prefer not to, given their shaky legal case and the additional publicity any litigation would give to the contents of the letters. Do yourself and them a favor. Say and write nothing further; simply proceed to publication."

Which is what I did. Not, I should add, without misgivings. I felt that a direct challenge to SCL, though it might have led to time-consuming, expensive litigation, could have yielded an important precedent useful to future scholars. I also regretted that Dr. Archer had never gotten the chance to read my unmailed final letter, especially the part in which I had asked him to spell out his specific reasons for deciding that publication of the Withers manuscripts would prove an "embarrassment." "For two men like Hammond and Withers," I had written Archer (hot tongue in hard cheek), "who have gone down in history as among the country's staunchest defenders of human slavery, I should think their reputations could only be enhanced by the playful, raucous—the humanizing—revelations contained in the two letters." Yes, I was being patently disingenuous, and, yes, it was unlikely I could force from Dr. Archer an explicit avowal of homophobia. Still, it would have done my soul good to try (it's doing it some good just quoting the unsent letter here).

Certain ethical considerations implicit in my decision to publish the Withers letters without authorization leave me the most uncomfortable: that familiar array of moral conundrums (in however diminutive a form) long associated with acts of "civil disobedience." To explain why I proceeded nonetheless, I have to step back a bit and approach the matter indirectly through some general observations.

There is a long-standing and long-sanctified notion that academia consists of a "community of scholars"—in the ideal sense of a disinterested collectivity of truth seekers. This is an exalted but, to my mind, illusory conceit. In practice, as I see it, the notion has served as a useful device for codifying professional behavior and a convenient rationale for denying credentials to those who might challenge the academy's entrenched values—women, gays, ethnic minorities. The conceit of a community of scholars, in short, has characteristically been a blind for parochialism and discrimination.

Yet the *ideal* of such a community remains attractive, as does the related notion that a genuinely unharnessed scholarship could provide needed data for challenging the status quo and nurturing alternative visions of the good society. In my view, a scholar's prime allegiance and responsibility should be to the ideal itself, not to those academic guilds that claim to represent it (even as they enforce standards for membership and employ definitions of "legitimate" inquiry that straitjacket and subvert it). Most of the scholarship emanating from universities functions primarily, if "unintentionally," to rationalize existing arrangements of power, and the academic guilds, in excluding or ostracizing mavericks, play an important role in perpetuating such arrangements.

What may seem obvious on an abstract level becomes less so when reduced to a personal one; then the whole question of "responsibility" becomes much stickier. As someone who chose to join the academic community and to remain in it (with attendant profit, such as a secure salary) I, and others like me, it could be argued, are obligated either to abide by academe's conventions or—if convinced we cannot—to resign. In response to that argument, I'd say that a scholar owes *primary* allegiance to what academe might be—to its promise, not its practice—and would add the specific observation that academe's own official standards about what constitutes "acceptable" professional behavior and proper scholarly inquiry are muddled and slippery. To give one example, there is no agreement among university-affiliated historians about what constitutes "correct" (or even preferred) research procedures, modes of analysis or styles of presentation: cliometricians battle impressionists, generalists disparage specialists, literary stylists war with statistical analysts.

Adding to the confusion is academe's own contradictory record in its treatment of dissenters. It is not a record of monolithic repression. Many principled and innovative academicians have indeed suffered grievously for their political, personal and professional nonconformity (as well as for belonging to a particular sex, class and race). But it is also true that academe has sometimes honored its eccentrics and insurgents, if belatedly: the political radical William Appleman Williams, for example, was elected president of the Organization of American Historians. While the academy is assuredly not the free-swinging arena of open inquiry its champions claim, neither is it as tightly sealed against novelty or as unvaryingly hostile to fractious upstarts as its detractors insist.

Academe's ambiguous traditions help persuade many intellectuals who by temperament, conviction or lifestyle are "deviant"—i.e., outside mainstream orthodoxy—to establish and maintain university affiliations. Some of these intellectuals would claim ("lull themselves into believing," left-wing skeptics might say) that academe is one of the few arenas in which innovative inquiry remains possible and that the "long march through the institutions" at present seems the only promising tactic available for creating substantive social change. But others among the group of "deviant" intellectuals do worry that by retaining their ties to academic disciplines and educational institutions that function essentially as "conservators"—preservers and transmitters of conventional knowledge and norms—they are putting their own values at risk. The danger of co-optation is always present; unorthodoxy and personal integrity can be gradually, sometimes indiscernibly, sapped. The best one can do to guard against that prospect is to try to stay vigilant—in touch with the different drummer within, resistant to the efforts to muffle it. But vows of vigilance, as we know, are more easily made than kept.

Anyway, that's about as close as I can come to delineating (and possibly idealizing) the relationship I myself have tried to maintain within the academic world, and also to conveying, however circuitous the route, some of the ingredients that went into my inner debate about publishing the Withers/Hammond letters. By finally deciding to publish them against the wishes of their official custodian, my own personal discomfort played a considerable role—discomfort at the prospect of yielding to the prevailing (and to my mind dangerously narrow) view of what is acceptable historical inquiry and, by implication, permissible norms of behavior. I also concluded, on more general grounds, that the public *does* have "the right to know"—and in regard to the Withers letters specifically, the gay public has a desperate *need* to know.

That last consideration proved decisive. I felt it was essential to challenge the tradition of suppressing information that might prove useful to gay people in better understanding the historical dimensions of our experience, the shifting strategies we've adopted over time to cope with oppression and the varied styles we've developed to express our special sensibilities. If the "lawless" tactics I've resorted to seem extreme to some, well, so is our need; more orthodox tactics (like polite letters of inquiry) have done little to meet it. The heterosexist world has long held a monopoly on defining legal and ethical propriety, has long imposed its definitions on the rest of us, using them as weapons for keeping us in line by denying us access to knowledge of our own antecedents. Let heterosexism take the blame then if, having finally despaired of gaining that knowledge by humble petition through proper channels, we now turn, by default, and in anger at the continuing impasse, to "improper" tactics. It seems better to stand accused of impropriety than to go on accepting someone else's right to control access to *our* history.

Power has created that "right" in the past. In the future, other claims to right must be pressed—like the right of a people to a knowledge of its own history (to *memory*), an indispensable prerequisite for establishing collective identity and for enjoying the solace of knowing that we too have "come through" as bearers of a diverse, rich, unique heritage. To press those claims, it may be necessary to defy entrenched conventions and to risk the attendant consequences, professional and legal, of doing so. Which is not the sort of thing one welcomes. Yet the alternative is still less palatable: to continue to accept and abide by anachronistic definitions of what constitutes "sensitive material" and "acceptable" areas of historical inquiry. To go that route is to collaborate in sustaining "things as they are"—to be complicitous, in sum, in our own oppression.

> *—this essay, in various versions, has been anthologized several times, most recently in John Howard, ed.,* Carrying On in the Lesbian and Gay South, *NYU Press: 1997*

The "Father" of the
Homophile Movement[*]

T wo crucial dates frame this story: 1951 and 1973.

In 1951 a book entitled *The Homosexual in America* appeared as out of nowhere, its author, Donald Webster Cory, entirely unknown. The book was the first full-scale nonfiction account of gay life in the United States, and its author spoke as an insider, an avowed homosexual. In opposition to psychiatric calls for "cure" and religious demands for "repentance," Cory's message to the homosexual was to "turn inward and accept yourself . . . You are what you are, and what I am—a homosexual. You will not outgrow it, will not evolve in another direction, will not change on the couch of an analyst."

---

*I've researched a variety of manuscript collections for this essay, the most important of which was the Mattachine Papers at The New York Public Library. In addition, some thirty or so Sagarin friends and colleagues agreed to be interviewed, and a number of them shared source materials and correspondence. Most did so, however, on condition of anonymity. Since many of the quotations in this piece must therefore go unascribed, I've decided to omit footnotes altogether rather than offer a truncated, incomplete set. I do, however, want to offer special thanks to certain individuals who provided advice, leads and data: John D'Emilio, Robert J. Kelly, Jim Kepner, John Loughery, John Richards and Peter Nardi.

We jump to 1973.

The January issue of *Contemporary Sociology* carried a lengthy essay reviewing some dozen books on homosexuality published in the wake of the 1969 Stonewall riots. The author was Edward Sagarin, professor of sociology and criminology at the City University of New York, a specialist in the study of deviance, president-elect of the American Society of Criminology, and the prolific author of a slew of books and articles.

In his acid essay, Sagarin derided the emergent view that homosexuals "are as healthy as anyone else," argued that "cure" was both possible and desirable, and denied that social oppression was the primary cause of such psychopathology as existed in the gay world. Children must continue to be taught, Sagarin insisted, that "it is better to have heterosexual than homosexual patterns."

Donald Webster Cory and Edward Sagarin were the same person.

Edward Sagarin was born in Schenectady in 1913 to Jewish Russian immigrant parents. The youngest of eight children, he lost his mother in the flu pandemic of 1918. After his father remarried, the family relocated to New York City, but Ed got along badly with his stepmother and eventually moved out. He then lived for varying lengths of time with different members of the extended Sagarin clan. His relationship with his father never recovered, and years later Ed had to be talked into showing up for his funeral.

Born with scoliosis, a lateral curvature of the spine, Ed had a noticeable hump on the right side of his back—his "posture problem," he would wryly call it as an adult. Frail, small, unathletic, intense and very smart, Ed grew up with the taunts of his cookie-cutter schoolmates ringing in his ears. Children thus stigmatized often become sensitive to the pain of others bearing marks of affliction, as well as fascinated with how they cope with the world's mean-spirited assaults. But sensitivity need not automatically manifest as compassion. It can also breed murderous disassociation—or an uneasy mix of empathy and repulsion, affinity for another outsider alternating with oddly erupting, unbidden distaste.

Though money was in scant supply, Ed did go to a good high school, and then managed to spend more than a year in France (where he met André Gide and learned French fluently—a skill that would prove important for his future business career). On his return to the United States, Sagarin enrolled at CCNY—in the late '20s and '30s notorious for its political passion and turmoil—and became active in left-wing politics. He felt special concern over the plight of black Americans (the concern would be lifelong), and the militantly left-wing National Student League sent Sagarin and two of its other young members (a second, ironically, also closeted—the poet Muriel Rukeyser) to observe the 1933 trial in Alabama of the "Scottsboro Boys," nine black youths falsely accused of raping two white women. After the three students were harassed by local sheriffs, Samuel Leibowitz, chief attorney for the Scottsboro boys, appealed to them to leave town—which they agreed to do.

In 1934, approaching his twenty-first birthday, Sagarin met another young radical, Gertrude Liphshitz. A shared interest in left-wing politics initially drew the two young people together, and would always be a strong binding force between them; but their involvement deepened beyond politics, and in 1936 they married. Gert came from a warm, caring, orthodox Jewish family—itself a powerful magnet for the love-starved young Sagarin. It was also a family of activists; her father was a staunch union organizer.

Those who *casually* knew the couple during their marriage of nearly fifty years tend to describe Gert as "a Brooklyn Jewish housewife, pleasant, level-headed, practical," a woman who took care of the home (the couple had one child, Fred), eschewed a career, and devoted her energies to her family. But those who knew the couple *well* shade the relationship quite differently. They agree that Gert assumed a traditional housewife's role, but insist she was far from the shyly hovering background figure described by those who saw the couple rarely and judged them superficially. Gert, her intimates knew, had strong opinions, freely verbalized them and strenuously argued with Ed over this public issue or that paragraph in something he was writing. An emotionally centered, deeply principled woman, she was powerful ballast for her husband's comparative fragility. She also remained politically involved, and astute, all her life—active in nuclear disarmament groups like Women Strike for Peace, and later participating in protests against the war in Vietnam.

The Sagarins' intimates also uniformly testify to the couple's mutual devotion: "Oh, the marriage hit some rough spots of course," one of their close friends told me, "but what marriage doesn't? The fact is, they adored each other."

In his 1951 preface to *The Homosexual in America*, Sagarin, writing as "Donald Webster Cory," put his decision to marry in less heated terms: In "later adolescence and early manhood . . . I struggled against my homosexuality . . . Homosexual love, I told myself, is a myth . . . At the age of 25, after determining that I was capable of consummating a marriage (In later life, Cory confided to a colleague that "Gertrude is the only woman I had ever had erotic feelings towards") I was wedded to a girl . . . who brought deep understanding to our union and who shared many interests with me."

The tone here is decidedly cool, not at all the stuff (or so we have been taught) of a promising union. The standard cultural script calls for surging rhythms of romance, pressing sexual passion; their absence (we are told) connotes inauthenticity and foretells disaster. Add in the fact that Sagarin, even after marriage, would lead a parallel life as an active homosexual *and* would keep that secret from most of the world (and for a time from his wife), and we would seem to be looking at a relationship destined to fail.

But the cultural script most sexologists agree on is full of equations too glibly drawn. Sex is not the same as love (though it risks un-Americanism to say so), nor does emotional satisfaction hinge on ecstatic passion, nor "honesty" guarantee a secure peace. Besides, the sexologists contradict themselves. They also tell us that the most reliable bedrock for an *enduring* union is not rapture and frank-heartedness but more prosaic (and scarcer) stuff: being a reliable listener, an enjoyable companion, a caring friend. And all of *that* Gert and Ed had—plus a periodic sex life as well. *They* viewed their marriage as a success. Should we presume to know better?

As for when, and to what extent, Gert became aware of her husband's second, homosexual, life, she has preferred in our several interviews to leave the details shrouded. One close friend of the Sagarins believes that Gert went into the marriage knowing, without ever probing for specifics, that Ed had occasional (no more than that) homosexual experiences. But other intimates believe that Gert put the pieces together at some point later in the marriage—after hearing enough rumors, or receiving an anonymous letter, or herself coming upon evidence of a homosexual tryst.

What Gert was willing to tell me was that when Ed was writing *The Homosexual in America* in 1950 (some fourteen years into their marriage), she was well aware of the nature of the project—though not, it would seem from other sources, of the extent of the personal "research" involved. Whenever it was that Gert learned the full truth, she will not discuss (with me, at any rate) the extent, if any, of her turmoil over the knowledge, the shape of the resolutions she made, the exact measure of her accommodation. Perhaps she no longer remembers. Or ever allowed herself to.

With the Great Depression, Sagarin, like many others, had to drop out of college. He held down a variety of jobs to make ends meet, including ghost-writing and editing other people's manuscripts. He also put his fluency in French to good use, handling the European correspondence for a cosmetics firm. Gradually, he branched out into sales and management, and in the process learned a great deal about the chemistry of perfumes and the technology of their production. Born scholar that he was, Sagarin turned that knowledge into the stuff of serious, deliberative inquiry. He published several consequential articles on the sense of smell, and then—characteristically eager to maximize whatever restricted opportunities came his way—managed to persuade Columbia University to let him teach an adjunct course on the chemistry of cosmetics. In the fifties he produced a massive, three-volume collection (*Cosmetics, Science and Technology*) for which he enlisted contributions from many of the country's leading specialists.

Sagarin stayed active in the perfume industry in various capacities into the sixties (for a while he was involved with a firm in which Lena Horne was a partner) without ever finding in it a true vocation or ever making much more than a decent living at it. Martin Rieger, a Sagarin associate from those years, vividly recalls him "with his old bound briefcase, schlepping through New York City, an intelligent type who didn't fit the business at all."

Neither Ed nor Gert ever cared much about accumulating possessions or money—it was almost a matter of political principle. The woman who edited several of Sagarin's later books, and knew the couple well, put it to me this way: "Ed never knew how to take care of himself," was "hopelessly naive about money" and "an easy mark" for the assorted sharks of the academic and publishing worlds; "Gert was the *more* practical of the two, but they were both babes in the woods."

Donald Webster Cory believed—and most sexologists would still agree—that Alfred Kinsey's two volumes, *Sexual Behavior in the Human Male* (1948) and *Sexual Behavior in the Human Female* (1952), were unmatched for their integrity, scope and influence. Cory made no claim that *The Homosexual in America* could "stand on the same shelf" with Kinsey's work. But he did claim—and there is no reason to doubt him—that he had "conceptualized [his own book] before I had ever heard of Kinsey." For years, Cory later wrote, "I had been impressed by the gap in the literature of homosexuality"—namely, how homosexuals "themselves felt, how they saw their lives, how they reacted to each other."*

Before Kinsey and Cory, penologists and psychiatrists had been the designated experts on the subject, and they had used their limited clinical samples to declare homosexuality pathological. In the sixties, the professional literature became more majestically moralistic and denunciatory still, as psychiatric "experts" such as Edmund Bergler, Irving Bieber and Charles Socarides joined journalists like Jess Stern (*The Sixth Man*) in producing a widely accepted portrait of homosexuality as a diseased and dangerous scourge. Hollywood would begin to confirm that image with the 1962 film *Advise and Consent*, followed by a legion of movies with simpering, vicious gay men and murderous or suicidal lesbians.

The only partial exception in the early sixties—there were none in the early fifties—were psychoanalyst Robert Lindner's several books (*Rebel Without a Cause; Must You Conform?*). Though Lindner refused automatically to conflate homosexuality with pathology (or nonconformity of any kind with mental illness), he also believed that more

---

*There have been word-of-mouth rumors for some time that Kinsey himself had had homosexual experiences. But the full extent of his involvement, especially as he grew older, has only recently been revealed; in other words, Kinsey was himself something of an "insider." See James H. Jones, *Alfred C. Kinsey* (Norton: 1997), as well as my essay, "Kinsey's Urethra," in this volume, evaluating Jones's revelations.

needed to be known about homosexuality—"the source of immense quantities of unhappiness and frustration"—so that it could be better "eradicated." For a less tepid and compromised view in those years one had to look to Europe and to the sympathetic works of Magnus Hirshfeld, Edward Carpenter and Havelock Ellis (all of which, from today's perspective, suffer from too much pseudoscience and too many confident overgeneralizations about "third sexes," and the like).

A good deal of fiction and poetry about lesbians and gay men *had* been published before 1951—from Gertrude Stein's *Tender Buttons* in 1914 to Gore Vidal's *The City and the Pillar* in 1948. But of "insider" nonfiction, there was almost nothing before Cory's 1951 book. The chief exception was *The Intersexes* (1908) by "Xavier Mayne" (the American novelist and scholar Edward I. Prime-Stevenson), a pioneering, underappreciated survey of homosexuality which Cory did not cite in his own book. He did, however, have high praise for Gide's *Corydon*, claiming it stood as a "great" philosophical discussion of homosexuality. It was in honor of Gide that Sagarin chose his pseudonym: Don Cory—a reversal of *Corydon*. He added the "Webster" to avoid the possibility, given the commonness of the name, of another Donald Cory suing him.

Cory had no team of assistants, no foundation support, no academic legitimization—none of the perks that today are the commonplaces of research in sexology. He did have one volunteer, a footloose, financially independent young man named John Horton, who had recently gotten his B.A. in anthropology at Columbia. Cory gave Horton two specific jobs: to look up all the laws in the forty-eight states that applied to homosexuality, and to write to each department of the federal government asking if they had figures on the numbers of homosexuals who worked for them. (The results are printed as appendices to *The Homosexual in America*.)

When I asked Horton why he thought Cory had turned to him for help, he replied, "Maybe because I had a black lover. Cory had had a number of affairs with black men. He used to boast of the frequency with which he was able to pick men up along the benches at Central Park West in the Seventies"—then a major gay male cruising ground. According to Horton, Cory would occasionally invite a sexual partner or friend he had grown fond of home to dinner, but he, Horton, was "the only one Gertrude thought was homosexual" (so she told her husband, who repeated it to Horton).

In the years Cory spent preparing *The Homosexual in America*, he (as he would put it in the book) "became more and more struck" by the notion that homosexuals were, like more established ethnic, racial and subcultural groups, a distinct and legitimate minority. This became the main thesis of *The Homosexual in America*, along with the implied corollary that homosexuals were entitled to the same rights as other citizens, and that majoritarian *mis*treatment—and not anything inherent in homosexuality itself—was chiefly responsible for whatever "pathology" could be found in the gay world.

Cory may not have been entitled to his claim of absolute originality in applying the minority concept to homosexuals. As early as 1921 Kurt Hiller, the left-wing German homosexual activist, had suggested something similar; and Harry Hay, the pioneering gay radical, expressed much the same notion at much the same time Cory did. Yet it remains indisputably true that *The Homosexual in America* gave the "minority" concept wide circulation for the first time, thus laying the cornerstone for what has come to be called "identity politics."

Read today, *The Homosexual in America* has its decidedly dated and conventional sections. For starters, its title: the book is not about *the* homosexual, it's about gay men, and the references in it to lesbian lives are perfunctory and ill informed. Other offhanded orthodoxies dot the pages: "the sexual instinct . . . is usually stronger in the male"; "a permanent relationship" is the surest guide to happiness; "promiscuity" represents a flight from intimacy; the aging homosexual is a "sad specter"; and so forth. Moreover, even as *The Homosexual in America* tries to demolish many of the reigning stereotypes about the gay world, it corroborates others. Denying the standard (and still current) view that homosexuals are more prone to depression and suicide than other people, Cory nonetheless maintains that "instability and restlessness" *are* defining features of gay male life. Though he was able—far in advance of his day—to see the iconoclastic stance as central to gay subcultural identity, he also negatively characterized the subculture as "fickle" and "rootless."

Yet the original, even visionary sections of *The Homosexual in America* outweigh the conventional ones and mark its true distinction. Against the current of his day, against the deep-seated tradition of American sex-negativism, Cory insisted that there was nothing dishonorable about sexual pleasure; that the human animal was "basically, instinctually, and naturally" bisexual; that biological theories about homosexuality were mostly bad science; that there existed a well-defined gay subculture which was all at once unassimilable to mainstream culture *and* "a banner-bearer in the struggle for liberalization of our sexual conventions." Cory urged homosexuals "not [to] fear the group life of the gay world . . . It is a circle of protection . . . Alone, you cannot change the world, but the combined efforts of many will surely effect a beneficial change."

Cory also sounded an astute—and astonishingly contemporary note—in insisting that "many homosexuals are, in the totality of their lives, not queer people at all, and many heterosexuals are extremely queer." He emphasized that "hard and fast categories"—homosexual, heterosexual, bisexual—are "rather meaningless oversimplifications." Four decades later, such views are at the ideological heart of what is currently called "queer theory"—the latest and purportedly new advance in gay self-understanding. Who would believe it?—the themes of contingency, change and fluidity being sounded in 1951, from the pen of a frail, gnomelike perfume salesman, trapped in a quixotic body, pulled in the deepest recesses of his being between anarchic Dionysian desires and the ordered virtues of Apollonian civics.

The civics part ("promiscuity is a flight from intimacy" et al.) might have been less strenuously declared had Cory written in a less fearful and suffocatingly conventional time. In the early fifties Joe McCarthy was in full vulturish flight, political and sexual nonconformists were being purged from public and private employment alike, and not even the ACLU would lift a finger on behalf of homosexuals. When Cory, among others, tried to win the ACLU's support in 1952, the organization informed him (as he later described it) that "if we feel our rights have been denied we should go to the district attorney and to the grand jury and fight without their aid."

Cory decided that "under the circumstances" the individual homosexual had little choice but to "take refuge behind the mask." For himself at least, he could not justify "subjecting those close to me to possible embarrassment or injury. . . ." Yet Cory made the decision for pseudonymity ruefully, aware that he was perpetuating a vicious cycle, realizing that "until we are willing . . . to identify ourselves . . . we are unlikely to . . . break down the barriers of shame or to change public attitudes."

But he hoped for the dawn of a different day, and at the close of *The Homosexual in America,* he struck a millenarian note: "In the millions who are silent and submerged, I see a potential, a reservoir of protest, a hope for a portion of mankind. And in my knowledge that our number is legion, I raise my head high and proclaim that we, the voiceless millions, are human beings, entitled to breathe the fresh air and enjoy, with all humanity, the pleasures of life and love on God's green earth."

Today such words may sound vacuous and trite, when for decades growing numbers have been coming out and joining up. But in 1951, secrecy and fear were in the saddle, and visionary calls to arms all but unknown. A handful, like Cory, were doing *something,* however locally or anonymously, to change the oppressive climate, but most gay people, having been dutifully socialized in self-disgust, were spending their energies and exercising their willpower in concealing or denying their sexual orientation—or trying to change it through psychotherapy. Even had the needed self-esteem and courage been in greater supply, there was, in 1951, scarcely any organized political movement to come out *into.*

A handful of gay men, led by Harry Hay, Rudi Gernreich (later famous as a designer) and Chuck Rowland, had just launched the tiny and secret Mattachine Society in Los Angeles—the name taken from a medieval fraternity of unmarried townsmen. That same year of 1951, the owners of a San Francisco gay bar, the Black Cat, won the landmark right from the state Supreme Court *legally* to serve gay customers. Then, in 1953, the homosexual magazine *ONE* (and subsequently its corporate entity, ONE, Inc.) was launched in Los Angeles, followed two years later by the birth in San Francisco of the first lesbian organization in the United States, the Daughters of Bilitis (DOB), the name taken from Pierre Louys's erotic poem "Songs of Bilitis." These organizations comprised by the mid-fifties the minuscule "homophile" movement. The choice of the name "homophile" over "homosexual" itself illustrates the nervous hope of these pioneers that if they emphasized the nonlustful emotions (*philia* = friendship/love) they might better win sympathy and support from the antigay mainstream—not that it was aware, or cared.

When *The Homosexual in America* was published, Sagarin's employer somehow found out about his double identity and fired him. As he lamented in a letter to Alfred Kinsey, "I lost my job . . . directly and exclusively due to the book. It is difficult to understand how any progress can be made if economic punishment is inflicted on all who protest." (Kinsey and Cory had met briefly back in 1951 and occasionally corresponded until Kinsey's death in 1956. By mid-1952 Sagarin was using his real name when writing to Kinsey, though the level of intimacy between the two men never proceeded very far.)

Upsetting though the firing was, Sagarin did soon find another job in the cosmetics industry. Besides, the book itself proved a success. It went back to press several times during the fifties, was translated into French and Spanish, and elicited 2,000 letters from readers—many of them versions of "thank you for a ray of hope."

Writing to a member of ONE, Cory contentedly summarized his newfound notoriety: "My correspondence is from all over the world, in many languages, people beg me to read a manuscript, leave it on my doorstep, threaten me with a lawsuit for failing to return it, take offense when I tell them how bad it is, and would not dream of paying for the return postage. Oh well, why think of the ungrateful, when so many have written me letters that reassured me, if ever I needed it, that my work was worth undertaking!"

The Homosexual in America did indeed prove a landmark for many, including a number of people who went on to play important roles in the pre-Stonewall gay movement. Randy Wicker, active in both the early black and gay civil rights struggles, has told me that he considers Cory's book "the most important thing in the early gay movement . . . I was like a religious fanatic underlining passages of the Bible . . . "

For young Jim Kepner, who joined the fledgling L.A. Mattachine Society in 1952 and became an editor of *ONE* magazine, *The Homosexual in America* was "a clarion call in the dark for gays all over the country." Cory's book, Kepner told me, "gave a shot in the arm" to the newly formed Mattachine Society. He leapt with excitement one day when he was passing Pickwick's (*the* Hollywood bookstore) and saw stacks of *The Homosexual in America* displayed in the front window.

Barbara Gittings was so stirred by the book when she read it a few years after it appeared, that she wrote the publisher (Greenberg, a small press which for two decades had been issuing gay novels, bringing down a post office suit on its head) for Cory's address, then went to New York City to meet with him several times. Cory told her about Mattachine and One, Inc., and in 1956 Gittings managed a trip to the West Coast, where she also hooked up with DOB; two years later, she helped found its first East Coast chapter in New York City, was elected its first president, and later edited the pioneering lesbian periodical *The Ladder*.

The impact of Cory's book carried beyond gay circles. Alfred Kinsey, pressed by Cory for some sort of endorsement, managed (with characteristic midwestern restraint) to call it "a worthwhile addition to the factual material that is available on the subject." Norman Mailer (with characteristic New York brio) hailed the book as revelatory. He even wrote an article about it for *ONE* in which he announced that "few books . . . [had ever] cut so radically at my prejudices and altered my ideas so profoundly . . . I found myself thinking in effect, "*My God, homosexuals are people, too.*"

In short order, *The Homosexual in America* became the Ur-text for the pre-Stonewall homophile movement. And Donald Webster Cory became widely regarded as its "father," an admired, celebrated figure—even if within limited circles.

Sagarin slowly began to involve himself further in the embryonic public gay world—always as Cory, not Sagarin. He also—using as a subscription base the large correspondence he had received in response to *The Homosexual in America*—set up in 1952 the Cory Book Service; it selected for subscribers a gay-themed title each month, usually of high quality (*The Poems of Cavafy;* Angus Wilson's *Hemlock and After,* Roger Peyrefitte's *Special Friendships*).

Further, Cory began to give public lectures as well, most notably a militant speech at the 1952 annual meeting of the International Committee for Sex Equality at the University of Frankfurt in Germany. In it, he excoriated the puritanical view of sex, and lauded Kinsey's work. But more, much more, had to be done, Cory argued at Frankfurt. He urged that efforts be made "to enlist friends among the medical, psychological, legal and other professions," and, as well, to educate homosexuals themselves away from *self-*condemnation and toward a realization of the necessity of struggling against social oppression—precisely the kind of work that the Mattachine Society would increasingly undertake during the fifties. What had been accomplished thus far, Cory said, might appear "meager." But he stressed the enormous importance of . . . beginnings . . . This is a new cycle and a dynamic one . . . "

When the gay magazine *ONE* made its first appearance in January 1953, Cory agreed to appear on its masthead as Contributing Editor, a position he held for more than three years. In the most notable of the articles he wrote for *ONE,* he denounced the contempt most homosexual men held for the effeminate among them, labelling the attitude "anti-feminist, anti-woman"—for the day, strikingly phrased. He underscored, too, the irony of homosexuals "pleading for acceptance from the world at large," yet refusing tolerance and understanding to those within their own ranks who differed from the norm. Once again, Cory was sounding themes rare in their day, and ones that continue to resonate.

Cory also distinguished between effeminacy and the "very distinctive [male] homosexual method of speech" with which it was often confused; the latter was a special argot, an "over-distinctive pronunciation of consonants, and lengthy pronunciation of vowels." Here Cory was building on his earlier argument that homosexuals constituted a definable subculture—a matter still contested today—itemizing as well what he took to be a distinctive gay walk, stare and handshake. He viewed these as reflexive, not conscious, and "neither masculine nor feminine, but specifically and peculiarly homosexual."

Back in 1951, after completing the manuscript for *The Homosexual in America*, Cory had asked Kinsey to approach Harry Benjamin, the pioneering transsexual researcher, about writing an introduction to the book. Benjamin had begged off, but had suggested Albert Ellis as a replacement.

Ellis at the time was chief psychologist for New Jersey's Diagnostic Center and had just published an iconoclastic book, *The Folklore of Sex*, in which he had mocked the American need to justify sexual pleasure with an overlay of romantic rhetoric and had made the unorthodox suggestion that "society makes sick people out of 'perverts'." Meeting Ellis would prove a milestone for Cory—liberatory according to some, disastrous in the eyes of homophile activists.

Ellis had agreed to write the introduction for *The Homosexual in America*—and it had proven a curious one. While applauding the book as "by far the best non-fiction picture of the American homosexual" available, and as a "well-warranted indictment of our smug and sadistic heterosexual persecution of homosexuals," Ellis had disputed several of Cory's views—and, in particular, his "pessimism concerning the possibility of adjusting homosexuals to more heterosexual modes of living."

Cory had argued in his book that homosexuality was "involuntary though not inborn," and therefore not susceptible to "change"— through psychoanalysis or otherwise. Ellis believed that *exclusive* male homosexuality denoted a neurotic fear of women, and thus could and should be treated. (In these years, almost nobody thought lesbianism was frequent or important enough to be worth much discussion.)

Ellis's treatment goal was not the standard psychoanalytic one of *annihilating* a male homosexual's drive, but rather adding heterosexual attraction to his repertoire of desire. He claimed a high success rate with his own patients, but never bothered to explore whether those who had successfully "expanded their options" had actually shifted the focus of their desire or merely their outward behavior—and even in terms of behavior, how many had subsequently "backslid." Similarly, nowhere in Ellis's voluminous writings, then or later, does he satisfactorily define the loaded terminology he casually employs ("neurosis," "disturbance," etc.), nor ever question his basic assumption that *some* degree of heterosexuality is a prerequisite for happiness. His logic remained self-enclosed: he simply defined "exclusivity" as "neurotic," without ever offering a cogent discussion of "normalcy" as a concept, or itemizing the criteria he used for recognizing it.

Today, over ninety and still in active practice, Ellis insisted when I talked to him that he had never argued that *all* exclusively gay men were "disturbed"—merely "most." Yet in tracking his writings through the decades, it becomes clear that he admitted the *possibility* of some exclusively homosexual men being non-neurotic only in the '70s, after the modern gay movement had come into existence. It needs to be added, however, that as early as 1954 (in his book, *The American Sexual Tragedy*), Ellis took the position—remarkable for that day, or this— that "what is scientific sauce for the goose should also be sauce for the gander . . . that exclusive heterosexuality can be just as fetishistic as exclusive homosexuality."

As early as 1951, moreover, Ellis, like Cory, had been arguing that heterosexual prejudice was itself of major importance in accounting for the psychological problems sometimes found in gay people. Moreover, both he and Sagarin were scornful of the monogamous ideal, seeing it as part and parcel of a sex-negative culture, and both argued for a reevaluation of prevailing moral values that disapproved of all sexual activity not (as Sagarin put it in a 1952 article) "romantic in origin and procreative in direction."

But for several years, some distance continued to separate the two men ideologically. Their disagreements centered on the degree to which homosexuality was "curable." Following Kinsey, Sagarin agreed that "people can and do change their patterns of sexual life over a period of years," and he was willing to believe "that certain psychologists can aid certain homosexuals in accepting a bisexual pattern of life." But (doubtless thinking of his own life) Sagarin continued to insist that those able to make a bisexual adjustment nonetheless went right on feeling "a major need for gratification with their own sex"—and therefore "cannot be said to be 'cured'."

Unlike Ellis, moreover, Sagarin continued to assert in the early fifties that many if not most homosexual men could *not*—even when they badly wanted to, and underwent prolonged psychotherapy—simply "add" heterosexuality to their repertoire of desire. He also insisted that the typical homosexual "can only make a satisfactory adjustment when he is prepared completely to accept himself and his way of life, without regrets, misgivings, shame, or unconscious defense."

By the end of the fifties, however, Ellis and Sagarin had come to hold nearly identical views about male homosexuality, with Ellis standing ideologically pat and Sagarin shifting his views in Ellis's direction. The likely explanation for the shift is that it resulted from Sagarin entering into therapy with Ellis. Ellis denies this ("It was a case of parallel evolution that we came to hold nearly identical attitudes about homosexuality") and even denies that Sagarin was ever in *formal* treatment with him. "The fact is," he told me, "Sagarin and I were never more than moderately close." From time to time, in the course of discussing other matters, Sagarin would talk over some of his problems, "but he was never an actual patient of mine."

But if Ellis wants no credit for either behavioral or ideological persuasiveness, several of Sagarin's intimates insist otherwise. One of his closest friends has strongly hinted to me that Sagarin turned to Ellis as a result of family pressure at a "tumultuous" moment in the marriage—perhaps when his son Fred was born: it was time, Sagarin was told, "to get control over himself." According to this same friend, Ellis's "repression technique"—which insists that one can learn consciously to control disruptive personal "obsessions" (what Ellis would later come to call "rational emotive therapy")—did help Sagarin curtail his homosexual "promiscuity." Sagarin believed enough in Ellis— by Ellis's own testimony—to send him "lots of referrals" throughout the 1950s, mostly "young men who had been his lovers."

On the other hand, we know for certain that Ellis was not Sagarin's first therapist. As he revealed in *The Homosexual in America* back in 1951, Sagarin had earlier realized that marriage had *not* "reduce[d] the urge for gratification with men," and "to rid" himself of it he had entered a "long analysis." To his surprise, Cory wrote in *The Homosexual in America,* the therapist had focused not on repressing or dissolving Cory's homosexuality but on overcoming his feelings of guilt about it—a goal, so Cory claimed in his book, that had been achieved. His guilt did diminish and he found himself enjoying homosexual relations *more* than before, even while feeling fewer "fears and repugnances toward sexual union with a woman." Thereafter, so Cory completes the tale in *The Homosexual in America,* he had adopted "a temperate and disciplined indulgence in homosexual affairs," and became entirely content with his "successful marriage" and "happy home."

Ellis agrees that Sagarin did have a good marriage, but disputes the rest of Cory's narrative. That first "long analysis," in Ellis's view, "didn't take": "When I met Cory he was an exceptionally promiscuous gay man." And remained so—though after *their* "few, informal sessions" together, according to Ellis, "Cory was able to get more pleasure from the sex he had with his wife." By 1959, in any case, after their views had become nearly identical, Ellis described Donald Webster Cory (in print) as "the best adjusted homosexual, by far, whom I have ever met . . ."

As part of his gradual involvement in the public gay world, Cory had joined the Veterans Benevolent Association, a state-chartered New York City gay male organization begun after World War II and serving its 75 to 100 members largely as a social group. The VBA ceased to exist in 1954 (it had "run into a little difficulty," was Cory's oblique reference to a correspondent). But the very next year saw the founding of a more overtly political organization: the New York City chapter of the Mattachine Society (MSNY). Cory had little involvement with MSNY during its first few years of existence, despite the fact that as early as 1953 he had praised Mattachine's work on the West Coast as "remarkable." He would occasionally attend one of MSNY's monthly meetings in its shabby rented loft space on West 49th Street, but it was not until 1957 that he agreed to be a guest speaker there. Soon after, he brought Ellis along to a meeting and before long Ellis, too, was invited to speak (this was at a time when most "experts" scornfully turned down Mattachine's invitations).

Ellis's talk at MSNY raised the hackles of at least a segment of his audience. Many members of Mattachine, though brave and unorthodox enough to join the organization or at least show up at some of its meetings, nonetheless were prone to defer to psychiatric authority and to agree with the profession's then commonplace equation of homosexuality with pathology. Yet Ellis's overbearing manner and dogmatic assertions—that "fixed" homosexuality was a sign of "disturbance" and that psychotherapy should be given "a fair trial" so that "repressed" heterosexual desires could emerge—brought even a few of the deferential to their feet.

When he finished speaking, "slings and arrows . . . flew thick and fast" (according to the *Mattachine Newsletter*) with several people in the audience challenging Ellis's view that some degree of heterosexuality was a prerequisite for happiness. Though Ellis—as always—held his ground, he was not only invited back for additional talks but was also asked to write for the *Mattachine Review*. After all, in the context of the psychiatric profession of the day Ellis was a decided liberal: he called for the decriminalization of homosexuality and was willing to testify in court against the common practice of police entrapment. By the late fifties, moreover, Ellis and Cory had joined forces to compile a comprehensive "Encyclopedia of Homosexual Behavior" (despite several years of work and the completion of dozens of in-depth interviews, the project, due to lack of funding, was never finished nor published).

After 1957, Cory's own involvement with MSNY quickened. He never took on much of the nitty-gritty organizational work, but he did speak at the fifth annual Mattachine convention in 1958, let himself be listed on the board of advisors and then elected to the more hands-on board of directors (where, up through 1965, he compiled the highest attendance record of any director).

Yet it wasn't until May 1962 that Cory finally took out formal membership. "After watching your valiant work for many years," he wrote in his application letter to Mattachine, "I have come to the conclusion that the movement for education and social justice deserves my active support. If I can be of some aid in this work, I shall feel gratified and honored."

Cory thereafter served on several committees, spoke before social and religious groups, and initiated dialogues with the YMCA on the treatment of homosexuals and with the New York Board of Health on venereal disease among the homosexual population. Randy Wicker remembers that at Mattachine meetings, he and Cory would, like competing auctioneers, try to outdo each other in exhorting members to increase their donations. By late 1962, Cory, with more than a touch of grandiosity, was writing Dorr Legg of ONE Institute, "There is a danger that the New York group might grow too dependent on me, and I do not want to exercise too much influence."

It was also in 1962 that Cory's real name became known in Mattachine for the first time. When a new book of his, *The Anatomy of Dirty Words,* was published, Randy Wicker remembers someone rushing into the MSNY office one day with a copy—with author Ed Sagarin's picture prominently displayed on the back. If Sagarin (like so many other members of Mattachine) had tried to conceal his name, he had never hidden the fact that he was married. As Frank Kameny, the pioneering Washington, D.C., gay activist, has told me, "Everyone was aware that Cory was married—[it was] known and accepted, no deal made of it. Almost nobody in Mattachine was out of the closet. People's private lives were considered their own business. Besides, Cory had short-circuited any distrust of him as a married man by having written that book."

Sagarin himself drew firm boundaries, never inviting any discussion of personal matters. Mattachine bigwig Curtis Dewees, who probably got to know Sagarin better than anyone else in the organization, was occasionally invited to the Sagarins' Brooklyn apartment—but not when Gertrude was there. Dewees and his lover, Al de Dion, viewed Cory (in de Dion's words) as "an icon, like a Godfather." Yet even so, they knew not to cross the line. As Dewees recalled, "My conversations with Cory were limited basically to the organization, the direction of the movement—that kind of thing; he *never* discussed his inner feelings with me."

Within Mattachine, Cory was regarded more with awe than affection. Not even Dewees was much drawn to him personally. "I respected the man's intelligence," he told me, "his capabilities, what he had done," but he "wasn't much fun to be around." He was too "dead serious," and when his opinion was challenged could be "thin-skinned, easily offended, aggressive."

Harry Hay, the founder of Mattachine and *himself* often called "the father of the homophile movement," actively distrusted Cory. Hay first met him (the two had corresponded earlier) when Cory went to the West Coast in 1955 to speak at the new ONE Institute of Homophile Studies. "I did not like him," Hay told me. Having himself been in the

Communist Party—and "astounded" when I told him that as an undergraduate Cory had had decidedly left-wing views—Hay had grown accustomed to sniffing the air and avoiding what he sensed might be risky people or places. "I never felt safe with Cory in the room. I had the sense I was dealing with someone shifty. I remember thinking, I wish he wasn't here at *ONE*. Who is he really?"

Young Barry Sheer felt no such reluctance. When the famed author of *The Homosexual in America* came across the room at an MSNY meeting to introduce himself, Sheer was delighted. He had read Cory several years earlier when, as an undergraduate at the University of Colorado in Boulder, Sheer had joined the tiny local Mattachine chapter. It was there that he had been introduced to *The Homosexual in America*. "It was," Sheer told me, "*the* book; we would read it and discuss it all the time." Sheer flunked out of Colorado after two years, returned to the east coast, enrolled in Farleigh-Dickinson College in New Jersey and quickly hooked up with New York Mattachine.

Sheer was a good-looking young man with a muscular body and (in his words) "an excess of testosterone." He discharged it generously into the less-laden bodies of the homophile leadership, gaining a reputation (applauded by some, deplored by others) as a "star-fucker." Cory spotted Sheer at a Mattachine meeting one night in 1960 and—never one to play the shrinking violet—invited him out for coffee. "If he hadn't written this book and been a famous person," Sheer told me, "I would have said, 'No,' because he wasn't a heck of a lot to look at. Small, a loud, high-pitched voice, bald, somewhat deformed and walked with a limp."

Yet Sheer quickly found himself involved in what he now calls "a 'Death in Venice' relationship . . . Cory would give me a little money and have me help him with some of his research and I would let him have sex with me . . . I couldn't be especially emotional, but he was quite happy with that, it seemed . . . He'd come and see me two or three times a week. This went on for about three years." The "comrades" in

Mattachine were not kind about Cory's relationship with Sheer. As one of them told me, "Sheer was generally regarded as predatory," and Cory was privately mocked as a john who had to pay for sex—and who then confused it with affection. Sheer soon learned that Cory's real name was Ed Sagarin, and he even met Gertrude once. He found her "a right and proper Jewish matron" and, in retrospect anyway, remains a little indignant at the way Sagarin was "two-timing" her.

Sheer enjoyed helping out with Sagarin's research, *was* attracted to his "powerful intellect" and enjoyed their frequent arguments about homosexuality and "the movement." By 1960 Sagarin's views had not only become indistinguishable from those of Albert Ellis, but were held no less rigidly. "We're a tree that's stunted," he would tell Sheer, "but even if a tree is stunted, does it not grow in its own way and offer shade and beauty? And shouldn't gays be treated that way?"

Sheer rejected that attitude as "condescending tolerance." He was part of a new generation emerging within Mattachine in the early sixties (epitomized by Frank Kameny and the militant Washington, D.C. Mattachine chapter), insistent that there was nothing to apologize for, nothing "stunted" about homosexuals, nothing—other than society's irrational prejudice—that needed "curing." Much of which, in a more tentative, diluted version, Cory had himself argued in *The Homosexual in America,* way back in 1951, before almost anyone else, before perhaps even *he* was fully prepared for the radical potential in his own message. In the interim had come Albert Ellis, a ton of psychoanalytic books "proving" that homosexuality was "pathological," Cory's growing doubts about the quality of comradeship available in the homophile movement and his growing ambition to find greater "legitimacy" as an intellectual in the straight world.

At this same time, in the early sixties, the ideological struggle was heating up in MSNY about whether homosexuality was or wasn't a "mental illness," and the emergent forces, forgetting or never knowing what Cory had once stood for, were increasingly targeting him as the epitome of the played-out Old Guard. Simultaneously, Albert Ellis (and family members as well) was encouraging Sagarin to follow his long-standing scholarly bent and formally pursue an academic career.

Sagarin in 1958, at age 45, entered an accelerated B.A. program for adults at Brooklyn College and completed his undergraduate degree in 1961—graduating in the same class as his son, Fred. He then, at age 48, entered the M.A. program in sociology and wrote his thesis on "The Anatomy of Dirty Words." Scandalized at so unorthodox a topic, Sagarin's department rejected the thesis, but Sagarin got it published as a book in 1962, thumbed his nose at Brooklyn College and enrolled in the doctoral program at NYU.

He had accumulated just enough money to put the perfume business permanently behind him. Against great odds, he would emerge by 1966, at age 53, with a Ph.D., an academic job, and a prolific future career as scholar, teacher, mentor. The orphaned, taunted, physically handicapped youth, the proto-intellectual toiling away uncomplain-ingly for decades in a business world for which he was temperamen-tally unsuited, the triply deviant (disabled, homosexual, left-wing) double-lived misfit—these burdensome, knotted earlier selves would never disappear but would recede, soften, inflict less internal pain, less centrally define a life that had refocused in the legitimizing, deeply gratifying new identity of PROFESSOR Edward Sagarin. Donald Webster Cory would remain alive in print, and in a corner of Sagarin's heart—but oh, the relief of not having him constantly tugging at the sleeve, demanding to share center stage.

Sagarin's personal transition during the early to mid-sixties took place at a time when cataclysmic events—the quickening civil rights struggle at home, the escalating war in Vietnam overseas—were pum-meling and reshaping American consciousness. The tug-of-war within the tiny homophile movement mirrored in miniature the larger social upheavals: the challenge to "expertise" (like those East Asian "specialists" who had gotten us into the Vietnam war) and the new value placed on "differentness" (like the heralding of "Black is Beautiful" and SNCC's rejection of the hallowed goal of assimilation).

Police harassment of gay bars had long been standard, and the clientele of those bars had dutifully cowered under the cop's club. But by the mid-sixties knee-jerk deference to authority had weakened, and when the police raided a gay bar in San Francisco in 1964, a new organization instantly sprang up—the Society for Individual Rights—to protest police harassment; by 1966 it had enrolled a thousand members, becoming the largest homophile organization in the country. That same year, a group of progressive heterosexual ministers joined with gay activists in forming the influential Council on Religion and the Homosexual to combat homophobia.

On the East Coast, too, militancy was on the rise. Under Frank Kameny's leadership, Washington, D.C. Mattachine brandished a new "Gay is Good" slogan that spelled an end to apologetics and prefigured the aggressive confrontational politics of the post-Stonewall period. At New York Mattachine, the conservatives dug in their heels and fought a rear-guard action, but the handwriting was on the wall. The Young Turks started to snicker about Cory "the closet queen," Cory "the old auntie," "Auntie Donnie." Where once he had been almost uniformly hailed for his pioneering role, he was now being ridiculed in *ONE* magazine as a "so-dreary goodykins."

Despite his new legion of detractors, Cory was more active in Mattachine from 1962 to 1965 than ever before, perhaps not least because he was *studying* it: the topic of his NYU doctoral dissertation was "Structure and Ideology in an Association of Deviants"—that is, the Mattachine Society. He sent the manuscript to Dorr Legg of One, Inc., who spent considerable time critiquing it and digging out additional source materials for Sagarin's use.

In these same years Sagarin also began his teaching career—on the Baruch campus of the City University of New York, where he offered a course on minority groups. One of his students at Baruch was Phil Goldberg (today a novelist), who was part of the countercultural coterie on campus; he and his friends had formed a Human Rights Society, raised money for SNCC, and gone South to help with the voter campaign drive.

According to Goldberg, Ed Sagarin was one of the few faculty members sympathetic to their activities, and they were delighted when he agreed to serve as faculty adviser for the Human Rights Society. Sagarin may have begun his retreat from the homophile movement, but he remained decidedly left-leaning in his politics. Barry Sheer recalls how heatedly Sagarin would insist that "the government should take care of you and give you a good start," and if you then failed, "society should still take care of you."

One of Phil Goldberg's close friends, Eddie Zimmerman, enrolled in Sagarin's "minority groups" course. Sagarin encouraged his students to write in a nonacademic, personal style (he rightly prided himself on the lucidity of his own prose), and so when it came time to do his term paper, Eddie decided to write about what it felt like to be coming out as a gay man. When he got the paper back, he saw that Sagarin had written on it, "This is very remarkable. Please see me." Eddie did drop by the office, and (as he tells the story today) Sagarin expressed "great empathy for what I'd gone through." "I've done a lot of research on this," Sagarin told him, "and I think you would benefit from knowing about a group I'm acquainted with—it's called the Mattachine Society."

Mattachine's monthly meeting, he told Eddie, was coming up, and it promised to be a lively one: the well-known writer Donald Webster Cory was scheduled to speak. Eddie decided to go to the meeting, and when he arrived was delighted to see "so many ordinary-looking, mainstream types who were gay. It was important for me." Then, with considerable fanfare, the speaker of the evening was introduced—and out from the wings strode *his* Professor Sagarin! As Eddie tells it, Sagarin came up to him afterward and simply said, "Look, I took a big chance inviting you here, but I thought I should. But it's our secret." They had little subsequent contact, though Eddie does remember Sagarin introducing him one day to a young, blond-haired man, who he later told Eddie was his lover.

Eddie, of course, told his friend Phil Goldberg the whole story, and the following term Phil—though not gay—decided he, too, would sign up for Sagarin's course. But he didn't much like the man ("he was strange, troll-like, put people on edge"), and planned a little theatrical coup of his own. For the section in the course on "the homosexual minority," Sagarin assigned reading from *The Homosexual in America*. Phil carefully rehearsed his plan for how the classroom discussion would begin. Raising his hand, smothering his glee, he boldly asked, "Mr. Cory says such and such. How do *you* feel about that?" Sagarin momentarily blanched, then said, "Mr. Cory and I are of one mind about it."

Sagarin's ongoing discussions with Barry Sheer had made it clear to him (as Sagarin wrote in 1963) that "I was no longer viewing the new homosexual scene from within . . . I was not of the generation that grew up after Kinsey (and Cory), the peer-oriented and other-directed youths" whose voices were beginning to be heard. Yet despite the growing disparagement of his views within Mattachine, Sagarin felt no need to adjust them. Instead, he decided to restate them in a new book, *The Homosexual and His Society*, and shrewdly asked young Barry Sheer to be its coauthor. (Sheer used the pseudonym "John LeRoy," under which he had earlier written articles for the gay press.)

The book appeared in 1963, and became known as "The Second Cory Report." In it, the authors argued that the homophile movement should primarily concern itself not with trying to get people to join up,

but rather with "trying to ease the difficulties" of those already involved and "to enlighten the public on its attitudes." That enlightenment would begin with the acknowledgment that homosexuality was
"a disturbance"—but not "antisocial in its nature."

The Homosexual and His Society bravely devoted considerable space
to what was widely regarded as "unseemly" topics—like hustling and
venereal disease. Moreover, the authors justified their inclusion in
words that have a decidedly contemporary ring: "The hustler, the
cruiser, the lonely and the distressed, the muscle flexer, the partner-
changer, the effeminate hairdresser, the closet queen who is frightened
and the clothes queen who is courting social ridicule: yes, even the
poor disturbed people who are caught up in the sad world of sadomasochism—they are all our brothers, and their cause is ours." This
defense, however partial and patronizing, of outsiders of every stripe,
was complexly at odds with the fact that Sagarin was simultaneously
fighting *within* Mattachine to hold homosexuals to a "responsible,"
nonconfrontational appeasement of the social and psychiatric authorities of the day.

"The Second Cory Report" was immediately and angrily attacked:
the reviewer in *ONE*, for example, denounced it as "pseudo-scientific"
and a mere "rehash of other people's ideas." Sheer himself, in retrospect, regrets having lent his name to those portions of the book that
claimed there was no such thing as a "well-adjusted homosexual," and
that homosexuality originated in "a pathological situation based on
fear, anxiety, or insecurity . . . "

Yet in the counterattack Sheer and Cory published at the time in
ONE, they gave no ground. Indeed, Cory never thereafter budged
from his now formulaic views: homosexuality was not inborn, but was
a "disturbance"; the homophile movement should "accept therapy for
some and adjustment within the framework of homosexuality for others"; the movement should not waste its energy either trying to argue
"the utter normalcy of the homosexual" or emulating "a monogamous,

romantic concept of sexuality" that derived from the official model of heterosexuality.

Cory left unaddressed most of the troubling questions a new generation of gay activists had begun to raise: By what criteria does one establish "disturbance"? Why, if there was "no such thing as a 'homosexual'," was there any such thing as a "heterosexual"? Why should an increased capacity to have sex with someone of the opposite gender be taken as *the* measure of increased health—or, for that matter, an increased capacity to have sex with someone of the same gender? What was a "normal" sex life anyway? And who decided? And on the basis of which fragment of the limited "evidence"? And who had the *right* to decide?

When Frank Kameny came up from D.C. to speak at New York Mattachine in July 1964, he pulled the plug on the epistemological torture machine. "We owe apologies to no-one," Kameny thundered. "Society and its official representatives owe us apologies for what they have done and are doing to us." He insisted that the homophile movement put less effort into trying to educate an indifferent heterosexual mainstream and more into direct demands for civil rights. He assailed the unproven assumptions behind the psychoanalytic model of homosexuality as a "disorder" and insisted that "the entire movement is going to stand or fall upon the question of whether homosexuality is a sickness, and upon our taking a firm stand on it."

Sagarin was in the audience the night of Kameny's speech and (according to Kameny) expressed his disagreement "courteously." But disagree he did, and proceeded to work hard against Kameny sympathizers taking over New York Mattachine. He even allowed his name to be placed in nomination for president on an opposition slate in the crucial 1965 election. Shortly before, Kameny wrote Sagarin a prophetic letter of warning: "You have gotten yourself associated with bad company . . . you have become no longer the vigorous Father of the Homophile Movement, to be revered, respected and listened to, but the senile Grandfather of the Homophile Movement, to be humored and tolerated, at best; to be ignored and disregarded, usually; and to be ridiculated [*sic*], at worst."

The militants won the 1965 election, and most of the Old Guard within New York Mattachine, Sagarin included, left the organization immediately and for good. Sagarin tried to adopt an attitude of resigned inevitability: it is in the very nature of social movements, he counseled his allies, to turn against their founders; but "the politics of rejection would one day lead to the possibilities of rehabilitation." This Olympian abdication concealed considerable indignation and hurt. Sagarin let some of it surface when writing to Dorr Legg the following year: ". . . the homophile movement is a hopeless mess . . . the biggest gang of potential blackmailers against real or alleged or ex-homosexuals in America consists of the leadership of the homophile movement . . . I should like to state that I regard the homophile movement as inimical to the interests of homosexuals."

During the last twenty years of Sagarin's life, much changed: he ascended the academic ladder; reveled in the interchanges, intrigues and joustings of the scholarly life; approximated his long-sought dream of working in harness with a group of like-minded comrades. He became an encyclopedic, adept teacher and for his favored students—mostly male—an admired mentor. And he became the proud paterfamilias: his son Fred, who had chosen to teach handicapped and autistic children as a career, married and had three children of his own, whom Sagarin doted on.

While much changed, nothing changed. "Edward Sagarin," his new alias, added volume upon volume to the already lengthy list of writings he had produced as "Donald Webster Cory" (none of which he would any longer formally acknowledge as his). A few of his many books remain in print and toward the end of his life he even got a novel published and a play produced.

Sagarin's nearly two dozen sociological works are (mostly) liberal in content and accessible in style. In his later years he often sounded themes (as he had in 1951) with a strikingly contemporary resonance: the malleability of the self, the need to historicize "expert" opinion and thus limit its claims to universality. ("Part of the changing process," Sagarin wrote in 1977, "is to believe in the possibility of change . . . in the interests of freedom of choice, one must reject identity.")

None of his many books, however, can be seen as formative, theoretically innovative or heretically heart-stopping. (On this, every sociologist I spoke to agreed—and every one requested anonymity.) Sagarin continued to champion outsiders and underdogs of various kinds (blacks, Jews, antiwar protestors, socialists, prostitutes, alcoholics, gamblers, pornographers, schizophrenics, dwarfs). He fought through his writing to rescue them from the categories of enemy, freak or sinner, stoutly defending their rights against the smug majoritarian morality employed against them.

And yes, he even defended homosexuals, that is, on the limited grounds learned at Albert Ellis's knee: homosexuality should be decriminalized, but not normalized. One should work toward alleviating the many injustices that gay people currently suffered, but "without accepting the traits that mark them as different." "In an analogy which I find striking," Sagarin wrote in a 1979 essay, "I have noted that blindness is undesirable but a blind person is not an undesirable." Homosexuality remained to him a "condition," a "pattern of adjustment" (as he put it in 1973) that represented, in essence, "a perversion of the instinctual drives." Sagarin felt no more need in the 1970s than he had in the 1950s to define the loaded, self-enclosed vocabulary that he continued to assert with such unabated confidence.

Yet his own sexuality remained unchanged—argue though he did in theory for the "malleability of the self." Barry Sheer dropped out of his life after some three or four years. Increasingly militant in the post-Stonewall years, Sheer wrote an article in 1970—"The Anti-

Homosexual in America: Donald Webster Cory"—in which he cuttingly denounced his old mentor, advising the newly empowered young to forget but *not* forgive him.

Sagarin always scrupulously avoided approaching any of his students sexually. But he would still—the frequency decreasing with age and declining health—do a bit of cruising here or there, have a brief encounter, engage the occasional Times Square hustler. One of his forays to Times Square in the late '60s had particularly dire repercussions.

The story centers on "Richard Stein," a young colleague of Sagarin's in the sociology department at CCNY. Stein was part of a group of New Leftist faculty whose politics had proved offensive to some of the older members of the department and who had therefore failed to get tenure. When Stein himself came up for a tenure decision, he felt that Sagarin's sponsorship would produce a positive outcome. But on the day the five person executive committee of the department met to vote on Stein, Sagarin failed to show up and the vote, by 3 to 2, went against Stein's tenure.

What had happened to Sagarin? The accounts vary. According to one of his colleagues (who feels certain that his version is the accurate one), Sagarin had picked up a hustler in Times Square and gone back with him to one of the fleabag hotels that then catered to trysts and transients. The trick had turned nasty, had mugged Sagarin and then fled. Sagarin had had a heart attack in the hotel bathroom and been taken to the hospital. His wallet gone, he could not be identified for a full day. Stein himself doubts the accuracy of this account, primarily because he "saw no bruises of any kind" on his mentor when he visited him in the hospital.

In any case, Sagarin felt terrible about missing the crucial tenure meeting, and after he got back on his feet, he took Stein to lunch to express his deep regret. During the lunch Sagarin spoke openly—as he almost never did, and had not before to Stein—of the fact that he was gay. That he did so—since the heart attack would itself have been sufficient explanation for missing the meeting—suggests intense guilt and remorse, giving added credence to the tale of the Times Square hustler. As for Stein, his career never truly got back on track.

By the early seventies, the "secret" of Sagarin's double identity had become known to a number of his colleagues and even to some of his students and friends. But those who were aware of Sagarin's other life, both sexual and authorial, mostly ignored it. As one of his most admiring graduate students told me, "There's a distinction between knowing and acknowledging. I felt it was impolite, not fair, nasty, to acknowledge Sagarin's homosexuality if he preferred not to discuss it."

But far from everybody "knew." Robert Bierstedt, for example, who had been chair of Sagarin's doctoral committee in 1966, was astonished when I revealed to him that Sagarin and Cory had been one and the same person; Bierstedt had never, in the intervening thirty years, heard any rumor or gossip to that effect.

Sagarin himself was still not publicly owning up to the double identity. The sociologist Vern Bullough told me that after Sagarin saw galley proofs in 1975 of Bullough's forthcoming *Sexual Variance*—in which he had said something like, "Donald Webster Cory is also known as Edward Sagarin"—Sagarin contacted the publisher, Wiley, and threatened to sue. Before Wiley would agree to go to press, they made Bullough get depositions from various individuals who had been active in the homophile movement affirming that Sagarin and Cory were one and the same person.

When the January 1973 issue of *Contemporary Sociology* appeared with Sagarin's denunciatory essay-review of a dozen recent gay liberationist books, Laud Humphreys, a professor of sociology at Pitzer College in California, hit the roof. Humphreys's own (by then notorious) 1970 book, *Tearoom Trade: Impersonal Sex in Public Places*, was not among those damned in the review, but Sagarin had managed glancingly to refer to Humphreys's "unconvincing" work.

The two men had some startling commonalities in their histories: both had come late to academia and sociology, both were left-wing in their politics—and both were gay men who had married and fathered children. The parallels may have fueled Humphreys's anger; he was feeling suffocated by his own half-opened closet door and enraged at the homophobic hypocrisy of his own university, which had tried to delay his degree and also the publication of *Tearoom Trade*.

After reading Sagarin's essay, Humphreys's first reaction was to send off a rip-snorting letter of protest to the editors of *Contemporary Sociology*. He accused them of having "ordered this mass slaughter . . . as a sort of 'protective reaction' strike to rid us of the troublesome 'homosexual researchers' and that embarrassing gay question all in one operation . . . a whole genre of contemporary sociology, not to mention a movement for human freedom, are scheduled for clever annihilation."

When Humphreys failed to get a response that satisfied him, he decided on a second line of attack: he would speak out publicly at the 1974 annual sociology convention in Montreal. Humphreys was scheduled to appear as a discussant on a panel ("Theoretical Perspectives on Homosexuality") where Sagarin was due to give a paper surveying the recent literature. In the paper, distributed to the panelists in advance of the session, Sagarin denounced those fellow sociologists who encouraged or supported homosexuals in "coming out." In particular, he denounced the respected "pro-gay" researchers Evelyn Hooker and John Gagnon as special pleaders who had falsified or misread their own data.

After reading Sagarin's paper, Humphreys contacted a number of sociologists who he knew to be gay and urged them to attend the panel on the following day. He then stayed up all night preparing his rebuttal. Humphreys would ever after refer to the next day's events as "Bloody Monday."

Sagarin read his paper exactly as he had prepared it; he attacked recent "liberationist" scholarship, and for good measure appealed to homosexuals to seek therapeutic counseling. According to *The Body*

Politic, a leading gay publication of the day, Sagarin's remarks "were greeted with disbelief and laughter from attending delegates."

Laud Humphreys then rose to respond. He began by fully coming out himself for the first time as "a gay man," and then—as he had rehearsed the night before—periodically inserted "fake slippage" into his responding remarks; that is, he would refer one minute to "Professor Sagarin," the next to "Mr. Cory"; at one point he addressed Sagarin directly as "Mr. Cory."

In all likelihood, most of the audience had never heard of Donald Webster Cory—just as today almost everyone I've mentioned the name to responds with a blank stare (my favorite: "Don Cory?—was he the Mafia owner of the Stonewall bar?"). But Sagarin himself got decidedly rattled. When Humphreys moved in for the kill and sardonically asked, "And where did you get *your* data?" Sagarin's hands clenched and his voice choked up. "I am my data," he finally said. Tears fell from the corners of his eyes.*

To no-one's surprise, Sagarin was not one of the participants when, soon after the 1974 convention and in part to protest it, the Sociologists Gay Caucus was formed. Laud Humphreys served on the original steering committee.

Edward Sagarin/Donald Webster Cory died of a heart attack in 1986 at age 73.

—*an earlier version of this essay appeared in* The Harvard Gay and Lesbian Review, *Fall 1997, Vol. 4, No. 4*

---

*Eyewitness accounts vary somewhat in describing Sagarin's reaction to Humphreys's attack. (One has Sagarin sobbing, pushing back his chair and leaving the session before it officially ended.) I'm grateful to Stephen O. Murray for calling my attention to the divergence in memory, and for catching several errors in a previous version of this essay.

Masters and Johnson

As has been clear for some time now, Masters and Johnson are not noted for their conceptual clarity or sophistication. In their first two books, *Human Sexual Response* and *Human Sexual Inadequacy,* their boldly modernist findings on physiology (the multiorgasmic and clitoral nature of female sexuality) were presented in jarring tandem with their highly traditional psychosocial assumptions (monogamous lifetime pair-bonding as the optimal condition for human happiness). But sympathy for the overall daring of their enterprise disarmed some critics, and their Olympian tone and forbidding technical vocabulary intimidated others. Besides, many hoped that Masters and Johnson's reluctance to speculate signaled the kind of stringent self-denial that might one day result in a carefully constructed theoretical synthesis that would subsume the earlier contradictions in their work.

With the publication of Masters and Johnson's *Homosexuality in Perspective* [1979], that hope must be foresworn. If anything, the conceptual fog has thickened, the intellectual evasions and simplicities multiplied. One now fears the problem is less presumption than obtuseness, for the most astonishing aspect of Masters and Johnson's altogether astonishing new study is their inability to distinguish the

banal from the noteworthy. They overvalue their more obvious findings and negate or misconstrue their most original ones.

Thus they announce, with considerable fanfare, the "discovery" that
no significant physiological differences exist between homosexuals and
heterosexuals in regard to "efficient sexual functioning," or in
amenability to treatment for occasional dysfunction. These findings,
they predict, will greatly dilute antigay prejudice. But why? It has never
been widely presumed that gay people are "sexually dysfunctional";
"performance" may be one of the few areas in which they have not
been negatively stereotyped. The opposite premise—that gays are too
sexual, too active in pursuit of pleasure—has been a far more commonplace assumption in the homophobic culture at large.

Just as Masters and Johnson are overemphatic in declaiming the importance of their most obvious findings, they fail to recognize and underscore their most genuinely startling ones. Though its significance
seems to have escaped them, they do offer data of immense importance in helping to advance debate on a number of longstanding (and
long-stalemated) issues: Is Freud's suggestion that we are all innately
bisexual accurate? Is the gay lifestyle sufficiently distinctive to warrant
designating it a "subculture"? Is sexual fidelity an essential ingredient
of emotional commitment? Is monogamous pair-bonding the likeliest
guarantee of human happiness?

The Masters and Johnson data on bisexuality are found in two sections of their book—those on "ambisexuality" and "fantasy." While re-
cruiting over the years for their various studies, Masters and Johnson
occasionally met men and women (ultimately they gathered 12 of
them, six of each gender) who reported frequent sexual interaction
with members of both sexes, showed "complete neutrality in partner
preference" and evinced "no interest in sustained relationships." These
last two attitudes convinced Masters and Johnson that these people
should be distinguished from bisexuals, and accordingly they designated them "ambisexuals." Possibly they should be distinguished from

the entire human race, if we can believe Masters and Johnson's further findings about them. Ambisexuals, it seems, infrequently fantasize, never feel "performance anxiety," are "confident in their approach to any sexual opportunity," "obviously enjoy" any presented to them, "embody a tremendous sexual appeal [and the] . . . freedom to express sexual interest without prejudice or bias that might neutralize the appeal." In short, transcultural, suprahuman beings.

Except we are not quite persuaded they actually exist, not, at any rate, in the pure form Masters and Johnson describe. No one has ever accused Masters and Johnson of exaggerating for theatrical effect (their prose is turgid beyond all reason or belief), but they have often been charged with imprecision—a charge certainly applicable to their discussion of "ambisexuality." At one point Masters and Johnson describe the ambisexual's interest in sex as "purely a matter of physical release"; at another, as "primarily for tension release." Which is it—"purely" or "primarily"? The point is not too fine, since "primarily" leaves room for a host of additional possibilities—including an interest in "relating" of which ambisexuals are purportedly devoid. Skepticism increases when we learn that one ambisexual woman has been married. Masters and Johnson try to reassure us: "the marriage was contracted purely for the convenience of her partner; she had no investment in the personal relationship." "Purely" again; Masters and Johnson seem bent on dichotomy.

Suspicions aroused, we read on about these fascinating extraterrestrials. They have "no histories of trouble with the law or with authority figures; no patterns of poor performance at work, school or in the military . . . no difficulty in functioning responsibly in most facets of their lives," no history of "psychological pathology" and "no physical or metabolic defects." Hmmm. Does the absence of "patterns of poor performance" imply the presence solely of "excellent" ones, or were mediocre performances turned in as well? If ambisexuals function "responsibly in most facets" of life, does that mean they fail to do so in "some"? How is "responsibly" being defined (or, for that matter, "authority")? Is it nit-picking to ask whether freedom from so grand a malady as "psychological pathology" presumes freedom from garden-variety neurosis as well? (Why did that woman marry a man solely for *his* convenience? Isn't submission of that magnitude tantamount to self-negation—and wouldn't that qualify as "psychological pathology"?) If Masters and Johnson have persuasive answers for such questions, they withhold them. One would think, if nothing else, they'd feel an obligation to their own reputations to transmit the needed definitions and distinctions.

Instead, they swoop away from the particular into a dizzying spiral of outsized generalizations. Short on answers, they are quick with moralisms. Lest the ambisexual lifestyle strike mere mortals as attractively varied and uninhibited, Masters and Johnson warn that it ends as "an intolerable burden," that "the unceasing parade of new faces and bodies" leads in time to "overwhelming" feelings of "social isolation." How do the good doctors know? During interviews, it seems, "the older ambisexuals" told them so. (One of them? Several? It's well to remember that the total study sample consisted of 12 people.) Is their "loneliness" different in degree or kind from what aging people generally feel? One would expect ambisexuals to experience that emotion less—if they are as free of affect and attachment to other people as Masters and Johnson have insisted. Anyway, isn't aloneness an inescapable fact of life, and during every phase of it (and regardless of the number and quality of live-in companions)? Isn't recognition of that fact—however un-American—the only plausible definition of maturity?

Masters and Johnson will have none of it. They have contended for far too long that a committed relationship is a stay—*the* stay—against despair, to tolerate any moral ambiguity toward the ambisexual lifestyle. Their agitation and flights of fantasy build apace. Ambisexuality, Masters and Johnson tell us, represents either "a prior point of departure or an anticipated end-point in our psychosocial structuring"—the vestige of an earlier "immature" stage in human development or a grim forerunner of what lies ahead. That covers the two polar bases—pleistocene and lunar—but the air remains a little thin. Without having ever convinced us that ambisexuality is indeed a separate phenomenon of being, Masters and Johnson proceed to endow it with symbolic importance of vast Manichaean dimensions. Then—as in all good morality plays—they close on a note of benign reassurance: "The research team is currently more comfortable with the speculation that ambisexuality represents more a prior point of departure than a societal end-point." What a relief! (But did you notice that ambivalent word "more"? Oh for God's sake—be grateful for small imprecisions!)

Moving right along, Masters and Johnson next try to defuse a second storehouse of bisexual explosives: our fantasy lives. They present data on sexual fantasies gathered over a 20-year period and although they try to muffle the materials' subversive impact, they still startle, challenging conventional wisdom on several fronts. To give a few samples: homosexuals (according to Masters and Johnson) show "greater psychosexual security" than heterosexuals; all four groups studied—homosexual men and women, heterosexual men and women—express a high level of interest in "forced sexual encounters"; the fantasies of homosexual men contain a greater amount of violence than those of heterosexual men (who envision themselves more frequently as rapees than rapists—as victims of "groups of unidentified women"); lesbian women record the highest incidence of fantasy, and are the only group that includes current partners in their fantasies to any significant degree; the most common fantasy pattern for both heterosexual men and women involves the replacement of their established partners with somebody else.

Masters and Johnson's single most intriguing finding is the high incidence they report in all groups of "cross-preference" fantasies.

Among gay men and lesbians, overt heterosexual interaction was the third highest fantasy; to an only slightly lesser degree, straight men and women fantasized about overt homosexual interaction. The last finding is especially remarkable, and for two reasons: the heterosexual subjects were overwhelmingly Kinsey 0 (that is, exclusively heterosexual) during face-to-face discussions and interviews, moreover, they described same-gender sex as "revolting" and "unthinkable." Yet the same men and women who vitriolically condemned homosexuality showed in their fantasies "a significant curiosity, a sense of sexual anticipation, or even fears for effectiveness of sexual performance."

If Masters and Johnson fully recognize the explosive nature of these findings, you would never know it from their brief and bland discussion of them. On the high incidence of fantasies involving force, their sole comment is to caution against "necessarily" assuming any desire exists to act on such fantasies in "real life"—a statement that exudes less the air of scientific scrupulosity than personal repugnance. Masters and Johnson have never shown—unlike Alex Comfort, say, or Kinsey—much tolerance or understanding of "perverse" variations on the missionary theme. For them to acknowledge the appeal of "force" would be tantamount to admitting that the household staples (coitus, partner manipulation, fellatio/cunnilingus) do not exhaust the imaginations or appetites of even the sexually proficient. It would also mean opening the Pandora's box of sadomasochism, exploring the rising incidence in our society of sexual scenarios involving domination and submission, retrieving the S/M phenomenon from the scummy fringe to which traditional moralists (like Masters and Johnson) have comfortably consigned it.

Their reaction to the "cross-preference" data they present is cut from the same tweedy cloth. They simply warn against assuming that such fantasies indicate "latent or unrealized" attractions. And no more said. Yet it takes no great insight to deduce other plausible readings. It strains neither the evidence nor the imagination to see in the high incidence of cross-preference fantasies confirmation of Freud's hoary suggestion that all human beings are potentially receptive to bisexual stimulation, that even when we have grown up in a homophobic culture and have long since declared ourselves gay or straight, the wish to be both retains a strong subterranean hold.

Masters and Johnson keep to the same adamantly bland posture in the face of their remarkable finding that for both heterosexual men and women, the single most common fantasy is displacement of their established partner. Five years ago [1975] in *The Pleasure Bond*, their only book aimed at a popular audience (an aim that required the services of a coauthor to translate hieroglyphics into basic English), Masters and Johnson sternly equated infidelity with immaturity. That same animus, in more muted form, pervades *Homosexuality in Perspective*—indeed pervades all of their work. Though enamored of their self-image as "objective scientists" and tireless in referring to their "neutral," "value-free" approach, their books have always been drenched in ideology. In choosing to deny this, they have merely ensured that their own personal values would contaminate their data more, not less; for when the subjective component is not acknowledged, its distorting effect is less easy to measure and contain.

As far back as 1975, Paul Robinson (in his book *The Modernization of Sex*) succinctly and brilliantly uncovered the ideological assumptions that underlay Masters and Johnson's work. The essential ingredient, he wrote, is an "aversion to all sexual relationships that violate the monogamous heterosexual standard." Their therapeutic concern firmly centers on the *couple*, with the needs of the individual subordinated to those of the marital unit. To maintain or salvage a committed relationship, the individual is expected to sacrifice a certain amount of freedom—especially in pursuing sexual pleasure. Pleasure and union, in this view, are apparently seen as at odds: the sexual drive inherently strong, the marital unit inherently fragile.

What then justifies the heroic effort to curtail the one in the name of saving the other? According to Masters and Johnson the marital unit is the only context in which something called "growth" can proceed. Does that mean "growth" and "pleasure" are discreet, even antagonistic entities? Unlike their Puritan forebears, Masters and Johnson seem never to have posed that question consciously, or thought through an argument for asserting the prior claims of "growth." All that is clear is that on a subliminal level, they link growth with safety—the kind associated with the security of lifetime bonding. But in substituting muddy hints for a reasoned exposition, they prove unconvincing advocates—especially for those who associate growth with the ability to remain open and take risks, with a willingness to explore the manifold, hidden recesses of desire.

Given Masters and Johnson's theoretical opacity and evasion, it comes as no surprise to find them unwilling to face the subversive implications of their own data. To do so might shake loose some foundation stones in their own wobbly value structure. To absorb the fact that heterosexual men and women involved in longstanding relationships frequently—almost obsessively, it seems—fantasize about displacing their established partners, might raise the feared specter that familiarity really does breed contempt (or, minimally, loss of erotic interest). For Masters and Johnson to digest their further finding that among the previously unattached couples they studied, "fewer functional failures" turned up during sex than among committed couples, might lead to speculation that people find excitement in the unfamiliar—that outside "spice" provides respite from the boredom and dysfunction that commonly assail long-term lovers. Rather than explore such implications, Masters and Johnson simply reiterate their belief in the prime importance of maintaining the marital unit—that "port-in-the-storm," that "retreat from social pressures." Security remains their supreme value, the ultimate benefaction, the essence and sum of human needs. We are in the landscape of the 1950s.

Masters and Johnson's deep distrust of pleasure when pursued out-side the context of a committed relationship is of critical importance in understanding the tone and tactics they adopt in discussing gay life. Their earlier studies contained only scattered references to homosexu-ality; they treated it, in Paul Robinson's words, "from only one per-spective: as a factor in the etiology of sexual inadequacy . . . as an impediment to successful marital relationships." If a sexually dysfunc-tional client revealed any history of homosexuality, Masters and Johnson tended to draw a causal link between the two and would bend their (formidable) energy to "restoring" heterosexual functioning and "neutralizing" homosexual impulses. The client was never encouraged to explore the extent of his homosexual drive, to consider whether he might not be happier abandoning heterosexual marriage and commit-ting to a gay partner or lifestyle. In their earlier books Masters and Johnson declined to undertake any extended discussion of the etiology of homosexuality. But they dropped enough incidental remarks to re-veal a strong commitment to an environmental (as opposed to biolog-ical) explanation for same-gender attraction; to view homosexuality as an "organic" predisposition, after all, would have precluded therapeu-tic intervention.

The same assumptions underlay *Homosexuality in Perspective,* ob-scured by the mountain of new findings. On the surface Masters and Johnson seem to be presenting data for building the most substan-tial—and implicitly revolutionary—case for gay chauvinism ever made. Early on, they tell us that their decade-long study comparing heterosexual and homosexual men and women has convinced them that gay people are "more related" and more fully involved in their sex-ual experiences. Gay people take more time; they make "each step in tension increment something to be appreciated"; they show markedly higher levels of "free-flowing" verbal and nonverbal communication. In contrast, heterosexual couples spend much less time in foreplay, show "greater psychosexual insecurity" and are "far more goal-oriented"—they want "to get the job done." In "only a few instances" did a husband seem "fully aware of his wife's levels of sexual excitation" or try to help her "expand her pleasure"—and these were couples purportedly prescreened for sexual proficiency and freedom from psychological or physical pathology.

But having catalogued the superior sexual and interpersonal skills of gay people, Masters and Johnson swiftly proceed to discount their own evidence with twisted logic, defensive calculations and *ex cathedra* pronouncements. They stress first the advantage gay people have of "intergender empathy." Perhaps—but is empathy a quality that adheres to gender rather than to individuals? Besides, how does intergender empathy, an "advantage" lesbian and gay male couples share, help to explain the very different qualities that often mark their relationships? As Masters and Johnson tell us, lesbian women achieve consistently higher levels of sexual excitement and show consistently greater consideration for their partners than gay men do. The latter, after all—a point Masters and Johnson fail to make—are often engaged in traditional male games, emphasizing competition over cooperation, goals over process.

Masters and Johnson assign still greater importance to a second explanation they offer for the "unusually high level of communicative interchange" between homosexual partners. It's the result—hold on to your hats—of necessity. Meaning? Only two "stimulative approaches" (partner manipulation and fellatio/cunnilingus) are "widely popular" among gay people, therefore "these techniques of necessity must be constantly varied and refined to the utmost to avoid the loss of stimulative effectiveness." If we follow this line of reasoning, should we then ascribe the frequent failure of heterosexual couples to reach "optimal" peaks of pleasure during coitus to a *lack* of necessity—to the presumably wider range of stimulative options available? But then why do they also fall short, in comparison with gay people, in the degree of excitement they manage to reach during fellatio/cunnilingus? Are they hoarding skills and pleasure for yet another day? If so, which day? "Partner manipulation"—general body contact, holding, kissing, caressing—is the only other "basic stimulative option" Masters and Johnson recognize, and there, too, heterosexual "accomplishment" is portrayed as comparatively slight.

As logic falters, as Masters and Johnson patently fail to explain away the advantages of a gay lifestyle which they themselves have itemized, their own dismay grows palpable. To counteract it, they resort to repeating—in ever more strident tones—that two and only two "basic stimulative techniques" are available to gay people, and that these, furthermore, are fundamentally "my turn–your turn" transactions (one person giving, the other receiving stimulation), unlike the "our turn" character of coitus. They concede that gay people can avail themselves of "the pseudocoital techniques of rectal intercourse and dildo usage, plus occasions of mutual masturbation." But these, according to Masters and Johnson, are theoretical options only. "Only a minority" of their homosexual study group (a grand total of 176 people, 94 men and 82 women) reported using those techniques with any regularity. Ergo: they are not real options for gay people anywhere—and thus require no further discussion. With that sleight-of-hand, Masters and Johnson are able to proclaim that certain "long-range disadvantages" in gay life are inherent—that's right: inherent—even in committed homosexual relationships. The tables have been neatly turned: what appeared to be certain advantages in the gay lifestyle have been reconfigured in the nick of time to be so in the short run only. But this conclusion comes at the cost of a characterization of gay sexuality that relies on arbitrary and self-enclosed definitions ("my turn–your turn") and an odious mix of misinformation and ingenuousness.

Such lunatic—and imperious—oscillations scramble the brain, to say nothing of affronting common sense. One would have to be fatuous (or malignant) not to see that every sexual act carries the potential for being a one-sided (my turn–your turn) or mutual (our turn) transaction. *Which* potential will become operative hinges on the consideration the two partners have for each other's needs and their willingness to let their needs be known. On both counts gay people win hands down—by Masters and Johnson's own reckoning. It is they who report that during coitus heterosexual couples only infrequently achieve any shared transaction worthy of the name. It is they—not some polemical gay pamphleteer—who report that a lesbian woman engaged in manipulating or sucking her partner's breasts (ostensibly a my turn–your turn transaction) "frequently reaches" a high level of sexual excitation herself (manages, in other words, simultaneously to receive and give pleasure—the essence of an "our turn" transaction).

It might also be well to remind Masters and Johnson of their own repeated warning in *Homosexuality in Perspective* that their study samples are too small and skewed to be taken as "representative" or to be made the basis for broad generalizations. Would that they had heeded their own warning. Would that—once the temptation to issue resounding pronouncements overtook them—they had at least consulted additional source materials to supplement their own limited samples. One would have thought scientific integrity would have dictated as much—or, failing that, an instinct for self-protection. Hubris apparently proved stronger than either.

A substantial library of additional source material *is* available. One recently published book—Karla Jay and Allen Young's *The Gay Report*, an 800-page compendium of lesbian and gay male sexual attitudes and practices—is alone sufficient to embarrass Masters and Johnson's characterizations. Based on 5,000 replies to a lengthy and sophisticated questionnaire (yes, 5,000—a somewhat larger sample than 176), *The Gay Report* undermines any confidence in Masters and Johnson's description of the "stimulative options" available to gay people; it even contains information suggesting that the range of options employed by gay people may well exceed that used by more timid (not "inherently disadvantaged") heterosexuals.

The Gay Report reveals that anal intercourse—a technique Masters and Johnson disdain as too peripheral to warrant discussion—is a "frequent choice of sexual pleasure for about half of the men" surveyed; a still larger proportion (70 percent) express "positive feelings" toward it. As for analingus—a practice Masters and Johnson never once mention (Dare They Not Speak Its Name?)—it turns out that a majority (54 percent) of gay males engage in it with "some frequency" (though nearly 70 percent of lesbian women have "never engaged in it at all"). *The Gay Report* does confirm Masters and Johnson's statement that dildo usage among lesbians is minimal. However, lesbians feel far more positively about the use of vibrators (again unmentioned by Masters and Johnson)—apparently because, as Pat Califia has suggested in her recent study, "Lesbian Sexuality," vibrators are more effective than dildos in stimulating the clitoris and do not carry the negative associations of male penetration.

With all this as background, we can now approach the single most publicized portion of *Homosexuality in Perspective:* Masters and Johnson's claimed success in "converting" homosexuals. In evaluating that claim, their view on the etiology of same-gender attraction is central. Essentially it is the same view expressed in their earlier studies, though now stated more explicitly and in more detail. Reviewing the recent research literature that has tried to identify possible hormonal and biological factors in the formation of a homosexual orientation, Masters and Johnson declare themselves (and I would agree) unimpressed; as yet, they conclude, such research has failed to produce any "secure information." They continue to believe that homosexuality is the product not of genes but of experience. But experience of a particular sort—negative experience. *Homosexuality in Perspective* contains numerous tales of how same-gender orientation resulted from prior heterosexual experiences that had been unsatisfactory. One woman "gravitated to homosexuality as a means of sexual release" only after her husband had made it clear that he was "not interested in sex."

Another woman, gang-raped at 20 and lacking "psychotherapeutic support," found herself "unable to cope"—which "led to total rejection of the male sex." This etiological perspective, in tandem with Masters and Johnson's long-standing assumption that the *summum bonum* for a happy life is monogamous, heterosexual, lifetime pair-bonding, made it predictable that their prime clinical concern would be to "neutralize" homosexual impulses and "re-establish" heterosexual ones.

Their treatment of "N" serves to illustrate their doctrinal and therapeutic approach. A 37-year-old Kinsey 4 (an individual "who has had a significant amount of heterosexual experience but whose sexual outlets have been predominantly homosexual"), N's history included marriage. But after falling in love with a man with whom he then lived for seven years, N shifted entirely to a homosexual orientation, one which (in Masters and Johnson's own words) "completely satisfied" him. That is, until rumors began to circulate at his place of work that he was gay, making him fear exposure and the destruction of his career. Though it had been many years since he had felt any interest in heterosexual contact, N went to the Masters and Johnson Institute in St. Louis determined to "convert" (or, in his case "revert"). They accepted him into the program. "Strong motivation," they believe, plus the availability of "an understanding opposite-sex partner" during treatment, are the best auguries for "success." They also believe that "the real or implied threat of social rejection or a constant concern for job security" is "good reasons" for an individual to change his sexual orientation. Just as Masters and Johnson have always given priority to the stability of the marital unit over the pleasure-seeking drives of the individual, so they opt for career security over any emotional or expressive needs that might jeopardize it.

During treatment, N's earlier "heterosexual effectiveness" was restored: he was soon able to perform with his female partner. Masters and Johnson then "explained the alternatives" (we are given no details) open to N, and he "evidenced no indecision in making a full heterosexual commitment." Masters and Johnson placed him in their "success" column (as they did 67 percent of the 54 men and 60 percent of the 13 women in their program). N, in their view, had "achieved" heterosexual behavior. Those percentages are remarkably high in comparison with the 10 to 25 percent rates claimed by other therapies, and Masters and Johnson allow themselves a little well-mannered crowing: "the current concept among health-care professionals" that the sexual orientation of "dissatisfied" homosexual males or females cannot be changed—a concept which "the homosexual community has also adopted and freely propagandized"—is "simply erroneous."

"Simply," it turns out, is more than a little bald-faced. Masters and Johnson's selection process, first of all, had been so rigorous it is not unfair to call it rigged. Recruitment for the program took place between 1964 and 1968, a period predating the gay liberation movement and the positive changes it has subsequently wrought in self-image and social acceptance, a time when many gay men and women felt desperate—and were, in Masters and Johnson's preferred terminology, "highly motivated" to change. Still, some were not thought highly motivated enough: nearly one-fourth of the original applicants were denied admission to the program. Those accepted were atypical in yet another important way: only five of the 67 men and women finally selected for treatment were Kinsey 6 (exclusively gay). The large majority were Kinsey 3 or 4—"bisexuals," as some prefer to call them. Further, 31 of the men and six of the women were married, and they entered the therapeutic program with their spouses (an additional two men and one woman were currently living in long-term heterosexual relationships).

To call such a sample "skewed" hardly does justice to the matter; the selected subjects were so ripe for change, they would have likely turned yellow at first glance; the real surprise is that more did not. Moreover, Masters and Johnson's longterm "success" rate is almost certainly inflated. It turns out that after treatment ended, 16 men and three women became "unavailable" for follow-up study. It seems logical to assume that unavailability connotes a degree of disenchantment. But not to Masters and Johnson. By indulging in some dubious legerdemain based on "prorating," they are able to "estimate" that only four of those lost to follow-up actually returned to their homosexual ways—which further enables them to declare a two-thirds success rate.

The manipulation of evidence at work here is troubling enough, but the underlying ingenuousness is more so. Masters and Johnson are remarkably uninquisitive about the philosophical premises on which their project rests and "innocently" indifferent to its ramifications. This imperturbability reflects enormous self-confidence. Yet given the nature of their enterprise (when closely scrutinized), assurance of that magnitude becomes an indictment, not a virtue.

For although Masters and Johnson will not see it, they are essentially engaged in promoting social conformity—the undertaking made more offensive for being paraded under the banner of liberation. They are bent on helping people pass muster, meet traditional social expectations, "achieve" heterosexual behavior. That this is often done in the name of protecting careers and social status merely compounds the conformism. Masters and Johnson seem never to question whether the emphasis on turning out secure and dutiful citizens is of ultimate advantage either to the individuals or to society (to self-actualization and to democracy); whether in helping their clients achieve a limited mechanical proficiency, they may not have disabled them emotionally, crippled their prospects for finding love; whether gain is best measured by a heightened ability to comply with prescribed sociosexual norms or by a heightened sense of inner integrity (success in living with oneself). Masters and Johnson are expert in creating a well-regimented band—and in muffling the different drummers within.

Recall the case of N, the man who "reverted" to heterosexuality—one of Masters and Johnson's success stories. But "success" by what definition, and at what cost? Those who believe that the continuing expansion of options is the best gauge of continuing vitality will see in N's decision to commit himself exclusively to heterosexuality not an advance—given the potential he had shown to relate fully to women *and* men—but a defeat, an artificial truncation wrought by social fear. Masters and Johnson tell us nothing about N's inner life (perhaps they never asked him). But it's possible to wonder whether his "conversion" produced a greater or lesser alignment between his outer behavior and his inner needs. In giving up homosexual activity, did N cease to have homosexual fantasies? A reversal in behavior is not the same as a reversal in desire. One can learn to perform sexually as a heterosexual and still not *feel* heterosexual; it is the difference between physiology and psychology—between the mechanics of fucking and the absorption of loving. A crucial distinction, if one wants to talk responsibly and with precision about "conversion" and "change." It's a distinction Masters and Johnson never draw. One gets the sinking feeling they may be unaware it exists.

—The New Republic, *June 16, 1979*

POSTSCRIPT 1999

It is now twenty years since Masters and Johnson insisted on the ease—and necessity—of changing a gay sexual orientation through therapeutic intervention. Given the shift in the public's acceptance of homosexuality over the past few decades, one would have thought that any (let alone sanguine) exhortations to "cure" a same-gender orientation would long since have been discarded to the dustbin, a distasteful relic of the Dark Ages.

But the call for "cure," and the claims for its feasibility, in fact continue to the present day. Have they at least diminished in number? Are there solid grounds for believing that the shift in public attitude is now too advanced to be reversed?

That the social stigma attached to homosexuality *has* to some significant degree lessened in mainstream culture is generally acknowledged; it is the extent and durability of the shift that remains in nervous contention. Within the psychotherapeutic community itself, many observers see the reversal as dramatic and permanent. Yet the debate about whether homosexuality is a pathology or a normal variant remains ongoing. Charles Socarides [see "Sex and the Military," in this volume] for one, has not budged from his insistence that same-gender eroticism is *always* pathological—and he continues to have a following among the older generation of psychotherapists.

In my reading, therapists who are themselves openly gay or lesbian are among the more optimistic that the-worst-is-far-behind-us. To give one example: in 1991, in a speech at the annual meeting of the American Psychiatric Association, I alluded to the APA's 1973 vote deleting homosexuality from the category of "illness," and expressed my own uneasiness about what the outcome might be today if that proposition was again put to a vote of the membership. Several people in the audience, to a general nodding of assent, assured me that my apprehension was unwarranted, more a function of my own miserable experiences in therapy during the 1960s (which I had recently recounted in my book, *Cures*) than of the progressive climate that currently characterized the psychotherapeutic profession.

At that point, my introducer, Richard Isay, took the microphone, told the audience that he shared my apprehension, and sternly warned against a blindfolded optimism. In Isay's and my view, there were—and are—real dangers in overstating the shift in the therapeutic perspective on homosexuality, dangerous because it encourages complacency where vigilance is needed and because it mistakes fragile progress for irreversible gain.

Since 1991, my apprehension has been further fed by the surfacing of the "reparative therapy" movement led by Joseph Nicolosi. In its essence, reparative therapy marks a return to the twin doctrines that dominated psychotherapy in the 1950s and '60s: that a homosexual orientation results from something having "gone wrong" in the developmental process (in Nicolosi's formulation, it is the child's failure properly to identify with adult figures of his/her gender; and—this was supposed to be the *good* news—that all could be set right, "repaired," through therapy). In the land of reparative therapy, the "truth" about homosexuality was established in the fifties.[1]

I'm not suggesting that Nicolosi's views are widely shared in the psychotherapeutic community, nor that they are in any immediate danger of recapturing the throne. But Nicolosi *has* a following as well as a larger number of therapists who agree with this or that portion of his resurrection of the Gospel according to Messrs. Bieber and Socarides. Heterosexuality, in short, continues to be equated with "normalcy" and homosexuality with malfunction—with something in the individual's developmental process having gone seriously "wrong."

However, too much doom and gloom will not do. Despite the Nicolosis, there is no gainsaying the remarkable shift in how professional therapists view homosexuality. As recently as this past December [1998], the board of trustees of the American Psychiatric Association unanimously voted that "reparative" or "conversion" therapy is misguided, and dangerously so: "the potential risks of 'reparative' therapy are great, including depression, anxiety and self-destructive behavior, since the therapist's alignment with societal prejudices against homosexuality may reinforce self-hatred already experienced by the patient."

That this shift has taken place in only a few decades is justifiable cause for satisfaction and celebration. Still, it might be well to keep an eye peeled on that shadow phalanx still hovering menacingly on the sidelines. It is a steely, determined band, an Iron Guard, eager to return us to a premodern age.

Kinsey's Urethra

Beware the facts; they can lead you away from the truth. James H. Jones has unearthed an enormous amount of new information in his biography, *Albert C. Kinsey*. Let no one underestimate the achievement. But let no one confuse it with an understanding of Kinsey's life and work. Diligence is the beginning of scholarship, not the end point. Through research, scholars discover what material exists. Then they must decide what it *means*. Jones gets high marks for industry, low ones for insight.

The most myopic moment comes near the beginning of his book and is repeated throughout: Alfred C. Kinsey was "a homosexual." Oh, really? By what definition? Jones presents evidence—full, incontrovertible, and previously known only to a small circle of insiders—that Kinsey often had sex and occasionally fell in love with people of his own gender. Yet Jones also tells us that Kinsey was lovingly married for some 45 years to Clara McMillen, and that their relationship was in no sense perfunctory, certainly not sexually. A decade into their marriage, Alfred and Clara were "eagerly" exploring various coital positions newly recommended by a friend, and they maintained a sexual relationship until Kinsey became ill near the end of his life. With Clara's knowledge, Kinsey also slept with other women during their marriage—as did Clara with other men.

Isn't it obvious that if Kinsey must be labeled, then "bi"- or "pan"-sexual is more appropriate than "homosexual"? For some unfathomable reason, Jones has chosen to ignore Kinsey's own famous 0–6 scale (0 = exclusive heterosexuality; 6 = exclusive homosexuality). By using that scale, the simplistic category "*a* homosexual" would be reserved for individuals whose sexual behavior was exclusively confined to their own gender. Or if not their behavior, then their fantasy life. Perhaps Jones meant to argue that Kinsey *self*-identified as a homosexual on the basis of his erotic fantasies, discarding as irrelevant his ability (and desire) to perform bisexually. *If* that's what Jones means, he's forgotten to provide the evidence or make the argument.

Insiders at the Kinsey Institute place Kinsey between a "1" and a "2"—more "straight" than "gay"—when younger, then shifting increasingly to the "gay" side of the scale as he aged, but never becoming an exclusive "6." In other words, whether the yardstick be behavior, fantasy or self-definition, Kinsey considered his sexuality malleable (and long before Queer Theory reified "fluidity" as the signifier of sexual, indeed personal, authenticity).

Astonishingly, Jones doesn't get it. He not only persists throughout his book in referring to Kinsey as "a homosexual" but he tries to force Alfred and Clara's relationship into the canned mold of "homosexual man seeks cover in a heterosexual marriage." Along with vitiating all that was special and brave about the couple, Jones can't even manage a complicated version of the gay man/straight woman arrangement, presenting instead a tired stereotype of lost souls (which he bases on a few outdated articles from 20 to 25 years ago that he nervily refers to as "recent studies").

The other slot Jones drops Kinsey into is "masochist." It is one of many terms—"voyeurism," "exhibitionism," "prurience," "pathology," "perversion"—Jones slings around, never pausing for close definition. Judging from his footnotes, Jones's guiding experts on "masochism" have been Havelock Ellis, Richard von Krafft-Ebing and Theodore

Reik, now partly or wholly superceded by recent scholarship. *None* of the vast literature on sado-masochism that has accumulated over the past two decades is cited, let alone argued with or theorized.

Still, *Alfred C. Kinsey* does contain a considerable amount of new information. Thanks to Jones's prodigious labors, we are now privy to aspects of Kinsey's sexual life previously known only to his family and a closed circle of associates and co-experimenters. Kinsey, it seems, found that tugging on his testicles provided pleasurable/painful sensations; later in life, the stimulus had to be increased to maintain the desired effect and he took to tugging on them with a length of rope. Kinsey also discovered that the urethra was, for him, an erogenous zone, and over time he teased and plied it with various instruments, culminating in the use of a toothbrush. Later in life, he was also drawn to watching various S/M performances, but he preferred looking to participating.

These were occasional practices, not exclusive, narrowly focused fetishes. Kinsey utilized many other, more conventional outlets for sexual pleasure. How we evaluate his more "extreme" (unconventional) practices will very much depend on our own sexual histories and our willingness to explore our own fantasies. In the process, we would do well to remain modest about our inevitable subjectivity and our limited imaginations.

James Jones is limited, but not modest. He is very sure what Kinsey's behavior means, and is very quick to characterize and denigrate it— usually with heavy-handed psychologizing. Kinsey's "inner demons" are given vast explanatory powers, catchall references to his "confusion," "anger" and "guilt" made to substitute for any sustained, persuasive analysis of the inner man. A few samples: "By late adolescence, if not before, Kinsey's behavior was clearly pathological, satisfying every criterion of sexual perversion" (the "criterion" are not provided); he was "an exhibitionist extraordinaire"; an "aloof loner"; headstrong, stubborn, highly opinionated, gruff and arrogant; a man of "iron will" whom few liked; an unpopular teacher (who somehow attracted droves of students), a thin-skinned, manipulative elitest; a self-styled martyr and would-be messiah.

Jones's crude psychologizing (which is really moralizing) is far too formulaic to inspire confidence. Indeed, several of Kinsey's surviving colleagues guffaw at Jones's reductive view of the complicated man Kinsey was. "It's nonsense," says C. A. Tripp (author of *The Homosexual Matrix*, and in my view the most rigorous and fearless disciple of Kinsey's sexual iconoclasm). "All that guilt and anger Jones keeps talking about—well, you could say that about anybody. Kinsey can't even get interested in gardening without Jones ascribing it to 'deep tensions' or explaining his scanty clothing while working the soil as a need to 'shock' people. And how naughty of Kinsey to stand nude in his own bathroom as he shaved!"

Where another biographer might, with justice, have emphasized Kinsey's remarkable capacity for open-minded exploration, Jones persists in negatively labeling nonconventional sexual behavior as "skating on the edge," as "compulsive" and "addictive" risk-taking. He can manage to credit the homophobic sexologist Richard von Krafft-Ebing as having been prompted "by deeply moral concerns," but pansexual Kinsey is merely "sex-obsessed." This is like calling Albert Einstein "physics-obsessed." And it leaves us wondering what to think about James Jones, who has devoted 27 years to researching Alfred Kinsey's "perverted" life.

Where all this becomes serious is when Jones uses his defamatory portrait of Kinsey, the man, to discredit his work as a sexologist. He does so through a morally slippery ploy: he generously quotes from Kinsey's antagonists (often mistaken), letting them do Jones's talking for him. Now and then, however, Jones's own indignant voice breaks through: "Despite his claim of coolly being disinterested," Jones hisses, "Kinsey was nothing of the sort . . . enthusiasm for sex was a fundamental tenet of Kinsey's thought, and it rang out loud and clear in his writing." Enthusiasm for sex? For shame!

Elsewhere, Jones refers to Kinsey's "facade of objectivity"—as if value-free social science has ever existed, or been more than approximated as an ideal. *Of course* Kinsey's "personal needs and motivations" influenced his findings; this is primer stuff in social science. Besides, subjectivity cuts both ways: what it often means is that the sensitized investigator is able to see and reveal much that had previously been closed off to less personally engaged scholars.

The bottom-line question is whether Kinsey's personality, and personal engagement with his material, led to serious distortions in his findings. The two most common accusations against his *Sexual Behavior in the Human Male* (1948) and *Sexual Behavior in the Human Female* (1953) relate to the statistical methodology he employed in arriving at his conclusions, and especially at the finding that 37% of the adult male population has had at least one homosexual experience to orgasm, and that 4% of the male population is exclusively homosexual. (Kinsey is often misquoted as saying that 10% of males are homosexual, a rating he reserved to males who score 5–6 on his scale *for three years* between ages 16 and 55.)

Jones repeats most of the long-standing critiques of Kinsey: "for all his posturing and bluster, Kinsey was chronically unsure of himself as a statistician . . . his sample was far from random," etc. But we are not told that Paul Gebhard (one of Kinsey's co-authors and his successor as director of the Institute for Sex Research), himself reacting to criticism leveled against the two volumes, spent years "cleaning" the Kinsey data of their purported contaminants—removing, for example, all material derived from prison populations.

In 1979, Gebhard, with Alan Johnson, published *The Kinsey Data*, and—to his own surprise—found that Kinsey's original estimates held: instead of Kinsey's 37%, Gebhard and Johnson came up with 36.3%; the 10% figure (with prison inmates *excluded*) came to 9.9% for white college-educated males and 12.7% for those with less education. And as for the call for a "random sample," a team of statisticians studying Kinsey's procedures had concluded as far back as 1953 that the unique problems inherent in sex research precluded the possibility of obtaining a true random sample, and that Kinsey's interviewing technique had been "extraordinarily skillful." They characterized Kinsey's work overall as "a monumental endeavor."

In his shrewd way, Jones sprinkles his text with periodic praise for Kinsey the master researcher, the brilliant interviewer, the daring pioneer, the debunker of conventional morality. No heavy-handed conservative frontal assault for Jones. We learn that Kinsey was an active, loving parent (perhaps that's why we hear so little about his four children), a concerned mentor who stayed in touch with many of his students for years, a man of childlike wonder and one capable of great warmth, gentleness and generosity. How does this Kinsey fit together with the near-monstrous one Jones more frequently portrays? It doesn't. Jones never manages a coherent portrait (and personality contradictions *can* intelligibly cohere); the pejorative assertions that dominate the book simply overwhelm occasional references to Kinsey's positive qualities.

Why this insistent pathologizing of Kinsey the man and, by implication, the devaluing of his work? The moral values that have guided Jones's choice of emphasis come into sharpest focus in the contrasting way he treats two of Kinsey's closest associates, Paul Gebhard and Wardell Pomeroy. Gebhard, who gave Jones four interviews and whose testimony is crucially enlisted against Kinsey at various points, appears to have been the only male staff member unwilling or unable to sleep with men; he is pronounced "a free spirit," "a very likable man" with "a terrific sense of humor." Wardell Pomeroy, who distrusted Jones and refused to see him (now, with Alzheimer's, he is unable to defend himself), loved all kinds of sex with all kinds of people; he is dismissed as a "sexual athlete or superstud . . . a randy boy in a man's body," with "a character of little substance."

Get it? The exclusively heterosexual Gebhard wins the kudos (Jones even dares to claim that among his associates "Kinsey probably respected Gebhard the most professionally"). Pomeroy, a man *by other accounts* of great charm, intelligence and warmth, is dismissed as a vain creature "whose taste in partners could be described only as broad, if not indiscriminate." "He fucks just everybody and it's really disgusting," says one of Jones's informants, who clearly speaks for Jones.

James Jones has added an enormous amount of information to our knowledge of Alfred Kinsey's life and research. But he has not understood, or does not approve, Kinsey's foundational message: erotic desire is anarchic and will necessarily break free of and engulf all simplistic efforts (like Jones's) to categorize, and thus confine it.

Kinsey's work will survive this book.

—The Nation, *Nov. 3, 1997*

III

Foreign Policy

Vietnam and American Foreign Policy (1967)

Each of the standard arguments used by Cold War warriors to justify our presence in Vietnam can be stripped to its essential vacuity: (1) "We are legally obliged to fight." Answer: The SEATO pact is full of escape clauses, and in any case no state has ever, will ever, or need ever, abide by a treaty harmful to its interests. (2) "We are responding to an emergency plea from the Vietnamese people." Answer: We have never heard from the Vietnamese people, only from the elitist groups that rule them. (3) "Our global reputation is at stake." Answer: It is, indeed, our once-proud reputation as symbol and champion of the aspirations of the common man. (4) "We are resisting an invasion." Answer: Even if one concedes that Hanoi created and continues to control the NLF, the basic question remains: why have so many South Vietnamese responded? Anyway, if the presence of foreign troops is sufficient to deflate an army's claim to nationalist revolutionary status, then what will we do with the fact that General Washington's troops were outnumbered at Yorktown by their French allies? (5) "If we fail to contain Them here, we shall have to contain Them some place else." Answer: This "domino" theory rests on a premise we have not acknowledged: that nationalism, especially the

Asian variety, threatens American economic imperialism. It rests, too, on the arrogant assumption that all the Vietnams are our possessions, to be disposed of according to our interests, even if these run counter to the aspirations of their own people.

Our intervention in Vietnam is only the latest, if most horrendous, symptom of the long-standing American view (perhaps best articulated by W. W. Rostow) that America, selfless and altruistic, is primarily interested in collaborating with the revolution of rising expectations throughout the world, in helping underdeveloped nations to import our technological know-how in order to improve the material well-being of the local populace.

Lovely in theory. And convenient as official rationale. But what about actual practice? The record is not lovely, nor convenient.

Consider Paraguay: U.S. aid is a major prop for the regime of dictator Alfredo Stroessner; regrettable, one of our Embassy officials in Asunción admits, but, after all, Stroessner is anti-Communist, and "a sure anti-Communist, no matter how despicable, is better than a reformer, no matter how honest, who might turn against us."

Consider Haiti: Duvalier's government has received more than $57 million in AID support and almost as much in loans from the World Bank and the Ex-Im Bank; his own person is protected by a 20,000-man palace guard trained by U.S. Marines. The Haitian people, in turn, have the lowest school attendance in the hemisphere, the fewest hospital beds, the lowest per capita annual income ($70).

Consider Jamaica: it is rich in sugar, tourism and bauxite, yet the country is in debt and 93 percent of its people earn less than $500 a year. Where is the wealth going? To American corporations, to Alcan, Alcoa, Kaiser and Reynolds.

There are numerous such examples. The list is depressingly long: our support in Brazil of the plutocrat opposition to Janios Quadros; our sale of F-86 Sabre-jet interceptors, C-47 and C-130B transports and Sikorsky helicopters to South Africa, whose racist policies we officially deplore; our successful attempt to overthrow President Arbenz in Guatemala because his agrarian reform program included taking over certain unused lands held by the United Fruit Company; our intervention in the Dominican Republic which, based on hysteria and hearsay, ended in destroying the democratic regime of Juan Bosch.

In short, the pretense that our foreign policy brings democracy and prosperity to the masses is simply that—pretense. This is not to say that our government is *never* involved in genuine efforts to produce social reform abroad. The Peace Corps does embody a wish to be of help to other people; the Asian Rice Institute in the Philippines does hold out hope of being of real value to the Asian masses; and it is worth pointing to Ronald Steel's recent observation in *The New Republic* that "the United States has not only accepted land reform and nationalization in such countries as Bolivia, Indonesia, and Algeria, but even aided the expropriating regimes with food and money."

But basically, overwhelmingly, America is not the friend but the enemy of revolutionary movements in the underdeveloped world trying to establish governments responsive to the needs of their people and committed to using resources to create a better life for the many. This seems to me an undeniably accurate description of our foreign policy of, say, the last twenty years. But when we carry the analysis further back it becomes less persuasive. And when New Left critics like Carl Oglesby call business profit the kernel of our foreign policy "from its earliest days onward," they are forced into some considerable sleights of hand with historical evidence.

When Oglesby writes (in *Containment and Change*), for example, that in our war with Spain in the late nineteenth century "we had no time for pietistic hogwash; we were openly in the business of protecting business," it can only be that he is ignorant of the widely accepted conclusions of historian Ernest May that we embarked on that war primarily because of popular indignation in this country over Spain's mistreatment of the Cuban people.[1]

Or when, still more sweepingly, Oglesby writes that "we were never isolated and never isolationist. . . . from the beginning, we had a Department of State and we were always directly interested in the power struggles of the commercial European states," he vastly under-estimates the determination (one could almost say the obsession) of our early statesmen to avoid European entanglements, fearing as they did that these would compromise our identity and our independence.

These distortions are chiefly disturbing not because they misrepre-sent this or that episode in our past but because they are part and par-cel of a larger distortion, namely, the view that human events can be accounted for almost wholly in terms of economics. "Reality" lies in questions of dollars and cents; if one wishes to know the actual as op-posed to the professed motives of human beings, look to the pocket-book. (Thus Oglesby can announce that it was "the more practical arguments about money and land that won the Revolution the deci-sive support of early American conservatives"; he doesn't specify whom he refers to here, but certainly John Adams, everybody's "early American conservative," will not fit the bill.)

Oglesby sounds very tough-minded, but only if one still wears the spectacles of the 1930s, seeing a munitions maker behind every states-man, a scheming capitalist behind every humanitarian reformer. At times Oglesby sounds like the very reincarnation of Charles Beard, as when, in a direct paraphrase of Beard, he refers to the American Civil War as our "national trauma to settle the dispute between the planters and industrialists"—a view that has not held currency for about twenty-five years.

Economic determinism seems to me a curious position for idealists like Oglesby to wed themselves to. For an idealist, supposedly, is one who believes in the possibilities of our better nature (such as the abil-ity of the ideal of fraternity to overbalance the drive toward material accumulation). But if human affairs have been exclusively character-ized through time by rapacity, aggrandizement, deception and greed, the record will not, to put it mildly, inspire much confidence in the possibility of a more benevolent future. Which is not to say the record should be falsified in order to give balm to our fantasies of perfectibility, but only that it can (accurately) be read more broadly.

There is yet another serious objection to economic determinism. Because it maximizes the role of profits and minimizes the role of ideas in history, it encourages us to believe that in the specific case of the Cold War, our leaders care nothing, or next to nothing, for the anti-Communist ideology they mouth. Yet it may well be that the deepest cause for concern is that they *do* believe what they are saying. Their talk of making the world safe for democracy is not simply a smokescreen to conceal their wish to make it safe for American business. Johnson and Rusk are apparently convinced (at least at times) of the truth of their rhetoric; indeed at such moments it is not rhetoric to them at all, but the expression of a sincere belief in the country's missionary role. They are dangerous not only because they have become the willing tools of American business, but because they are also the unwilling prisoners of their own altruistic fantasies. It is hard to know which is worse: a statesman who cynically uses the rhetoric of benevolence to conceal his self-interested policies or one who genuinely believes that rhetoric but then consistently chooses policies that run counter to it. It is, if you like, the choice between Scylla and Charybdis. The point is that both the monster and the whirlwind are elements in our foreign policy, and if we are ever to survive the double hazard, to steer that narrow course between, we must be aware of both, and not merely one.

—The Village Voice, *May 11, 1967*

The Havana Inquiry (1974)[1]

Hans Magnus Enzensberger's *The Havana Inquiry,* a documentary play about the Bay of Pigs, needs to find a wide audience in this country. Yet I hesitated before agreeing to write this introduction to the printed version of the play. I've never been to Cuba. My Spanish is minimal. I have no expertise in Hispano-American affairs.

While debating the advisability of writing this essay, I took Samuel Flagg Bemis's *A Diplomatic History of the United States* down from my bookshelves. It was the text we had used when I was an undergraduate at Yale in the early 1950s for a course on American Foreign Policy taught by Bemis himself—then widely regarded as the "dean" of American diplomatic historians. I turned to the sections in the book on Cuba and was startled at their jingoistic content and embarrassed to see that I had not scribbled a single note of protest in the margins. At the time, obviously, Bemis's views in no way offended my understanding of the world and of our country's historic role within it. Yet among his statements are the claims that our "trusteeship of Cuban independence . . . has stood as a notable example to the powers"; that we intervened in Cuban affairs and set up provisional governments "with great reluctance"; that the Cuban people "who had not submitted to 200,000 Spanish troops in 1898, made no resistance to a handful of soldiers in the second American intervention because they had confidence in its righteousness"; and that our special relationship with Cuba had allowed its people to enjoy "a rousing economic prosperity."[2] I decided to write this introduction.

In reprinting Bemis's words, it isn't my intention to hold him up to special scorn (for all I know he has changed his own opinions in the last twenty years as much as I have mine), but rather to illuminate the consensus view of our benign role in world affairs that has long dominated both the historical profession and popular opinion. In the past decade, events in Southeast Asia and the revisionist work of such scholars as Gabriel and Joyce Kolko, Lloyd Gardner, Ronald Steel, William Appleman Williams, and Walter Lafeber, have shaken that consensus view to its roots. Students have grown more skeptical of their professors' textbooks, and citizens of their government's professed benevolence.

Yet perhaps not skeptical enough. The dimensions of our historic imperialism are still not widely known or, if known, not widely credited. As regards our relations with Latin America in general, the long-standing ignorance—a compound of disinterest and disbelief—still holds. As regards Cuba in particular, our lazy susceptibility to the limited materials fed us through government channels, the media and those few popular histories—preeminently, Arthur Schlesinger, Jr.'s *A Thousand Days*—which under the guise of objective analysis are in fact suffused with unacknowledged value judgments, helps to maintain the image of the United States as a kindly parent and of Cuba as a mere Soviet satellite.

Yet as revisionist scholarship has made clear, the 1961 invasion at Playa Girón has a long, dishonorable ancestry; it was but the latest in many direct interventions on our part in the internal affairs of other countries in this hemisphere, itself illustrative of our continuing sense that we have a divine right to determine other peoples' futures.

As regards Cuba itself, if we dig into the history of our relations with that country at almost any point, we unearth an appalling stench.[3] The malodorous high point in the pre–Civil War period was probably the famed "Ostend Manifesto." In their eagerness to secure Cuba from Spain, President Franklin Pierce and his advisers arranged a conference of the American Ministers to London, Paris and Madrid. The three worthies duly conferred, and issued to the world a "memorandum" bluntly declaring that if Spain refused to sell the island of Cuba to the United States, "then by every law human and divine, we shall be justified in wresting it from Spain, if we possess the power." Most of the world read those laws differently. Indignation was so widespread (an indignation shared, it should be said, by many Americans— "Manifesto of the Brigands" was the New York *Tribune*'s title for the memorandum) that President Pierce backed down and American rapacity was thwarted for some forty years.[4]

But at the end of the nineteenth century, as Cuba's great poet and revolutionary José Martí feared, independence from Spain was no sooner achieved than it rapidly gave way to almost total dependence on the United States. In 1901 our government forced the "Platt Amendment" into the Cuban constitution, affirming Cuba's obligation to sell or lease lands to us for coaling or naval stations and our right to intervene "for the protection of life, property, and individual liberty." That right has since been exercised many times and under many guises, from landing the marines in 1906, 1912 and 1917, to FDR's more "liberal" approach of simply sending warships into Cuban waters to register our displeasure with (and thereby bring down) a government of which he disapproved.

Business, as usual, followed the flag. American corporations moved into Cuba soon after the 1898 war with Spain, and the investment from such giant firms as the United Fruit Company and the First National City Bank of New York rose from $50 million in 1895 to $1 billion in 1959, the year Castro came to power. By then, it is no exaggeration to say, American interests had long since come to dominate all strategic sectors of the Cuban economy, turning the island into a giant plantation and the vast majority of its citizens into servants of American corporate enterprise. That Castro would change all this was immediately apparent to the American power structure. In a confidential memorandum written in April 1959 for distribution to the CIA, the State Department, and the White House, Richard Nixon suggested that a force of Cuban exiles be armed to overthrow the Castro regime. President Eisenhower adopted this suggestion in 1960, and President Kennedy implemented it in 1961 at Playa Girón. Of Kennedy's advisers, only Senator Fulbright openly opposed the invasion.[5]

The landing at the Bay of Pigs, in short, was not an aberration, an inexplicable deviation from our traditionally benign stance toward Cuba. Instead it was of a familiar piece with our long-settled view that we have the right to intervene—and by force—in the internal affairs of other countries whenever our "interests" appear to be threatened. And *we* define the nature of those interests and the reality of the threat. Sadly, it's questionable whether the fiasco at the Bay of Pigs has taught us anything—other than the need to be more circumspect in our tactics and more determined upon our goals. Only recently has information come to light that in 1970 the CIA gave covert advice to the agents of the giant conglomerate ITT on how to prevent President Allende from taking office in Chile. There's no evidence that anyone questioned our *right* to topple a legitimately elected government. Cooperation between the CIA and ITT was, to be sure, indirect and limited. Not even Washington is wholly unable to learn from history.

The literature currently [1976] available in English on the Cuban Revolution contains huge discordancies: vilified in some books, Castro is elevated to sainthood in others. What has most surprised me, though, has been the range of views expressed among my own friends, good leftists all. Like Hans Magnus Enzensberger, they deplore the historic role the United States has played in Cuban affairs and regard the Bay of Pigs invasion as wholly disgraceful. But many would disagree with the exclusive stress Enzensberger places (in his own introduction to the *Havana Inquiry*) on economics as a sufficient explanation for our country's role; and many would also question the surety of his confidence in all aspects of Castro's Revolution.

My own views have wobbled back and forth from book to book and conversation to conversation, and I don't pretend that I've unraveled them, even to my own satisfaction. This in part reflects the abrupt, sometimes contradictory shifts in the Cuban Revolution itself. On two matters there seems to me (and to almost all those on the Left to whom I've talked) no dispute: the abysmal conduct of the U.S. government in attempting all at once to destroy the revolution and to manipulate the revolution's enemies; and the enormous accomplishments of Castro's Cuba to date in improving the material well-being of its people.*

Disagreement begins over Enzensberger's assumption that this country's imperial pursuits have always centrally, even exclusively, pivoted on matters of profit, trade, and markets. I find this analysis too narrow. It fails to take account of the missionary zeal to spread (or defend) "democracy" and "Christianity" that has always been a significant element in the American character and has always encompassed passions beyond the monetary.

"Missionary zeal," to be sure, has sometimes been no more than a convenient cover for greed. But not always. "Philanthropy," however misguided we may consider it, has played a significant and independent role in the formation of policy decisions. Even as regards the war in Vietnam, I think it's an oversimplification to assume that the vocabulary of "anti-communism" that our leaders use in justifying their

---

* In the twenty-some years since this essay was written, that material well-being has sharply declined. The collapse of the Soviet Union, which had provided significant economic support to Cuba, in combination with the continuing American blockade of the island, have resulted in a much-lowered standard of living.

murderous policies is merely a cynical smokescreen designed to conceal their real aim of protecting markets and investments. The Johnsons and the Nixons have unquestionably been sympathetic to the view that what's good for American business is good for the world—and their policies have reflected that sympathy. But saying that does not *summarize* their ideology—nor unravel its complex strands.

Our leaders, like most of us, are capable of sustaining varied loyalties: in their case, to "free enterprise," American profits, God, "individualism" and parliamentary democracy. That these loyalties have almost always been mutually reinforcing does not justify the assumption that they are interchangeable. To recognize, moreover, that Johnson, Kennedy, Nixon et al. have certain *non*-material commitments is not to soften the indictment against them but to clarify it. Marxists tend to see ideas (except those of Marx) as having no authentic or independent life apart from the "material relationships" that brought them into being and for whose protection they are publicly employed. Not only does this undervalue the powerful role that a "mere" idea (such as "manifest destiny"—or Freud's concept of the unconscious) can play in human affairs, but it minimizes as well the ability of individuals to act other than along predictable socioeconomic lines. That Castro and most of the other guerrilla leaders in the Sierra Maestra came from the middle class should alone give pause to the dialecticians among us.

Which brings us to the Cuban side of the equation. Enzensberger's categorization of the invaders at Playa Girón as representatives of the deposed ruling class seems, from independent evidence, a well-substantiated description of the large majority.[6] But the category isn't subtle enough to allow for a full accounting of motives or social composition. Moreover, it serves, paradoxically, to minimize the profound impact of Castro's revolution on his own countrymen.

This last point is clarified in Geoffrey E. Fox's recent studies of *working-class* refugees from Cuba. These people did not flee their homeland because their property had been expropriated, their privileges taken away, their previous power curtailed. They had had no property or power. They were the people—the poor—in whose name the revolution had been made. Why then did they flee? Because the world no longer made sense to them. Women were leaving the home to work and study. Children were being taught at state-run boarding schools. Blacks were intermingling socially with whites and were even being assigned positions of authority. "Moral incentive," not the need for money, was being declared the reason one worked—for the good of the collectivity, not the survival of the family.[7]

No one, it goes without saying, had to persuade the poor that disease, illiteracy and lack of decent food and housing were undesirable. Yet those afflictions had been central to life for so long as almost to seem a definition of it—with the Church encouraging the view that misery was part of God's inscrutable plan for the universe. Castro's Revolution challenged that ancient view and as well upset (in some cases, reversed) long-accepted definitions of what it meant to be a man or woman, a white or black, a worker or boss, a parent or child, an official or a citizen. The ensuing sense of confusion, even of loss, has nothing to do with rational or material definitions of what makes for contentment and peace of mind.

This may only be another way of saying that a true revolution cannot happen in a day, or a decade, or possibly in a generation. Dislocations in Cuba have been psychic as well as material. Members of all classes have felt the strains of readjustment, however different the strains characteristic of each class. And this itself is an index to the depth of change, to the basic rearrangements in understanding that the revolution has produced. Discontented elements in Cuba included people not readily reduced to the classic Marxist category of a "parasitic elite." Dominated though the invading brigade at the Bay of Pigs unquestionably was by middle- and upper-class elements, it included a number of men (the San Román brothers, for example) who had earlier tried to overthrow Batista or had initially been strong supporters of Castro as well as some fifty blacks and one hundred white workers.[8]

Since the Bay of Pigs, the continuing need (and willingness) to reevaluate revolutionary tactics has further fed internal upheaval. The shift between moral and material incentives, the vacillating relations with Moscow, the debates over Che Guevara's tactics for setting off a chain reaction of revolution throughout Latin America and over the dangers of a centralized bureaucracy—these and other fluctuations have made change the chief constant in Cuba's "march toward socialism." Not everyone can live with perpetual motion. And those who cannot are not confined to a single class. Edmundo Desnoes's novel, *Inconsolable Memories*—to give an example of another sort—describes the trauma of an upper-middle-class man of "worldly," "esthetic" interests who feels sympathy for the revolution and yet cannot live comfortably with it on a daily basis.[9]

If Enzensberger minimizes the profound impact of the revolution on all classes in Cuba, his implication that the victory at Playa Girón marked a conclusive triumph risks the danger of overconfidence. True, Yankee imperialism was turned back, the counterrevolutionaries captured and convicted, the revolution saved from external subversion. But saved for *what*? The victory at Playa Girón signified only that the revolution would continue, not that its many contradictions had been resolved. I doubt if it's accidental that Enzensberger fails to cite any of the left-wing critiques of Castro's Cuba that have been published in recent years—especially the telling commentary of K. S. Karol, René Dumont and Allen Young.[10]

It's still difficult, a dozen years later, to identify the revolution's central thrust—to grasp whether its brand of socialism is peculiarly Cuban (its Marxism derivative, superficial, original, confused, or cynical) and whether the pivotal role Castro plays in making policy is a substitute for or a necessary transition to popular control. Some of the revolution's central contradictions seem to have intensified with time. Thus Castro, a confirmed believer in (and prime exemplar of) the importance of the individual in history, has periodically narrowed the definition of acceptable individual deviation: the publication of the avant-garde *Lunes* has been suspended; the poet Heberto Padilla has been made to confess publicly his literary/political sins; homosexuals were at one point rounded up and put in isolated prison camps (a repression that has now given way to subtler but still real forms of coercion and ostracism). As Miguel Angel Quevado, the editor of *Bohemia*, wrote in 1960, "To carry out a profound social revolution, it was not necessary to install a system which degrades man to the condition of the State." Angel suspended his journal, sought asylum—and died by his own hand in Caracas in 1969.[11]

A revolution made in the name of the masses, one that has taken enormous steps in eliminating the vast inequalities that earlier existed between rich and poor, white and black, urban and rural Cubans, has yet to find institutional means for ensuring that the people can have a direct and continuous voice in deciding national policy.[12]

I'm persuaded by Fidel's argument that *before* the revolution, elections and political parties had served only to legitimize and preserve the interests of the privileged. But I'm not persuaded that the exploitative purposes for which these institutions were used under an oligarchy need automatically discredit their potential value under socialism. The fact that some of Castro's policies—preeminently, his support of the Russian invasion of Czechoslovakia—have never had to stand the test of popular ratification does not encourage the belief that present-day Cuba has yet found substitute channels for the expression of dissent. We know that political parties and elections bring with them the dangers of counterrevolution. We know, too, that a "free press" is often the handmaiden and alter ego of the privileged elite in power. But as Salvador Allende showed in Chile, we also know that parties can serve as authentic alternatives to, rather than mere echoes of, privilege. And as the *New York Times* demonstrated with the Pentagon Papers and the *Washington Post* during the Watergate scandal, we also know that far from being a mockery of justice, a free press can sometimes be its agent.

A devoted friend of the Cuban Revolution has asked me to remember that it must be judged not from where we are, but from where

Cuba *was*. It's an injunction bewildering on several counts. No one (on the Left, that is) would want to deny that Cuba has made impressive headway against the vast disparities that once existed in income, job opportunity, health services, diet and education. No one would want to claim that the United States, proportionate to its resources, has made comparable strides. It therefore hardly makes sense to patronize a country whose performance has been superior to our own.

Unless, that is, other kinds of costs seem to overbalance the material gains. And unless the material gains themselves seem in danger of becoming the resting place—rather than the starting point—of the revolution. Hugh Thomas has written, "Health and education are only aids to the good life. . . . The multitudes in uniform are surely supposed to be marching to a spot where they can disband."[13]

A growing number of people no longer locate that spot, or even the march to it, along the older utopian continuum of "man free from material want." They search for a new utopia in the area of psychosexual transformation, envisioning a gender revolution in which "male" and "female" have become outmoded differentiations, individual human beings instead combining in their persons the qualities previously thought the preserve of one sex or the other. It's possible to argue that this new vision, when most of the world still goes to bed hungry at night, is a luxury and an illusion, the decadent yearning of a society already sated with possessions—but not with the satisfactions they were supposed to have brought in train. I myself think not. But that argument is for another place.

The point here is that those who see the redefinition of gender and sexuality as the cutting edge of the newest revolution tend also to regard the contours of Castro's "new man" as distressingly old. "Honor" and *machismo* on the one hand, and statism and authority on the other, combine to suggest an image that may not do justice to Castro's *ultimate* intentions but does seem descriptive of his current emphases.

Perhaps he has no choice. Doubly beset as Castro is by the ingrained aggressiveness of our country and the ingrained gender stereotyping of his, he may think it neither wise nor possible to push the revolution into still further areas of innovation. The danger is that he may not want to. Or that he may be a willing prisoner of the Marxist paradigm that sees changes in material relationships necessarily preceding changes in culture. Or it may be that even if his ultimate goal *is* a sexually liberated, State-less communism, he may find, as have so many visionaries before him, that ultimate goals forever recede as they forever approach.

We do not know. For the vast majority of people in the world, the "older" vision of freedom from material want is still so distantly utopian that perhaps only a citizen of the United States could be provincial enough to doubt its continuing centrality. Or arrogant enough to suggest that a more encompassing vision, the redefinition of gender roles, awaits us, that the redefinition cannot proceed without absolute freedom of inquiry and expression, and that it is in the presumed heartland of counterrevolution, the United States of America, that we are beginning to glimpse its emerging contours.

—*Introduction to Hans Mangus Engensberger,*
The Havana Inquiry, *1974*

The Gulf War
(1991)

Remember Anita Bryant and her campaign to "Save the Children?" Gay people knew that she was really trying to save her own narrow traditionalism, that if she cared about children she would have been campaigning against heterosexual males who do 98 percent of the child molestation and would have been working to create educational and job opportunities to rescue the minority young from despair.

Well, strong women and gentle men, get ready. The fake sloganeers are back in force, "Saving the Peace" with carpet bombing, "Bolstering Democracy" by censoring the news, "Liberating" Iraq and Kuwait by destroying them. And in the process, once again making our own land safe for macho militarism.

The notion of strong women may fare better than that of gentle men in the war climate. Women are being allowed to drive jeeps, run supply depots, service aircraft and—to the horror of our patriarchal Saudi allies—appear in full uniform on the nightly news making appropriate gung ho noises, their fears and doubts either nonexistent or temporarily erased by the responsibility felt during their ten-second bite to Say the Right Thing—the thing that will make the folks back home Proud.

This time around, the young men in uniform, interestingly, *are* being allowed to express fear (though not doubt). Repeatedly on the TV screen, a sweet-faced, earnest twenty-year-old will confide to a reporter, "Yes, I'm scared." The jaw will be set, of course, and the confession will be quickly followed with a reassuring, "We'll get the job done we've been sent here to do." But apparently it is now okay for men to acknowledge that killing is not something they do with spontaneous relish. One might even be tempted to claim this new male expressiveness as a victory for feminism.

The United States has never been able to go to war and, at the same time, preserve (not to mention extend) free speech and dissent. During the Civil War, Lincoln suspended the right of habeas corpus. During World War I, President Woodrow Wilson—he, too, wanted to make the world "safe for democracy"—had radicals like Emma Goldman rounded up and deported (to Russia, of course, and on a leaky vessel that had been condemned as "not seaworthy"). And during World War II, as even Hollywood has gotten around to showing, Japanese Americans were confined to prison camps—just in case they *might* to be tempted to dissent.

We're about to see more of the same. George Bush and the mirror-image boy/men who surround him—all, like the boss, cold, shallow and vindictive—feel wonderfully vindicated by the triumph of traditional "virtues": by our ability once again quickly to mobilize resources for war, to outperform everybody else in the technological wonder of our killing machines, to reassert our claim to be the toughest kid on the block, to *matter.* Everything worth doing, in the Bush hierarchy of values, we have proven we can still do superlatively well. That excludes, of course, waging war against poverty, discrimination and disease.

None of which is to say that Saddam Hussein is not a bloody tyrant and, probably, a psychopath. But he is *not* as direct a threat to our national well-being as are the undernourished children, despairing teenagers, AIDS-infected young people and homeless multitudes. Nor is Saddam a threat of Hitler-like proportions to the globe—not when all he could manage after an eight-year war was a stalemate with neighboring Iran.

Clearly, our decision to intervene had to do with more than defending democracy (the "democracy," mind you, of Kuwait, where no women and only 8 percent of the male population are allowed to vote). Like wanting to protect our oil supply, say. Like making it necessary for Germany and Japan to deal directly through us, as the next century's resident power in the Middle East, for their energy sources. Like, perhaps most basic of all, allowing the elite of white men who control our country once again to confirm and assert that they cannot be bypassed or supplanted. Neither patiently waiting for sanctions to work nor joining a general Middle East peace conference would have served those ends nearly as well as a screeching, terrifying display of brute power.

And to reassert this macho meanness of spirit, many must die—including multitudes of Iraqis no less innocent than the many American soldiers forced to an impossible choice between their wish to win certification at home and their own humane instincts. Abroad we will become hated conquerors, a hate that will pursue us for generations. At home we could see the containment (or outright suppression) of nonconformity, especially of challenges to heterosexist white male standards.

The body bags and VA hospitals will soon be filling. And Anita Bryant is singing in the wings.

—The Village Voice, *Feb. 19, 1991*

PART TWO

Sites of Resistance:
The Sixties and Seventies

I

The Black Struggle

"Moderation" versus "Militancy" (1964)

There is a widening chasm between the white "moderate" and the Negro "militant." The moderate position is epitomized by the *New York Times:* concerned and well-intentioned, but willing to tolerate only polite forms of protest. The militant position is epitomized by a Harlem minister: "Freedom is never voluntarily given up by the oppressor. We're going to have to be out on the streets a long time." The argument between moderation and militancy represents contrasting attachments to order and justice. The moderate, who already shares in some of the "good things" of life, prefers to believe that social justice can be achieved without unduly disturbing social order. The militant, who sees little in that order worth preserving, believes that considerable tension, conflict and *dis*order are unavoidable concomitants of meaningful change.

There is a growing impatience with the built-in evasions of the moderate position. In practice, "gradually" has often meant "glacially," and even were the phrase now to carry overtones of real advance, it might no longer be sufficiently rapid to satisfy Negro impatience or to sustain hope. Certainly "gradualism," even if genuine, would not be enough to win back those Negroes who have become convinced of the

Muslim contention (all too reasonable) that whites will never fully "make good." To this extent, white racism has already created its own virulent counterpart.

Aside from being "too little, too late," the moderate position suffers from the optimistic defect of placing too much faith in man's "conscience." An appeal to morality, a reliance on the white man's guilt, is in itself an insufficient guarantee of reform. Conscience has brought some improvement in the Negro's status, but only some. If fundamental change is to come—and nothing less will do—"the movement" must organize and demonstrate its power. The hostile or apathetic white majority will not surrender its privileges unless frightened or forced into doing so.

In this sense the militants are tough-minded realists. Their refusal to place entire faith in an appeal to conscience, or in the benevolent workings of time, separates them from the genteel mainstream of the American reform tradition. That tradition has always been grounded in a double optimism—that the world can be made better, and that this can be done through an appeal to "right reason" rather than force and fear. The militants share the belief that the world can be made a better place, but they put their faith for change in power, not goodwill. To this degree, they are more in the tradition of European radicalism than American reform.

The civil rights struggle is growing more radical in ends as well as means. There is a growing view among civil rights leaders that merely trying to win full partnership in American life is not enough. The view has two sources, one intellectual and one tactical. The first, represented by James Baldwin and Lorraine Hansberry, is that partnership may not be desirable because the firm is corrupt. The root fear of the Baldwins, in part based on a reification of Negro-hipster-slum life, is that Negroes might exchange whatever cultural uniqueness their sufferings have given them for the desiccated rituals of middle-class white life.

A second source of protest against aiming the civil rights movement solely at assimilation comes from tactical rather than ideological considerations. The view here is that although full participation in American life may be desirable, it will not materialize unless the basic assumptions of our society are first challenged. The Negro will never be fully accepted until the value structure which has so long denied him is itself overhauled. Until then, he will be given partial concessions only, just enough semblance of good faith to pacify the gullible—or the tired.

Both these sources—the intellectual and the tactical—are moving Negro protest into a deeper form of social criticism, one that sees racism as a symptom as well as cause of our social rot, and that calls for fundamental political and economic changes beyond civil rights. Specifically, the federal government must be brought to exercise its powers in a full-scale assault on poverty, unemployment and education. The problem of poverty underlies the problem of civil rights; the inequalities of American life are phenomena of class as well as color. And it is essential for the under-privileged and poor of all colors and backgrounds to recognize their kinship. A neo-Populist alliance is needed—one that would unite the American underclasses in a concerted drive to acquire power in the name of making fundamental changes in our society.

Yet the obstacles to a coalition of the poor are formidable. Low-status whites are often those most hostile to Negroes. Their prejudice is part of their essential protective equipment; it could be surrendered only if a new scapegoat could be found for their frustrations—possibly the wealthy and privileged. The Negro poor, on their side, may be too preoccupied with survival issues to think in terms of potential alliances. In addition to the specific obstacle of color prejudice, there is also the inhibiting effect of our middle-class value structure (not confined to the middle class), with its emphasis on what is safe and secure, as well as our reform tradition of piecemeal adjustment.

There are fundamental inequities in American life which call for fundamental reforms; these reforms require the full weight and support of the federal government behind them; the government cannot be brought to exercise its power unless "encouraged" to do so through political pressure from below; the best way to exert such pressure is through an alliance of the poor. Such an alliance may be the only real hope for revitalizing the country—which makes its unlikeliness all the more depressing.

—Book Week (The New York Herald Tribune), *Aug. 9, 1964*

James Meredith
(1966)

J ames Meredith is the man who integrated the University of Mississippi. Needless to say, I was prepared to find his book *Three Years in Mississippi,* admirable. It has not been that easy.

Like almost everyone of my age, education and region, I regarded Meredith's assault on the state of Mississippi as heroic. And still do. But one can admire an act without being attracted to the man who performs it, and certainly without thinking well of the account he subsequently writes of it.

One part of my trouble is that I do not believe in Divine Missions, let alone Divinity. The other part is my distaste for the military personality. Meredith is convinced of the former and personifies the latter. I take him here at his own evaluation; the emphases are his, not mine, and he places them relentlessly lest we be tempted to inquire into other aspects of his personality and experience. Again and again he speaks of his "Divine Responsibility," of pursuing his Destiny, of carrying out his Mandate: "At a very early age I had established the . . . goals to be achieved on the way to my final destiny"; ". . . it appeared to me that the particular steps that I had chosen to take in an effort to carry out the mandate of my Divine Mission had been proper and timely"; ". . . my belief in my super-natural or superhuman powers was another important factor. Whether it was true or not, I had always felt that I could stop a mob with the uplift of a hand . . . Because of my 'Divine Responsibility' to advance human civilization, I could not die."

In the very first paragraph of his book, Meredith announces that he is "a soldier at heart" and goes on to say that if there was anything he ever wanted to be "it would have been a general." Throughout he employs military terminology: he is the aggressor in a war, he plots his strategy, he knows his enemy, and when in the end he finally wins his degree, it is his "battle citation." Meredith of course *was* in a war, and no doubt only a man of his intensity and certitude could have seen it through successfully. But the pervading element of grandiosity, à la MacArthur–de Gaulle, is nonetheless disturbing. That Meredith's Napoleonism is self-admitted makes it less, not more attractive, for it is proclaimed with a guilelessness that suggests self-delusion. He seems unaware that there could be grounds for embarrassment in viewing himself as The Chosen Vessel of the Lord.

"I have never made a mistake in my life," he asserts, "because I never make arbitrary or predetermined decisions. Every decision made and every action taken is always an impersonal result of the processing of every available bit of data." (Once, though, Meredith does admit to "an arbitrary decision"—the result of "failing to apply my decision-making formula.") The computerized mentality so candidly, so proudly, displayed carries some eerie echoes of *Dr. Strangelove*. That movie, it is said, was hyperbolic, but no sentence in Terry Southern's screenplay is more improbable—or shocking—than this one from *Three Years in Mississippi:* "I not only want the right to participate in an established government, but I have the desire to fashion a better government . . . not only the right to be an employee in a nuclear plant, but the desire to build a better and more effective bomb."

The deterministic tone of Meredith's narrative, the stolid, resolute quality of his prose, reflect his impersonality. He believes Society must be placed above Self, and that events are shaped by forces larger than the individual. The result is that all the people in his book, including himself, emerge as cardboard figures. Thus Constance Baker Motley, a key figure in the Ole Miss fight, is not to any degree brought to life as a person. She, like everyone else in the book, plays out her assigned role in the inexorable historical process—one more cog in the machine. There is a curious irony in the fact that Meredith, an individual who did so much to change long-standing patterns, has little belief in the importance of individuals.

If we could excise the postures and banalities from *Three Years in Mississippi*, we would have a work of considerable value as a primary source. Meredith has given us a case-history of one of the key episodes of recent decades; he not only narrates the events but also prints many of the central documents—court decisions, correspondence with university officials, depositions and testimony, excerpts from his own speeches, articles, TV appearances and private mail. Much of this information only Meredith could have provided, and at many points he fills out our understanding of events with new details. Thus he makes it clear that his temptation to leave Ole Miss was not due primarily to bad grades; he shows that the pistol Cleve McDowell (the second Negro student to gain admittance to the university) carried and that ultimately led to his dismissal, was necessary for self-protection; and he rehashes the controversy surrounding his 1963 speech to the annual convention of the NAACP (though in this instance his justifying comments are not persuasive: reading his declaration in the speech that the pending March on Washington would "not be in the best interest of our cause," and his Horatio Alger preachments to Negro youth on the supreme importance of establishing good credit ratings, I was not surprised that many in his audience were offended).

Throughout the book I kept being brought up short by the astonishing parallels in rhetoric and attitude between Meredith and any earnest, high-minded American of the mid-nineteenth century: his optimism, religiosity, boot-strap theory of self-help, his belief in our country's "manifest destiny," in ethical absolutes and man's power to control and change his world. There is an antique (and appealing) ring to Meredith's statement that "the very existence of the human being makes everything possible"—yes, even rapidly changing the Southern status quo. There is an almost antediluvian (and less appealing) ring to Meredith's perfervid patriotism: "America is a great nation. It has led the world in freedom for a long time . . . I have read widely and have traveled a good deal, and I am firmly convinced that the American nation is truly the greatest among nations."

—Book Week (The New York Herald Tribune),
April 24, 1966

I wrote this second piece on Meredith less than two months after the article printed above, on the occasion of his having been shot while on a one-man march in the South.

James Meredith set off on his march to demonstrate that Negroes had "nothing to fear." Could he have believed this? It seems inconceivable that a man brought up in Mississippi could really think that we have now reached the point where Negroes no longer need worry about physical violence. Only a few years ago, when trying to integrate Ole Miss, Meredith personally experienced the Anglo-Saxon wrath that awaits those who boldly challenge established mores. Surely Meredith does not actually believe that in the three years since then, white attitudes have been so revolutionized that Negroes in Mississippi could troop off to the polls without any fear of retaliation. What then was in his mind?

At the risk of both presumption and oversimplification, it is possible to see in Meredith's act a rationale and significance apart from his stated purpose. What Meredith was saying to *me*, when he set out for Mississippi, was not that reasons for fear no longer exist, but that because they are still present, they must be continually faced. Danger, death, must be risked. Not to risk them, to bow to the implied threat, is to guarantee a continuation, perhaps even a worsening, of inequality. And the risk, Meredith seemed to be saying when be set off alone down the road from Memphis, must be assumed on an individual basis. The government can pass laws, the official forms of compliance can be registered, but significant change comes when individuals, facing their own fear, inspire similar self-confrontations in others.

What would have happened had Meredith not been shot, had he completed his march without being harmed? Would he have thereby demonstrated—in accord with his stated purpose—that Negroes no longer have grounds for fear? Hardly. The common reaction, I suspect, would have been that he was lucky, protected by fame and media coverage. The average Negro tenant-farmer would never have been foolish enough to imagine that his own anonymity and helplessness would prove safeguards of equal weight. Indeed the shock with which news of Meredith's shooting has been received was based on the widespread feeling that in his case "they wouldn't dare!"

But they did dare—or someone dared. Death in the civil rights struggle has almost always come at the hands of one, or a few individuals. If most white Mississippians would never "go that far," the important point is that the Mississippi ethos turns up the Byron de la Beckwiths with enough regularity to cast doubt on whether they can accurately be called "exceptions."

If Meredith had not been harmed, in other words, his march would have demonstrated little more than his own courage, a quality we have long been familiar with. Now that he has been shot, the effects of the march are likely to be more extensive, though not in the direction Meredith hoped for. That is, few Mississippi Negroes will now be encouraged (if they ever could have been) to believe either Meredith's stated or implied purpose: that they have little to fear or that a confrontation with their fear, however "soul-enriching," will be unaccompanied by physical injury.

Few men have the inner resources (whatever their complex origin) to face up to such consequences. And one would be as sanctimonious in telling men that they should, as one would be naive in expecting that they will. The more likely and probably more human (there is something suprahuman about Meredith) response in the Negro community will be a redoubling of fear. And anger. And disillusion with the benefits of continued reliance on the tactics of nonviolence.

The civil rights movement, under the weight of accumulated frustrations, had begun to shift ground before James Meredith's march, a shift dramatically symbolized by the recent change of leadership in the Student Nonviolent Coordinating Committee (SNCC). Given the usual distortions of the press, it is not easy to know what the assumptions and goals of Stokely Carmichael's "Black Panthers" really are, but their rejection of "politics" and their emphasis on "blackness" are unmistakable signs of heightened alienation. And who can say that their discouragement, their refusal to participate further in official assaults on segregation, is other than an appropriate response to the seemingly endless evasions of white America? Unfortunately their own approach seems even less promising, based as it is on a black variation of the separate but equal theme, on a suicidal rejection of allies.

Promising or not, the ranks of the disaffected are bound to be swelled by the abrupt end of James Meredith's march. His intended purpose was to encourage further participation by Negroes in "the American way," to kindle their hope in the possibilities of participation. The effect is likely to be the reverse. It is hard to feel encouraged at the prospect of a bullet. It is difficult to feel hopeful when even a James Meredith can be shot down. Meredith, the congenital optimist, has unwittingly given fuel to the growing pessimism within civil rights ranks.

—The Village Voice, *June 16, 1966*

Taking Stock (1967)

The civil rights coalition is in disarray, the mood of the country has turned conservative and the energies of the federal government have been diminished by its uncertain mandate and its own divided will. The accurate words are "played out," not "completed." Like the First Reconstruction of the 1860s, the second one of the 1960s has stopped tragically short of the hopes once held out for it.

I do not mean that nothing has been accomplished. Something has been, and those who deny any advance falsify the evidence almost as much as those who claim we are already standing on Mt. Pisgah and in sight of the Promised Land. Still, the record of achievement, on balance, is depressingly slight.

First, there is the matter of public schools. It took ten years, following the Supreme Court decision of 1954, to place 2.5% of Negro children in the Deep South in previously all-white schools. Then, from 1964 to 65, the figure shot up to about 12%. Recent gains are largely due to Title VI of the 1964 Civil Rights Act, which gave the federal government a new weapon to use against segregation: it allowed federal funds to be cut off from any program in which discrimination was found to exist.

The utilization of Title VI, while producing comparatively rapid progress in the last two years, has still not radically altered the existing pattern of segregation. A survey released by the Office of Education in July 1966, shows that 80% of white children in first grade attend schools that are 90% or more white, while 65% of all Negro first-graders attend schools that are 90% Negro.

Even if the federal government was to combat school segregation to the full extent of its powers, the battle could not easily be won. In most urban centers it will be maintained simply because it is a direct reflection of residential segregation, which is itself on the increase. In 40 of the 45 largest southern cities, the index of residential segregation has shown a net gain since 1940. In the North, as a Lou Harris poll released in *Newsweek* in August 1966 reveals, 46% of the white population still objects to having a Negro family live next door (as do 69% of southern whites). Moreover, touted urban renewal programs have done almost nothing to create racially integrated areas—the Negro ghetto has simply been removed to a new location. Only widespread busing can break the pattern of segregated schools, and resistance to that expedient is fierce.

Another obstacle to integration is a new phenomenon known as "segregation by flight"—that is, in order to avoid sending their children to desegregated schools, whites will either flee the city for a suburb or, alternatively, will enroll their children in parochial and private schools. The most notorious example is Washington, D.C., where 85% of public school students are now Negro. But the pattern is widespread in the North. In Philadelphia, to give another example, 57% of public school pupils (as of April 1966) are now nonwhite in a city that is 70% white; indeed white enrollment is greater in Philadelphia's private schools than in the city's entire public school system.

Turning to economic matters, the picture is even less reassuring. It is true that opportunities have expanded for the small number of Negroes qualified for white collar employment, but the great mass of Negro workers hold unskilled or semiskilled positions, and for these people, future prospects are dim. By 1970 our labor force will have been further swelled by the babies of the postwar "boom" who are now reaching employment age; at the same time, automation and technological advances will further shrink the number of available unskilled jobs. Thus while the tiny Negro middle class will continue to find unprecedented opportunities, the vast majority of Negro workers will find their economic position increasingly in jeopardy. As Daniel Moynihan has put it, "in terms of employment and income and occupational status, it is quite possible the Negro community is moving in two directions, or rather that two Negro communities are moving in opposite directions."

In the area of political rights there have been undeniable gains, but as the number of Negro voters has increased, so, ironically, has the realization that the vote, once thought a panacea, in fact provides only limited leverage with which to exert pressure for change. Even if Negroes should some day vote in proportion to their numbers, only 85 out of 1,139 southern counties have Negro voting-age majorities. Moreover, many of the basic ills from which Negroes suffer—inadequate housing, lack of job opportunities, inferior education—cannot be solved on the county level. These are national phenomena requiring national resources for their solution. Whether these resources will be allocated in sufficient amounts in turn depends on the strength of the civil rights coalition.

Yet no new "populist" coalition seems likely. Civil rights organizations are themselves divided and feuding, with SNCC and the Congress of Racial Equality (CORE) increasingly committed to black nationalism and separatism. This development, in turn (along with riots like Watts and the feeling that the two recent civil rights bills have "solved the problem"), has led to a decline in white sympathy. Finally, those groups thought to be the likeliest candidates for a reform coalition are either politically impotent (like the campus activists of Students for a Democratic Society [SDS]) or (like the organized labor movement) increasingly identified with the establishment. The defeat in Congress of the 1966 civil rights bill is only the most dramatic example of this loss of a national consensus over civil rights. The Lou Harris poll of August 1966 shows that no less that 70% of whites think Negroes "are trying to move too fast." This shift in white attitudes works to convince many in the Negro community that integration is impossible or undesirable, to increase the apathy or anger that alternately displays itself in "dropping out" or in turning to the slogans of Black Power.

All of this is gloomy enough. Yet it's possible to hold to some measure of optimism. It is at least true, for example, that the South is no longer a unit behind the doctrine of white supremacy. In a few states—notably Mississippi, Alabama, Georgia and Louisiana—the white majority remains overwhelmingly racist, but in others, like North Carolina and Tennessee, a pattern of real change can be detected. It is not change sufficiently great to allow for large-scale optimism; equality is hardly making giant strides.

Nor is it the stuff, God knows, of which moral revolutions are made—and ultimately nothing less than that is required. Yet if it turns out that we have *time* to await slow, piecemeal advances, they may yet, in their cumulative effect, produce that revolution.

A second cause for comfort is the Negro's own determination. Though the disappointments of the past few years have undoubtedly fostered additional cynicism and fear in the Negro community, much faith, remarkably, does seem to remain. Two out of three Negroes questioned by Lou Harris in his August 1966 poll felt that life had improved for them since 1963, and the blandishments of Black Power, separatism, nationalism and violence continue to have only marginal appeal.

Finally, it's possible to argue that Northern whites have a deeper commitment to equality than they had during the First Reconstruction. This argument, to be sure, is highly vulnerable—as the figures in Lou Harris's poll make clear. Moreover, to the extent Northerners *have* been converted to egalitarianism, the conversion may be more rational and willed than emotional and felt. I am not sneering at this; if everyone in the country had at least arrived at an intellectual commitment to equality, we would be far better off than we are. But I do think it's important to keep in mind that on a visceral level, even many "liberals" are uncertain of their feelings and, because of that, cannot be consistently relied on. Intellectually they may have outgrown the racist assumptions of their culture, may have become aware of the falsity and cruelty of those assumptions and disciplined themselves into acting accordingly. Yet, chiefly at an unconscious level, they cannot wholly root out some lingering anti-Negro sentiment. After all, in our racist culture such feelings were ingested with our pabulum and cannot be entirely exorcised simply by wishing to do so.

And we would be foolish to expect that they can be. This is a point worth stressing. We must not hold out the unrealistic hope that this generation can achieve true *feelings* of brotherhood. We will do well if we can bring it to *act* according to the principles of brotherhood. Perhaps some future generation, brought up in a more truthful and humane spirit will move beyond outward conformity to inner conviction. But the myths and assumptions of white supremacy are too central a part of our heritage to expect that, on a deep emotional level, we can wholly uproot them in a single generation.

To achieve even the limited goal of equality before the law, we must be prepared to exercise force. We must also be prepared, as a result, for a fair amount of social upheaval. Despite the powerful elements working against legal equality, there are grounds, as I have argued, for qualified optimism. But if racism is to be overcome, we must have not only additional legislation, but legislation that is actually enforced—unlike the record compiled with the federal acts of 1964 and 1965.

It is often argued that egalitarian legislation cannot be imposed upon an unwilling people. We can agree, of course, that it would be better if change came voluntarily; enforced legislation is not the ideal way. But given the lateness of the hour and the intransigence of the opposition, it is apparently the only way. It will be said in answer to this that if change is imposed, it cannot produce lasting results; one cannot legislate against prejudice: stateways cannot change folkways.

But this argument mistakes the primary intention of egalitarian legislation, which is aimed not at eradicating prejudice but at curtailing its outward expression. And this much legislation *can* do effectively (if enforced): it can insist that people obey the law, regardless of their feelings about that law. There is even evidence that in the long run legislation can affect the prejudice itself. As the psychologist Gordon Allport has argued in his book *Becoming,* when you force a man to change his outward pattern of behavior, you may eventually change his inner attitudes and feelings. This is probably not true of what Allport calls "compulsive bigots." Such people must simply be forced to obey the law; we cannot hold out the hope that by so doing they will undergo a gradual inner conversion as well.

I do not believe, however, that most white Americans are confirmed bigots—except in a few and increasingly isolated areas. Or perhaps it might be better put this way: I believe that the racial bigotry of most Americans is offset by their belief in Christian and democratic ethics, and the resulting tension between their prejudices and their values produces the guilt that can creatively respond to egalitarian legislation. For these Americans, their private consciences are at least partly in line with the legal prods being exerted upon them. Most Americans, after all, *have* been weaned on the precepts—or at least the slogans—of Christianity and democracy, that is, the idea that all men are brothers, that we should love one another, that every life has unique value and every man the natural right to make of his life what he can. These ideas conflict basically, disastrously, with racial intolerance. And somewhere most Americans know it. They may try to bury the conflict between their practices and their values, but the conflict will not stay buried. When legislation is passed that forces them to honor their own democratic and Christian assumptions, to conform, as it were, to their better selves, they often greet the legislation with something like relief—that is, after an initial display of fury which is in part real, in part a concession to what they take to be local mores.

Much of what I have said about the prospects of achieving justice for Negro Americans is highly problematic: speculations about the future always are. My own feelings waver very much between doubt and hope, sometimes coming down on the latter side, more often in recent months, on the former. It is true that there are signs of progress all around us, slow, agonizing progress. But progress—though American mythology dislikes dealing with the fact—is reversible (as the First Reconstruction proves). History is not the story of inevitable and continuing improvement, though Americans have a special fondness for that assumption because it helps to excuse them from active exertion on behalf of change.

We must be alert to the fact that the reform impulse can spend itself before reaching its goals, that a reverse trend can set in and erase previous gains. In 1967, as in 1877, signs of reversal are again apparent. If the trend is not resisted, it may well accelerate. In short, we can hardly afford to rest on our laurels—pitiful as they are. If further gains toward racial equality are to come, they will result from hard work, not from reliance on the presumed benevolence of Time and the Deity.

—*Foreword to* The Civil Rights Reader
(Leon Friedman, ed.), Feb. 1, 1967

Black Power and the American Radical Tradition (1968)

T he slogan of "Black Power" has caused widespread confusion and alarm. This is partly due to a problem inherent in language: words necessarily reduce complex attitudes or phenomena to symbols which, in their abbreviation, allow for a variety of interpretations. Stuart Chase has reported that in the thirties, when the word "fascism" was on every tongue, he asked 100 people from various walks of life what the word meant and got 100 widely differing definitions. And in 1953 when *The Capital Times* of Madison, Wisconsin, asked 200 people "What is a Communist?" not only was there no agreement, but five out of every eight admitted they couldn't define the term at all. So it is with "Black Power." Its definition depends on whom you ask, when you ask, where you ask and, not least, who does the asking.

Yet the phrase's ambiguity derives not only from the usual confusions of language, but from a failure of clarity (or is it frankness?) on the part of its advocates and a failure of attention (or is it generosity?) from their critics. The leaders of SNCC and CORE who invented the slogan, including Stokely Carmichael and Floyd McKissick, have given Black Power different definitions on different occasions, in part because their own understanding of the term continues to develop, but in part, too, because their explanations have been tailored to their audiences. The confusion has been compounded by the press, which has frequently distorted the words of SNCC and CORE representatives, harping on every connotation of violence and reverse racism, minimizing the central call for racial unity.

For all these reasons, it is still not clear whether "Black Power" is to be taken as a short-term tactical device or a long-range goal, that is, a postponement or a rejection of integration; whether it has been adapted as a lever for intimidating whites or organizing blacks, for instilling race hate or race pride; whether it necessitates, permits or encourages violence; whether it is a symptom of Negro despair or of Negro determination, a reaction to the lack of improvement in the daily lives of Negro-Americans or a sign that improved conditions are creating additional expectations and demands. Whether Black Power, furthermore, becomes a constructive psychological and political tactic or a destructive summons to separatism, violence and reverse racism will depend at least as much on developments outside the control of its advocates (like the war in Vietnam) as on their conscious determination. For all these reasons, it is too early for final evaluations; only time, and perhaps not even that, will provide them. At most, certain limited, and tentative, observations are possible.

If Black Power means only that Negroes should organize politically and economically in order to improve self-regard and to exert maximum pressure, then the new philosophy would be difficult to fault, for it would be based on the truisms that minorities must argue from positions of strength rather than weakness, and that the majority is far more likely to make concessions to power than to justice. To insist that Negro-Americans seek their goals as individuals and solely by appeals to conscience and "love," when white Americans have always relied on group association and organized protest to achieve theirs, would be yet one more form of discrimination. Moreover, when whites decry SNCC's declaration that it is tired of turning the other cheek, that henceforth it will actively resist white brutality, they might do well to remember that they have always considered self-defense acceptable behavior for themselves: our textbooks view the refusal of the revolutionaries of 1776 to "sit supinely by" as the very essence of manhood.

Although Black Power makes good sense when defined to mean further organization and cooperation within the Negro community, the results that are likely to follow in terms of political leverage can easily be exaggerated. The impact is likely to be greatest at the county level in the Deep South and in the urban ghettos of the North. In this regard, the "Black Panther" party of Lowndes County, Alabama, is the prototype.

There are roughly 12,000 Negroes in Lowndes County and 3,000 whites, but until 1964 there was not a single Negro registered to vote, while white registration had reached 118 percent of those eligible. Negro life in Lowndes, as Andrew Kopkind has graphically recounted,[1] was—and is—wretched. The median family income for whites is $4,400, for Negroes, $935; Negro farmhands earn $3.00 to $6.00 a day; half of the Negro women who work are maids in Montgomery (which requires a forty- to sixty-mile daily round-trip) at $4.00 a day; few Negroes have farms, since 90 percent of the land is owned by about 85 white families; the one large industrial plant in the area, the new Dan River Mills textile factory, will only employ Negroes in menial capacities; most Lowndes Negroes are functional illiterates, living in squalor and hopelessness.

The Black Panther party set out to change all this. The only path to change in Lowndes, and in much of the Deep South, is to "take over the courthouse," the seat of local power. For generations the courthouse in Lowndes has been controlled by the Democratic party; indeed there is no Republican party in the county. Obviously it made little sense for SNCC organizers to hope to influence the local

Democrats; no white moderates existed and no discussion of integration was tolerated. To have expected blacks to "bore from within" would have been, as Carmichael has said, "like asking the Jews to reform the Nazi party."

Instead, Carmichael and his associates established the separate Black Panther party. After months of work SNCC organizers (with almost no assistance from federal agents) registered enough Negroes to hope for a numerical majority in the county. But in the election of November 1966, the Black Panther party was defeated, for a variety of reasons which include Negro apathy or fear and white intimidation.[2] Despite this defeat, the possibility of a better life for Lowndes County Negroes does at last exist, and should the Black Panther party come into power at some future point, that possibility could become a reality.

Nonetheless, even on the local level and even in the Deep South, Lowndes County is not representative. In Alabama, for example, only eleven of the state's sixty-seven counties have black majorities. Where these majorities do not exist, the only effect independent black political parties are likely to have is to consolidate the whites in opposition. Moreover, and more significantly, many of the basic ills from which Negro-Americans suffer—inadequate housing, inferior education, limited job opportunities—are national phenomena requiring national resources to solve. Whether these resources will be allocated in sufficient amounts will depend, in turn, on whether a national coalition can be formed to exert pressure on the federal government—a coalition of civil rights activists, church groups, campus radicals, New Class technocrats, unskilled, un-unionized laborers and certain elements in organized labor, such as the UAW or the United Federation of Teachers. Such a coalition, of course, would necessitate Negro-white unity, a unity Black Power at least temporarily rejects.[3]

The answer that Black Power advocates give to the "coalition argument" is of several pieces. The only kind of progressive coalition that can exist in this country, they say, is the mild, liberal variety which produced the civil rights legislation of recent years. And that kind of legislation has proven itself grossly inadequate. Its chief result has been to lull white liberals into believing that the major battles have been won, whereas in fact there has been almost no change, or change for the worse, in the daily lives of most blacks.[4]

Unemployment among Negroes has actually gone up in the past ten years. Title VI of the 1964 Civil Rights Act, with its promising provision for the withdrawal of federal funds in cases of discrimination, has been used in limited fashion in regard to the schools but not at all in regard to other forms of unequal treatment, such as segregated hospital facilities. Under the 1965 Voting Rights Act, only about forty federal registrars have been sent into the South, though many areas have less than the 50 percent registration figure that would legally warrant intervention. In short, the legislation produced by the liberal coalition of the early sixties has turned out to be little more than federally approved tokenism, a continuation of paper promises and ancient inequities.

If a *radical* coalition could be formed in this country—that is, one willing to scrutinize in depth the failings of our system, to suggest structural, not piecemeal, reforms, to see them executed with sustained rather than intermittent vigor—then Black Power advocates might feel less need to separate themselves and to concentrate on local, marginal successes. But no responsible observer believes that in the foreseeable future a radical coalition on the Left can become the effective political majority in the United States; we will be fortunate if a radical coalition on the Right does not. And so to SNCC and CORE, talk of further cooperation with white liberals is only an invitation to further futility. It is better, they feel, to concentrate on encouraging Negroes everywhere to self-respect and self-help, and in certain local areas, where their numbers warrant it, to try to win actual political power.

As an adaptation to present realities, Black Power thus has a persuasive logic. But there is such a thing as being too present-minded;

by concentrating on immediate prospects, the new doctrine may be jeopardizing larger possibilities for the future, those that could result from a national coalition with white allies. Though SNCC and CORE insist that they are not trying to cut whites out of the movement, that they merely want to redirect white energies into organizing whites so that at some future point a truly meaningful coalition of Negroes and whites can take place, there are grounds for doubting whether they really are interested in a future reconciliation, or if they are, whether some of the overtones of their present stance will allow for it. For example, SNCC's so-called position paper on Black Power attacks white radicals as well as white liberals, speaks vaguely of differing white and black "psyches" and seems to find all contact with all whites contaminating or intimidating ("whites are the ones who must try to raise themselves to our humanistic level").[5]

SNCC's bitterness at the hypocrisy and evasion of the white majority is understandable, yet the refusal to discriminate between degrees of inequity, the penchant instead for wholesale condemnation of all whites, is as unjust as it is self-defeating. The indictments and innuendos of SNCC's "position paper" give some credence to the view that the line between Black Power and black racism is a fine one easily erased, that, as always, means and ends tend to get confused, that a tactic of racial solidarity can turn into a goal of racial purity.

The philosophy of Black Power is thus a blend of varied, in part contending elements, and it cannot be predicted with any certainty which will assume dominance. But a comparison between the Black Power movement and the personnel, programs and fates of earlier radical movements in this country can make some contribution toward understanding its dilemmas and its likely directions.

Any argument based on historical analogy can, of course, become oversimplified and irresponsible. Historical events do not repeat themselves with anything like regularity; every event is to a large degree embedded in its own special context. An additional danger in reasoning from historical analogy is that in the process we will limit rather than expand our options; by arguing that certain consequences seem always to follow from certain actions and that therefore only a set number of alternatives ever exist, we can prevent ourselves from seeing new possibilities or from utilizing old ones in creative ways. We must be careful, when attempting to predict the future from the past, that in the process we do not straitjacket the present. Bearing these cautions and limitations in mind, some insight can still be gained from a historical perspective. For if there are large variances through time between roughly analogous events, there are also some similarities, and it is these which make comparative study possible and profitable. In regard to Black Power, I think we gain particular insight by comparing it with the two earlier radical movements of Abolitionism and Anarchism.

The Abolitionists represented the left wing of the antislavery movement (a position comparable to the one SNCC and CORE occupy today in the civil rights movement) because they called for an *immediate* end to slavery everywhere in the United States. Most Northerners who disapproved of slavery were not willing to go as far or as fast as the Abolitionists, preferring instead a more ameliorative approach. The tactic that increasingly won the approval of the Northern majority was the doctrine of "nonextension": no further expansion of slavery would be allowed, but the institution would be left alone where it already existed. The principle of nonextension first came into prominence in the late 1840s when fear developed in the North that territory acquired from our war with Mexico would be made into new slave states. Later the doctrine formed the basis of the Republican party, which in 1860 elected Lincoln to the Presidency. The Abolitionists, in other words, with their demand for immediate (and uncompensated) emancipation, never became the major channel of

Northern antislavery sentiment. They always remained a small sect, vilified by slavery's defenders and distrusted even by allies within the antislavery movement.

The parallels between the Abolitionists and the current defenders of Black Power seem to me numerous and striking. It is worth noting, first of all, that neither group started off with so-called "extremist" positions (the appropriateness of that word being, in any case, dubious).[6] The SNCC of 1967 is not the SNCC formed in 1960; both its personnel and its programs have shifted markedly. SNCC originally grew out of the sit-ins spontaneously begun in Greensboro, North Carolina by four freshmen at the all-Negro North Carolina Agricultural and Technical College. The sit-in technique spread rapidly through the South, and within a few months SNCC was formally inaugurated to channel and encourage further activities. At its inception SNCC's staff was interracial, religious in orientation, committed to the "American Dream," chiefly concerned with winning the right to share more equitably in that Dream and optimistic about the possibility of being allowed to do so. SNCC placed its hopes on an appeal to the national conscience and this it expected to arouse by the examples of nonviolence and redemptive love, and by the dramatic devices of sit-ins, freedom rides and protest marches.[7]

The Abolitionist movement, at the time of its inception, was similarly benign and sanguine. It, too, placed emphasis on "moral suasion," believing that the first order of business was to bring the iniquity of slavery to the country's attention, to arouse the average American's conscience. Once this was done, the Abolitionists felt discussion then could, and would, begin on the particular ways and means best calculated to bring about rapid, orderly emancipation. Some of those Abolitionists who later became intransigent defenders of immediatism—including William Lloyd Garrison—were willing, early in their careers, to consider plans for preliminary apprenticeship. They were willing, in other words, to settle for gradual emancipation *imme-*

diately begun instead of demanding that freedom itself be instantly achieved.

But this early flexibility received little encouragement. Neither the appeal to conscience nor the willingness to engage in debate over means brought results. In the North the Abolitionists encountered massive apathy; in the South, massive resistance. Thus thwarted, and influenced as well by the discouraging British experiment with gradualism in the West Indies, the Abolitionists abandoned their earlier willingness to consider a variety of plans for prior education and training and shifted to the position that emancipation had to take place at once and without compensation to the slaveholder. They also began (especially in New England) to advocate such doctrines as "Dis-Union" and "No-Government," positions that directly parallel Black Power's recent advocacy of "separation" and "decentralization," and that then as now produced discord and division within the movement, anger and denunciation without.

But the parallel of paramount importance I want to draw between the two movements is their similar passage from "moderation" to "extremism." In both cases, there *was* a passage, a shift in attitude and program, and it is essential that this be recognized, for it demonstrates the developmental nature of these—of all—movements for social change. Or, to reduce the point to individuals (and to clichés): "revolutionaries are not born but made." Garrison did not start his career with the doctrine of "immediatism"; as a young man, he even had kind words for the American Colonization Society, a group devoted to deporting Negroes to Africa and Central America. And Stokely Carmichael did not begin his ideological voyage with the slogan of Black Power; as a teenager he was opposed to student sit-ins in the South. What makes a man shift from "reform" to "revolution" is, it seems to me, primarily to be explained by the intransigence or indifference of his society: either society refuses reforms or gives them in the form of tokens. Thus, *if* one views the Garrisons and Carmichaels as "extremists," one should at least place the blame for that extremism where it belongs—not on their individual temperaments, their genetic predispositions, but on a society that scorned or toyed with their initial pleas for justice.

In turning to the Anarchist movement, I think we can see between it and the new turn taken by SNCC and CORE (or, more comprehensively still, by much of the New Left) significant affinities of style and thought. These are largely unconscious and unexplored; I have seen almost no overt references to them either in the movement's official literature or in its unofficial pronouncements. Yet the affinities seem to me important.

But first I should make clear that in speaking of "Anarchism" as if it were a unified tradition, I am necessarily oversimplifying. The Anarchist movement contained a variety of contending factions, disparate personalities and differing national patterns. The peasant Anarchists, especially in Spain, were fiercely anti-industrial and anti-urban and wished to withdraw entirely from the State to live in separate communities based on mutual aid. The anarchosyndicalists of France put special emphasis on the value of a general strike and looked to the trade unions as the future units of a new society. Michael Bakunin advocated violence; Leo Tolstoy abhorred it. Pierre-Joseph Proudhon believed in retaining individual ownership of certain forms of property; Enrico Malatesta called for its abolition in every form. Max Stirner's ideal was the egotist engaged in the war of "each against all"; Prince Peter Kropotkin's was human solidarity, a society based on the union of voluntary communes.

These are only some of the divisions of strategy, personality and geography that characterized the Anarchist movement. What bound these disparate elements together—what makes plausible the term "Anarchism" in reference to all of them—is their hostility to authority, especially that embodied in the State, but including any form of rule by man over man, whether it be parent, teacher, lawyer or priest. The Anarchists were against authority, they said, because they were for life—not life as most men had ever lived it, but life as it might be lived. Anarchists argued, in a manner reminiscent of Rousseau, that human aggression and cruelty were the products of imposed restraints. They insisted that the authoritarian upbringing most children were subjected to stifled spontaneity, curiosity, initiative, individuality—in other words, prevented possession of themselves. If they could be raised "free"—freed economically from the struggle for existence, intellectually freed from the tyranny of custom, emotionally freed from the need to revenge their own mutilation by harming others—they could express those "natural" feelings of fraternity and mutual assistance innate to the human species.

The Anarchists' distrust of the State as an instrument of oppression, as the tool by which the privileged and powerful maintained themselves, is generally associated with nineteenth-century "classical" liberalism, with John Stuart Mill and, in this country, with the Jeffersonians. But by the end of the nineteenth century and increasingly in the twentieth, liberals began to regard the State as an ally rather than an enemy; only the national government, it was felt, had the power to accomplish regulation and reform, to prevent small groups of self-interested men from exploiting their fellows.

Today the pendulum has begun to swing back again. In the liberal—but more especially in the radical—camp, the federal government has lost some of its appeal; veneration is giving way to distrust; from an instrument of liberation, the central government is once more being viewed as a bulwark of conservatism. This shift is the result of accumulated disappointments. The regulatory agencies set up to supervise the monopolists have been discovered to be operating in the interests of the monopolists; farm-subsidy programs have been exposed as benefiting the richer operators while dispossessing tenant farmers and sharecroppers; the urban renewal program seems to be aggravating rather than alleviating the housing problems of low-income groups; civil rights legislation has added to the sheaf of paper promises without making any notable dent in existing inequities; the poverty program begins to look like one more example of the fallacy of treating symptoms as if they were causes; and the traditional hostility between big government and big business has given way to a cozy partnership whereby the two enterprises have become almost indistinguishable in their interests.

The Anarchists believed that man was a social creature—that is, that he needed the affection and assistance of his fellows—and most Anarchist versions of the good life (Max Stirner would be the major exception) involved the idea of community. The Anarchists insisted, moreover, that it was not their vision of the future, but rather society as presently constructed, which represented chaos; with privilege the lot of the few and misery the lot of the many, society was currently the essence of *dis*order. The Anarchists envisioned a system that would substitute mutual aid for mutual exploitation, voluntarism for force, individual decision-making for centralized dictation.

All of these emphases find echo today in SNCC and CORE. The echoes are not perfect: "Black Power" is above all a call to organization, and its acceptance of politics (and therefore of "governing") would offend a true Anarchist—as would such collectivist terms as "black psyche" or "black personality." Nonetheless, the affinities of SNCC and CORE with the Anarchist position are substantial.

There is, first of all, the same belief in the possibilities of "community" and the same insistence that community be the product of voluntary association. This in turn reflects a second and still more basic affinity: the distrust of centralized authority. SNCC and CORE's energies, and also those of other New Left groups like SDS, are increasingly channeled into local, community organizing. On this level, it is felt, "participatory" democracy, as opposed to the "authoritarianism" of representative democracy, becomes possible. And in the Black Panther party, where the poor and disinherited do take a direct role in decision-making, theory has become reality (as it has, on the economic side, in the Mississippi-based "Poor People's Corporation," which to date has formed some fifteen cooperatives).[8]

Then, too, SNCC and CORE, like the Anarchists, talk increasingly of the supreme importance of the individual. They do so, paradoxically, in a rhetoric strongly reminiscent of that long associated with the Right. It could be Herbert Hoover (or Booker T. Washington), but in fact it is Rap Brown who now reiterates the Negro's need to stand on his own two feet, to make his own decisions, to develop self-reliance and a sense of self-worth.[9] The two ends of the political spectrum in this country have started to converge—at least in terms of vocabulary, if not in terms of interests or goals. But the Anarchist tradition is not of equal relevance to the New Left and to the traditional Right, except that it feeds their shared distrust—in one case burgeoning, in the other diminishing—of centralized power. The Right has never been so much anti-authority, as simply anti-one kind of authority—that associated with the federal government. To the Right, authority has been bad when it emanates from Washington, but good when associated with the Church, the Law, the schoolroom, the home, the Anglo-Saxon way. Far from being hostile to established opinion, the Right galvanizes its legions in its defense.

A final, more intangible affinity between Anarchism and the entire New Left, including the advocates of Black Power, is in the area of personal style. Both hold up similar values for highest praise and emulation: simplicity, spontaneity, "naturalness" and "primitivism." Both reject modes of dress, music, personal relations, even of intoxication, which might be associated with the dominant middle-class culture. Both, finally, tend to link the basic virtues with "the people," and especially with the poor, the downtrodden, the alienated. It is this *lumpenproletariat*—long kept outside the "system" and thus uncorrupted by its values—who are looked to as a repository of virtue, an example of a better way. The New Left, even while demanding that the lot of the underclasses be improved, implicitly venerates that lot; the desire to cure poverty cohabits with the wish to emulate it.

The Anarchist movement in the United States never made much headway. A few individuals—Benjamin Tucker, Adin Ballou, Lysander Spooner, Stephen Pearl Andrews, Emma Goldman, Josiah Warren— are still faintly remembered, but more for the style of their lives than for any impact on their society.[10] It is not difficult to see what prevented them from attracting a large following. Their very distaste for organization and power precluded the traditional modes for exerting influence. More important, their philosophy ran directly counter to the national hierarchy of values, a system of beliefs, conscious and otherwise, which has always impeded the drive for rapid change in this country. And it is a system which constitutes a roadblock at least as formidable today as at any previous point in our history.

This value structure stresses, first of all, the prime virtue of "accumulation," chiefly of goods, but also of power and prestige. Any group—be it Anarchists or New Leftists—which challenges the soundness of that goal, which suggests that it interferes with the more important pursuits of self-realization and human fellowship, presents so basic a threat to our national and individual identities as to invite almost automatic rejection.

A second obstacle that our value structure places in the path of radical change is its insistence on the benevolence of history. To the average American, human history is the story of automatic progress. Every day in every way we have gotten better and better. *Ergo,* there is no need for a frontal assault on our ills; time alone will be sufficient to cure them. Thus it is that many whites today consider the "Negro Problem" solved by the recent passage of civil rights legislation. They choose to ignore the fact that the daily lives of most Negroes have changed but slightly—or, as in the case of unemployment, for the worse. They ignore, too, the group of hard-core problems that have only recently emerged: maldistribution of income, urban slums, disparities in education and training, the breakdown of family structure in the ghetto, technological unemployment—problems that show no signs of yielding to time, but that will require concentrated energy and resources for solution.

Without a massive assault on these basic ills, ours will continue to be a society where the gap between rich and poor widens, where the major rewards go to the few (who are not to be confused with the best). Yet it seems highly unlikely, as of 1968, that the public pressure needed for such an assault will be forthcoming. Most Americans still prefer to believe that ours is either already the best of all possible worlds or will shortly, and without any special effort, become such. It is this deep-seated smugness, this intractable optimism, which must be reckoned with—which, indeed, will almost certainly destroy any call for substantive change.

A further obstacle facing the New Left today, Black Power advocates and otherwise, is that its Anarchist style and mood run directly counter to prevailing tendencies in our national life, especially those of conformity and centralization. The conformity has been commented on too often to bear repetition, except to point out that the young radicals' unorthodox mores (sexual, social, cultural) are in themselves enough to produce uneasiness and anger in the average American. In insisting on the right of the individual to please himself and to rely on his own judgment (whether in dress, speech, music, sex or stimulants), SNCC and SDS may be solidly within the American tradition—indeed may be its mainstream—but this tradition is now more central to our rhetoric than to our behavior.

The Anarchist focus in SNCC and SDS on decentralization, on participatory democracy and on community organizing likewise runs counter to dominant national trends. Consolidation, not dispersion, is currently king. There are some signs that a counterdevelopment has begun—such as the pending decentralization of the New York City school system—but as yet the overwhelming pattern continues to be consolidation. Both big government and big business are getting bigger and, more ominous still, are coming into ever closer partnership. As Richard J. Barber has recently documented, the federal government is not only failing to block the growth of huge "conglomerate" firms by antitrust action, but it is contributing to that growth through procurement contracts and the exchange of personnel.[11] The traditional hostility between business and government has rapidly drawn to a close. Washington is no longer interested in restraining the giant corporations, and the corporations have lost much of their fear of federal intentions. The two, in happy tandem, are moving the country still further along the road to oligopoly, militarism, economic imperialism and greater privileges for the already privileged. The trend is so pronounced, and there is so little effective opposition to it, that it begins to take on an irrevocable, even irreversible, quality.

In the face of these monoliths of national power, Black Power in Lowndes County is minuscule by comparison. Yet while the formation of the Black Panther party in Lowndes brought out paroxysms of fear in the nation at large, the announcement that General Motors's 1965 sales totaled $21 billion—exceeding the gross national product of all but nine countries in the world—produced barely a tremor of apprehension. The unspoken assumption can only be something like this: it is less dangerous for a few whites to control the whole nation than for a local majority of Negroes to control their own community. The Kafkaesque nature of life in America continues to grow.

B lack Power is both a product of our society and a repudiation of it. Confronted with the continuing indifference of the majority of whites to the Negro's plight, SNCC and CORE have lost faith in conscience and time, and have shifted to a position which the white majority finds infuriating. The nation as a whole—as in the case of the Abolitionists over a hundred years ago—has created the climate in which earlier tactics no longer seem relevant, in which new directions become mandatory if frustration is to be met and hope maintained. And if the new turn proves a wrong one, if Black Power forecloses rather than animates further debate on the Negro's condition, if it destroys previous alliances without opening up promising new options, it is the nation as a whole that must bear the responsibility. There seems little likelihood that the American majority will admit to that responsibility. Let us at least hope it will not fail to recognize the rage that Black Power represents, to hear the message at the movement's core:

> *Sweethearts, the script has changed . . .*
> *And with it the stage directions which advise*
> *Lowered voices, genteel asides,*
> *And the white hand slowly turning the dark page.*[12]

—Partisan Review, *Winter 1968*

POSTSCRIPT 1969

In its Spring 1968 issue, Partisan Review *asked a dozen people to comment on some of the issues this essay had raised.*

Of the four black commentators (Ivanhoe Donaldson, Charles V. Hamilton, William Melvin Kelley and Dr. Nathan Wright, Jr.,) all but Dr. Wright expressed resentment at the idea of a white person writing on the Black Power movement. Only Charles V. Hamilton offered a detailed critique of my views. He began by objecting to self-styled "ghetto-watchers" who spend their time "nit-picking with Black Power" instead of devoting their energies to combating racism within the white community—a point well taken only if one believes that white radicals must allocate their energies in an either/or way, which I do not. I am more ready to accept Hamilton's other main objections to my essay: that I do not give sufficient weight to Black Power's emphasis on "the culture and heritage of black Americans"; and that I focus too much on the positions taken by a few highly visible black leaders and seem ignorant of less publicized and perhaps more constructive developments which also characterize the Black Power movement—like the burgeoning organizations of black teachers devoted to developing "relevance" in the curricula of ghetto schools, and the recent meeting of black, middle-class professionals in Chicago to "map ways they can bring their skills to bear on the development of the black community."

Among the white commentators in *Partisan Review*'s symposium, Norman Mailer pressed for recognition of the fact that blacks "have become on the average physically superior" to whites, a view which Irving Howe and Dr. H. Jack Geiger took issue with in *PR*'s succeeding two numbers. They pointed out that if one uses the usual criteria of proneness to disease, infant mortality or life expectancy (which may not have been those Mailer had in mind), the statistics prove the opposite of Mailer's contention.

Another commentator, Tom Kahn, raised an important issue about "coalition politics." Though thinking I was "rightly critical of the inadequacies of recent liberal legislation," Kahn felt my pessimism about "radicalism's immediate prospects" left us "stranded"; needlessly, he argued, for the organized labor movement, in his view, was more available for a new coalition on the left than I had suggested—certainly as available as the New Class technocrats or unskilled, un-unionized laborers whom I had mentioned as possible allies. Kahn may be right that I overstated the availability of the latter two groups, but if so, that would leave me more, not less, pessimistic about the prospects for coalition politics. On the basis of the limited evidence I've seen, I don't think it means much (in terms of a *radical* coalition) to say, as Kahn does, that organized labor has "the most advanced economic policies of any major institution in American life." By "advanced," Kahn means a concern with "full employment, higher wages, expanded housing construction and increased federal spending for social purposes." These seem to me "advanced" goals only by New Deal definitions— though Kahn is surely right that no major institution in America has moved beyond them. In any case, organized labor seems interested in advancing those goals chiefly for its own limited membership.

II

Radicalism on Campus

"The Dissenting Academy"

The colleges of our country, in contrast to those of most of the world, have a long tradition of quiescence. They have been islands of passivity and irrelevance rather than centers of ferment and innovation. The faculties have tended their scholarly gardens of rare herbs and leafless plants. The students, like dutiful inmates, have put in their time.

In the past few years this has begun to change, most, though not all of the change, for the better. A growing minority of students is no longer willing to settle for mechanical exercises in which it has little interest and less control. Younger faculty have begun questioning both the traditional forms of education—lectures, grades, requirements, exams—and the traditional emphasis on morally neutral research and on the withdrawal of the scholar from active participation in public life. Meanwhile, senior faculty have begun to find their expertise in wide demand by government and industry, and have gained proportionately in status and income.

It is this last development which gives grounds more for worry than for congratulation: with the jet schedules of some faculty members, especially in the physical and natural sciences, beginning to rival those of Princess Pignatelli's set, there is growing concern that teaching is being shortchanged and that the academic's "search for truth" has become compromised by his association with the centers of economic and political power.

Theodore Roszak, editor of *The Dissenting Academy*, has summed up the indictment of university practices as "mindless collaboration on the one hand and irrelevant research on the other." The first charge, that of indiscriminate collaboration by the academy with the American military-industrial establishment, is well documented. At the University of Pennsylvania, biologists have worked—under secret contract—on chemical-biological weaponry. The Army's counter-insurgency Project Agile in Thailand enlisted a group of anthropologists, and the notorious Project Camelot, designed by our government to subvert the revolutionary aspirations of Latin America's underclasses, attracted a flock of social scientists. The professed ideal of the academic community is the relentless pursuit of truth, a pursuit that cares nothing for established piety or organized privilege. But our academics, more often than not, have been co-opted as defenders of the status quo, delighted to be on the Great Stage even if it means carrying a spear in some modern dress *Götterdämmerung*.

Sordid as this state of affairs is, no simple cure is available. Are all ties between government and the academy offensive, and should all be ended? If so, where will needed research funds come from? From the business community? From the foundations? From trustees? Are these sources likely to be any less pernicious in their influence? Besides, if we close the lines of communication between the academic community and the government, will we have any right to complain if our government then suffers from lack of information and expertise? If we do want the campuses to contribute personnel and ideas to Washington, what boundaries should we set, and who should set them?

The second half of Roszak's indictment is no less valid than the first—and no less troublesome. The social sciences and humanities are rife with what he calls "mindless specialization and irrelevant pedantry." The anthropological journals, for example, are full of articles on the Tzental words for "firewood," but, as Kathleen Gough has pointed out, they almost never contain speculation on such crucial matters as the dynamics of colonialism or the genesis of guerrilla movements.

The economists are doing little better; most of them assume rather than test the validity of doctrines central to the economic tradition of the West—free markets, efficiency, growth—and concentrate their energies instead on improving quantitative methods of measurement and on tinkering with peripheral matters like the manipulation of interest rates. All the disciplines, to quote Robert Engler, are characterized by a deplorable combination of "small-scale research backed by large-scale grants."

Since a value-free social science is impossible anyway, its practitioners should be ashamed rather than proud of their moral detachment, for the pride is based on a misunderstanding of both the limitations and responsibilities of their profession. Pseudo-scientific, pseudo-objective pretensions must be replaced by an ideal dating back at least as far as the Enlightenment: How can we as intellectuals "help men to live more fully and creatively and to expand their dignity, self-direction, and freedom"?

The problem comes when we get down to specifics, for although the indictment against today's academy is well-substantiated and well-deserved in general outline, it has at its core, some uncertain definitions. Roszak, for example, calls for an end to "fastidious but morally undirected research" and charges the scholar "to intervene in society for the defense of civilized values," to "clarify reality" so that his fellow citizens "can reason toward the solution of their problems." But what does it mean to "clarify reality," and exactly what kind of research should we discard as "fastidious but morally undirected"? Roszak himself explicitly rejects the notion that we should abandon all scholarly research that does not relate immediately to social policy; such a call, he says, would be "little more than philistine."

Yet another scholar has come very close to sounding that call when he recently disparaged the announcement of a new Henry James Journal as an example of the "more exquisite levels of absurdity" scholars continue to attain. But I see nothing inherently absurd in such a journal, though its topic is of interest to only a few and though its relevance to social problems is probably nil. The fact is it will give pleasure to those few, and to banish it haughtily from our Brave New World is to inaugurate a brand of Puritanism different in content perhaps from that of Anthony Comstock, but no less pernicious.

In short, it is not at all clear what kinds of knowledge a scholar would be pursuing, and in what ways he would pursue it, if he were indeed functioning for both his own and his society's best interests.

What is beyond dispute is that most academics are careerists: they will accept any offer or, alternatively, slight any responsibility (to their students, their profession, their society) in the name of augmenting their own prestige. In the meantime urgent social problems go unresolved, basic questions of international responsibility go unasked, and the older view of an intellectual community devoted to keeping alive the tension between what man is and what he might and ought to be, goes untended.

We would probably all agree (all but the Ayn Rands, that is) that nothing in man's genetic make-up forces him to behave in so self-enclosed a manner. The academy's failures are due to culture, not nature. One can hardly grow up in the American ethos of each-against-all individualism, in an atmosphere which emphasizes the virtue of accumulation (goods, power, prestige), and at the same time develop concern for one's neighbors, profession or community. The corruptions of the academy are, writ small, the corruptions of our society. A change in society's values must therefore precede (or at least parallel) any change in those of academia.

That a parallel re-evaluation *has* begun can be seen in the growing discontent of both students and younger faculty with traditional practices. They are finding a common voice, a voice that calls for value-oriented research, for teaching that concentrates on fundamental issues rather than marketable skills, for an interaction with the powers-that-be based on a critical rather than worshipful stance. This new, more humane spirit needs what nourishment it can get. For in our colleges, as in so many areas of our national life, an internal conflict is being waged: an increase in knowledge, compassion and social consciousness is being matched, and is currently dwarfed by the growth of pedantry, neutralism and careerism.

Academia, in other words, like so much else in our country, is in both better and worse shape than it was a generation ago. The worst tendencies at present have the upper hand. But it is good to know that the others exist and have entered the fray.

—The New York Times Book Review,
March 17, 1968

On Misunderstanding Student Rebels

The young, it is becoming clear, are regarded with considerable condescension in our country. Resentment against them cannot be explained simply as a reaction to the style of a particular generation, for in recent years the young have been attacked on such divergent grounds that the grounds themselves take on the appearance of pretext. In the 1950s we denounced students for their inertia, their indifference to public questions, their absorption in the rituals of fraternities and football, their dutiful pursuit of "achievement." In the 1960s we condemn them for the opposite qualities: for their passion, their absorption in public questions, their disgust with the trivia of college parties and athletics, their refusal to settle for mechanical processes of education.

Since the past two college generations have been denounced with equal vehemence for opposite inclinations, it seems plausible to conclude that it is not those inclinations but the very fact of their youth that makes them the target for so much abuse. This conclusion may seem to contradict the fact that American society, above all others, is known for its adoration of the young. But that itself, paradoxically, is one cause of adult hostility: our youth-obsessed elders resent the eighteen-year-old's easy possession of the good looks and high spirits they so desperately simulate.

Adult anger at the physical superiority of the young has usually been contained by the comforting assumption that eighteen-year-olds are at least the moral, intellectual, and emotional inferiors of their elders. College students have traditionally been viewed as apprentices, almost as supplicants. And until recently they accepted their role as dutiful petitioners for entry into the world of adult insight and skill.

As no one needs reminding, they no longer accept that role, though most of their elders continue the struggle to confine them to it. Today's eighteen- to twenty-year-old considers himself an adult, by which he does not mean (as so many forty-year-olds unconsciously do) that he has ceased growing, but that he has grown up enough to make his own decisions. In every sense, even statistically, his case is a strong one.

The weight of recent physiological and psychological evidence establishes the student claim that today's eighteen-year-olds mature more rapidly than those of earlier generations. Physically, they are taller and heavier than their counterparts at the turn of the century. Boys reach puberty around age fourteen, and girls begin to menstruate at the average age of twelve years, nine months (in both cases almost two years earlier than in 1900).

Moreover, there is much evidence that this earlier physical maturity is matched by emotional and intellectual precocity. According to Dr. C. Keith Conners, director of the Child Development Laboratory at Massachusetts General Hospital, both emotional and intellectual growth are today largely completed by age eighteen. By this Dr. Conners means that the difficult trials of adolescence are over, the basic patterns of personality have become stabilized, and the ability to reason abstractly—to form hypotheses and make deductions—has been established. This does not mean, of course, that no further maturation is possible after age eighteen. Additional information and experience do (or at least should) provide material for continuing re-assessments. But that, of course, is (or should be) true of all of us.

In terms of knowledge already possessed, moreover, the graduating high school senior of today, thanks both to the media and to the stepped-up pace of academic work, is well informed on any number of topics—the new math, say, or the physical properties of the atom—of which his elders are ignorant. And as for experience, I am not at all sure that the eighteen-year-old who has had his senses activated by early sexual relations, strobe lights, pot, soul, and rock, and his political instincts honed by Vietnam, the draft, and the civil rights movement, should not be considered more vitally alive, more instinctually sound, than the typical forty-year-old who has spent his additional twenty years glued to the tube, the routinized job, the baseball and stock statistics.

It is bad enough that we have refused to extend to students the rights and responsibilities that their maturity warrants. What is perhaps worse is that many of those who hold positions of power or prestige in our universities have learned so little from the upheavals which that refusal has produced. A recent spate of books and articles by such men demonstrates anew their uneducability; they make it clear, by their continuing patronization and belittlement, that students still have an uphill fight in their struggle to be taken seriously.

One case in point is George F. Kennan. In an article, "Rebels Without a Program" in *The New York Times Magazine* (January 21, 1968), he refers to the "massive certainties" of the student left on campus, to their "screaming tantrums," their consuming interest in "violence for violence's sake," etc. I've often argued with members of Students for a Democratic Society (SDS) over particular points or attitudes, and have found them far more knowledgeable and sophisticated than the average undergraduate. Because they believe there can and should be less suffering in the world hardly makes them naive utopians.

True, they have no "blueprints" for creating a better world. If they had, the charge of naivete *would* apply. But if Kennan and other patronizing members of the older generation will actually *read* the position papers frequently issued by SDS, they would find any number of proposals for "constitutional amendment or political reform" as well as that very wealth of "reasoned argument and discussion" which Kennan claims is absent.

Kennan further lectures student activists on their "inability to see and enjoy the element of absurdity in human behavior" (adding, gratuitously, that he suspects their love lives, no less than their politics, are "tense, anxious, defiant and joyless"), on their "social science" rhetoric and on their indifference to "nature as a possible compensation or sustaining factor in the face of social or political frustration." Kennan fails, however, to make clear how the merit of the issues the students raise in any way depends on the "inadequate" manner in which they might raise them. I, for one, cannot see how the Vietnam War or the plight of those who live in our ghettos might become more attractive or tolerable if viewed with an awareness of "the element of absurdity in human behavior" or described in a rhetoric free of social science jargon or escaped from by periodic trips to the wilderness.

Kennan insists that the students' obliviousness to nature, and so forth, is symptomatic of their "lack of interest in the creation of any real style and distinction of personal life generally," by which he means, as he goes on to specify, their lack of "manners," their untidiness, their "personal hygiene," their refusal to cultivate the "amenities." It is debatable whether this description is accurate or significant as applied to the nonpolitical, drug-oriented "hippies," but it is certainly not a valid description of campus activists, the ostensible subjects of Kennan's critique.

The main point, of course, is not that the new generation lacks "any real style," but that Kennan is unable to perceive much of its distinctiveness. Kennan is a good eighteenth-century *philosophe,* distrustful of "enthusiasm" and preoccupied with the rationalist credo of restraint and temperance in all things. Since "passion" is suspect, it follows (albeit unconsciously) that no injustice warrants fervent protest. What the new generation believes, and Kennan apparently does not, is that "moderation" can itself become a form of paralysis, even of immorality—like the moderate protest of Pope Pius XII against the extermination of the Jews.

If Kennan's condescension toward the different lifestyle of the young was peculiar to him, it could be more readily ignored. But in fact his attitude is the characteristic response of the older generation to the young. Any number of other examples are possible, but I will mention only two of the more prominent: Sidney Hook and Jacques Barzun.

Hook has published two statements on recent student protests at Columbia: a long article, "The Prospects of Academe," in *Encounter* for August, 1968, and a brief note in the *Psychiatry and Social Science Review* for July 1968. It is difficult to choose between them in deciding the high point to date for gray-bearded arrogance. In the shorter piece Hook flatly states that the Columbia rebels "had no grievances" and that they were interested solely in "violence, obscenity and hysterical insult." In the longer article Hook characterizes the protesters as "callow and immature adolescents" whose dominant mood, like that of all adolescents, is "irrationalism." While denouncing students for their passion, this self-appointed defender of "reason" and of the university as the "citadel of reason," himself indulges in a rhetoric so inflamed ("Fanatics don't lack sincerity . . . They drip with sincerity—and when they have power, with blood—other people's blood") that by comparison the most apocalyptic students seem models of sobriety. Hook even declares that "there are some things one should not be moderate about," which is exactly what the student activists (and Barry Goldwater) have said. The students, of course, mean it is acceptable to be passionately against war and racism. Hook (and Goldwater) mean it is acceptable to be passionately against those who passionately protest war and racism.

Hook's themes—that college students are adolescents, that the best proof of their childishness is that they are "emotional" and that emotion (in others) is bad—are to be found in their most explicit form in Jacques Barzun's recent book, *The American University*. In its preface, Barzun, who was dean of faculties and provost at Columbia from 1958 to 1967, explains that the manuscript was in the hands of the publisher six weeks before the student outbreak on April 23, 1968. But lest we be tempted on that account to excuse some of the positions he adopts in his book, Barzun further adds that despite the outbreak he has "found no reason to change or add to the substance of what I had written months earlier." Among the views he has found no need to modify is his statement that Grayson Kirk, President of Columbia, has always shown himself "ready and eager for progressive changes." Barzun does not pause to define "progressive," but one can't help thinking he uses the word in its original sense to describe the reforms that preceded World War I. Certainly nothing in his (or Kirk's) attitude toward students would place him beyond the year 1915.

Barzun begins his discussion of the college population by adopting the Olympian view: they are, after all, young men, and that means "turbulence is to be expected, heightened nowadays by the presence of girls . . ." In other words, a certain amount of anger is inherent to being young, and anger must find its outlet. The nature of the outlet is almost a matter of indifference: if "the people of the town" do not provide a convenient target, well then, it might just as well be politics.

Still in the Olympian vein, Barzun further suggests—it is as close as he ever comes to implicating society—that "perhaps our lack of proper ceremonies for initiation into the tribe leaves the young to devise their own proof of manhood." Barzun loves dismissing the young with this kind of casual irony. Its elegant offhandedness is a useful device for keeping a proper distance between the generations. It is also useful—though of this Barzun seems unaware—for expressing the savagery which he likes to think is confined to the student population. Barzun claims that the undergraduates would themselves welcome rites of initiation, for what they really want, he insists, is more, not less, discipline. When they speak of the impersonality of the university, they mean, it seems, "the looseness of its grip upon them." Kennan makes the same point in almost the same words: students are currently objecting to parietal rules, he asserts, because "the rules have relaxed too much rather than that they have been relaxed too little." According to both men, students are starved for structure. In Barzun's phrasing, they are looking for "order," for "intellectual habits"; they sense that this is the balance they need, for like all youngsters they are in a "fever and frenzy," "their mind is monopolized by their inner life."

To meet this "rage for order," Barzun and Kennan posit an antiseptic university, a place of "respite and meditation" whose "proper work," in Barzun's phrase, is "in the catacombs under the strife-torn crossroads." He fills this subterranean cemetery with properly lifeless figures; they are "somewhat hushed," they give pause, as at Chartres, to the "spiritual grandeur of their surroundings." Yet just as one begins to feel, in the rush of Christian imagery, that Barzun has spent so many years surrounded by campus Gothic as to have lost all sense of distinction between the university and the church, he stoutly declares that *his* catacombs will not be peopled by early Christians. He dislikes that breed; it was marked by the same distasteful qualities he associates with today's young radicals: "indifference to clothes and cleanliness, a distrust and neglect of reasoning . . . a freedom in sexuality, which is really a lowering of its intensity and value . . . and—most symptomatic—a free field given to the growth of hair."

Barzun also shares with Kennan and Hook the proposition that "emotion" has no place on campus and that since student rebels tend to be emotional, it can be safely assumed they are also unreliable. All three men equate (and thereby confuse) "emotion" with "irrationality," and all employ a vocabulary of neat opposites—"reason" versus "emotion"—that separates what our experience combines. They see education as "the cultivation and tempering of the mind" but fail to see that "enthusiasm" is one path by which tempering proceeds.

Barzun is also huffy at the "nonsense" currently being peddled about teaching, especially the idea that teacher and student should explore together, each learning from the other. This view, he asserts, has done "immense harm to both parties. The teacher has relaxed his efforts while the student has unleashed his conceit." And of what does that "conceit" consist? Barzun is quick to tell us: the conviction that they (the students) have something to contribute. "Only rarely," he declares, with a hauteur appropriate to the century from which most of his ideas spring, does a teacher "hear from a student a fact he does not know or a thought that is original and true . . . to make believe that their knowledge and his are equal is an abdication and a lie."

And so we are back, as always in Barzun's schema, to the confinement of his starting assumption: students are children and, usually, fools. His contempt for undergraduates is pervasive. They are, very simply, not to be trusted; "student reliability is at a low ebb," he warns, and especially among radical students, who have but one purpose: to destroy. The evidence Barzun marshals to justify his contempt is so exasperatingly trivial (as well as suspect in its accuracy) that it demeans its compiler far more than the students it purports to describe. The undergraduates, he asserts, cheat a lot on exams and papers; they obtain pocket money by stealing books from the college bookstore; they keep library books out as long as they like and let fines go unpaid; they deny their roommates "the slightest considerateness"; students of both sexes live "pig-style" in their dormitories; their conversations "usually cannot follow a logical pattern," and so on.

The first thing to be said about these accusations is that Barzun has seized upon the occasional practices of a few undergraduates in order to damn a whole generation. The second is that even if these qualities did characterize a whole generation, they hardly seem heinous when compared with the sins of the fathers—when compared, that is, with racism at home and imperialism abroad.

The distressing consequence of this obsession with the peccadillos of the young is an avoidance of those genuinely important problems to which the young are calling attention. Mandarins like Barzun, Kennan and Hook are so preoccupied with manners that they forget matter. They blind themselves (and others) to the serious questions this new generation has raised—questions about the nature of education, the proper functions of a university, the very quality of American life.

The problems confronting the university involve difficult and interconnected questions. For example, the relationship of the university to the surrounding community hinges on a definition of what kind of an institution the university is. Is it best seen as a corporation? A family? A public agency? A combination of these? An entity *sui generis*? Linked to these questions are others: What are the sanctions and restraints of power within the university structure? Who legitimately holds and/or actually exercises that power? What, ideally, should be the roles played by state and federal governments, trustees, administrators, faculty and students? Are the latter children to be watched over and disciplined, or consumers whose needs must be heeded, or constituents whose voices must be heard? The radical young are raising these complex questions for the first time in at least a generation.

Much as I admire these campus activists, I want to make clear that I think some tendencies in some few of them are to be guarded against: using civil disobedience as a first rather than as a last resort (a precipitousness shared by most administrators when calling the police); interfering with the free speech of others; employing the rhetoric and sometimes the fact of violence; talking glibly of the advantages to be gained from right-wing repression; arguing that the university is the incarnation of evil—the *chief* enemy—rather than an antique institution whose renovation might well provide a major power base in the struggle for a new society. Though real, these tendencies are characteristic of only a small number of student activists and should not be used, as so many have used them, to slander the entire movement.

A dozen or so studies have been made of student activists at a variety of universities, and the findings have been conveniently summarized in a recent essay by Stanford's Nevitt Sanford. The group portrait that emerges (confirmed by Kenneth Keniston's book, *Young Radicals*) is strikingly different from the slanderous one being peddled by Messrs. Kennan, Barzun and Hook.

The activists, first of all, constitute only a small minority, though a growing one, of all college students: at Berkeley, for example, their number is put at about 15 percent. Second, there are important differences, in almost all measurable categories, between activists on the campus and other students. The activists score consistently higher on a wide variety of personality tests, including theoretical skills, aesthetic sensitivity, degree of psychological autonomy, and social maturity. They are also the better students, with significantly higher grade-point averages than the nonactivists.

One set of grievances among activists relates to the college classroom itself. As David Riesman has written, "Colleges on the whole have been very backward as compared with industry or the Army in their curiosity about their own inner processes." Until recently colleges have accepted lectures, grading and examinations as part of the Natural Order of Things and have seen no reason to question the long-standing assumptions that Teacher is the possessor and arbiter of Truth, that his function is to transmit knowledge (narrowly defined as accumulated information) to students and that their function is to memorize it.

Any challenge to this conventional wisdom is still viewed with scorn by the vast majority of faculty and administrators—and of the student population as well. Barzun, for example, gives short shrift to any protest against grades and tests: "no person by way of being educated," he announces, "resents examinations; they are so instructive." Should a student activist or one of his allies among the younger faculty reply that exams and grades chiefly instruct students in how to please their professors, in how to compete with one another, in how to settle for orthodox questions and answers and in how to suppress their own originality, Barzun's answer would be—hogwash.

By way of proof, Barzun triumphantly recounts a recent episode in a large Midwestern university: when students in a philosophy of education class of three hundred complained that they had little say in their own education, the professor asked how many did in fact want to take responsibility for their work, and only ten hands went up. The moral, as Barzun draws it, is that students calling for self-regulation merely "ape the advertiser's soapy mind." But that is not the moral at all. Our educational system has been so successful in turning out automatons that the vast majority of its products are terrified at the thought of taking over responsibility for their own lives. The fact that only ten hands went up is itself an indictment of our educational practices. Instead of proving that "all is well," it proves that we are in desperate trouble—that maybe only 3.3 percent of our *citizens* are interested in making their own decisions.

And what is the answer of men like Barzun to the growing resentment of the lecture system? That the protesters do not understand the true nature of their dissatisfaction. The real trouble, Barzun declares, is that the university has "let lapse the *formality* of lecturing—its form—which was its principal merit." What is wanted by way of change, in other words, is not to dismantle the lecture system but to return it to its pristine shape, to reintroduce "formal presentation" and even "staginess and rhetorical effects," since these impart something Barzun labels "didactic energy." Given this gross misreading of student discontent, it might be well to remember in speaking hereafter of the "generation gap" that incomprehension is not confined to one side.

Discontent with teaching practices in our universities embraces more than the lecture system. Even where small seminars or discussion groups prevail (an expensive device few universities can afford), the needs of the students are not given anything like equal consideration with the needs of teachers. As two students in the *Yale Daily News* recently put it, the present system fails to help undergraduates appropriate facts and skills "in the interest of making lives, not just livings." In assuming that the university's main, almost exclusive, function is to produce and transmit information, we have given top priority to promoting those faculty members most likely to assist in the manufacture of knowledge. This means, of course, that the university has come to be staffed chiefly by those concerned with research and writing rather than those concerned with educating the young—that is, with helping them to discover what their interests and talents are. As Alfred North Whitehead said long ago, "So far as the mere imparting of information is concerned, no university has had any justification for existence since the popularisation of printing in the fifteenth century." Yet most professors regard the imparting of information as the sum and substance of their responsibility. They make little or no effort to show, either in their subject or in their person, how knowledge can influence conduct and inform action (which, as the classicist William Arrowsmith has pointed out, is not really surprising, since they are themselves products of the same noneducation).

Most professors are interested only in students who are themselves potential scholars; they are concerned with training future colleagues, not with helping the individual young person grow in his own directions. The lack of interest taken by most professors in most students and their refusal to reveal or engage more than a small share of their own selves, have made many of the best students cynical about knowledge and about those who purvey it. They hoped to find in their professors models on whom they might pattern their lives; instead they find narrow specialists busy with careers, with government contracts, with the augmentation of status and income. They hoped to find a curriculum that would help them to uncover and pursue their interests; instead they find one primarily tailored to the needs of the faculty specialists. They hoped to discover a mode of living that would help them to integrate their intellectual curiosity with the demands of their senses and emotions; instead they find, in Erich Fromm's words, an education "more and more cerebral . . . [where] people are taught concepts, but are not taught or confronted with the experience which corresponds to these concepts." They hoped to find some acknowledgment of their worth and some encouragement toward its further development; instead they find disinterest, patronization, overt dislike. They find, in short, what Nietzsche called "the advancement of learning at the expense of man."

With considerable justice, therefore, the students, particularly the more talented and sensitive ones, reject the university and its faculty as self-serving, self-justifying, self-enclosed. They learn to seek their education—the expanding of insight and option—outside the formal academic curriculum, to seek it in talk and games with friends, in films, clothes and cars, in "Sergeant Pepper's Lonely Hearts Club Band," in the lyrics of Bob Dylan, in the Doors, in pot and acid. And if some of these sources prove as phony or dangerous as the mechanical exercises of the campus, surely much of the responsibility lies with an academic community that has encouraged, almost forced its students to look for life enhancement where they can.

Most of the powers within the academic community will not even acknowledge the right of students to complain, let alone the cogency of those complaints. To the request that they be allowed a voice in planning the curriculum, Jacques Barzun replies that they have done nothing to "earn" a voice. To the lament that their studies seem outmoded or irrelevant, Barzun retorts that "relevance is a relationship in the mind and not a property of things"—which apparently means that although students might want to study urban affairs, if they will instead study cockle shells *in the right way,* they will discover all there is to know about life in the ghetto. And to the students' suggestion that they have some formal power in such matters as choosing faculty, passing on applications for admission, or helping to decide on the expansion of the physical plant, Barzun responds with hoots of derision and George Kennan with cold anger.

Both gentlemen remind the undergraduates that the university is not, and was never meant to be, a democracy. Barzun does believe that students should have the right of self-government in their own dormitories, for he acknowledges that they are "socially mature enough not to need domestic proctoring" (a curious and seemingly arbitrary departure from his usual premise that undergraduates are children). But Kennan will not go even this far in extending power to undergraduates. The university, by virtue of its position as owner of the dormitories, has no choice in Kennan's view but "to lay down certain minimal norms for the manner in which that use can proceed. This would be true," he insists, "even if the inhabitants were older people." But it is not true, for Kennan's (and my own) university, Princeton, owns a great deal of faculty housing, and in none of it are the tenants subjected to the demeaning regulations in regard to visitors, and so on, that are imposed upon the students.

With the exception of this disagreement over parietal rules, Barzun and Kennan are firmly united in their contention that the university cannot and should not be a democracy. Kennan, in this instance, is the more peremptory of the two. "Even if university trustees and administrators had a right to shift a portion of their responsibilities for university affairs to the student, which they do not," he writes, the student would in any case "be unqualified to receive it." The very suggestion, he warns, is part of the current tendency of American society "to press upon the child a premature external adulthood."

Barzun rests most of his case on the grounds of impracticality. The university cannot function as a democracy, he argues, because it is "extremely difficult to get from student bodies either a significant vote, or a council or committee that is representative . . . Add that student newspapers have long ceased to purvey anything approaching a public opinion, and it is clear that democracy is the last name a political scientist would apply to the government by outcry which has lately gained favor as an extracurricular activity."

The absurdity of this argument (and its loaded terminology) is best seen when placed in another context. Is it *easy* to get a "significant" or "representative" vote from the U.S. Congress? Do our commercial newspapers "purvey anything approaching a public opinion"? Shall we, on those accounts, abandon both the Congress and the public press as unworkable institutions? In trying to make a case against democracy in the university, in other words, Barzun has forced himself—I assume, inadvertently—into making a case against democracy in general. The "insurmountable obstacles" which he finds to democratic institutions on the campus are likewise in the path of democracy within the larger society. Indeed, they loom less large on campus; given the limited size of a university, the opinions of its constituency could be canvassed and tabulated far more easily than in society as a whole—that is, if the will to do so existed.

The other argument most often heard for denying students any say in university affairs is that they are "mere transients." True, but so are many professors, and so (to change the context) are members of the House of Representatives, who are elected for only two years. Besides, the *interests* of the student population do not shift as often as the population itself; Clark Kerr, in fact, detects signs that students are beginning to look upon themselves as a "class." But even if the interests of the undergraduates did continually change (and they probably should), life does, after all, belong to the living, or, in the case of the universities, a campus to its *present* constituents.

In addition to student grievances over what happens in the classroom and on the campus, there is another major source of disaffection:

the university's relationship to the world around it—its role as landlord of neighboring property and, on the broader canvas, its role as the recipient of government largesse and the provider of government expertise.

The upheavals of last spring at Columbia brought to focus the problem of the university's relationship to the society at large. One of two key issues during that upheaval was Columbia's pending construction of a gym in a public park used by Harlem residents. This issue by itself might be thought of minor importance (if, that is, one is not a resident of Harlem), but in fact it was the latest of a long series of encroachments by Columbia into the surrounding ghetto, an encroachment which usually involved evicting tenants with little concern for their wishes and welfare. Even now Columbia continues its encroachment. It is still secretly extending its real estate holdings in Harlem, and its "relocation office" is still forcing families out of buildings it wants to tear down.

Various groups, including students, faculty, Harlem residents, and the city, had appealed to the Columbia administration to review its policies on the gym construction—all to no avail. It is simply false to say, as Sidney Hook has, that "instead of seeking peacefully to resolve them [grievances] through existing channels of consultation and deliberation, the SDS seeks to inflame them." Not only did student groups, including SDS, attempt to get a peaceful hearing, but they had to make those attempts against formidable obstacles, for as Amitai Etzioni, professor of sociology at Columbia, has written, "due process, even in the loose sense of established channels for expression and participation, is not institutionalized at Columbia or at most other universities."

Even after the upheavals of last spring, the suggestion that precise channels be established for student participation continues to infuriate men like Barzun. One would think that anyone who so deplores student "immaturity" would at least recognize the standard argument of psychologists that immaturity is prolonged, even heightened, by an exclusion from responsibility. But apparently, despite his rhetoric in defense of "orderly process," Barzun prefers occasional barricades to regularized communication.

He even goes so far as to deny the reality of such issues as the gym construction. Universities must expand, he argues, and expansion inevitably brings conflict with the university's immediate neighbors. But shall the needs of several hundred citizens, he rhetorically asks, "prevail over the needs of . . . a national university?" Besides, the area around a university is usually a "deteriorating" one (as regards Columbia, Barzun has elsewhere referred to its surrounding neighborhood as "uninviting, abnormal, sinister, dangerous"), so it is a matter of simple "self-protection" for the university to take "steps." The "steps," as Barzun defines them, include "bringing in the police against crime and vice, hiring special patrols, and buying real estate as fast as funds and the market permit." This might look, Barzun concedes, like "waging war on the inhabitants," but what they forget is that with the university's expansion goes "increased employment and trade." The residents of Harlem apparently do not see it that way. In his long book, Barzun has almost no discussion of Columbia's relations with Harlem; when I came to a chapter entitled "Poverty in the Midst of Plenty," I thought I had finally come to a detailed review of those relations, but the chapter turned out instead to be about the financial problems of the university.

The second major issue in the Columbia dispute last spring concerned the university's affiliation with the Institute for Defense Analyses (IDA), an affiliation which in turn symbolized the university's dependence on government grants and involvement with government research. Barzun and others like to defend the university as a "center of research," and they contrast that "proper" function with the "misguided" one of the university becoming a center of "experience." But it is one thing to defend the university theoretically as a research center, and quite another to ask specifically "research in what and for what?"

The multiple and tangled relationships that have developed between our leading universities and large corporations and the federal government raise doubts about the proper boundaries of "research." This is especially true of what James Ridgeway calls the university's "war machinery"—its complicity in everything from antisubmarine-warfare research at Columbia to counterinsurgency planning at the University of Michigan. Today more than two-thirds of university research funds come from agencies of the federal government closely connected with defense matters, and about one quarter of the two hundred largest industrial corporations in the country have university officials on their boards of directors. It is certainly an open question these days whether the university is engaged in research in order to pursue "truth" or to acquire status, power and profit.

There are, I should stress, no simple formulas for establishing the "right" relationship universities should form with public corporations and governments. It is *because* there are no easy answers that the matter should be subject to open debate, with all interested parties bringing to bear their insights and perspectives. And by "all," I include students. They are rightly disturbed over the university's entanglement with war and with private profit, and they ask that their concern be registered and their views considered. They are entitled to nothing less, for until students began to protest such matters as IDA affiliation, the universities were doing business as usual, blind to the implications of their own actions. The same is true of the university's record regarding innovation in education and the procedures of campus government—I mean real innovation, not the substitution of blue tape for red. Before student activists began forcing a variety of campus and classroom issues into the open, the university's concern was minimal.

What we are witnessing, then, is not a sporadic and superficial, but a sustained and far-reaching attack on the university's smug and antique bearing. Student activists are not rebelling against their parents' values, as so many glibly say, but applying those values to the institutions with which they find themselves involved. They are not confused children, uncertain of their motives or aims, but determined adults who have found their education and their society seriously wanting.

I doubt if we have ever had a generation—or at least a minority of one—that has engaged itself so earnestly on the side of principled action, that valued people so dearly and possessions so little, that cared enough about our country to jeopardize their own careers within it, that wanted so desperately to lead open, honest lives and to have institutions and a society that would make such lives possible. It is a generation for which we should be immensely grateful and of which we should be immensely proud. Instead, we tell them that they are frenzied children; that we will try to be patient with them but that they should not push us too far; that they too in time will grow to understand the *real* ways of the world. To say that this condescension or blindness on the part of the older generation is a "pity" does not fit the dimensions of the case. It is a crime.

—The Atlantic Monthly, *November 1968*

An Experiment in Education

In the fall of 1966, at the beginning of a new term, I received permission from the Course of Study Committee at Princeton University to drop all grades from my undergraduate seminar "American Radicalism." It was agreed that the record of each student taking the course would show only an asterisk in the space where a grade would ordinarily appear, and that the attached explanation would read: "experimental course; no grades given." It was further agreed that the experiment would be for a single term only and that at its end I would present a formal report to the committee describing the results. This is my (excerpted) report:

I have been an educator for ten years, but I have really been interested in education only for the past year or so. Before that I was chiefly interested in my career. I still am, but having got tenure three years ago, it became possible for me (this was not conscious: I see it only in retrospect) to concern myself solely with how I evaluated the success of my teaching and not how the senior members of my department did. My experience with teaching bears out the central point that I will be trying to make about learning: that only when the necessity to please others is removed, can the main job of *self*-evaluation begin. Most young teachers, like most students, are afraid much of the time they are in class, and fear guarantees that energy will go into defensive strategies rather than creative explorations.

Various threads besides the "release" that tenure gave me helped to produce my new concern with teaching and learning. Perhaps the original germ had been planted in 1962, when some students suggested that I read A. S. Neill's *Summerhill*. I did, and was moved by Neill's candor and exhilarated by his demonstration that children flourish when they are allowed freedom. After discovering Neill, I read Paul Goodman, Edgar Z. Friedenberg and, most significantly and most recently, John Holt—in other words, the "romantics" of educational theory, as they have been dubbed by their critics. I had also, within the past two years, read a great deal about Anarchism, in line with a play I was then writing on Emma Goldman. I strongly identified with anarchism's antiauthoritarian basis; it was the closest I had come to feeling at home in a philosophical tradition.

Much of what I have outlined thus far became clear to me belatedly. At the time I petitioned the Course of Study Committee for permission to drop grades, I knew only that my dissatisfaction with traditional methods of teaching had accumulated to the point of irritability. I wanted something more and different from my classroom experience. I felt that most students did also. For years I had heard graduating seniors speak unhappily of their education ("I still don't know who the hell I am"; "I still don't know what I want to do with my life"; "I don't even know if such questions matter to me any more"), and express bewilderment at how eager, curious freshmen had been turned, four years later, into prototypes of articulate emptiness.

The job of self-discovery is never, of course, complete; it is hardly surprising that twenty-one-year-olds do not fully know "who the hell they are." But the point is that they have not begun to know. In many cases, four years of college do not initiate or further but dampen or destroy efforts at self-exploration. This may not be the intent, but it is nonetheless the result of the tactics employed by those who administer and teach in a university. They make certain that the student's energies are directed toward fulfilling tasks set by others; they encourage him to define his worth in terms of his success in winning their approval: high grades, good letters of recommendation, departmental honors, prizes. He is taught to regard these tangible signs of election as the only important evidence or kind of achievement, and as the indispensable precondition, almost the guarantee, of a satisfying life. What he is not taught is that orientation toward gaining the approval of others carries high costs: the acceptance of disguise as a necessity of life; the unconscious determination to manipulate others in the way one has been manipulated; the conviction that productivity is more important than character and "success" superior to satisfaction; the loss of curiosity, of a willingness to ask questions, of the capacity to take risks.

It is often said that grades are necessary "training for life," for the competition that defines and measures all aspects of adulthood. While one may agree that competition is omnipresent, one can question its desirability and necessity. To the extent that we know anything about "human nature," and we don't know much, there is little reason to believe that the competitive drive is an instinctual and therefore inevitable component of behavior. Competition continues to be the hallmark of our society because we continue to train our youth to act competitively, to measure their worth in terms of how successfully they dominate others rather than themselves.

The grading system also trains the young to be more adept at judging others than at understanding them, and at judging, moreover, on the basis of limited qualities: how well an individual "performs" in public, how readily he assimilates established values, how responsive he is to pressure situations, how adept he is at memorizing and verbalizing, how mechanically he can provide "right" answers, how obediently he can avoid "wrong" questions.

I do not doubt that tests and grades prepare the student for the American lifestyle. The question is whether we approve of that style and wish to perpetuate it.

When the coercive power of the grading system is eliminated, can we rely on any alternative stimulus to motivate students to learn?

Quite a few members of my 1966 seminar felt that "natural curiosity" was a sufficient motivating force for learning, but a number of rebuttals were and can be made to this assumption. First of all, even if "natural curiosity" is innate, it can be argued that the deadening procedures of most early schooling will have bred that quality out of many undergraduates long before they arrive at college. Those whose curiosity has at least partially survived are then subjected to, and often defeated by, the rituals of campus classrooms.

Moreover, there is reason to doubt, as Bernard Z. Friedlander has recently argued, whether "natural curiosity," "hunger for learning," or "joy in knowledge" can be relied upon as a sufficient incentive for academic learning. Friedlander points out that young children are chiefly curious about matters that relate to sexuality and that such curiosity is not automatically transferable, as the child grows older, to scholastic topics. Indeed, if curiosity about sex is not satisfied—and in our society it is more usually disapproved and suppressed—the child's interest in asking questions may be permanently destroyed. Having been given no answers or false answers to questions of pressing urgency, he is not likely to consider raising questions about matters of less potent interest.

All of which raises the pessimistic possibility that curriculum reform on the college level may be an enterprise of marginal value only. By age eighteen, it could be said, it is too late to salvage curiosity. One could answer that those who arrive as freshmen at college, especially at a "prestige" college, can be assumed to be those whose early craving for information was satisfied and encouraged. This answer is not, however, very persuasive. The arrival of freshman Joe Brown at Princeton's portals means only that he has distinguished himself in a secondary school, that he has performed better in meeting its requirements than most of his classmates. Since those requirements are usually geared to satisfying the needs of teachers rather than students, Joe Brown's high grades may directly reflect, in inverse ratio, the slow strangulation of his own curiosity.

At discouraging moments during the 1966 seminar, one thought kept occurring to me: Anyone interested in education should teach on the primary-school level, where there is still some chance of it mattering. At other moments, however, I preferred this more sanguine syllogism: The curiosity of many students arriving at Princeton has already been destroyed; it is too late in any significant degree either to harm them or to help them; nevertheless, some freshmen are still eager and alive, and it matters very much whether they are subjected to destructive discipline or encouraged to seek, without fear of retribution, honest answers to honest questions.

The removal of grades is necessary, but in itself hardly sufficient for reversing standard classroom practices. Grading is but one way in which we turn potentially creative individuals into data-processing machines, adapting them to their society but alienating them from themselves. More than grades must go. The entire superstructure of authoritarian control in our schools must give way if we are to enable people to assume responsibility for and to take pleasure in their own lives. We cannot expect aliveness and involvement when we are busy inculcating docility and compliance.

In this regard, the false distinctions that separate student from teacher must be broken down. What do we think titles like "professor," "sir," or "mister" achieve? Perhaps the illusion of respect, but certainly not its reality. Those qualities that are worth admiring in a given person—perception, experience, honesty, empathy, openness—will be admired regardless of title, and no title can create admiration when such qualities are absent. But a title can—and often does—establish a pattern of formality that prevents free exchange and the common pursuit by student and teacher of understanding. Titles also provide the professor with a subtle means of discipline and a false sense of self-importance, neither of which is conducive to communication—or humanness.

Then there is the matter of "requirements." John Holt has written a brilliant critique of the notion that certain bits and pieces of knowledge are "essential," that adults know which these are and at what point and in what way they can best be fed to the young. It seems to Holt, and to me, that this is dangerous nonsense. There is no agreement as to what knowledge is essential. Should everyone read *Crime and Punishment*? Understand ego psychology? Study Greek civilization? Learn about quasar theory? All of these? Some of these? None of these?

The individual young have their own interests and timetables and if these are stifled by the teacher's imposed demands, the result may be a certain number of facts temporarily absorbed, but at the cost of knowledge becoming irrelevant and curiosity being destroyed. Schools, as Holt puts it, should be places where students "learn what they most want to know, instead of what we think they ought to know." In any given seminar, it is far less important to convey the particular body of information that the professor happens to care about than to seek the information that the student cares about. It is far more valuable for the student to let a course on, say, the American Revolution wander off during a given session into a discussion, say, of war, of the "utility of violence," than to insist on the day's set topic of the British Navigation Acts; the latter will stick for about as long as it takes the student to walk out the door, while the former could provide grist for a personal reevaluation of lasting significance. Moreover, if knowledge is made relevant to the student's current needs, it is henceforth viewed as a desirable commodity. A student who is allowed to ask questions that matter to him soon learns the habit of self-generating inquiry.

The chief defect of our current college classroom, it seems to me, is that we acknowledge only one form of interaction: rational discourse concerned with the mastery of factual detail and the interpretation of it. I have no wish wholly to minimize the importance of this function. My point is that other levels of interaction are also present in every classroom, though we do not choose to acknowledge them, and that these—if acknowledged—could be of immense value in advancing what I take to be the basic purpose of education: self-discovery. These other levels of interaction are often nonrational, nonverbal, even unconscious. They involve all those processes that currently go under the rubric of "group dynamics," that is, "what happens" when a group of five or more people come together—how each individual presents himself and his ideas, what roles he chooses to play, what roles he projects onto others, how he reacts to challenge and debate, what forms of discussion he finds most congenial (or most threatening), etc. We are all, as teachers, necessarily involved in group dynamics, whether or not we like the idea. Since we cannot escape that involvement, it seems to me we should try to deal with it more responsibly than we do. That would mean facing the fact that a variety of interactions do take place in our classrooms; that these interactions influence the form, the content and the retention of "rational discourse"; and that they are therefore important to excavate and understand.

The central point, it seems to me, is that a classroom setting necessarily involves more than intellectual exchange. Indeed, opinions and values are most likely to be honestly revealed when the atmosphere encourages rather than suppresses emotional interaction. Beliefs, never shaped solely by reason, are always influenced by personal relationships and encounters, themselves freighted with emotion, and thus are most likely to be exposed and examined in an environment that contains an emotional dimension. We want students to "reexamine their beliefs"; that, we like to say, is the whole point of education. Since those beliefs were first formed in a multidimensional setting, they cannot be successfully explored in a setting that is one-dimensional.

Perhaps someone might object that I had confused the purpose of a university seminar with that of a group-therapy session, that my function as a professor was not to treat personalities, but to develop minds. I would answer such an accusation in part by denying it and in part by embracing it. I would deny that the 1966 seminar was chiefly designed to encourage members to reveal pathology, that our purpose in coming together was "medicinal." Yet neuroses were revealed, and something which could be called "therapy" did take place. In the process of actively engaging one another, the students exposed personality traits of all kinds. To the extent that a given individual became aware of what he had revealed about himself and chose to ponder it (I do not mean openly, in seminar, but privately, with himself), some personality changes could have ensued. Henry Anderson has said: "Any experience that is humanizing might be called psychotherapeutic." If my course did partake of psychotherapy, I would therefore not only welcome the news, but consider it the best possible vindication of the seminar—for I do not know what "education" is if not self-examination and change.

This does not necessarily mean that I believe education and therapy should henceforth become interchangeable processes. I do feel, however, that the simple dualism which pretends that education is concerned solely with "informing the mind," and therapy with "understanding the emotions," falsifies our everyday experience. No one actually functions on the basis of such neat categories; our emotions always color our intellectual views, and our minds are continually "ordering" our emotional responses.

It would be grotesque and dangerous for a professor of history to claim the insight and skill needed to conduct group-therapy sessions, just as it would be foolish for a therapist to conduct a seminar on Plato for his patients. But this is not to say that a university seminar does not influence the emotions of its members. We need to recognize that when a seminar is functioning well, the emotions of its members *are* engaged and, once engaged, will be transmuted.

Intellectual development does not, cannot, take place *in vacuo*. Indeed, it can be argued that intellectual development is predicated on the simultaneous development of the emotions. By intellectual development, I do not mean the amassing of facts (we all know walking encyclopedias who are emotional infants), but rather what William Kessen, professor of psychology at Yale, has called the individual's "delight in the solution of problems, pursuit of the orderly, joy in his own active inquiry, the relief and excitement of setting his own goals." For that kind of intellectual development, one needs emotional growth as well. The two are inextricably linked, and it is because we have tried to separate them—have tried to exclude emotion from the classroom—that we have turned out many more pedants and parrots than human beings.

Finally, there is the matter of leadership. A crucial distinction must be made between authority and authoritarianism. The former represents accumulated experience, knowledge, and insight. The latter represents their counterfeits: age masquerading as maturity, information as understanding, technique as originality. Authoritarianism is forced to demand the respect that authority draws naturally to itself. The former, like all demands, is likely to meet with hostility; the latter, like all authenticity, with emulation. Our universities—our schools at every level—are rife with authoritarianism, all but devoid of authority.

In any given seminar the teacher, expounding on the subject of his choice, almost always knows more facts than anyone else. He is also older and has had more professional training. These are the raw materials—information, experience, discipline—out of which authority can come, but they do not guarantee authority. If information has not been digested and personalized, if years have added more grayness than growth, if training has submerged the person in the specialist, then the potential authority turns into a mere authoritarian. And it is the rare authoritarian when given power—when put, say, in charge of young people—who can resist the satisfaction of reducing them to his level. So it is that one generation, desperate lest its own achievement be exceeded, corrupts the next—all the while protesting benevolence. Fathers are not known to encourage patricide—and few youths grow to manhood.

But let us look at the authority, rather than the authoritarian. Even the genuine authority—no one realizes this better than he—is limited in perspective. The ideal Professor Jones, a master of both Shakespeare and himself, knows that he can be surprised. He knows that Joe Smith, freshman from Dubuque, has some special experience that can illuminate a word or passage from *Hamlet*. Joe may be oblivious to generations of scholarship, but he knows something about sons. And he will tell it—if the climate is right, if Professor Jones has made it clear that no one has a corner on truth, that competence is never across the board, and that therefore leadership (in a classroom discussion, in life) should shift as areas of competence shift. If he can convey that much to Joe Smith, Professor Jones will have given him the one encouragement essential to true education: Ultimately each man can, must, become his own authority. This is the one path to adulthood—and democracy.

—Daedalus, *Winter 1968*

—— POSTSCRIPT 1969/1999 ——

I tried the experimental course described in the preceding article for two years. At the final session of the second year, the students and I spent more than three hours evaluating the course; it was a discussion that helped greatly to clarify in my own mind what still needed doing in the way of classroom reform. It led me to formulate plans for a new experiment which is best described in a memo I circulated to members of my department at Princeton. It read in part:

> Most undergraduates, I believe, are starving on the standard diet of course work which is tailored more to the professors' interests than to their own and which concentrates on the absorption of information.
>
> My tentative view is that in the long run we can best change this situation by giving all graduate students, regardless of their field of specialization, training in group dynamics. This would give them some of the insights and skills needed, when they become seminar leaders, to deal with certain non-rational classroom processes which are now handled by evasion, both conscious and otherwise.
>
> I should stress that I do not wish to abandon or minimize the intellectual content of university work but on the contrary to find out more about those hidden transactions which inevitably influence intellectual exchange. I feel I know a good deal at this point in my life about what it means to be a professional historian, about research and writing in the field of my special interest. I feel I know very little about what it means to be a teacher of history (or of anything), about what kinds of strategies succeed with what kinds of students, about what can be exchanged between teacher and student.

To move the experiment to what I felt was a needed next level, I decided it would be useful to have someone trained in group dynamics sit in on the seminar; their job would be to help us understand and untangle problems in communication (but not to join in or comment on the content of the discussions). My department, after first rejecting my proposal, eventually approved it, but it was then vetoed by the Princeton administration on "financial and pedagogical" grounds—though I had offered to teach it free. I tried to set up an appointment with the president of the university, Robert Goheen, to further explain the rationale for the course, but he refused even to see me. Thanks to Robert Cross at Hunter College, I was able to teach the course there in the spring term of 1969. Unfortunately the group therapist I got to sit in on the course as our "process person" proved inept; he was far more interested in joining our discussions (and in a showoffy, pontifical way) than in facilitating them.

My outrage at Princeton's hidebound and peremptory rejection of my course—at its lack of interest, though an educational institution, in exploring what education was or could be all about—contributed to my decision to resign my position as a tenured full professor and accept an offer to teach at CUNY, a university that proved far more welcoming of educational experimentation.

Young Radicals:
Politics or Culture?[1]

E pigrams cannot do the work of analysis, but it is tempting to say of the Left in the United States that as its numbers grow, its strength ebbs. More Americans are currently [1969] dissatisfied with our society than at any time since the thirties, yet as the ranks of the discontented swell, they simultaneously break into fragments.

Black activists of CORE reject cooperation with white radicals of SDS; Marxists in the Progressive Labor party scorn the ideological flabbiness of members of the Peace and Freedom Party; the columns of *The New York Review of Books* are filled with radicals denouncing radicals (Harrington vs. Macdonald, Genovese vs. Lynd); *Hard Times* regards *The New Republic* as old hat; *Dissent* worries about the responsibility of *The Village Voice*, which in turn scolds hippies and "crazies," who couldn't care less so long as the Mexican pot fields don't go up in flames. The closest all come to a common voice is when faced with The Enemy—who is not, as the uninitiated may suppose, George Wallace or Max Rafferty or General Westmoreland—but rather that latest figure of Left demonology: The Corporate Liberal.

In sorting out divisions on the Left, one critical index is electoral politics. Though many of the young retain their faith in the ballot—

like the students who worked in the Kennedy and McCarthy cam-paigns—the more radical among them increasingly doubt its useful-ness for promoting change. Black militants became cynical about politics as far back as 1964, when the Mississippi Freedom Democratic party was denied its rightful place at the Democratic Convention. Many campus activists have never been attracted to pol-itics as the top order of business, arguing that that priority must go to building a radical constituency through community organizing.

Distrust of the electoral process is far less pronounced among older radicals. They, too, applaud community organizing and political edu-cation, but argue that the best way of curtailing corporate and military power is to use the ballot for gaining control of the only larger power complex in the country—the federal government.

Two organizations are currently bidding for the allegiance of those who believe in the strategy of electoral politics. The first, the New Democratic Coalition, came into existence during the closing hours of the Chicago Convention and now has chapters in about half the states. The NDC believes in working within the Democratic party in the hope of ultimately capturing it (though its antagonists charge that a "capture" would only result in more of the same welfare statism), and has already drawn to its banner such men as Julian Bond, Allard Lowenstein, Paul Schrade, Michael Harrington, Arnold S. Kaufman and Adam Walinsky. The second organization calls for the formation of an entirely separate party (the New Party); thus far it has less strength and fewer well-known names than the NDC, but does in-clude among its advocates Marcus Raskin and Dr. Benjamin Spock.

Christopher Lasch has also recently announced his belief that some form of a new party will eventually be necessary (though he feels it must be preceded by a good deal of theoretical and practical work of the kind that the Fabian Society did in an earlier generation.) And Lasch's opinion carries weight. Over the past few years his essays have won wide respect for the way they combine a devotion to understanding the past with a passion for informing the present. Five of those essays—one each on Populism, Socialism, the Congress for Cultural Freedom, Black Power, and the concluding piece, "The Revival of Political Controversy in the Sixties"—which has as its main theme the need for a new party—have been collected as *The Agony of the American Left.*

Though *Agony* contains any number of provocative insights, I want to quarrel with some of Lasch's judgments and prescriptions for social change. I particularly want to take issue with his assumption that the formation of a new party is the most practical and promising of the political options available. I found his description of that party's potential shape so vague as to leave me unconvinced that it holds any decisive advantage over working for a progressive coalition within the old Democratic party.

Lasch argues that a new party, by "daring to call things by their proper name," would gather to itself the widespread discontent that currently exists. But the proper name that Lasch employs for the party—Socialist—is one that produces instant trauma in most Americans. Perhaps it's possible to define "Socialism" in such a way as to make it a feasible political label in this country, but Lasch does not provide that definition.

He rejects the "ugly overtones of bureaucracy, centralization and forcible repression" which the term has acquired from its association with existing "Socialist" regimes in the Soviet Union and in various underdeveloped countries, and he also disavows the diluted "social democratic" (or welfare state) connotations with which Socialism has been identified in industrialized countries like Sweden or Great Britain. But he offers us nothing in place of those definitions other than the hint that the basis for a new Socialism might come from an "indigenous tradition of radical populism"—which he describes as "decentralization, local control and a generally antibureaucratic outlook."

But this is not very helpful, since that same tradition is claimed by the American Right. Moreover, a definition that relies on "decentralization," etc., seems to confine Socialism to a matter of means rather than ends. Yet if that is to be the case, why is there no discussion of the possible necessity of nationalization? Is its omission meant to imply that nationalization is too obvious—or too outmoded—to mention? And in any case, what does Lasch then mean when he refers to "social planning"? Can that be achieved without state ownership, or at least state regulation, and if not, how would he then avoid the bureaucracy and centralization he so deplores?

It would be unfair to expect from Lasch a fully satisfying redefinition of Socialism, since no one else has been able to provide one. When C. A. R. Crosland made his notable attempt a dozen years ago, he insisted that the constant in Socialism was its goals not its means, but he was reduced to so broad a definition of those goals—"a high priority for the relief of the unfortunate"—that any welfare-stater could qualify as an adherent. Before the idea of a new party is embraced, its intentions will have to be made less obscure.

Besides, I am not convinced that electoral polities is going to prove the most significant catalyst or even the chief conduit for social reconstruction. I think what is most impressive about the radical young is not their politics or their social theories, but the cultural revolution they have inaugurated—the change in lifestyle. If that revolution develops, it may well express itself politically (and to some extent already has), but that is not the same as arguing that the new culture must rely on political expression for its development.

The sources and manifestations of the revolution lie elsewhere—in a bewildering grab bag that includes hallucinatory drugs, bisexuality, communal pads, dashikis and bluejeans, rock and soul, Eastern mystics, scientology, encounter groups, macrobiotic foods, astrology, street theaters and free stores. One may loathe some of the ingredients (as do many of the young themselves), or argue that they have not yet (and never will) crystallize into anything distinctive enough to be called a culture. But though the mix be unpleasant, shifting and inchoate, if it continues to locate its center in the senses and emotions, in participation and sharing, in the unexplored, the spontaneous, the casual, the experimental, we may well be witnessing a decisive break with our society's hitherto dominant values of rationalism, puritanism, materialism and individualism.

I think Lasch pays insufficient attention to this side of the youth revolt, though he has much to say about young radicals and much of value. Some of it is complimentary: he credits them with having communicated to many people a sense of crisis and an awareness that our system is unresponsive to the needs of millions of its citizens. Some of it is disparaging: he is angry at their tendency (present in only a few, it seems to me) to turn public questions into tests of personal "authenticity" and to talk glibly of guerrilla warfare or the advantages of right-wing repression.

Though Lasch is as eloquent in defense of their virtues as he is stern in censuring their failings, he nowhere credits the young with what may be their most revolutionary contribution—the forging of a new mode of living. This is the more ironic because Lasch himself, in the very last page of his book, calls for "an alternate culture and vision." It may be that his temperament, with its unqualified faith in rationality (historical analysis, he writes, is "the best way, maybe the only way, of gaining a clear understanding of social issues") and its distrust of what he calls the "spiritual and philosophical chaos of American life," has blocked his access to the particular kind of alternate culture the radical young are in the process of creating.

One quality Lasch assuredly shares with them—and it sets both apart from welfare-state liberals or the NDC—is uncompromising anti-Americanism. That attitude in the main cannot be faulted—certainly not as regards the horrors of our war machine, our ghettos, our corporate greed, our violent, inequitable society. Yet even so, the case against us can be made too all-inclusive, and Lasch is sometimes guilty of this excess.

When he writes, for example, "The American press is free, but it censors itself. The university is free, but it has purged itself of ideas. The literary intellectuals are free, but they use their freedom to propagandize for the state," one is willing to credit the statement only if Lasch has in mind some narrow definition that would exclude (to give only a few of many possible examples) *The New York Review of Books* from membership in the "press," would eliminate Harvard from the category of universities and would deny the editors of *Partisan Review* (whom he elsewhere praises) the right to be called "literary intellectuals."

I doubt if Lasch himself believes that dissent is as "illusory" in this country as he sometimes seems to argue, for he implores radicals to guard against the suppression of free speech, and unless he is thinking only of its future potential rather than its current value, he could not call for so determined an effort in defense of so "meaningless" a cause. It may be that in speaking of "illusory dissent" Lasch only means to deplore the fact that dissenters do not have the impact on official policy that they would like or that their numbers would sometimes justify. But as Johnson's decision not to seek reelection shows, that is not the same as saying dissent has no impact whatsoever.

Or it may be that Lasch only means that our society does not value free inquiry to the extent that it claims. But as the flood of anti-American books and periodicals demonstrates, that does not mean we *habitually* prevent free inquiry from proceeding. It is one thing to recognize that freedom of speech and of the press are diluted by self-censorship, by government indifference or harassment and by vigilante attacks, but quite another to suggest that those freedoms do not exist at all. The distinction is not trivial. It would be tragic if radical critics, having taken the lead in challenging our country's mindless anti-Communism, encourage the substitution of mindless anti-Americanism.

At one point in his book, Lasch refers to Marx's insight that political issues must be seen in their social context. That same insight can be used to inquire into the determinants of our own rabid anti-Americanism, for it, too, is a social product—not only in the sense of being a response to our society's serious shortcomings, but also in being a reflection of our society's furious self-hate (which alternates with indiscriminate self-congratulation). Our self-esteem as a nation has often rested on pride in material affluence. We have recently (all too recently) learned that millions of Americans do not share that affluence and, more heart-rending still to defenders of the faith, that additional millions of our middle-class youth who *have* shared in that affluence not only do not prize it, but consider it a positive handicap in the search for personal identity and national integrity.

Yet our worth as a people never did depend solely on our riches. It may be too late to recapture other qualities in our national character—our dynamism, openness to innovation, generosity, optimism—but one way of trying is to divert some of the energy that now goes into frenzied self-contempt into the very different and more promising channel of self-examination. Men like Christopher Lasch, Howard Zinn and Noam Chomsky are providing the materials for that self-examination. Now, if only people will read them.

—The New York Times, *March 23, 1969*

The Shifting Mood
on Campus
in the Seventies

I'll call her Tina. She's a Hispanic student of mine at Lehman College, the Bronx campus of the City University of New York. Tina came by my office recently to tell me the triumphant news of her acceptance at a prominent graduate school. She talked with shy exuberance—and residual disbelief—of the opportunities and rewards that now lay ahead. But then, her voice quieter, her words less coherent, she started to describe her fear that she would forget—that she may already have forgotten—her original goals: "to use my education for my people . . . to help them . . . to work in the community." The glow left Tina's face, her body sagged. It was as if some unbidden force within had broken through the confident crust, swallowing up her happiness. She put her head down and cried.

That's what I most want to tell you about: the pain that lies just below the surface of this so-called "me" generation.

Most students at Lehman College are drawn directly from the Bronx, the poorest of New York City's boroughs and the only one with a majority of black and Puerto Rican residents; 61 percent of the freshmen entering Lehman in the spring of 1977 came from families with an average annual income of less than $6,000 (the city-wide average is \$9,682). With few exceptions, my students are the first in their families to attend college; often they're the first to have graduated from high school. Understandably, they're impatient with courses that don't provide a direct avenue to good jobs (business and accounting being in far more demand at Lehman than ancient history or the nineteenth-century novel).

Despite these commonalities, Lehman's students are otherwise remarkably diverse: in lifestyle, age, ethnic background, values, allegiances, aspirations. The two seminars I teach—"The History of Radicalism in the United States" and "The History of Sex Roles and Sexual Behavior"—attract the full range. Because I keep classes small, unstructured and concentrated (three-hour sessions), a maximum amount of personal material tends to emerge. Not everyone takes to the informal climate; initially, almost no one does. Lehman students are used to the protective anonymity of large lecture courses; close contact can be threatening, especially when the material is potentially disruptive and the ethnic/ideological mix potentially volatile.

This year in the "History of Radicalism" seminar we were lucky in our "chemistry," or whatever one calls that mysterious emergence of trust among people of widely differing temperaments. It became possible to risk disagreements without creating lasting dislike. And on some topics disagreement proved sharp. Those are the sessions I want to describe in some detail, because I feel they provide clues for a generational portrait applicable beyond the Lehman campus.

The topic "Utopias, Past and Present" inaugurated the most intense of our discussions, opening up a set of interlocking questions and spiraling contention. The basic disagreement throughout was between Janet, strongly committed to radical feminist values and scornful of politics as an agency of change, and Tony, a macho, twenty-year-old Italo-American, furious at the "system" that had kept his hard-working family bound to a wretched tenement in the South Bronx.

Tony had early announced that he *thought* he was a socialist—adding, with honorable precision, that he hadn't done enough reading to be sure and wasn't affiliated with any Marxist group. A strong woman and a strong man with differing outlooks on the world, Janet and Tony had steered clear of each other for most of the term. The discussion of utopias brought them into direct conflict.

It began when Janet described the satisfaction she'd felt the previous summer while living in a commune in upstate New York. As a one-shot experience, that seemed acceptable enough to everyone. But then Janet went on to say that she intended to become a regular member of the commune after graduating in June. Tony, the wavering socialist, instantly stopped wavering.

"You're *what*! A commune—in 1977? What's that gonna change?"

"My head."

Deep groan from Tony. From the others: grimaces of dismay, blank amazement, superior sighs, assorted accusations and a few (very few) smiles of encouragement. Tony coordinated and vocalized the opposition by initially focusing on what a "tired" option communal living was. "The media's tired of it; I'm not," Janet said. I threw in some figures that I'd seen recently which suggested there were more communes today (and more kinds: publishing collectives, food co-ops, child-care groups, etc.) than had existed during the late '60s, the supposed height of their popularity. Claims about "bringing a new world into being" have been toned down, but the trend toward collectivization has accelerated.

"But collectivization in the name of *what*?" Tony broke in, shooting me a look as if to say, "you've probably made up the statistics, and if not, you're an enemy of the people for disseminating them." He turned on Janet.

"How the hell can you go off and plant vegetables when the country's falling apart? For Chrissake! Unemployment's 40 percent in the ghettos, the corporations are getting bigger and fatter every day while the rest of us grub for rent money, ecological disaster is—"

"—I can't solve any of that. Nobody can."

"You can damn well try."

Some sniper action started on Tony's right: exceptions were taken to his figures (40 percent of *teenagers* in the ghettos), halfhearted interjections were made on the order of "where is it any better? Russia? China? Ha!" Still, almost everyone bought Tony's description of our society as one in which the privileged few exploit the many. Janet bought it too. She simply reiterated her view that nobody knew what to do about it. The mess had gotten out of control. The only way to lead a decent life was to get the hell out, find some kind of meaning within oneself and with a few close friends. She didn't mean drugs, sex, and discos, but several nods of agreement in her direction seemed prompted more by visions of hedonism in the streets than ascetism in the woods.

Because Tony himself seemed at an impasse at that point—unable to translate his anger into a set of political propositions—we decided to move directly into a discussion of "the theory and practice of socialism." It lasted a month. Tony began it with a description and analysis of our assorted social ills that roused little opposition. Since many Lehman students come from low-income families and are also members of minority groups, they're well aware of the vast disparities of income and opportunity that Tony pointed to, and even those students from more privileged backgrounds expressed dismay and discomfort over those disparities. Nor was a large majority in the seminar slow to buy Tony's argument that the blame for our assorted ills should be placed directly on the interlocking alliance of hereditary wealth, federal officialdom, Pentagon brass, and multinational corporations. They were only a little slower in agreeing that the whole package could accurately be labeled "capitalism."

It was when we tried to sharpen and extend Tony's initial indictment that the seminar consensus broke down. Some of the students (pre-eminently Tony) argued that capitalism's defects were functional: the direct result of private ownership of the means of production. Others thought the defects incidental: the failure of government to curb the "excesses" of big business. The few conservative students preferred to cite the cosmos: "the poor always ye have with you."

Tony's insistence that only socialism offered the needed vision and tactics for change led to a prolonged squabble over definitions that fragmented opinion still further. Was the chief identifying feature of "socialism" public ownership of the means of production and distribution? If so, wouldn't that make the Soviet Union the epitome of socialism—though it suppresses those basic freedoms of speech, et al., which everyone agreed (no defenders here of the view that such freedoms are mere window dressing) were essential aspects of any society worth inhabiting? Besides: public ownership by exactly whom and of precisely what? Should the "public" be defined as on-the-job worker collectives, or as local communities, or as state and federal political assemblies? Should "ownership" be of basic industries and utilities only, of small businesses as well, or of all private property?

Trying to cut through the thickening knot, someone suggested socialism might best be defined not in terms of outright ownership of production but as "increased social planning." That opened up a different, but no less difficult set of questions. Who would do the planning? And to whom would they be accountable? Wasn't there a danger of concentrating power—and the potential for its abuse—still further? Of inflating an already swollen bureaucracy? Of multiplying regulatory agencies that had long since proved their susceptibility to co-optation by the very special-interest groups they were meant to control? But perhaps it was possible, someone said, to accomplish planning on a local level, to decentralize decision-making. Objections arose to that, too. Many felt that such problems of national scope as racism, poverty and gender discrimination could not safely be left to local initiative, resources—and prejudice.

Yet another shift followed: perhaps socialism should be defined in terms of ends not means: that is, by its focus on the plight of the unfortunate, by its insistence that highest priority be given to the needs of the least privileged. That seemed to bring us back full circle: how to devise a strategy for achieving those goals? Even if we succeeded, someone asked, what made us think that those in power would voluntarily relinquish it? And if they didn't, what then? Should we rely on a process of reeducation? Attempt violent overthrow? Pursue the "long march through the institutions"? Most thought the first tactic naïve, the second immoral, the third impractical. Discussion of the last unearthed additional complexities—and a further babble of discord. Given the ethnic and racial divisions in the country and the average American's distrust of collective action, how could we hope to get the needed marchers? And even if we somehow managed, what would prevent outright government repression?

As conundrums multiplied, spirits sagged. Having run into my own roadblocks on these questions for a decade, I wasn't of much help. I told them that we'd recapitulated in a month the essence of a debate that has been in process for a hundred years and (putting the best face on it) that we had to accept the frustration of realizing that no easy answers were available. "You mean *no* answers," someone shot back—to a general, melancholy nodding of heads.

"Typical American impatience!" Tony yelled impatiently. "If we can't get instant results, the hell with it! The revolution happens Wednesday at 5:00, or it's down to the disco!"

"Yeah, keep on dancing! Smoke more, think less!"

"Very funny," Tony said morosely. "You're dancing on your own graves."

"And what are you gonna do, Karl Marx?"

"Build a bomb shelter in the backyard."

That bit of gallows humor wound up the month-long discussion, give or take a few pep-talk platitudes I felt impelled to throw in (mostly because Tony looked so miserable) about this being "a creative period of dissolution . . . have to expect conflict over strategy . . . clarification emerges during the process of struggle . . ." I think I even said, "where there's a will there's a way," blanching less at the cliché than at the knowledge that when all ways seem blocked, the will atrophies.

Janet picked up the beat. There *was* a way, she said, but we'd been looking in the wrong places. "With typical male fanaticism, you've poured energy into a hyper-rational analysis of who has power and how to get it. Even if you managed to come up with some blueprint for a brave new world, I wouldn't want to live in it."

Tony (angry): "Meaning?"

Janet: "Meaning you'd shift rulers, not values. Any lasting social transformation has to be preceded by *self*-renovation."

Tony (angrier): "Meaning?"

Janet: "As radical feminists have been saying for years, we have to reclaim the world of the senses and emotions. Men—some women too—have to rediscover their capacity for tenderness and intimacy, a capacity now submerged under the patriarchal imperatives: tabulate, accumulate, dominate—imperatives perpetuated by the institutions of marriage and the nuclear family."

An elegant summary, I thought to myself. Before I could say so, Tony jumped in: "More bourgeois subjectivism!"

Janet: "And what's your anger—*objective*?"

Tony: "You bet your sweet—!"

Janet (and ten others): "—sexist pig!"

Tony (and two others): "—self-indulgent child!"

We got beyond the name-calling pretty fast. Apologies were offered all around, and some ideological ground—but only some—given. Tony declared his agreement with the feminist demand for "equal pay for equal work" and also his support for ERA—despite his feeling that "*most* women lacked the stamina and aggressiveness needed to perform well in certain fields." ("We're not interested in becoming professional football players," one of the women snapped back.) On her side, Janet acknowledged that the classic socialist goal of ending material want should be high on everyone's list of social priorities. Somewhat less readily, she conceded that where material deprivation was severe, it might be premature to talk of the need for a psycho-sexual revolution.

These concessions aside, Janet and Tony remained fervently at odds. Tony continued to insist that the radical feminist call for an end to traditional marriage and the nuclear family and its insistence that there were no innate biological (and thus psychological) differences between the sexes was "simply foolish." Janet quoted Marcuse in support of her view that the sexual liberation movements (feminist and gay) were the potential cutting edge of revolutionary change. Tony blanched briefly at one of his heroes being used against him, but rapidly rebounded. With millions starving, he said, it was "irresponsible" to put primary emphasis on destroying sex-role stereotypes and downright "moronic" to think (Janet had also quoted Norman O. Brown and Wilhelm Reich) that "resurrection of the body," "polymorphous perversity" or any of that "bisexuality/androgyny junk" could be a matter of even remote importance to *serious* people.

Janet and Tony's antagonistic views represent in pure form a debate that currently engages many more students (and on many campuses) than our official opinion processors seem to have noticed. The resurgence of interest in socialism has gone particularly unreported. That resurgence can be exaggerated (and often is by students directly involved). It isn't a stampede; nowhere near that. But the mere fact of its existence represents a significant departure from campus attitudes of recent decades.

In the '50s, interest in (let alone commitment to) socialism or to any ideology was considered aberrant, a sign of personality disturbance, perhaps derangement. In the '60s, the orientation of activist groups on campus was almost entirely, if not often self-consciously, anarchist—which is to say, deeply distrustful of authority in any guise, institutional *or* theoretical. The '70s have brought renewed interest in systematic analysis and encompassing generalization. Those on campus drawn to Marxism-Leninism have thus far more typically joined informal reading and discussion groups than any of the proliferating political organizations (Young Socialist Alliance, New American Movement, Progressive Labor, Democratic Socialist Organizing Committee, etc.) bearing the socialist banner.

The number of self-designated socialists on campus is small. But that may not be a reliable gauge of their potential influence. A tiny minority can initiate a movement that eventually wins wide support and has considerable impact (for example, the Abolitionists). It's too soon to know if this will prove to be the case with the new (new, that is, since the '30s) campus interest in socialism. What can be said is that all the current socialist groupings—despite the factionalism traditional on the Left—share a positive orientation toward the working class. And this is in marked contrast to the '60s, when SDS and hard hats viewed each other as bitter antagonists. Today, as in the '30s, almost all young Marxists look to an eventual mass movement led by the working class itself.

Therein lies ground for potential unity. And also for a greater numerical strength that could be further augmented by recruits from those unions (for example, the Hospital Workers) where a parallel upsurge of interest in socialism has been developing. Moreover, students like Tony—currently holding back from organizational affiliation while continuing to study the classical Marxist texts—could be galvanized into an active commitment by the force of events (another Vietnam, say, or a major depression). I myself think that the chances for the emergence of a significant socialist movement in the near future are slight. But then, no one expected the sudden and massive campus uprising in the '60s, either; political prophecy has not been noted in recent years for its fine calibrations. What remains true is that socialism—however inchoate, ill-defined and politically ineffective in its current form—is showing more signs of life than it has for several decades. Whether it can manage an accommodation with feminist analysis—the two coalescing into a vision of radical originality and widespread appeal—seems to me the key imponderable.

The debate between Tony and Janet, ending as it did in minimal concessions or sympathy, exemplifies the obstacles to coalescence. Like many male Marxists I know, Tony is a cultural conservative. He'll fight the establishment tooth and nail (yes, tooth and nail: the male style) on economic issues, but otherwise tends to share the reigning patriarchal values. Tony believes in the importance of hierarchy, reason, authority (in his case, Marx), leadership, order, discipline. He tends to over-rationalize experience, is impatient with personal idiosyncrasy ("subjectivism"), inattentive to realities (like intimacy) that cannot be precisely measured. He wants to expand access to material goods, but not definitions of humanness. He wants to destroy distinctions between the classes, but is wary of challenging those that separate the sexes. Reverse all the above, and we see the alternate strengths—and limitations—of Janet's vision.

Most of the young in my seminars (and throughout the country) are not absorbed by Tony's or Janet's concerns. They don't raise (let alone dwell on) issues posed by socialist or feminist analysis. Yet it would be inaccurate to say (as many have) that they're indifferent to them. During our discussions, Janet and Tony hardly had the floor to themselves. Almost everyone joined in at some point, a nerve struck, an old allegiance challenged, a new option clarified. What surprised me wasn't the amount of passion (of which this generation is supposedly devoid) that got invested in the debate, but the extent to which opin ion clustered on Janet's side. I hadn't expected students from working-class families that tend to stress traditional values to be drawn to an "extreme" feminist position. Well, I thought, that's New York City—it *is* different. But then I read some surveys of campus attitudes elsewhere, and Lehman didn't seem so atypical after all.

As early as 1973, Daniel Yankelovich's analysis of the views of a broad cross section of young people between the ages of 16 and 25 on sex roles and sexual mores revealed what he called a "startling" shift in values. It was perhaps predictable that he'd find a majority of young people in favor of equal pay for equal work and in agreement with the proposition that women "should be free to take the initiative in sex." But less predictably, Yankelovich also found a majority in agreement with the radical premise that men and women "share the same essential human nature" and with the view that certain traditional notions of masculinity (the need to be "physically strong" and "handy around the house") should be de-emphasized.

His study documented a decisive shift in attitudes toward sexual behavior as well. Those on campus who said they "would welcome more acceptance of sexual freedom" rose from 43 percent in 1969 to 61 percent in 1973. Among *non*-college youth the figure climbed from 22 percent to 47 percent. (The shift in that segment of the population was still more dramatic in response to more specific propositions: "casual premarital sexual relations are morally wrong"—down from 57 percent in 1969 to 34 percent in 1973; "relations between consenting homosexuals are morally wrong"—a drop from 72 percent to 47 percent.)

Additional studies have confirmed and extended Yankelovich's findings. A poll taken by the undergraduate newspaper at Princeton in 1976 found no significant differences in sexual experience between male and female students, a widening acceptance of "recreational" sex (40 percent said they knew of no valid arguments against "promiscuity"), and a growing disaffection from the monogamous model (nearly one-third saw no reason why even intimate relationships *had* to be sexually exclusive). This attitudinal shift is apparently still more pronounced among the generation waiting in the wings. Planned Parenthood has recently released figures showing that the nationwide rate of nonvirginity among teenage girls is up from 27 percent in 1971 to 35 percent in 1977. In the San Francisco area—presumed seedbed of the new day—the figure is now close to 60 percent.

It's clear that certain suppositions about "human nature" which have long had the status of axioms are increasingly being viewed as something considerably less than that—as culture-bound norms subject to scrutiny and redefinition. What does (or should) it mean to be "male" or "female"? Is sexual fidelity in a "primary" relationship either necessary or desirable? Does sexual pleasure require the justifying context of a "love relationship" or is pleasure its own justification? Is same-gender love and lust in any sense "abnormal"? Do marriage and family life provide optimal conditions for human happiness? Some new models of "optimal" behavior are also emerging—preeminently bisexuality (sleeping with individuals not genders) and androgyny (combining in every person traits hitherto thought to be the "natural" preserve of either men or women).

Such attitudes have rarely surfaced in the past, and never among so large a percentage of the population. The radicalism of the '60s engaged more people, but that of the '70s is engaging a set of questions previously so immune to inquiry—because not viewed as questions at all, but as immutable givens—that it may represent a more profoundly innovative departure.

Not many see it that way. Certainly not the young Marxists currently struggling to build a movement. They regard the shift in campus interest from economic analysis and political organizing to gender and sexual exploration as merely the logical (and misguided) extension of hippie concerns of the '60s. And they deplore it as yet another of those "personalistic" diversions that time and again in our history have fatally sapped the strength of movements for social change, detouring energy from the proper work of objective analysis, collective organizing, and structural renovation into the illusory (and peculiarly American) pursuit of individual "self-fulfillment."

This critique can hardly be dismissed. It will be generations before we know whether the current assault on traditional definitions of "personhood" will bring in train the destruction or reinforcement of traditional arrangements of power; whether the challenge to sex-role stereotypes and normative definitions of sexual morality will prove the cutting edge for a broad social transformation or a self-indulgent dead end for a privileged few. I myself think the former—but wouldn't want to hang on the proof.

The challenge to patriarchy and the challenge to capitalism are the only two radical games in town (the challenge to racism having long since receded). Currently they view each other (with individual exceptions) with deep suspicion. Both have made significant gains in the past few years, with the feminist momentum more pronounced. But neither feminists nor socialists have captured the allegiance of the campus majority. Nor, unlike previous minorities (SDS, say, or the hippies), have they succeeded in setting a generation's agenda or style.

The majority on campus is much more of an enigma than the activist groups competing for its attention. Most students seem to me to be so uncertain and volatile in their attitudes that any generalization about them becomes suspect. The temptation is to grab on to one thread in the tangle—alienation, careerism, ethnicity, religiosity et al.—and insist that *it* provides the key. It does—if one is willing to believe a side corridor is the same as the main entrance.

What I see over the main entrance (carved, of course, in sand) is the word "Emersonian." This may be foolishness: overdignifying and overelaborating an essentially banal set of generational characteristics.

Perhaps. Let's therefore call it *my* thread through the maze and see where it leads.

Emerson has always been a most unmanageable figure. The problem is his plenitude, his multiplicity of insights and personae. He's the silly-putty of American letters. No sooner does his image seem fixed than it dissolves. No sooner does he seem to declare decisively on this or that question than he shifts ground—and often the question. This can be especially galling because of Emerson's serene acceptance of his own equivocations, his apparent belief that elusiveness is a virtue and consistency a failure of imagination. He will disavow no mood, even after it passes. He retains affection for all his opinions, however much they change, for he views all as aspects of his singular self. This is highly offensive in a culture dedicated to categorizing and intolerant of ambiguity.

Through the years, most of my students have dismissed Emerson as a hopeless hypocrite; and in drawing that indictment, they've had no trouble finding innumerable instances of contradiction in his thought. On the one hand, Emerson asserts the absolute claims of the self, the need to reject the world's "conspiracy to importune you with emphatic trifles"; the illusion of change ("dream delivers us to dream"); the misplaced emphasis of social reformers ("it is easy to live for others; everybody does"). "Stand apart" seems to be the sum of Emerson's philosophy: "in silence, in steadiness, in severe abstraction, let him hold by himself."

And yet . . . turn a page in Emerson's writings, pick up another essay, and the disdainful Olympian transforms into the egalitarian democrat, the elitist praises the insights of the common man, the hermit scholar disdains books as "crutches, the resorts of the feeble and lame," the radical individualist demands that attention be paid to the claims of the world and action be taken against social injustice ("It is in vain you pretend that you are not responsible for the evil law, [to] seek a temporary peace by the diversion of . . . thoughts from politic or vexed questions, hiding . . . like an ostrich . . . ").

Is this a spirit at war with itself, a temperament unable to choose? Or is it a multitudinous nature large enough to contain opposites, and refusing to reduce itself to a single impulse, a fixed identity? In the '50s, my students couldn't have cared less. They simply found Emerson boring: too serious, too introspective, too abstract. In the '60s, they found him repellent: overcultivated, indifferent to suffering, smothered in self-importance. The '50s' hero was Daniel Webster: sonorous patriot, skillful aggrandizer, sophisticated power broker. Webster "understood" that ethical absolutes had no place in politics; that those calling for radical change were misguided fanatics; that national power required national unity; that the democratic process was "working" when interests had been compromised, passion defused, ideology discredited; that Truth was any white line running down the center of any road.

The '60s' hero was William Lloyd Garrison. He came up so fast on the outside track that Webster was thrown clear off his horse (an animal groomed for generations in the thoroughbred stables of Eastern Academe). Garrison was Webster's polar opposite. He disdained politics as innately corrupt, the trading of spoils. He insisted that moral considerations took precedence over all others, denouncing "pragmatic compromise" as an evasion of principle. He freely attacked any established authority—the church, the political parties, the law, the Constitution, the Union itself—complicitous in the sin of slavery. He had a profoundly optimistic view of the perfectibility of human nature and human society. Within a very few years in the mid-'60s, Webster, prototypical insider, yielded his place in the pantheon to Garrison, archetypal outsider.

And their contemporary, Emerson? He languished still in Concord, no one's Representative Man. The infinitude of the private soul, the illusion of "reality," the need to cultivate indifference to circumstance, the importance of becoming "a system instead of a satellite," the sense that the demands of community are at odds with the development of a sovereign self—these were themes without takers. For a time, I gave up trying to plead Emerson's case, increasingly uncertain he had one.

It was only this past year that I decided to act on the hunch (probably several years overdue) that Emerson's time had finally come. My hunch proved—within limits—to be right.

The limits were considerable. Emerson's basic belief in a benign universe, his basic conviction that an underlying "moral order" automatically converts transient evil into ultimate good, met with astonishment and anger (New York not being a benign universe). "Patrician complacency" is how one student characterized his view. I think she pinpointed the main reason for Emerson's long decline in popular favor and why even a generation sympathetic to certain aspects of his thought still sees him as being on the other side of an immense divide.

Janet and Tony, needless to say, found little in Emerson worthwhile. To them he remains what he was to the '60s' generation: a remote, fastidious figure, unable to translate his ideas into action, unwilling to try. But almost everyone else—the centrist majority, that is—found something to identify with in Emerson, something to admire. Sometimes a single line spoke to them: "Society is a masked ball where everyone hides his real character, and reveals it by hiding." ("He must have known Nixon!" somebody quipped.) The more conservative students latched on to "Many a reformer perishes in his removal of rubbish"; the more liberal ones liked "Men in all ways are better than they seem." But far and away the favorite was "Perhaps all that is not performance is preparation, or performance that shall be."

I may be overinterpreting, but I think the deep response that line produced is an important index of the dominant mood on campus. Or at the least, a gauge of how most students these days would *like* to see themselves: that their concentration on preparing for careers will someday justify itself in terms of performance. And performance of a particular kind: one that will bring a measure of income and status—but in tandem with a measure of "self-fulfillment" and "service."

Tina comes back to mind, the day she cried in my office. Like so many others, she desperately wants to believe that she can combine personal advancement with public responsibility. She cannot be comfortable, as students in the '50s were, with the former alone. Nor can she devote herself, as could the activists in the '60s, to the latter alone. A divided consciousness—the Emersonian double vision that prevents single-minded commitment either to personal goals or to public ones. Like Emerson, Tina fears to participate, and fears not to. She sees corruption everywhere and tends to think it unsolvable; she sees, too, that its subtlest form may be the refusal to try. But the serenity with which the Sage of Concord could regard such ambivalence is no longer available. The Tinas of today are not confident that they can balance indefinitely the competing loyalties, pressures, and claims that tug at their lives. Nor that they can rely on a "beneficient moral order" to draw the balance for them. Thus their pain. And tears.

—Liberation, *Fall 1977*

--------- POSTSCRIPT 1999 ---------

Having been much less active in the last twenty years in educational reform and campus politics than I had been earlier, it's difficult for me to offer any confident generalizations about recent developments. I read and hear about a budding new commitment on campuses to the cause of labor, but I don't see any of it at the City University of New York, where I teach. Yet there's no doubt that a political revitalization is underway in the colleges. *The New York Times*, for example, has reported (March 29, 1999) "the biggest surge in campus activism in nearly two decades" [since the early-1980s protest demanding that colleges divest from companies doing business with South Africa].

Most of this resurgence in activism *has* focused on improving working conditions for labor—the call for a living wage, an end to sweatshops and so forth. (See Marc Cooper, "No Sweat: Uniting Workers and Students: A New Movement is Born," *The Nation,* June 7, 1999.) Important as these protests are, they rarely are embedded in any critique of corporate capitalism nor do they often include any call for a structural revamping of our economic system.

If fiery socialists like Tony or counterculturalists like Janet still exist (and I know some *must*), they haven't been registering on my radar. Nor have I spotted many Tinas, torn between career ambitions and wanting to "give back" to their own communities. What does register loud and clear is the career part of the equation. These days most of my students—against ever more difficult odds of balancing family commitments and work with getting a degree—are aiming for credentials in fields like accounting, engineering or computer science that promise good future incomes. And who can blame them, given a shrinking job market that rewards only certain skills in certain fields?

What I also see is a pervasive cynicism—even though students in the nineties are no less aware (and are possibly more so) than were those in the seventies of social inequities, the growing gap between rich and poor, endemic corruption and ongoing racism and sexism. I think I also see, simmering just below the surface, endemic anger about a system where the privileged few skim off an ever larger share of the nation's wealth. It is an anger that could once again coalesce and erupt in response to some galvanizing public event. Or so I would like to believe. And there *is* evidence to warrant that belief.

CODA
(1996) The Multicultural Curriculum

Allan Bloom would have hated Lawrence Levine's new (1996) book, *The Opening of the American Mind*. So will Lynn Cheney, William Bennett, Gertude Himmelfarb, George Will and Dinesh D'Souza. Arthur Schlesinger, Jr., will be judiciously appalled.

Here alone are grounds surely—unless one is a benighted fan of those smug and swollen pooh-bahs—for rejoicing. Other grounds are readily available. Lawrence Levine's *The Opening of the American Mind* (a play on Bloom's *The Closing of the American Mind*), confronts the conservative critics of multiculturalism with the rigorous scholarship and lucid analysis usually absent in their own work. And he does so in a tone I can only call awesomely moderate.

I myself would have preferred a few more wrathfully bloodied noses—as just recompense for the rancorous invective D'Souza and his comrades have themselves indulged in, and the unwarranted pain they have meted out. Not that Levine ever hesitates in naming individuals or carving up their poorly documented and shabbily argued works. But his is a temperate spirit. Who better, after all, than a cool-hand Luke to subdue the West?

The central purpose of Levine's book is to rebut those critics who view a recently expanded curriculum that includes subjects long tabooed and voices long silenced as the equivalent of the invasion of the Gauls (usually equated with '60s New Leftists who lost the battle in the streets but have now "captured" the university).

Levine anchors this debate in a historical context. He proves in rich detail how much of the conservative nostalgia for the university's pristine past is based on a shallow understanding of that past. The "canon" currently being defended by the anti-multiculturalists has in fact not been around very long. No canon, moreover, has ever been fixed through time nor been modified without fierce resistance from the old guard—always in the name of a set of "universal truths" themselves of recent vintage.

The university curriculum in the colonial period focused on a limited number of Greek and Latin classics—and they were read not as literature but as rote grammatical exercises (to the infinite boredom of the students). It was little more than a century ago that such subjects as science and "modern" (meaning post-Roman) languages, literature and history were allowed to enter the curriculum—to howls of protest from defenders of the classics of antiquity and to dark predictions of an imminent descent into barbarism. And it was only after World War II that such now-revered works as *Moby-Dick, Leaves of Grass,* and the poetry of Emily Dickinson were considered worthy of the attention of American undergraduates.

Though conservatives, moreover, tend to regard Western Civilization survey courses as the very backbone of the national spine, the truth is they were only introduced in the post–World War I period and had declined as the dominant feature of the humanities curriculum as early as the 1950s. Nor were these courses apolitical, as conservatives like to presume when contrasting them to today's "ideological" curriculum. To the contrary, "Western Civilization" was mostly taught parochially as the culminating and superior end product of world history, and without reference to entire hemispheres or epochs. The professors who dominated the university in the fifties—a homogenous group of conservative white males—liked to think of themselves as engaged in a value-free pursuit of truth. But no. As mere mortals, they mirrored, as do we all, the values of their time, which then meant the smug assumptions of Anglo-Saxon superiority.

That the curriculum *has* recently expanded is undeniable. Topics relating to gender and sexuality, previously ignored, are now widely discussed. Whole continents—Asia and Africa—either previously bypassed or allowed into view solely to demonstrate the triumphant Anglo-Saxon march across the earth's surface, are now studied and valued within their own cultural frameworks. And in regard to the literature and history of the United States, we are hearing a lot more of those nonwhite, nonmale, nonheterosexual voices that comprise the actual complexity (as opposed to the official simplicities) of our national narrative.

To the Himmelfarbs and Bennetts this amounts to a betrayal of all that is worthwhile in our past, a threat to the common (read "privileged") good, an ominous foretaste of our country's fragmented future (as if the lauded "melting pot" has ever been more than an exaggerated myth). In their enflamed Manichean scenarios, the expansion of the university curriculum has been due to a deliberate conspiracy on the part of the have-nots and know-nothings—to the radical feminists (Allan Bloom likened feminism to the Terror following the French Revolution), the critical race theorists, the poststructuralists, the new historicists, the degenerate queer theorists (Bloom, poor old queen, longed for a university where the students' sexual energies were diverted into metaphysical study).

Yet as Levine so ably demonstrates, the multicultural impulse is at bottom an effort—finally, belatedly—to tell the truth about our country's past (and present). It seeks to broaden understanding of our peculiarly fluid, dynamic, transnational society by paying due attention at last to the diverse cultural contributions and interactions that have created it. Conservative critics have labeled this trend "political correctness," cleverly trying to convert an opening up into a closing down—just as they have tried to reduce multiculturalism to an ahistorical exercise in "feel good" therapy.

These critics, like true believers of any sort, champion the static view that a set of "universal values" exists that transcend time and place, that these can be ascertained by objective truth-seekers, that they always have and always must form the basis of our society and can (must) be transmitted uncontaminated to the young through certified texts that embody our cultural heritage. "Our" is the key word, and its definition is not self-evident.

What we are witnessing—on university campuses, in society as a whole—is a struggle over legitimacy. Those who believe, for example, that "classical" music alone is worth listening to (let alone studying) are bound to be discomforted, as Levine eloquently argues, at current claims being made on behalf of jazz, blues, folk, country, rock, punk and rap music as significant forms of cultural expression worthy of inclusion and analysis.

Automatically to disdain such claims is to do several disservices all at once: to the way in which a dynamic, democratic society like "ours" has always renewed itself; to the way in which the university has always functioned as a mirror (more than as a causative factor) of changes underway in the larger society; to the fact that previously silenced minorities, having discovered their voices, are rightfully insisting that they be heard.

"They," after all, *are* "us." That is the whole point. Though official culture is loath to acknowledge the fact, various races, ethnicities, genders and classes—plus some charming folks who refuse to fit into any category—*have* long been part of the country's fabric, and acknowledgment of their contributions to it is long overdue. As Levine succinctly puts it, "The debate over the canon is now, and has always been, a debate over the culture and over the course that culture should take." And to that insight, he shrewdly adds another: "The fact is, of course, that teaching subjects in schools and colleges gives them cultural legitimacy."

A few people have long understood all this. As far back as 1915, Horace Kallen, a Jewish American professor at Columbia, wrote two articles in the *Nation* pronouncing the "melting pot" a theoretical misconception and a practical failure, and he introduced in its place the concept of "cultural pluralism." And the scholar Milton Gordon argued some thirty years ago that immigrants coming to the United States did undergo considerable behavioral assimilation (in language, dress, manner, and so forth) but they entered mainstream institutional structures much less completely, adhering instead (due to a combination of exclusion and choice) to their own ethnic church, social and service organizations. The mainstream and the periphery have constantly interacted, affected and shaped each other in a process of unceasing change.

Melting pot celebrants fail to recognize the complexity of this historical course. They prefer a "we allowed *them* to join *us*" version of assimilation, descrying all forms of refusal as "un-American." But as Kallen saw, diversity is not a curse but a blessing—the very ingredient that has given U.S. culture its distinctively vital, ever-evolving, ever-changing mix of old and new. Only in recent decades, and to mounting, predictable protest, have we begun to relearn Kallen and Gordon's lesson that America's identity (and strength) *is* its heterogeneity, and to realize that we must honestly come to grips with the full spectrum of who "We" actually are.

In a widely read pamphlet in 1834, Samuel F. B. Morse (yes, that one) denounced the arrival of Irish and German Catholic immigrants in the Mississippi Valley as a conspiracy to destroy American republicanism. In an even more widely read work in 1987, Allan Bloom condemned the introduction of non-Western materials into the university curriculum; he saw Western culture as synonymous with Civilization and raged against any move that might destroy "the West's universal or intellectually imperialistic claims, leaving it to be just another culture."

Bloom's *The Closing of the American Mind* was on *The New York Times* bestseller list for thirty-one weeks and in hardcover alone sold some 800,000 copies. Lawrence Levine's *The Opening of the American Mind*, a forceful, cogent challenge to Bloom's dogmatic, sullen, insular work, deserves to sell as well. But of course it will not. And the reason is sadly obvious: Not enough mainstream Americans are yet willing to acknowledge that many different kinds of people, in dynamic interaction, have produced and continue to reshape that complex set of identities, values and cultural products we call American Civilization.

—The Nation, *October 7, 1996*

III

The Emerging Gay Movement and Feminism

Sex and Love:
Mailer/Miller/Millett

G*enius and Lust,* Norman Mailer's "journey through the major writings of Henry Miller," is a stupefying mishmash of sense and nonsense—the latter predominating. The book contains nearly five hundred pages of Miller's writing which Mailer has selected mostly from the earlier, better work. The anthology's stated purpose— to persuade us that Miller is a neglected "genius" of the first rank—is not accomplished.

Some will view Mailer's claims for Miller as a disguised plea for what he likes to call the "title." They will cite Mailer's characteristic conversion of aspects of his subject into aspects of himself, and will point further to the real resemblance between the two men—their shared view of sex (and writing) as a form of warfare, their endearing (these two tender, neo-Victorians) insistence that they are monstrous Toughs.

Those of us who admire Mailer have learned to take his extravagance as a concomitant of his gifts. But Mailer's attempts to define his respect for Miller are sloppy, swollen, tautological. "It would be tempting to say," Mailer tells us, that Miller "writes well about everything but his enthusiasm." Since the whole volume is designed to demonstrate that lust is *the* enthusiasm, Mailer has thus carelessly made him-self say that Miller rarely writes well. Elsewhere Mailer sounds giddy (though many will not be amused): Miller's "insights smack the brain like a bouncy tit which plops full of fucky happy presence over your nostrils." As we ponder whether to draw a breath, comes the news that Miller is "the Grand Speleologist of the Vagina—out of the sensations of those caverns will he rediscover every item in the world." If so, he didn't bring them back; I can think of few writers as tiresomely mono-chromatic in subject matter or rhythm.

Mailer prefers to celebrate Miller's liberating influence—itself un-deniable—than to linger on its limitations. He praises Miller for "ex-ploring the vast watershed of sex from that relatively uncharted side which goes by the name of lust"—but does not pause over his own in-sight that for Miller "sex and filth were components of the same equa-tion, as related as mass and energy." Mailer's haste is understandable. In his own earlier work he has already identified himself with Miller's perspective. As he wrote in *Armies of the Night*, "sex . . . was better off dirty, damned, even slavish! than clean, and without guilt." And in *The Prisoner of Sex*, he showed no sympathy for Kate Millett's cogent ar-gument that although Miller deserves credit for being honest enough "to articulate the disgust, the contempt, the hostility, the violence, and the sense of filth which our culture, or more specifically, its masculine sensibility, surround sexuality," he has played no role in "freeing us from such afflictions."

There is no evidence in *Genius and Lust* that Mailer yet sees the need to "free ourselves." If anything—perhaps because his investment in defiance can prevail over his actual views—he seems to embrace Miller's vision of sexuality more fiercely than ever. He acknowledges that "a part of Miller has been amputated forever from any comfort in the idea that woman has a character as large as man," but then blames Miller's distancing mother for his inability to see women as other than "disembodied cunts"—indeed gratuitously broadens the indictment to blame the "anti-sexuality" of *every* man on "all the cold and disinterested women of childhood." He would have us believe that every time Miller says the equivalent of "take that, you cunt!", he is slaying "social artifice and hypocrisy . . . all the cancers of bourgeois suffocation."

No. He is slaying women. And Mailer outdistances Miller (who has no talent for philosophy) in providing a justifying polemic. "Something in a woman," he tells us—the lack of embarassment is awesome—"wishes to be killed . . . she would like to lose the weaker part of herself, have it ploughed under, ground under, kneaded, tortured, squashed, sliced, banished, and finally immolated." At latest count, no advocate of "innate female masochism" has gone this far; they speak of every woman's desire to be raped; Mailer seems to add—raped to death. When Miller wrote, in the 1930s and '40s, his denigrating views of women were commonplace in the culture. Mailer, writing in the '70s, lacks that sociological justification.

To some modest extent, Miller needs to be rescued from both Mailer, his staunchest defender, and Kate Millett, his sharpest critic. Though the two are usually seen as polar opposites, their characterizations of Miller at certain points sound interchangeable—and interchangeably diminish him. When Mailer (Millett agreeing) locates the focus of Miller's writing on "the vagaries and outright contradictions of a stiff prick without a modicum of conscience," he is intending a compliment (Millett not agreeing), but it comes at the expense of ignoring the modicum (no more) of conscience that Miller did have: "it was truly abominable the way I treated her," Miller writes of one woman in *The World of Sex*—"contemptible." Or when Millett says (Mailer uses almost identical words, though not—again—for an identical purpose) that Miller yearned to effect "a complete depersonalization of woman into cunt," she can do so only by ignoring the many modifying, humanizing nuances in the hundreds of pages he wrote about his second wife, June Edith Smith.

Both Millett and Mailer likewise ignore what might be called the "experimental" side of Miller's sexuality—those occasional, impressively casual references to tickling another man's balls during a threesome, getting an erection while dressing up in women's clothes, feeling deeply aroused ("on the verge of coming") when listening to the tale of a "big horse cock" shooting off. It's curious that Millett, ordinarily so responsive to variegated forms of sexuality, and Mailer, ordinarily so insistent on the "mysteries" at the heart of sex (and writing), should reduce Miller to so flat and one-dimensional a level.

Most curious of all—the alliance here is dizzying—is the sharp dichotomy both draw (not in their lives, apparently, but when writing about Miller) between lust and love—as if the one was composed of an entirely different set of attributes from the other. When Mailer expatiates on how lust "dominates the mind, appropriates loyalties, generalizes character," the description seems as applicable to the obsessive, exclusionary, projective aspects of love—or at least of what we are learning to call its "early," "romantic" phase. When Millett describes Miller's seven-year marriage to June Smith as "less a love story than the case history of a neurotic dependence," does she mean that "dependence" (the need for support? the wish for complementation?) is not a significant ingredient of love?

It may be—though I doubt many psychiatrists would agree (which doesn't invalidate the proposition)—that the apparent absence in Miller of a need to be "completed," his inability (as both Millett and Mailer have it) to fall in love, should be seen as a sign of mental health, of an already achieved personal wholeness, of a remarkable freedom from those romantic expectations which in our culture have dominated—and poisoned—intimacy. It may even be that the process of looking to another person for qualities we feel lacking in ourselves is better seen as the central component of lust (which we've been taught to dismiss, much too glibly, as a "merely physical" attraction) and not as an appropriate description at all for that companionable sharing and mutual concern which characterize a "love" relationship of any sustained duration.

Because this is a jumble for all of us right now, my complaint is not so much against imprecision as against premature simplification. Since we are at some distance from that halcyon day when we can talk with confidence of the distinctions between "love," "lust," "affection," "dependence," "sex" et al., I prefer the way Miller confines himself to describing an act to the way Mailer and Millett attempt to categorize it.

—The New Republic, *Nov. 27, 1976*

Feminism
and Gay Men

A. The Gay Academic Union

One day in April 1973, I got a phone call inviting me to join a group of gay academics who had begun to talk together informally about our situation in the university world. I accepted enthusiastically. About twenty people gathered in an Upper West Side apartment, most of them graduate students and junior faculty, and most of them not yet "out" professionally. We started talking about whether as a group we had some special function to perform and after lengthy discussion came up with several: we could pressure the American Association of University Professors and other academic organizations to protect the rights of openly gay faculty; we could serve as a support network for the many isolated gay people on campus; we could pinpoint needed areas of scholarly research; and we could originate pilot programs for course work in lesbian and gay studies. The group excitedly decided to meet again in two weeks, and I could hardly wait, eager to throw myself into the kind of organizational work for which I had always claimed temperamental distaste.

From this point, we began to meet frequently, soon named ourselves the Gay Academic Union, and soon after that decided to plan a national conference for the fall on "The Universities and the Gay Experience" as a way of announcing ourselves and providing a rallying point. The speed with which we formed the organization, mapped out strategies, and debated national, even international, ramifications led one of the few women in the group to say, acerbically, "You guys may be oppressed faggots, but you show the same comfort with power and the same confidence that you'll gain access to it as any other gathering of men I've ever witnessed." She was not at all sure, she added, that she liked the pace or approved the tone.

And indeed from then on the issue of how and whether women would affiliate with GAU became a constant and contentious topic. Within a few months of our organizing, forty or so people were attending the meetings, with twenty to twenty-five showing up regularly. But very few were women. The men agreed from the start that women should have equal representation on GAU's steering committee, but claimed the principle was difficult to implement: women were scarce in academia, and open lesbians scarce among women. Some of the men vocally disclaimed any interest in making a special effort to encourage women to join GAU, an attitude that several of the women who did attend the meetings rightly took to be sexist.

To try to combat the sexism, a dozen of us met separately for an evening of frank talk about whether men and women *could* hope to work together successfully in GAU. We all acknowledged some variant of sexism within ourselves. Several of the men admitted that machismo turned them on erotically even though, politically, they fervently disapproved of it. Other men conceded that their preference for the company of women hinged on endowing them with stereotypic "compassion" and "sensitivity." Some of the women acknowledged that they tended automatically to see *all* men as the enemy, even though many of the men in GAU had shown genuine sympathy for the feminist struggle.

Andrea Dworkin, with whom I'd earlier gotten friendly, gave an angry, intransigent rap against women working in "integrated" organizations. When some of the other women replied that the goal *was* feasible and in this case desirable because the consciousness of most (though certainly not all) of the men in GAU was higher than average, Andrea insisted that "our sense of primary emergency does not coincide; for women, feminism takes precedence as an issue over homosexuality." But why should that prevent us, I asked, from combining forces where our concerns genuinely did coincide—as surely they did on campuses, where gay men and lesbians shared similar discrimination because of their same-gender sexual orientation. Even if the hope that we could work together was slim, didn't we owe it to ourselves to seize the possibility instead of presuming failure? At some point gay men and lesbian feminists *would* be able to combine their efforts, and that point might just be now.

I would subsequently come to feel still more strongly that a natural alliance between lesbians and gay men did exist, even though the two subcultures were in some important ways at variance (for example, in the greater value many lesbians placed on monogamy and permanent pair-bonding). Lesbians, in my view, were far more nonconforming in their gender roles and much more marginal in the culture than were heterosexual women, and that gender nonconformity and cultural marginality were precisely what connected lesbians to gay men. That connection, however, had been infrequently recognized and had rarely gotten translated into sustained political alliances.

What had prevented the alliance from maturing, in my opinion, was a growing denial on the part of many gay men—and particularly the white, middle-class contingent that had already come to dominate the organized political movement—of their own marginality and gender nonconformity. Many of these middle-class men might not in fact play stereotypic male/female roles in their relationships, or might luxuriate in the anonymous, promiscuous pleasures of the baths and the backroom bars, yet would publicly insist—and even in their own psyches continue to believe—that they were "just folks." The wish to buy into heterosexual white male privilege over an honest avowal of the actual dimensions of their differentness would increasingly come to take precedence for many gay men. Seeing that eagerness to conform to traditional male roles and institutions, many politically minded lesbians would choose to keep a wary distance—and to ally instead with the feminist movement.

After months of further discussion, the women in GAU finally proposed that we list the organization's *first* purpose as the desire "to combat oppression against women." Several men angrily attacked the proposal. The women, they said, were "demanding impossible proofs that they were welcome," and their proposal, if adopted, would make GAU a mere appendage to the feminist movement. Despite the opposition, the resolution was voted on and carried by a large majority. Even so, the gender issue continued to agitate the group. At the following meeting, one of the men who had opposed the resolution patronizingly announced that he hoped its passage "would ensure *no* further discussion of the woman question—we have *important* work to do." Some of the women took that comment as proof that the men in GAU had no intention of honoring the commitment they had just made, and a few, including Andrea, walked out.

As we prepared for the conference, the volatility of our meetings sometimes made us doubt whether we could hold together as an organization, let alone carry off a successful event. Not only did the role of women in GAU continue to agitate our working sessions, but the issue of bisexuality soon proved divisive as well. I basically agreed with those who argued that to have sex with both genders in the same way—to be *always* dominant, *never* yielding—worked against the realization that we contain many, sometimes contradictory selves. But my traditional side wanted to relegate bisexuals to some distant category of indecision, wanted to see their lifestyle not as a function of free-spirited polymorphous perversity but rather as a paralysis of will, an impaled inability to break away from the security of a traditional marriage and take on the still onerous image of being homosexual.

It was precisely that argument that raged within GAU. Most of our group regarded bisexuality with suspicion. It was a cop-out, they argued, a failure of nerve. It rendered being gay provisional, made it seem a varying impulse rather than a steady state. But that attitude also struck me as simplistic and I went with the minority side of the debate, with the view that a bisexual capacity was probably intrinsic to human nature (before socialization bred it out of most of us). Still, I cautioned that such an assumption—seemingly on the side of human liberation—could become the latest "scientific" dictum used to intimidate and control "deviants"—in this case exclusive homosexuals *and* heterosexuals. Having been made to feel guilty for most of my life about my homosexuality, I was trying not to yield too readily to the new cultural imperative that threatened to instill guilt instead for *exclusive* homosexuality.

By October, with a hundred last-minute chores to be done, we put aside high philosophy and grappled with the immediate issues of registration forms and coffee cake. Though we still had no idea how many people would show up, acceptances to speak arrived from Edgar Z. Friedenberg, Wilson Carey McWilliams, Barbara Gittings, and Richard Howard, and their likely drawing power seemed to guarantee at least a minimal turnout.

Barbara Gittings and I were chosen as the keynote speakers. In the weeks preceding the conference, I put in long hours preparing my remarks, going through several drafts, determined to get it right, to speak my mind as fully and cogently as possible.

On the morning of November 23, the members of GAU gathered early and nervously at the City University of New York's John Jay College, the site of the conference. The vast lobby looked ominously empty, and as we set up the registration tables and took our assigned places behind them, we anxiously wondered whether we hadn't over-reached ourselves.

But then they started to come, even before the official 9:00 A.M. opening time for registration, and in a steady, happily noisy stream that continued for hours, overwhelming the registration tables, throwing the organizers into a tizzy of delight. In the end, 320 people actually registered, and it was clear that another hundred or so, preferring not to sign their names to anything, simply milled anonymously about, surreptitiously sitting in on an occasional workshop or panel. Equally gratifying, more than 70 women showed up—far more than we had dared hope. Throughout the two-day conference, a separate women's caucus met at regular intervals, and at the end a majority (35 to 22), satisfied that GAU was at least not *blatantly* sexist, formally voted to affiliate.

When it came time for my keynote address, I mounted the podium with my heart in my mouth. I began by telling the overflow crowd that "a seemingly absurd phrase" had been haunting me ever since I began preparing my remarks: "Honored Rabbi, dear parents, relatives, and friends . . ." The phrase was the opening of my bar mitzvah speech, delivered at age thirteen to the congregation of Sinai Temple.

That speech had marked my official rite of passage to manhood, and the phrase had haunted me, I said, because "today, too, is a rite of passage. Not for me alone, but for us together—not into manhood or womanhood as those states have been traditionally defined; not sanctified by supernatural doctrine; not blueprinted by centuries of ritualized behavior; not greeted by kinship rejoicing and social acceptance; not marked by the extension of fellowship into the established adult community"—but nonetheless a rite of passage, that historic point in time when gay women and men decided to organize themselves around their skills, using them to fight homophobia, to protest the notion that same-gender love and lust affront the laws of nature, to place ourselves "in the forefront of the newest and to my mind most far-reaching revolution: the recharacterization of human sexuality."

I expressed the hope that the conference would mark the beginning of "the long march through those particular academic disciplines and institutions with which we find ourselves affiliated." But marching, I warned, "is notoriously hard work. And institutions are notoriously resistant." Neither dedication nor competence guaranteed success. In the short run, they probably guaranteed heightened resistance. "Because we challenge the exclusive heterosexual lifestyle by which the majority in this country all at once defines biologic truth, social necessity, and personal essence, our work will be difficult and frustrating. Because we are asserting our own worth and our special perspective, the work can be joyful."

But, I further warned, self-worth was not a function of self-congratulation: "If we mean seriously to challenge sexual stereotypes, we cannot assume any automatic truths. If we wish to inaugurate a profound debate on sexuality, we cannot set the topics or terms, nor announce in advance the nature of the conclusions. Nor can we afford to dismiss out of hand information or arguments that might discomfit our own theoretical models—we cannot, that is, if 'liberation' is to be more than a slogan and 'revolution' more than a posture."

As a case in point, I argued that we should welcome, not shun, current research investigating whether homosexuality had a hormonal or genetic component, even though we recognized that the scientific world's continuing concern with the "causes" of homosexuality was propelled by the assumption that homosexuality was an "error" to be corrected. As scholars, I said, we must never support the suppression or avoidance of evidence—"not under the most severe ideological pressure nor in the name of the most sublime political advantage." Our function was to welcome research and then to insist that it not be misused for repressive purposes. If, for example, future studies did prove that homosexuality had a genetic component, we would need insistently to remind the scientific world that that discovery merely provided insight into how certain sexual patterns got formed, *not* whether a particular pattern was "good" or "bad"—the latter was a moral judgment reflecting cultural, not scientific, imperatives.

I then turned in my speech to a consideration of the risks and gains of "coming out." I spoke of the risk of losing jobs or never being hired; the risk of laying ourselves open to categorization as that "thing"—a homosexual; the risk of our public avowal being treated as a vaguely unclean bit of exhibitionism. In my own case, I reported, the risks had proved minimal because of my secure, tenured position. I "stood in awe," I said, "of the courage of those students and untenured faculty who are coming out in increasing numbers; indeed, the untenured among us—those with the most to lose, as the world measures loss—have been setting the pace for their more privileged and protected colleagues."

Though the risks were heavy, I went on, they were perhaps inescapable by-products of becoming political, "of openly uniting with others—no less frightened, complex and private—to end the common oppression." And the personal gains of doing so were profound: the quieting of self-doubt, the comfort of becoming part of a community. That emerging community would be shaped, I cautioned, as much by process as by ideology—as much by how coworkers treated each other as by how they fronted on the world.

The internal feuding and divisions that already characterized the gay movement were, I submitted, to some extent unavoidable: the diversity of lifestyles among gay people required a diversity of expression. Besides, we were in the ambivalent position of being products of the same set of cultural values that we were organizing to protest against—"values that confuse maleness with machismo, femaleness with docility, bisexuality with indecision, and sexuality with orgasm."

But if the gay movement was destined to be marked by controversy, perhaps it need not, I argued, be marked by mutual recrimination and contempt. And I used the close of my speech to make a plea that we "at least try to proceed as friends reinforcing each other's confidence, instead of as adversaries assailing each other's deviations. The former builds community, the latter perpetuates powerlessness. The one does the work of the revolution, the other the work of the oppressor."

My hope for GAU in particular, and the gay movement in general, I concluded, "is that we can serve as a genuine alternative to the sexist models that dominate our culture; that we will refuse to talk of human beings—gay or straight—as single impulses, fixed essences, judgable objects; that we will offer, in opposition to the current vision of homogenized humanity, our celebration of human diversity.

"The goal is utopian, and must partly fail. But only utopian goals, I believe, will allow us partly to succeed."

Just how utopian was amply demonstrated in the immediate aftermath of the conference. Six of us, three men and three women, had been elected at the conference as GAU's steering committee. At our first meeting a month later, one of the men didn't show up at all and the second arrived stoned, launched into a lyric account of how much he was turning on a woman friend in bed—"she's letting herself go enough to moan and make noises"—and suggested that we prepare *now* for the eventual split of GAU into male/female factions. It was as if our enemies had sent in an *agent provocateur.* The women were furious at what amounted to a caricature sexist monologue, but decided, "for now," to try to get done the organizational work for which we had been empowered. How long they would remain committed to GAU, however, remained to be seen.

In the weeks and months following the conference, moreover, as committees and rhetoric proliferated apace, the danger loomed that GAU would simply turn into one more liberal academic talkfest. Gay academics, it became apparent, were academics first and gays second— that is, they loved to talk and argue; were cautious by inclination and training; shied away from class analysis, confrontational politics, and interracial cooperation; and were wedded to mainstream notions—petition and pressure the government for legislative action—of how to achieve social change.

Indeed, by 1974 the gay movement in general was heading into the same set of interlocking dilemmas that have characterized protest movements throughout our history. How to prevent a radical impulse from degenerating into reformist tinkering? How to mobilize a constituency for substantive change when most of the members of that constituency prefer to focus energies on winning certain limited concessions, like civil rights legislation, and show little interest in joining with other dispossessed groups to press for systemic social restructuring? How to appeal to a country on behalf of an oppressed minority when the country's instincts are deeply conservative, when, in the aftermath of the black struggle and the Vietnam War, it was sick to death of moral demands, when it smugly assumed its prejudices and values were somehow divinely ordained?

Knowing that my own expectations were always too high, I tried to resist feeling discouraged. But that was hard to do in the face of continuing hostility both within and without the movement. It hurt when the leading gay literary magazine, *Gay Sunshine,* printed a dismissive article on the conference, claiming that the large attendance was simply due to the academic penchant for networking ("They were looking for contacts . . . their gayness a gimmick to push their careers"). And it was sobering when the head of the American Association of Teachers of French (and publisher of the *French Review*), in declining to print a notice of GAU activities, sent us this bit of invective: "Please do not expect any cooperation from our organization for the publicizing of your philosophy of life. Self-restraint is one of the necessary qualities of all mature adults, and pampering, publicizing, and advocating a weakness such as yours would be a pathetic indication of the decline of our society."

Infighting among our own ranks would prove at least as frustrating and take as large a toll as would the struggle against homophobia in the outside world. GAU's second conference, in 1974, drew some six hundred people, and by 1975 the organization had broadened from its New York City base to additional chapters in Boston, Philadelphia and Ann Arbor (and, subsequently, in Chicago, Los Angeles and San Francisco as well). All the standard signs of success were present. Yet within a year of GAU's founding, I had developed a queasy feeling that the victory might be pyrrhic. From the beginning, GAU had drawn many more men than women, and the women continued to express disappointment in the lack of feminist consciousness among many of the men.

Some of the GAU men, myself included, self-identified as radicals; we not only agreed with the feminist analysis, but also with the criticism already being sounded by radicals outside the university that the middle-class white male mentality dominant in GAU meant the organization was in danger of replicating rather than challenging the academic world's patriarchal attitudes, hierarchies and rituals—right down to constructing its conferences around "panels," a format likely to perpetuate already suspect divisions between "experts" and audience, teachers and students, haves and have-nots. Instead of working to broaden standard definitions of what intellectual work *was,* and to break the connections between academic research and established bastions of power, GAU was, so the critique went, in danger of becoming such a bastion itself (or at least it seemed to be earnestly trying to).

Sympathetic to these warnings and complaints, I decided, when asked to give the concluding speech at the second GAU conference, to use the occasion as a vehicle for talking openly about my own fear that the organization was moving in dubious directions.

I expressed disappointment, first of all, that while GAU was largely male, few *tenured* male faculty had affiliated. I suggested that we probably needed to face the fact "that in a very real sense a generation of gay men has largely been lost to us—that they have been superbly, probably irretrievably indoctrinated and cowed by the patriarchal culture. If community *is* to come, the work and rewards alike are going to belong to the young."

What I didn't point out, and probably should have, was that there weren't enough *non*-tenured faculty involved with GAU either. Anyone who wanted to attend a GAU function had been welcome—there was no other way to build the organization—so as time went on, GAU had become increasingly attractive to well-educated gay white men looking for a congenial environment in which to come out and to find partners and friends. After the first year, these men probably out-numbered the graduate students and junior faculty who actually had university affiliations. Which meant that GAU was handicapped nearly from the outset in its specific mission to change the climate on the country's campuses.

In my closing speech at the second GAU conference in 1974, I also expressed discomfort over how much of the organization's energy dur-ing the previous year had gone into social events and consciousness-raising sessions. I realized how necessary such activities were: "For most people consciousness-raising is a needed prelude to active polit-ical commitment. And continuing social contact is a valuable device for keeping that commitment human—oriented to the needs of peo-ple rather than to the dictates of ideology."

But the *amount* of time invested in social events and CR sessions, I argued, had been excessive to the point of self-indulgence. True, much of the consciousness-raising work had come about in response to crit-icism from GAU women that many of the gay men were sexist; yet sexism had not been consistently addressed during most of the CR sessions. And except for the issue of sexism, I wasn't convinced that we needed as much consciousness-raising as we were lavishing upon our-selves.

Most of us were college-educated, middle-class, and white—in other words, as I pointed out, "already over-privileged when compared with the majority of our gay brothers and sisters." And most of us, I added, perhaps overstating, "are in better shape psychologically than we sometimes care to admit to ourselves. The argument that we 'have to get our heads together before we can do any political work' can become a standing rationale for doing nothing: our psyches are somehow never quite ready, our motors never quite tuned up. I think a lot of this has to do with American perfectionism, and even more to do with male selfishness."

We were in danger of talking too much and doing too little. And talking, moreover, about a limited set of issues. We had heard almost nothing during the second conference—indeed, during the whole second year—about the class and race divisions that characterized the gay community no less than the society at large. It was time to face those divisions, I argued, and to do something about their root causes. As matters currently stood, we were in danger of becoming an organization that gave a conference once a year. "And at that, a conference modeled rather closely on those genteel gatherings we're already familiar with in our respective professional caucuses."

I also voiced concern over the contempt I had heard expressed for those whose style differed from that of the gay mainstream—for bisexuals, transvestites and transsexuals, and for those involved in sadomasochism. That intolerance, I said, was to me tantamount to playing "a version of the same game the larger society plays with us. Namely: 'Either do it *our* way or be prepared to find yourself ostracized.' It comes down to the same contempt for individual differences that we deplore in the culture as a whole. If we try to humiliate those who deviate from our norms, how do we protest when those who adhere to the heterosexual norm choose to hound and humiliate us? To my mind, we have to oppose *any* prescription for how consenting adults may or must make love."

I strained to conclude the speech on a more upbeat note, praising us for coming together and staying together, for at least beginning the work of combating homophobia in society at large and sexism within ourselves. And I talked glowingly about the potential contribution GAU could make toward the creation of a strong and richly diverse gay and lesbian community.

This closing pat on the head did little to dilute the considerable anger subsequently leveled at me for having stringently criticized the white male contingent that dominated GAU councils. I was surprised at some of it, and particularly at the letter I got from the writer George Whitmore, himself on the left and a friend. George (the author of *The Confessions of Danny Slocum* and *Nebraska*, who died of AIDS in 1989) took me to task for what he characterized as my "ill-advised and over-stated" remarks, and made passing, scornful reference to "bisexual chic." That, I wrote back, struck me as precisely the sort of "reductive phrase for conveniently demeaning the lifestyle of others" that I had been protesting in the first place.

George and I soon patched things up; our politics *were* basically similar. The larger problem was that our shared vision of a broad-gauged movement devoted to substantive social change, a vision forged during the radical optimism of the sixties, had itself faltered and fragmented in the changed climate of the early seventies. Globally, *the* issue for the vast majority of the world's population was still the one that had engaged socialists for generations: how to ensure freedom from material want, how to improve the terrible conditions of daily life endured by most people. But little progress had been made toward that goal—and by the early seventies little will seemed to remain for pursuing it.

Richard Nixon may have been forced from power but, as I saw it, his arrogant assumption of our entitlement to dictate the affairs of the globe remained alive and well in national councils, accompanied, as it had long been, by a firm commitment to the "traditional" values of male power, black inferiority, and homosexual pathology. Mean-spir-ited, vindictive bigotry was flourishing anew in the land by the mid-seventies. Los Angeles police chief Ed Davis showed neither embarrassment nor hesitation in 1973 when he spoke out against law reforms that would extend rights to those "predatory creatures" called "gays." And the *Chicago Daily News* columnist Mike Royko seemed equally assured when, in a 1974 column entitled "Banana Lib," he described how "men in love with monkeys" were winning acceptance by "coming out of the cage."

GAU was not immune to the conservative national trend. A growing number of men with less than progressive views became more visible and active in the New York GAU, with the result that most of those (myself included) who self-defined as radical and who had founded the organization began to drift away. Almost all the women—who from the first had thrown in their lot with GAU uneasily and tentatively—became disaffected (with the growth of lesbian separatism, they were simultaneously withdrawing from other cogender gay organizations as well).

Probably the best-known of the conservative men who moved into prominence in GAU was Wayne Dynes, a professor of art history at Hunter College. He was surely among the most vocal. As early as the second GAU conference in 1974, Dynes had locked horns with Charlotte Bunch, a leading lesbian-feminist writer and organizer. In her speech to the conference that year, Charlotte had expressed the view that gay men insufficiently acknowledged the rights and needs of women. To end lesbian separatism, Bunch said, we had to end the reasons that had made separatism necessary: the failure of the gay movement to fight male supremacy.

Dynes indignantly replied that this was nothing more or less than an invitation to male self-flagellation. He was tired of being told what was wrong with him, he said, tired of "obligatory therapy" that at bottom undermined the self-esteem of gay men, and, he added ominously, he rejected any purported self-examination that came at the "expense of mind"—whatever that meant. Dynes insisted that GAU's proper mission was simple and straightforward: to pursue cases of antigay discrimination in academia and to increase the amount of reliable scholarship on gay lives.

Barbara Gittings, the longtime lesbian activist, also took issue with Charlotte, though the cordial tone of her criticism and her underlying wish to build bridges were light-years away from Dynes's sardonic divisiveness. Gittings deplored the growing mystique about "vast differences" between gay men and lesbians, fearing it would minimize our very real commonalities and thereby our ability to join forces against shared oppression. "Nothing would suit anti-homosexual bigots more," Gittings said, "than that we fragment." Separatism, she added, "seems to me uncomfortably close to the notion that anatomy is destiny."

Though I basically agreed with Charlotte, I shared some of Barbara's fears. In particular, I felt that Charlotte had failed to acknowledge that some gay men—not enough, certainly, and obviously not including Wayne Dynes and his growing cohort—had been trying to incorporate feminist values in their lives and work—almost certainly more gay men than straight men.

Yet basically I believed, with Charlotte, that fighting sexism had to become central to our movement work. Only an infusion of radical feminist insights, I believed, could keep the gay male movement from edging ever closer to a narrowly gauged agenda that would simply allow gay white men to take their place beside straight white men at the apex of privilege.

The gulf between Bunch and Dynes, and the positions they espoused, continued to widen. In a letter to me in 1975, Dynes characterized feminism as "a rickety ideology with an astonishing affinity for mythos . . . I believe it to be playing a parasitic and negative role in the gay movement." Two years after that, he launched a public assault on Bunch. In a letter to the national gay publication, *The Advocate*, Dynes characterized her as "virulently homophobic and man-hating," insisted she had a "considerable history of anti-male thinking" and even suggested that "her activities would make a good subject for investigation."

This seemed to me cranky even for Dynes. I decided his misogynistic outburst needed a response, and I wrote a letter of my own to *The Advocate*. I suggested that instead of "investigating" Bunch, Dynes might try investigating her writings. If he could "get beyond his own prejudgments," I wrote, he would find a wise and humane attempt "to point out how much *all* of us still adhere, at some semi-conscious level (to put it in the most favorable light) to patriarchal and hierarchical values—the very values that stand in the way of the psycho/sexual 'revolution' we call for out of the other side of our mouths. I suppose it's predictable that such insights would prove threatening to many. But the fault, dear Horatio (Dynes) is not in the stars but in ourselves."

Although intensively involved in the first two formative years of GAU, by the time the third annual conference came around in 1975, I had moved myself to the sidelines. Indeed, along with almost all the women and radical-minded men, I was more than halfway out the door, distressed at the increasingly mainstream (male) tone and goals of the organization. Perhaps those of us who dissented from that trend should have stayed and fought the good fight longer. But the odds seemed poor, our energy limited, and the need to get on with other work compelling.

The focus of my own energy had, by the early seventies, already gotten reinvested in a new organization, the National Gay Task Force . . .

B. THE NATIONAL GAY TASK FORCE

In October 1973, I had been asked to serve on the first board of directors of the National Gay Task Force (NGTF), and I readily agreed. Though pleased to lend my name and energy to NGTF—and its board of directors did turn out to be very much a working board—I had serious doubts about the new organization from the beginning. I set down my conflicted feelings in my diary:

> NGTF clearly wants to pattern itself on the ACLU or NAACP—which means it can make a valuable contribution, but in the liberal, reformist mode: "let us in" rather than "let us show you new possibilities." Structurally, too . . . it's not clear in whose name we're speaking, the nature of the constituency, its ability (once existent) to implement decisions, to countermand the board. All hands assure me that a constituency (à la CORE or NOW) *will* develop and will have power. We'll see . . .

NGTF's limited frame of reference and practical-minded emphases offended the utopian side of my politics that had been shaped in the sixties and was devoted to the possibility of a revolution far more encompassing than the limited though important right to fall in love and have sex with members of one's own gender. Even if NGTF proved successful in its political strategy, I feared that the net effect might be to win recognition of gay people as a legitimate minority, but a minority wedded to dominant mainstream values. A new world would not be ushered in, but the old world reaffirmed—with the addition of a few prosperous, well-educated, middle-class, white queers.

But if my utopian side made me wary, other elements in the mix drew me in. For one thing, I saw few other available political options. After a fire of suspicious origin in October 1974 gutted the headquarters of the Gay Activist Alliance (GAA), it was reduced to a shadow organization. Minuscule gay socialist and anarchist groups did exist, and I felt closer to them philosophically than to the Task Force, but they were confined to a few dozen people, barely made a blip on the political screen and seemed doomed to ineffectuality.

But it wasn't simply for lack of options that I joined the Task Force board. I did have a strong practical side that coexisted with my utopianism and it attracted me to NGTF's can-do agenda. By the mid-seventies, with the country again heading into a right-wing deep-freeze, utopianism of any kind had scant chance of winning converts or making gains. Probably the most that gay activism could hope to accomplish in these years would be to win some limited (and desirable) legislative and judicial victories, and to expand its own subcultural institution-building.

A cumulative set of accomplishments did seem to be having some effect in slowly, very slowly, changing entrenched mainstream views that equated homosexuality with pathology or with what the pope in 1976 described as "a serious depravity." But if any number of gains in mainstream acceptance could be pointed to, they were often paralleled by demonstrable losses, making it difficult confidently to draw a positive balance.

Thus in 1974 a federal gay civil rights bill was introduced into Congress for the first time—a moment of real symbolic importance—but the legislation had few sponsors and no chance of passage. And although by 1976 sixteen states had repealed their sodomy laws (and by 1979 twenty-five had), the repeals mostly came about as the result of a general overhaul of penal codes—the result, that is, of a legal mindset changing in advance of public opinion. Similarly, two states and some forty cities had, by 1979, implemented job protection for gays and lesbians, but in most cases this was through executive order and confined to municipal and state employees.[1]

Similarly, the U.S. Civil Service Commission ruled in 1975 that homosexual applicants would no longer be *automatically* disqualified from employment, and a State Department directive in 1977 instituted a policy of considering gay job applicants on a case-by-case basis. But neither ruling could guarantee that such cases would be objectively evaluated and that an actual shift in hiring policy would result.

Not, that is, when the dominant climate in 1977 still allowed the City Council of New York to defeat a gay rights bill; let the national columnist George Will condemn gay rights ordinances as "part of the moral disarmament of society"; enabled the Toronto police to raid the offices of Canada's leading gay publication, *The Body Politic;* and allowed Florida governor Reubin Askew—who had a *liberal* reputation—to announce that he would not want "a known homosexual" teaching *his* children.

Not when vandals could ransack the feminist Diana Press in Oakland, California. Not when *The New York Times* could publish a virulently antigay op-ed piece, and then, when I protested it in a private letter to the editorial-page editor (whom I knew slightly), have her justify it to me as part of the paper's standing policy of trying "to give the full range of ideas a chance." Indeed, she added in her letter to me, the *Times* had the "obligation" to publish pieces "most thinking people" might not agree with. I acerbically replied that the "full range" was represented in *The Times* in regard to certain issues only and that it was hypocritical to claim comprehensiveness as a general policy: "You have given ample space," I wrote her, "to what someone has called 'Hitler's viewpoint' on homosexuality, but not on, say, blacks, Chicanos, women, et al. When was the last piece you ran arguing that the cranial size of blacks is on average smaller than that of whites? When the last piece debating whether Jewish greed is congenital or merely cultural? These views *are* held by a large number of Americans—probably at least as many as think gays are diseased or demented—but their opinions, *that* segment of the 'range,' has been carefully excluded." This time I got no reply.

The seventies did see real gains but they remained tentative, incomplete and—especially to those who were not white, did not live in big cities, did not hold secure jobs or salaries—of marginal significance or none at all.

No, heterosexuality remained decidedly the national measure of health, the sum of well-being. Even in liberal straight circles, homosexuality could be accommodated only when seen as a pale shadow of the superior heterosexual way. Any suggestion that homosexuals, with their special historical experience, had a unique and valuable perspective to contribute—especially in regard to nonconformist gender roles—was perceived (accurately) as a threat to the established psychosexual order and treated, at best, with uneasy, patronizing scorn. To insist, as the Gay Liberation Front had, back in 1970, that "we must release the homosexuality in heterosexuals and the heterosexuality in homosexuals" would be, in the mid-seventies, to talk into the wind.

Like so many others, I longed for less qualified progress, a more sweeping mitigation of straight bigotry and gay self-hatred. But to achieve that, my radical lobe insisted, required an across-the-board assault on the country's manifold inequities. To fight for anything less— to try to win rights within a profoundly corrupted system—was mere tinkering around the edges. Worse, to focus on a limited civil rights agenda that left institutionalized heterosexism and racism in place would simultaneously guarantee that such rights would never amount to more than superficial toleration *and* create a false expectation of full acceptance that would shore up the very system needing demolition. But the pragmatist (and optimist) in me kept responding, "To hold out for a full-scale revolution that, in this conservative, conformist country, is unlikely ever to come, is to surrender the chance of making at least *some* lives better now."

It was a debate—within me, within the country—that has never had a satisfying resolution. Did the effort to end the slave trade, by raising the value of those already enslaved, in fact rejuvenate the institution? Did the struggle to win the right to vote for women come at the expense of a more encompassing assault on gender roles? Did the nineteenth-century movement for an eight-hour workday sap—and thus ultimately betray—the Socialist effort to destroy a capitalist system in

which the brutalized many worked for the exorbitant profits and pleasures of the few?

In the face of immediate suffering, it is difficult *not* to want and to
work for piecemeal change. Where misery is rampant, visible and concrete, Revolution can seem a distant, even heartless abstraction.

No, the Task Force, with its limited civil rights agenda, its willingness to play ball with the heterosexual powers that be, was never going
to usher in a libidinal revolution that featured androgyny and polymorphous perversity as its starring attractions. But if NGTF could
achieve some legislative and judicial victories, that would at least
shrink the legitimate boundaries of public homophobic expression
(which is all civil rights legislation can ever do) and thereby reduce to
some extent the daily toll that hatred and violence took on gay and lesbian lives. Even more, perhaps, it would encourage gays and lesbians
to feel better about themselves, to band together for mutual support
and to work for a more hopeful future. That was surely not everything—but, just as surely, it was something. As I wrote in my diary
several years after joining the Task Force board, "For all NGTF's 'reformism,' it *is* at least reforming."

One must also remember the difficulty of the obstacles faced, the
entrenched homophobia that continued to circumscribe even the most
dedicated efforts; to remember, too, that many gay men and lesbians
were "otherwise engaged" in the seventies—the men with their pleasure domes, the women with building separatist institutions. An organization like the Task Force, which held to the vision (even though
sometimes failing to implement it in practice) of gay men and lesbians
continuing to work together, did so in the face of a divided community largely indifferent to politics.

Which isn't to say that the initial doubts I and others had had about
the Task Force were ever laid to rest. We would still involuntarily
twitch at the periodic charge that NGTF was an "elitist" organization
out of touch with the needs of ordinary lesbians and gays and their

grass-roots communities, and was unwilling or unable to embrace nonwhite or working-class cultures. In this regard, nothing made us more uneasy than when the West Coast millionaire David Goodstein (who had purchased the national gay publication, *The Advocate,* in 1974) expressed his favorable opinion of the Task Force. Goodstein was known to deplore radical gay "obstructionists" who might conceivably derail or delay our acceptance into the American mainstream—a theme he continued to pound home in his *Advocate* columns. Middle-class respectability was Goodstein's totem; he wanted those of us who might qualify (namely affluent white men) to take their place on the assembly line of the American Dream, and those of us who couldn't qualify, to get out of the (his) way. By 1979 Goodstein was claiming that "moderates" were responsible for all the movement's successes to date, and the "left-wing radicals" responsible for nothing but "noise . . . an enormous amount of friction in the gay community and a lot of unhappiness."

Several early resignations from the NGTF board hinged on racial issues. The first African-American member of the board, Jon L. Clayborne, stayed but a short time, making clear his dissatisfaction with efforts to involve Third World gays in the official movement and insisting that the elimination of racism in the gay world "should be as much a consideration" as the elimination of sexism. And Clayborne was certainly right that it was not. Thomas Dotton, another African American, wrote in an angry 1975 article, "Nigger in the Woodpile," that after five years of working in the movement he still found racism "unseen" and had become fed up with "the endless apologies and excuses." Or, as the black lesbian writer Pat Parker put it in her poem "Have You Ever Tried to Hide?", the white lesbian's foot might well be smaller than the white man's, "but it's still on my neck."

Just as in the early feminist movement, the early gay movement could not seem to focus its attention on issues relating to race and class. Its *in*attention kept most nonwhites (and most nonurban working-class whites as well) unwilling to set aside their own agendas and their sense of multiple identities and loyalties in favor of a single-issue political movement. Even a radical publication like *Gay Community News* (which began in Boston in 1973), though devoted to broad analyses and alliances, and with a substantial readership of eight thousand by the mid-seventies, proved unable to attract more than the occasional nonwhite staff person.

Besides Clayborne, who stayed just briefly, the only other African American on a Task Force board that by 1976 had thirty members was Betty Powell, an instructor at the Brooklyn College school of education; she was soon elected cochair. And before the end of the decade, the board had implemented as formal goals that a minimum of 20 percent of the body should consist of minority members and that the ratio between men and women should be fifty-fifty. But the awareness that such goals were desirable was not tantamount to meeting them; as regards minority inclusion, especially, the accomplishment was (and in most gay organizations remains) woefully incomplete.

Disagreements over gender-related issues continually agitated board meetings. By the mid-seventies I had formed friendships and a loose political alliance with several of the women on the board, especially Betty Powell and Charlotte Bunch. Our alliance was based on the shared perception that NGTF's continuing focus on winning powerful mainstream allies in order to foster a civil rights agenda was insufficient.

By then I had become convinced that the women of NGTF were far more impressive, politically and humanly, than the men. I was especially taken with Pokey Anderson from Houston, Jean Crosby from San Francisco, and Dorothy Riddle from Tucson; all three, I felt (as I wrote in my diary), had "a forceful grasp of the larger political context, the radical commitment that should underlie our reformist activities"—precisely what I felt was lacking in most of the men. But as I was told at the time (and since), I have a way—a deplorably "essentialist" way—of over-categorizing and overcriticizing "middle-class white men" (that is, people like myself) and, in contrast, overgeneralizing about the superior political insight and all-around wisdom of lesbians. I persist in this, I am told, even while well aware that the lesbian community has itself been racked with factionalism and ideological warfare through time. And so I try, like a good analysand, to work on my bias about the superior virtue of lesbians—of women in general. Yet it stubbornly holds.

By the mid-seventies, the women on the Task Force board had formed a women's caucus and had made it clear that the organization would henceforth function on a coalition ("women *plus* men") not a unity ("people") model. That might not represent the optimal hopes some of us—including some of the women—had, but it did represent the current reality of how gay men and lesbians could best work together.

The fact was that by then a significant portion of the lesbian community had concluded that the male-dominated gay political movement could not represent its needs. They were convinced that most gay men were mere reformists; were repelled by gay male rhetoric about the "wonders of promiscuity" and the "absurdity of monogamy"; and—at a time when cultural feminism, with its insistence on the fundamental differences between women and men, had eclipsed radical feminism within the women's movement—considered the "lurid" gay male style (which they sometimes exaggeratedly attributed to all gay men) as at odds with their own values. This did not mean, as many younger lesbians today assume, that the lesbian-feminists of the mid-seventies were antisex prudes. But it is true that they defined lesbianism less as a *sexual* identity (in contrast to the way most gay men regarded themselves) and more as one centered on their gender interests as women.

The women of NGTF were somewhat unusual in the mid-seventies in their continued willingness to work with gay men, but they were not willing to keep letting lesbian-feminist issues take a backseat to gay male ones. As Charlotte Bunch put it in a 1976 essay, "Lesbian-feminists assert that homosexual oppression is intricately connected to women's oppression through the patriarchal institutions of male supremacy and heterosexuality, and therefore heterosexism and sexism must be fought together."

This outraged Frank Kameny—who in the pre-Stonewall years had played a heroic, militant role—above all others. Frank would periodically explode during board meetings over the "intrusion" of feminist values. After a weekend board retreat in June 1976, I wrote in my diary, "Every time one of the women talked of the need to end lesbian invisibility or insisted upon the semantic propriety of 'gay men and lesbians,' Frank, leaping to apoplectic cue, would either shake his head with vigorous displeasure, mumble something about the 'fanaticism of revolutionaries,' or do some of his furious (and infuriating) speechifying about the need to maintain a clear separation between the feminist and gay movements."[2]

The hoped-for transformation of the Task Force proved tough sledding. And probably because, at bottom, transformation—personal or social—was not what most gay Americans (any more than most straight ones) have in mind. "We-want-in" politics were, and still are, far closer to what the majority of gays and lesbians desire than are the views of us self-styled radicals. Most gays, after all, see themselves—and want others to see them—as good mainstream Americans, believers in the essential "rightness" (indeed superiority) of Our Way; and NGTF's strategy of working through established channels for piecemeal change was, and is, entirely consonant with their own goals.

Attempting to remain at least marginally optimistic—for how else does one remain political?—I managed to find *a* bright side even when the Supreme Court in the 1976 "Doe v. Commonwealth" decision essentially declared that the states could constitutionally punish sodomy between consenting adults; that night I wrote in my diary "The decision does make clear—and most gays need to see this, too—that we're not struggling against a phantom oppression or overstating the obstacles in the path of acceptance. Despite the backlash, I find it hard to believe we'll be thrown back (in New York at least) to the days of widespread police entrapment. Indeed, the establishment clampdown is an almost infallible sign that a certain level of change *has* been achieved."

And I tried remembering two other things as well: That movements for social change are always subject to fluctuating fortunes; the graph never traces linear upward progress but rather peaks and valleys of varying, maddening, unpredictable duration. And that for all the "one step forward, one step back" nature of the gay (or any) advance in the United States, progress here seemed infinitely greater than elsewhere in the world. In Barcelona in 1977, the police fired rubber bullets into a gay pride march. In London that same year, the editor of *Gay News* was convicted on charges of blasphemy. In 1978, when Australia finally managed to field a gay rights march of two thousand people (more than a quarter million turned out that year in San Francisco), the police moved in and made arrests for "indecent behavior." And in Iran in 1978, six men were executed by firing squad for the crime of homosexuality—with thousands of additional executions to follow under the Khomeini regime.

—*excerpted from* Cures *(1991) and*
Midlife Queer *(1996)*

Sex and the Military: The Matlovich Case (1976)

Leonard Matlovich, tech sergeant in the Air Force, was in 1975 relieved of his duties after coming out publicly as a homosexual. A Langley Air Force Base hearing in late September of that year was the first round in a protracted struggle for reinstatement, a struggle that ended in 1981, when Matlovich accepted a cash settlement of $160,000 in back pay, a promotion, and an honorable discharge. Matlovich died of AIDS in 1988. The headstone he chose for his grave reads: "A Gay Veteran. When I was in the military, they gave me a medal for killing two men, and a discharge for loving one."

To write this 1975 essay, I talked at length with Matlovich and sat in on every session of his week-long hearing that year at Langley Air Force Base in Hampton, Virginia.

If there has ever been a son of mid-America, it is Lenny Matlovich. He believes in God, duty, his country, monogamy, competition and hard work. He volunteered for three tours of duty in Vietnam because "that's where my nation needed me." He erected an eighteen-foot flagpole in his front yard. He voted for Goldwater. He always did more than his share on the job, pushing himself to excel—and then took on additional jobs. He was never comfortable with sexuality; in his conservative Catholic family, "anything relating to sex was not discussed." His politics were right-wing: when the Air Force became integrated, he protested being housed with "niggers." He considered Walter Cronkite a "flaming liberal."

That is, until two years ago, when Leonard Matlovich, aged thirty, lost his virginity. To a man.

One doesn't want to claim too much for the transforming power of sex—or even of self-acceptance—but if the causes can't be neatly charted, Matlovich today is clearly a different man from the superpatriot of a few years back. He is now deeply ashamed of the stand he took against integration, and his eyes water when he notes the irony that blacks at Langley have formed his chief support group since he publicly came out. On the front door of his apartment a placard reads: "Trust in God—She Will Provide."

Some of his earlier values remain intact or have only marginally changed. He still disapproves of those who would "destroy the country." He would still "turn in immediately any gay individual harming security." He says that if he had the choice—and he is adamant that homosexuals never have the choice—he would rather be straight (when he first realized he was gay and before coming out, he "cried a lot, prayed a lot," begged the Lord to "make me like everybody else"). He still believes in monogamy, still hopes to find the "one right person." He still insists that duty impelled his decision to come out: he had sworn to uphold the Constitution, with its guarantees of equal rights for all citizens. He still loves the Air Force and is still optimistic that he will be allowed to serve in it.

The board of inquiry convened at Langley in late September 1975 for a week-long "fact-finding hearing" (the Air Force's preferred phrase for "trial") has ended with the recommendation that Matlovich be discharged, but he plans a string of subsequent appeals. The final outcome of those appeals will not, it seems to me, hinge on the human or legal merits of the case, but on certain assumptions about sexual behavior—the causes and permissible limits of erotic expression—that dominated (albeit unintentionally) his first hearing and seem likely to dominate subsequent hearings, however concealed by the rational mode of courtroom discourse.

Before attending the hearing I had expected and hoped to see a simple morality play, having already cast the leading heroes and villains. The event has proven more complex. The defense witnesses did not embody all available enlightenment and persuasiveness, nor did the prosecution prove to have a monopoly on condescension and confusion.

On the very first day of the trial the chief attorney for the defense, David Addlestone, conducted a *voir dire*—an examination of the jury to determine its impartiality. The jury—the "board of inquiry"—consisted of five majors and colonels. Each was questioned separately, out of hearing of the others, and it seemed to me that all—give or take the usual quotient of human evasion—were candid, even earnestly so, in their responses (though the higher the rank, the more monosyllabic the replies). Four of the five said they had read little or nothing about homosexuality. All five felt that their religious training, Protestant in every case, had not influenced their views on homosexuality.

That was the first time I blanched. True, Roman Catholicism and Orthodox Judaism have been more explicit and virulent in their homophobia, but it's also true that until very recently all institutional religion in the West has uniformly viewed same-gender sex as sinful. That these Air Force officers insisted to the contrary did not seem to me part of a deliberate intention to deceive but rather a lack of self-consciousness about the sources and extent of their own ideology.

I say this because they revealed that ideology with almost ingratiating innocence. In response to particular questions relating to the "immorality" or "sickness" of homosexuality, the board, taken as a whole, was decidedly more inclined to the former view—suggesting a greater adherence to the traditional religious rather than the traditional psychiatric model of homosexuality (though a full 50 percent of all answers were some version of "I don't know").

The liberal civilian press corps tut-tutted a great deal among themselves over the officers' equivocation, ignorance and bigotry, and I joined in the general derision. Still, "I don't know" isn't the worst state of mind with which to approach some of the formidable questions about sexuality that came up at the hearing and that are currently at issue in the culture—assuming, of course, that the officers' uncertainty wasn't feigned. My own impression is that it was not. Which isn't to say that they sounded enlightened, but only that in their unenlightenment they're in the mainstream of public opinion and that some of them, in certain particulars, seemed a little in advance of it. It's too easy to ascribe the verdict in the Matlovich case to the "retrograde mentality" of the military—too easy because this interpretation far too casually disparages "them" and far too conveniently congratulates "us." Through some limited private soundings I learned that at least three members of the board agreed during the deliberations that Article 125 of the Uniform Code of Military Justice (which forbids "any unnatural carnal copulation") was "ludicrous, antiquated" and perhaps unconstitutional. If the Article indeed offended their sense of what is just and reasonable, one might argue that they acted with insufficient courage in abiding by the narrow parameters that the Judge had set. But it would be more difficult to argue that homophobia pure and simple was responsible for their decision to recommend Matlovich's discharge.

What was most fascinating about the trial, what gives it a larger significance, were the broad questions, and the attempts to answer them, raised during the hearings about our current assumptions regarding gender identification and sexual orientation. The defense attorneys called a number of expert witnesses whose testimony provided intriguing insight into the range of scientific opinion on sexual behavior. What does science currently claim to know, the specialists were asked, about the "causes" of homosexuality? (Three of the board members, during the *voir dire,* ascribed it, without hesitation, to "environment.") Is there a critical point at which sexual orientation becomes fixed? If so, is that point during gestation? Within the first few years of life? During adolescence? Later still? Never? Are erotic patterns, once fixed, subject to change? If so, marginally or totally?—and as a result of what experiences? Is "bisexuality" a modish fantasy or a biological reality? What is "perverse" in sexual behavior, and what is "normal"? Does society have any stake in insisting on the maintenance of certain standards of sexual "morality," and, if so, through what agency should intervention proceed?

The experts testified on these questions with a good deal of conviction, impressive erudition and a notable paucity of "I don't knows." Much information was elegantly packaged and dispensed, various "myths" challenged, new "truths" revealed. Those rooting for Matlovich were greatly heartened. A more humane world seemed indubitably on the way. And yet . . . some of the new truths seemed less than conclusive; some of the certitudes seemed to conflict with each other; the will to do good was sometimes more apparent than the hard evidence needed to prove that good must be done. The testimony of John Money was the most significant case in point.

The famous head of the psychohormonal research unit at Johns Hopkins, author of a dozen books and hundreds of articles, president of the Society for the Scientific Study of Sex, John Money was the most commanding figure to appear as a defense witness. Austere, lucid, formidably at ease, he performed with the taut resolve and polished reserve that transport all fans of Sherlock Holmes into instant rapture. The courtroom seemed full of such fans. By the end of Money's testimony, there wasn't an empty notebook in the room—or an unscrambled brain. The one moment when I felt any rush of sympathy for the prosecutor was when—a weak smile on his face, his shoulder tilted deferentially—he asked Money the addlepated question, "Is it true that the closer one is to genius, the more likely one is to be homosexual?" Money flashed a charming smile. "I don't subscribe to that theory."

What Money said he did subscribe to is worth attending in some detail, for his views carry enormous (though not uncontested) weight in the scientific community. And they have also—thanks largely to the semi-popular book *Man & Woman, Boy & Girl,* coauthored with Anke Erhardt—been widely disseminated in educated circles. Money's research in endocrinology and his studies of transsexualism have had special impact on the ancient controversy over the comparative influence of nature (the biological givens) and nurture (the social expectations) in determining personality structure.[1]

The thrust of Money's testimony seemed on the side of predestination—physiological, not divine. At one point he went so far as to say that "once the die is cast hormonally, it cannot be reversed." Unfortunately, he never made clear what "it" referred to: the establishment of "gender identification" ("I am male"; "I am female") or the development of "sexual orientation" ("I am erotically aroused by members of the same—or opposite—sex"). His references veered between the two without specifically mentioning either. "Prenatal hormones," he said early on, "can predispose bi- or homosexual development" (a reference, clearly, to sexual orientation). Later he declared that we are "psychologically undifferentiated or neutral" until roughly eighteen months of age (a reference, apparently, to the onset of gender identification). At yet a third point, he claimed that "by adulthood, we don't have the potential any longer to be other than what we are—homosexual, bisexual or heterosexual" (a matter, again, of sexual orientation).

A trial, of course (even when called a "fact-finding hearing") is essentially a political, not a scientific, occasion. Legal strategy, the pressure of the moment, the eagerness to be helpful, the lack of opportunity to expand and qualify remarks, all encourage simplification and even misstatement; indeed, they may be in evidence in direct proportion to the witness's humanity. All that said, Money's apparent emphasis during his testimony on the paramount importance of biology came as a considerable surprise to anyone familiar with his writings on the subject.

If Money meant that the "die" of gender identification cannot be reversed after a certain age, then what he said on the stand was consonant with his published findings. His work with transsexuals (those convinced, contrary to all anatomical and genetic indices, that they are members of the opposite gender) has persuasively demonstrated that after age five, at the very latest, an individual's psychological conviction about his or her gender cannot be changed—just as he has also shown that in an *infant* the "die" *can* be recast (in one of his most famous examples, a male baby accidentally castrated was not only successfully reassigned as a female, but, under the pressure of stereotypical socialization, became a little girl obsessed with cleanliness, hair ribbons and dolls).

But if Money meant to imply during his stated testimony that the die of *sexual orientation* cannot be recast, then he would have to square that statement with the anthropological data he has himself often cited, data that suggest that we all have "a bisexual capability which is either *culturally* encouraged or suppressed." Money's emphasis on the stand on the congenital and the predetermined is important, I think, because it reflects a general resurgence, a renewed acceptability in our culture, of the belief that biological considerations are the basic ones in any explanation of human behavior.[2] This shift in cultural consciousness—it is nothing less—is especially startling in a country that for so long has insisted on the malleability of behavior and has touted the ability to "change" as a cardinal social value (even as a test of personal authenticity).

Like most "revolutions in consciousness," this latest one seems less a breakthrough into the previously unknown, than a retreat to the recently forgotten. The vocabulary ("bias on the neural substratum"), the units of measurement (neonatal "startles") and the techniques (pituitary grafts), all seem miracles of modernity. But thus far the modern mountain has brought forth only the proverbial mouse—sorry, rhesus monkey. And it seems to be squeaking an ancient tune. For in fact many of the assumptions about sexual behavior that are suddenly prominent again are the same ones that guided the earliest—only a hundred years ago—self-conscious theorizing about sex. In the late nineteenth century, almost all sexologists agreed that male homosexuality (women, as usual, were rarely considered) had a constitutional base; behavior was inborn, not acquired. Before Freud, almost no one (the French psychologist Binet may be the one important exception) stressed the possible importance of environmental factors. Considerable disagreement did exist as to which constitutional factors were most salient and which secondary symptoms most revealing. Among the favored "causes" were "embryonic malformation," "degenerated genes," a "woman's brain," epilepsy and anemia, climate and altitude, masturbation, an absence of spermatozoa and the presence of "genital nerves" around the anus. Among the most telltale symptoms were small glans, a smooth rectum, a penchant for dirty books and luxurious living, left-handedness, an inability to spit and whistle.

Despite these disputes over the distinguishing organic and somatic marks of male homosexuality, almost universal agreement prevailed that the condition itself was incurable (one couldn't be cured of that which was innate) nor should one be punished—and this marked a humane advance—for that which was involuntary. What *could* be expected of the afflicted was that they remain celibate (a position Norman Mailer, that revolutionist of modern consciousness, has more recently flirted with in *The Presidential Papers*). Should willpower prove insufficient to the task, the nineteenth-century physician could recommend such popular devices of the day as the spiked penile ring—guaranteed to discourage any threat of tumescence.

Far removed from 1975 and the climate surrounding the Matlovich case? Hardly. Not only did the hearings demonstrate that the congenital theory of homosexuality is rapidly gaining ground again, but the government's attorney actually invoked the nineteenth-century remedy. "Sergeant Matlovich," he asked, "would you sign a contract never to practice homosexuality again?" Matlovich blanched in disbelief—then declined.

On the fourth day of the testimony Dr. Wardell Pomeroy, Kinsey's associate and coauthor, took the stand. A man of less intellectual brilliance than John Money, Pomeroy's presence—warm, rumpled, grandfatherly—was altogether more benign. His testimony coincided with Money's on many counts, but was most provocative when it did not. The two agreed on much: that Matlovich the individual was stable, bright and self-assured; that the great majority of homosexuals did not wish to "convert" heterosexuals; that they are not prone to molesting children; that they stand up as well (or badly) as anyone else under pressure.

When asked whether they viewed homosexuality as "unnatural" or "immoral," both men concurred that the terms had to be clarified before the question could be considered. "Strictly speaking," Money said, "anything that occurs in nature is 'natural'—and homosexuality is recorded among all primates." He aptly redefined "morality" as "ideology"—the value set and rules of behavior that characterize a given culture at a given time. "In our civilization since Christianity," he conceded, "we've chosen to define homosexuality as immoral," but "society is now in the process of making up its mind whether this long-standing stigma any longer makes sense—just as it has recently made up its mind to take mad people out of dungeons and to stop treating left-handedness as a disease." (Another witness, Michael Valente, Professor of Religious Studies at Seton Hall University, testified to the shift currently taking place within the churches themselves: not only are they moving away—at a glacial pace—from the view that homosexuality is immoral, but away from the Augustinian/Thomist tradition which holds that all sex is tainted with evil, the evil merely counteracted—not nullified—when the partners intend procreation.)[3]

Pomeroy amplified on possible definitions of "normalcy." The statistical norm simply means "what is common"—what more than half the people do. By that standard, using the familiar Kinsey finding that about a third of all adult American males have had a homosexual experience to orgasm, male homosexuality is on the borderline of "normalcy." If we use as our gauge "What do we as mammals do?" then the verdict on homosexuality is "normal," since it is "ubiquitous" among mammals. According to our Judeo-Christian cultural values and legal pronouncements, homosexuality is judged to be abnormal—but both attitudes and laws are changing.

The Money/Pomeroy approach to the questions of "normalcy" and "morality," I would have thought, would strike most reasonable or reasonably well-informed people as so obvious as to be banal. So I thought, that is, until I started reading some of the "reasonable, well-informed" press commentary on the hearings. To take only two (prominent) examples: Edwin A. Roberts Jr. in *The National Observer* and William Safire in *The New York Times* have written columns that all at once express sympathy for Matlovich the individual, declare the Air Force misguided in not retaining him, and make pronouncements about "normalcy" that exude all the confidence and most of the prejudices of the Council of Constantinople (A.D. 381).

"The acts that homosexuals indulge in," Roberts writes, "confound the natural purpose and structure of sex." If among "acts" he means to include kissing, fellatio and anal intercourse, a fair number of Roberts's heterosexual friends should be keeping their eye out for notices of excommunication. Safire, in his column, is not a whit less confidently categorical: "Homosexuality is a sin . . . to practice it is to break all moral codes." To men so parochial and ethnocentric, it's probably futile to point out the high incidence of homosexuality recorded in the historical and anthropological literature—the conclusion, for example, of the anthropologists Clellan S. Ford and Frank A. Beach that 64 percent of the societies they surveyed regarded homosexuality as a normal variable. The information would make as much impression as the news that ancient Greece, where intergenerational male/male sex was an accepted commonplace, also had a "moral code."

Since both Roberts and Safire have publicly declared that they advocate civil rights for gay people, I shudder at the likely sentiments of those who regularly lobby and vote against bills that would extend those rights. At one point during his trial Matlovich exclaimed, "It's hearts we have to change!" Alas, no expert has yet found the lobe specific for heart-change, nor even the endocrine gland that bathes it.

In one area, as I said, Pomeroy and Money disagreed in their testimony. A critical area, involving the central question "When and how does sexual orientation become fixed and to what degree can it thereafter be changed?" Money claimed to have found "a great deal of evidence" to support the view that prenatal hormones play a significant role in "predisposing postnatal sexual behavior." Pomeroy said he has found almost none. Neither man was pressed during the hearings for details, but Money did point to research on pregnant women under stress as indicating one way that hormonal imbalances could be created and the child's later sexual orientation affected.

But as Naomi Weisstein, professor of psychology at the State University of New York at Buffalo (and herself engaged in basic brain research) pointed out to me when we talked over Money's statement, almost all women (and most men) in this culture are under considerable stress much of the time. What critical density has to be reached before which specific behavioral results can be predicted? And what other hormonal levels—and behavior—are or are not affected? Not only is the stress variable difficult to isolate and measure, but even were it possible to do so, we would still have to explain why so many "stressful" pregnancies apparently produce heterosexual offspring.

It also needs to be noted that hormonal research is in its infancy. Because the available data are minimal and contradictory, dogmatic statements about the effect of hormones on behavior are suspect. Besides, hormone levels in a given individual seem to vary according to environmental circumstances; a study of American soldiers in Vietnam, for example, showed a sharp drop in testosterone levels. We are apparently dealing with a fluctuating phenomenon, not a fixed state. As C. A. Tripp has written in *The Homosexual Matrix,* "[T]he idea that definite chemical substances might account for homosexuality incorrectly assumes that heterosexual and homosexual responses are discrete and that they differ in some fundamental way. On one level, it might be easy to postulate such differences—but not differences which would be compatible with how easily a homosexual response can develop and can coexist with heterosexuality." To add the words of another student of endocrinology: "What is really needed is for some good, controlled studies in man—or some well deserved silence in the absence of them." In the interim, Pomeroy's skepticism seems warranted.

Which is not to preclude the possibility that subsequent experiments may establish a significant or even controlling role for prenatal hormones in programming postnatal sexual behavior. Nor does such a possibility pose any necessary threat to gay people (as many seem to feel). The possible discovery that hormones, or other aspects of our biochemical and genetic inheritance, may be responsible in whole or part for influencing sexual orientation carries no automatically negative judgment. That is, if—and it's a big "if" in a culture as insistent as ours (despite rhetoric to the contrary) on homogeneity—"differences" are not equated with "deficiencies."

One reason gay people—and women and blacks, too—have been so distrustful of the current resurgence of interest in "innate" differences, is their awareness that in the past such "discoveries"—the homosexual's presumed inability to whistle and spit, the female's presumed lack of interest in sex, the blacks' presumed smaller cranial capacity—have been spawned not by science (as claimed) but by ideology, by the need to justify and extend the existing patterns of power. Knowing the repressive uses to which "scientific" findings have been put in the past, many gay people have understandably decided that the safest tack for the present is to refuse to be drawn into any discussion of the "causes" of homosexuality.

That stance is neither safe nor wise. Even if we grant that scientific discoveries do emerge from a particular social context, it doesn't and needn't follow that they must always be put to repressive uses. Even if scientific inquiry often has reflected and served the interests of those already in control of social resources, it's difficult intellectually to justify a demand for an end to scientific inquiry per se. To do so would put us in the company of those who brought on the Scopes trial.

What we (gays, women, blacks et al.) can do is play a double watchdog role: point out, first, that subjective assumptions significantly influence scientific findings and the uses to which they are put; and second, continue to insist that "differences," if cultivated rather than suppressed, are a potential source of personal and social enrichment. That watchdog role needs to be maintained not only against the biological view of sexual behavior currently gaining in popularity, but also against the older environmentalist position, which itself continues to sprout new variations. Pomeroy, for example, reported during his testimony on research currently in progress on the "play groups" of pre-adolescent boys, research that he thinks may demonstrate *one* way homosexuality becomes established. According to this view, when a boy is excluded from his play group because of, say, poor coordination, he may develop an erotic interest in the very group that excludes him.

It is as easy, and necessary, to be skeptical of this latest wrinkle on the environmentalist side of the argument as of the biological—easier, since nature theory has held sway for so long, been used so destructively and, recently, been challenged so sharply. The inadequacies, for example, of the "binding mother/absent father" theory of male homosexuality most closely associated with Drs. Irving Bieber and Charles Socarides have lately become so apparent that the theory has been all but relegated to the dump heap—though not in time to save a generation of parents from disabling guilt and a generation of sons and daughters from the tortures of the talking cure.

Unlike Drs. Bieber and Socarides, Wardell Pomeroy is neither homophobic nor judgmental. His research is worth noting, not to recommend or disparage it but only to demonstrate that the search for the "causes" of homosexuality continues unabated on both sides of the nature/nurture controversy, and does so with infinitely more zeal than has ever characterized any investigation into the origins of homophobia—or heterosexuality.

In any case, where John Money feels "that by adulthood, we don't have the potential any longer to be other than what we by then are," Pomeroy believes that sexual orientation is never wholly fixed—that within limits, the range of our erotic interests can be changed at almost any point in the life cycle. In elaborating that view during his testimony, Pomeroy referred to the familiar Kinsey scale of 0 to 6—0 designating an exclusive heterosexual, 6 an exclusive homosexual, the others some mix of bisexual experience. It is impossible, he believes, for a 6 to ever become a 0, or vice versa. And he wryly recalled that he had long ago challenged those psychoanalysts and behavioral therapists who claim "cures" involving total transformation to produce a single such case. The challenge has never been taken up.

Short of such a complete reversal in erotic patterns, however, Pomeroy believes that considerable realignment is possible: a 0 can become a 5, a 6 can become a 1. It is, as he put it, like adding right-handed dexterity to left-handedness—not switching completely from one to the other. But to accomplish that, one must first be comfortable with left-handedness; the degree of self-acceptance about what one already is, directly affects the ability to become something more. A poor candidate would be a heterosexual man disassociated from his sexuality who is compulsive about proving and re-proving that he is, indeed, "all man." In that state of mind, obsessed with inadequacy, he is not receptive to other internal impulses.

In listening to Pomeroy, I was reminded of the number of gay men who have told me that since coming out they've developed—for the first time in their lives—erotic interest in women. I'm reminded, too, of the number of women I know who, after becoming active feminists, adopted a bi- or homosexual lifestyle. My own anecdotal evidence has recently had some indirect statistical confirmation. In their book *Male Homosexuals,* Martin Weinberg and Colin Williams, research sociologists at the Institute for Sex Research, have concluded that gay men who are publicly "out" are less rigid, fixated and anxious—have fewer inhibitions of all kinds—than those who remain closeted. When fear and shame occupy the core, there isn't much energy available for exploring the periphery. Being constantly armed and at attention doesn't exactly inspire others to make friendly advances, or oneself to receive them.

Needless to say, all such "findings" by sexologists should be taken with a ton of salt. Societies typically tend to produce "expert opinion" that clarifies and consolidates already acceptable assumptions about how the world works. Though specialists usually view themselves as pioneers driven by "the need to know," fearlessly exploring the frontiers of Truth, the typical role they play is to confirm, not challenge, dominant social attitudes. Only the greatest in each generation—often to their own surprise, sometimes contrary to their own expectations—reexamine experience in a sufficiently original way to unsettle familiar notions. (Even they, it could be argued, are responding to social cues—to the microcosmic ones, those needs in the culture so new and tentative that they elude all but the most sensitive antennae.) Moreover, it's only with the passage of time that we can distinguish with any confidence between approaches that mark a genuine passage to the "newness" and those that—however novel the packaging—serve essentially to rationalize existing arrangements.

At this confused moment in time, we can confidently say only that growing numbers of Americans no longer find serviceable the traditional formulas used to categorize sexual behavior, nor the conventional morality used to judge it. We can also say that new—in at least the minimal sense of not having been recently fashionable—explanations and norms have begun to assert themselves. What is much less clear is why the argument from biology—one among several competing views—has jumped to sudden prominence; why, despite the paucity of evidence, the theory of the importance of prenatal genetic or hormonal influence on postnatal sexual orientation has captured so much attention and allegiance. If, as I think, it's not a case of the theory persuading through the sheer weight of evidence, then how else do we account for its growing appeal? By looking at the set of values that would be confirmed if the biological view triumphed.

To step back a bit:

Until recently we have—perhaps more than any other people in history—stressed our ability to shape our destiny according to whatever design we deemed desirable. This has been true of us at least since the decline of Calvinism (with its emphasis on *pre*-destination and man's *in*ability)—a decline completed by the end of the eighteenth century but probably underway from the day of the first settlements, when it seemed, in this vast solitude of space, that man could indeed start anew, unimpeded or regulated by previous rules. Certainly during all of the nineteenth century and for most of the twentieth, it seemed axiomatic that "we" (meaning white males) could become whatever we wished to become. Neither human history (the accumulated force of tradition) nor human biology (the genetic givens) was seen as a significant counterweight to human will. Divine Intention did, to be sure, carry weight, but in sending us out to populate an "empty" continent, He had made manifest *our* specialness and *His* decision to renovate the world. We have thus been, through time, the most optimistic—and most petulant—of people; convinced of our birthright to do as we pleased, we have treated any effort to thwart our will as an affront to Nature. That frame of reference has shifted dramatically in the last decade—most notably under the hammer blow of our defeat in Vietnam, most recently [1975] under the prolonged insecurity of an economic recession. We've lost confidence not merely in our ability to "renovate the world" but to control our individual lives. As a result, the conviction that change is a difficult process, and radical change a dangerous one, may have greater currency in our society at present than at any previous time in our history. And as judged by the emergence of a movement like Werner Erhard's training institute, "Est," many are now willing to reaffirm Dr. Pangloss's vision: Whatever is, is right.

It's comforting to be granted respite from that relentless American injunction to "arise anew," to transform ourselves yet again in response to yet another set of social dicta about what is optimal behavior. Both Money and Pomeroy, despite their difference emphases, are encouraging us—all of us, regardless of sexual orientation—to be whatever we are rather than to become what someone else tells us is desirable. Which is to say, both are on the side of self-acceptance—and diversity. This is a humane shift in emphasis, a shift away from an inflated sense of self-mastery and from a demeaning conformity to social expectations. It may well mark a profound passage in national consciousness: an end to our inordinate confidence in Will and to our missionary zeal to homogenize the planet; a belated and welcome dilution of American arrogance.

As with every passage, there's some sense of loss, and foreboding. When Matlovich heard that the verdict had gone against him, he held up a Bicentennial 50-cent piece with the inscription "200 years of freedom." "Not yet," he said. "Maybe some day, but not yet." Can we believe "some day" might still arrive if we lose *entire* confidence in the human capacity for self-transformation? The question should be considered without reference to the immediate issue of sexual orientation—for it transcends it.

—The New York Times Sunday Magazine,
November 9, 1975

Postscript 1975

When the article on Matlovich appeared in the Times, *it elicited a considerable response. Two of the letters came from Dr. Irving Bieber and Dr. Charles Socarides, the psychiatrists I had singled out as tenacious upholders of outmoded views. The* Times *did not print my exchange with Socarides (he denied permission to publish it in this volume). The letters between Dr. Bieber and me, which appeared in the* Times *on Dec. 28, 1975, are reprinted below.*

Irving Bieber:

In just two sentences, Martin Duberman made three misstatements about my work, clumsily attacked psychoanalysis and attempted an inept, *ad hominem* thrust against Dr. Charles Socarides and me . . .

He confused data with theory and inaccurately referred to our findings on the fathers of male homosexuals. A research team of 10, including myself, found that the fathers were mostly detached and hostile, not absent. Had Mr. Duberman read our book he would know that, of the 106 homosexuals studied, only three had absent fathers. He would also know that not one subject had had a loving, constructive father. In 1969 Evans and, independently, Snortum et al., using our questionnaire to study samples of nonpatient homosexuals, found the same parental configuration. Over the past 12 years I have personally interviewed more than 900 homosexual men, and all the information gathered continues to support our original findings. The data are incontrovertible, though some colleagues have differing theories as to causal variables. I have concluded that given a good father-son relationship no boy develops a homosexual pattern . . .

Mr. Duberman has erroneously associated Dr. Socarides with our study. As it happens, he worked independently and did not know of our research until it was published as a book. Dr. Socarides is not affiliated with our sponsoring organization, the Society of Medical Psychoanalysis.

The view that our study has been relegated to the dump heap is wishful thinking. It won a research award from the American Psychiatric Association in 1964, was later translated into Spanish, is now being translated into Italian, and Basic Books, Inc., has just issued another, 1,000 copies—developments that do not suggest an ignominious end.

As to psychoanalysis, he warns against "the tortures of the talking cure." If he got that idea from an unfortunate personal experience, he would do well to give it another try. I would gladly recommend any number of competent, painless analysts.

Mr. Duberman refers to Dr. Socarides and me as homophobic, a description he would likely attach to anyone who views homosexuality as other than a variant of normal sexual behavior. This is a typical *ad hominem* technique when avoiding a more cogent engagement with substantive issues. Mr. Duberman is a historian, a pursuit that does not qualify him to make authoritative judgments in another field where he is strictly a layman. A homosexual adaptation does not, in itself, provide the background and training required of experts in the biology and psychology of sexuality.

My Reply:

Dr. Bieber is being deliberately naive. He knows perfectly well that "binding mother/absent father" has become standard shorthand for describing the theory of homosexuality with which he and Dr. Socarides are identified. "Binding" and "absent" are umbrella terms— like "homosexuality"—that should indeed be broken down into their component parts when intricacies of definition are under discussion; that was not, however, the purpose of my essay. Bieber is being equally evasive in stating that I "erroneously associated Dr. Socarides with our study." I did not say in the article that the two men worked together on the same book. I said that they are associated with a common set of findings—namely, that a particular family configuration will produce homosexual children. Like Dr. Socarides, Bieber continues to insist that those findings are "incontrovertible." To which I can only say that he must have given up reading the medical journals after he won that prize.

. . . Bieber feels that a "layman" has no right to express an opinion on the subject. Who are the laymen? Leaving aside the legion of fellow specialists who have challenged Bieber's data, it is surely time to ask whether gay women and men might not themselves qualify as "experts" on their own lives. Perhaps Dr. Bieber remembers the time when white liberals—always with the "best intentions"—tried to explain to blacks the meaning of their own experience. Perhaps he also remembers the aftermath . . .

It's good of Dr. Bieber to recommend a "painless" analyst for me. I assume he means the kind that gives gas. I've had several, thanks. A dozen years of inhaling the fumes of "disease theory," "character disorder" et al., did quite a job on my ability to breathe. Having left the consultation room four years ago, my lungs are now clearing up nicely—in part, I might add, because of a therapist who concentrated on helping me to understand, rather than to berate, myself.

Another of Dr. Bieber's kind offers is still fresh in my memory. When Dr. Bieber and I debated the subject of male homosexuality several years ago before an audience of college counselors, he made the same statement I find repeated in his letter: he has never known a

"subject" (the choice of words is not unimportant) who "had had a loving, constructive father." An undergraduate took the microphone to
say that he was gay and had had just such a father. Clearly used to such
"distorted self-evaluations" during his long clinical practice, Bieber offered to give the young man a proper battery of tests if he would present himself at the office. At which point I grabbed the microphone
and, in an equally kindly spirit, offered to test Bieber for advanced
symptoms of homophobia if he would present himself at *my* office.
The doctor seemed startled, which I took to be a considerable advance.
The offer still holds.

Postscript 1999

As late as the 1980s, a therapist's admission of his/her own homosexuality predictably led to ostracism and a damaged career; for one such
frightening experience, see Richard Isay, *Becoming Gay* (Pantheon:
1996). It wasn't until 1991—thanks in no small measure to Isay's per-
sistence—that the American Psychoanalytic Association prohibited its
training institutes from denying admission on the basis of sexual orientation (a practice which up to that point had been standard). As of
December 1998 there are 35 to 40 openly gay and lesbian candidates
training in 29 psychoanalytic institutes, and 15 (out of 1,000) faculty
members are now openly gay. (*The New York Times,* Dec. 12, 1998).

Even this marginal shift has been strongly resisted by some analysts.
In 1992 a group of them—led by Joseph Nicolosi and the redoubtable
Charles Socarides—founded the National Association for Research
and Therapy of Homosexuality (NARTH), which continues to advo-
cate changing homosexuals into heterosexuals through therapy. (See
Nicolosi's 1991 book, *Reparative Therapy of Male Homosexuality,* Jason
Aronson, Inc.) NARTH receives its support primarily from right-
wing religious groups.

Back in 1974, Socarides led a campaign to reverse the APA's 1973 removal of homosexuality from the list of pathological conditions; with over ten thousand members voting, a full 37 percent sided with Socarides. Since then, his influence has receded considerably within the profession. But neither his marginalization nor even the coming-out of his own son, Richard (an official in the Clinton administration), has produced any shift in Socarides's views nor ended his campaign to turn the clock back (his chief comrade-in-arms, Irving Bieber, died some years ago). Which means Socarides and his sympathizers will almost certainly ignore or disparage the findings of a new book, *Psychoanalysis: A Contemporary Introduction,* coauthored by two Chicago analysts, Dr. Robert Galatzer-Levy and Dr. Bertram J. Cohler. The two, after comprehensively reviewing the scientific literature on homosexuality, have concluded that "homosexuality is not associated with any psychopathology in any way" and that "there is no evidence that any form of therapy, including psychoanalysis and the Christian therapies, can change sexual orientation."

The Anita Bryant Brigade (1977)

Robert Hillsborough, aged 33, has been killed. A husky, gentle man, he lived in a small apartment in San Francisco's Mission District. As the newspaper accounts have it, he claimed to have had only two ambitions in life: to work as a gardener and to live quietly with someone he loved. Two years ago he got a fulltime job as a city playground gardener and called himself "the happiest man in the world." Until recently he lived with Jerry Taylor and on the night of June 21 the two had gone out to discuss resuming their relationship. They stopped off at a local Whiz-Burger. In the parking lot a group of teenage toughs baited them with taunts of "Faggots! Faggots!" (initial provocation, if any, unknown; perhaps the two had dared to hold hands, had been seen kissing in their car). To avoid a confrontation, Hillsborough drove off. Four of the teenagers followed, caught him outside his apartment and stabbed him 15 times in the chest and face. He died within minutes.

Two weeks earlier, Anita Bryant had won her spectacular victory in Dade County against a gay rights bill. She had told audience after audience that homosexuals were an abomination to the Lord. I could tell you stories about these people," she liked to say, "that would turn your stomach." I doubt that Anita Bryant will add the story of Robert Hillsborough to her repertoire.

Simple equations between her inflammatory rhetoric and Hillsborough's murder should be avoided. Homosexuals, after all, had been beaten, tortured and burned to death for centuries before Anita Bryant began her crusade. The sixth-century Emperor Justinian blamed homosexuals for the natural disasters of plague and famine; the fourteenth-century clergy linked them to sorcerers and "misbelievers"; the eighteenth-century legal experts—notably Blackstone in his *Commentaries* of 1765–69—cited against them "the voice of nature and reason." The preferred form of punishment also changed through time; burning at the stake, an early favorite, gave way to stoning and castration. The Swiss, noted for their precision, liked to cut off one limb at a time over a period of several days—a finger here, a leg there—until the lifeless trunk was eventually ready for the flames.

Today the politicians sometimes seem to be in advance of their constituencies on the issue of gay rights. It was Dade County's elected officials who had passed the original ordinance banning discrimination in jobs and housing based on sexual orientation; it was the citizenry, by a vote of more than two to one, who rescinded that ordinance. This is hardly to say that our politicians can be counted on to lead and enlighten the public. During the Dade County struggle, Senator Alan Trask read *Leviticus* aloud in the state senate, warning that "we must never pass a law that is contrary to the teachings of God." Governor Reuben Askew went out of his way just before the climactic vote in Dade to announce publicly that he has "never viewed the homosexual lifestyle as something that approached a constitutional right."

Sometimes when public officials do climb out on a limb, they rush to slide back down the tree should their constituents make any move to shake it. In New York City a few years back, passage of a gay rights bill in the city council seemed assured—until pressure from the Catholic hierarchy (and to a somewhat lesser extent from Orthodox Jewish rabbis) led to the sudden reversal of several critical votes. The Catholic hierarchy did its bit in Dade as well. A letter from Archbishop Coleman Carroll urging repeal of the ordinance was read aloud in Catholic churches on the Sunday preceding the referendum.

But the Catholic vote alone could not have provided Anita Bryant with her wide margin of victory. She was heavily supported as well by Protestant fundamentalists, the Cuban community, and a coalition of right-wing activists who had worked together many times previously to block measures that "threatened the American Way"—busing, ERA, the public school ban on prayers and liberalized abortion and marijuana laws.

What assumptions and fears bind together these antigay forces? Why would people of such seemingly disparate backgrounds, status and interests—a working-class Cuban, say, a Baptist farm wife, a Catholic prelate, a wealthy advertising man—find a transcending commonality in homophobia? Are their stated, public reasons for opposing civil rights legislation for gay people their real reasons? Or are these reasons buried in some tangled web of inarticulate fear and illogic?

Sharing the normative values of our culture, social scientists have put infinitely more effort into elaborating "explanations" and "cures" for homosexuality than for homophobia. Most authoritative work has concluded that those who are against human rights for gay people cluster in the "most bigoted" category on a wide variety of other issues as well. They are deeply racist and sexist, abhor nonconformity of any kind, fiercely reject all manifestations of the "sexual revolution" (feminism, abortion, pornography, extramarital sex, etc.), are patriotic to the point of xenophobia, and in general show marked fear of all that is "other" or "different." New ideas are threatening—and especially to those middle-aged or older, with a low level of education, living in rural areas and from authoritarian family backgrounds.

The public arguments Anita Bryant has resorted to in opposing civil rights for gay people have struck a deep chord in many Americans, and it seems to vibrate on an emotional frequency not susceptible to information or logic.

The official antigay argument clusters around surprisingly few points. Foremost is the issue of "immorality," the judgment deriving from a literalist reading of the Bible. One Baptist evangelist, echoing many others, has put the matter succinctly: "We are facing the Devil himself in these homosexuals." A state senator, Marion Manning of Minnesota, has even managed a bizarre role reversal of victimizer and victim when he declares that gay people are a "threat to my personal rights, a threat to my religious beliefs."

The favorite citation accompanying such pronouncements is *Leviticus 18:22:* "And if a man also lie with mankind as he lieth with a woman, both of them have committed an abomination: they shall surely be put to death; their blood shall be upon them." But fundamentalist Christians seem unable to grasp the fact that interpretations of Holy Writ have undergone almost as many permutations as Supreme Court pronouncements on the Constitution—and in both cases, the most recent "truth" stands in direct contradiction to the official word that immediately preceded. As the Jesuit scholar John McNeill has pointed out in his book, *The Church and the Homosexual,* most contemporary biblical scholars have become convinced that the "sin of Sodom" originally connoted "inhospitality," and its current equation with "homosexuality" is the accumulated result of centuries of garbled translations and corrupted texts.

Try telling that to the fundamentalist marines. Biblical exegesis is not their strong point, nor are scholarly findings among their sources of inspiration. For obvious reasons. To acknowledge recent biblical scholarship would be tantamount to subverting their basic understanding of the Universe; Galileo, it will be remembered, was not hailed as a liberator. For people like myself, who don't derive our moral principles from the Bible, theological debate is irrelevant. But for those who do—the vast majority of our countrymen—it's fair to insist that they at least be consistent, that they live in a manner comporting with their own literalist interpretation of biblical morality.

Yes, *Leviticus* condemns "sodomy." It also condemns swearing, covetousness, jealousy—and shaving. Adulterers, according to the same book, should be stoned to death. Fundamentalists are free to reject the view that ethics, like all spin-offs of the human mind, are subjective and changeable. They are free to insist, rather, that moral precepts are static, transcending time and culture, and free to insist that behavior conform to the prescriptions enunciated 2,000 years ago in the Bible. But they are not free to pick and choose among those precepts as to which ones they will follow. Not, that is, without opening themselves to the charge of hypocrisy. It is fair to expect that if biblical fundamentalists are going to follow the dictates of *Leviticus* to the literal letter, they will show equal nicety in adhering to the rest of the "original" (preexegetical) biblical code of behavior. Which means they will no longer break the Sabbath by attending movies or by joining bowling parties. That they will no longer accumulate worldly goods beyond providing for basic needs (one doubts if Anita Bryant's $300,000 mansion will qualify). That the men among them will grow luxuriant beards and the women silken hair on their legs. That they will no longer engage in any sexual act other than missionary intercourse—and then only when procreation is the goal. Perhaps on one matter a little hypocrisy should be tolerated: since Kinsey has shown that more than half the male population has extramarital relations, we nonfundamentalists would not demand that adulterers be stoned to death in the streets. We, too, after all, are patriots; we do not wish to see the country decimated.

When not being denounced for offending against Heaven, gay people are excoriated for the baneful influence they exert on Earth. And especially on children. Here the indictment is in two parts: we spread subversive ideas and we serve as invidious role models. Anita "Save Our Children" Bryant has taken out full-page ads to denounce gay people as recruiters, seducers and molesters of children.

This depiction of us as child molesters has probably been the most potent weapon in the antigay arsenal—and the most impervious to factual refutation. The clinical studies and statistics about the actual nature of the sexual abuse of children have been well publicized and are incontestable. All the studies agree that the vast majority of such cases involve offenses committed by heterosexual men against young girls. Vincent De Francis's *Sexual Abuse of Children* summarizes the matter. He estimates that of the 100,000 children sexually molested each year, 92 percent are female and 97 percent of their victimizers are male—thus making it statistically impossible for more than a minuscule fraction of child molestation cases to involve same-gender assault.

As for gay people as role models, no one knows precisely why or how a particular sexual orientation develops, nor the extent to which, once developed, it remains fixed. Specialists who have spent decades studying these matters are far more tentative in their views than the strident advocates on either side of the nature/nurture debate. Not that the specialists need be automatically deferred to. The history of scientific thought on matters relating to sexuality is sobering evidence of how the opinion of "experts"—at any given moment in time trumpeted as definitive—has in fact oscillated wildly, conforming far more to changing social attitudes than to actual accretions of knowledge.

Today we know far too much in some fields (cross-cultural studies, for example) and far too little in others (the barely inaugurated research in endocrinology) to indulge in the confident sophistries of the past. Currently, the nature vs. nurture debate in scientific circles is more polarized and clouded than it has been for decades. Where some of the new findings from hormonal research suggest the possible influence of prenatal factors, the accumulating data from anthropology suggest the contrary conclusion—that the incidence (and kind) of same-gender sexual contact is centrally shaped by social learning. No one with even minimal information (perhaps I mean integrity) would say—as has Mike Thompson, the "brains" behind the Save Our Children campaign in Dade County—"all the evidence indicates that homosexuals aren't born; they're made. They choose." Thompson's prescription for those who cannot or will not "choose" to change their sexual orientation is predictably merciless: They should "suppress their drive."

Perhaps more disheartening than the professional bigots, with their claims on a monopoly of truth and their narrow definitions of the permissible limits of humanness, are those professional intellectuals who disassociate themselves from the crude polemics of an Anita Bryant even as they disseminate in subtler form the basic prejudices that animate her cohorts. Most public intellectuals are maintaining silence (and silence, as we should have learned from what happened in Nazi Germany, is a political act) or expressing agreement—modulated and selective, to be sure—with the crusade to withhold even minimal civil rights protection from gay people.

Two such examples are George F. Will, the syndicated *Newsweek* columnist and Pulitzer Prize winner, and the political theorist Michael Novak, heterodox defender of "differentness," that is, when ethnic not sexual. I single out Will and Novak not because their commentaries on gay rights have been uncommonly intemperate or venomous, but precisely because they have not. Their pained thoughtfulness, their more-in-sorrow-than-in-anger tone, better represents the stance thus far taken by well-educated, well-placed heterosexuals than does the outright malice of a John Simon, say, or a William Buckley, and is because of that, dangerous. Nothing persuades like "sweet reasonableness."

George Will entitled one of his *Newsweek* columns "How Far Out of the Closet?" Noting that the American Psychiatric Association had removed homosexuality from its list of mental disorders, Will questioned whether the decision had been wise. Did it not encourage a view already too prevalent that "all notions of moral normality are 'mere' conventions, or utterly idiosyncratic"? Was there not a danger that the notion would gain ground that "no form of sexuality is more natural, more *right* [his italics] than any other . . . "? Well yes, I might answer, but isn't that best viewed as a hope, not a danger—the hope that we might become a less hypocritical and conformist, a more comfortably diversified society?

Why does George Will feel otherwise? Because in his mind the prospect looms "of the repudiation of the doctrine of natural right on which Western society rests," a doctrine that allows us to know and encourage "some ways of living that are right because of the nature of man . . . more human ways of living . . ." The doctrine of natural right? The nature of man? Human ways of living? Large concepts, those. Not easy to grasp or evaluate, especially since Will provides no specific definitions, does nothing to elucidate the particular meaning he attaches to such grandly vacuous phrases. Instead, he heaps on further abstractions. Not even a liberal society, he tells us, can leave everything to chance. Certain "essential values" must be safeguarded, shored up by law. "Surely healthy sexuality is one: the family, and hence much else, depends on it."

Apparently Will equates "healthy sexuality" with "family." But instead of providing evidence and argument (a formidable task, given all we've learned of late about marital disorder and child abuse within the home), he issues papal pronouncements that do much to clarify the sources of his inspiration but nothing to authenticate them. One example: "surely homosexuality is an injury to healthy functioning, a distortion of personality." Since almost all the recent scientific literature—including the opinion of the American Psychiatric Association, which Will himself cites—points to the opposite conclusion about homosexuality, it's not surprising that the sole "evidence" he offers in support of his statement is a tired stereotype: "Homosexuality often reduces sex to the physical . . . [it is a] subculture based on brief, barren assignations . . ."

One might ask George Will—since parody begets parody—if he has ever heard of the notorious "subculture" of traveling heterosexual businessmen, famed for their "brief, barren assignations"? Should we assume he would want to deny them access to jobs and housing, too, since they too—by his standards—threaten society's "essential values"? But then those men *do* have families, no matter the quality of their relationships, no matter the extent of deceit and oppression operative within their households. One comes away from Will's camouflaged sanctimony with a decided preference for the foot-in-mouth rantings of Anita Bryant. Both associate homosexuality with a threat to traditional sex roles and the institutions that embody them, and with a "dangerously" elastic view of the permissible range of sexual pleasure. Anita uses the words. George Will, perhaps aiming at the subliminal crowd, moves his lips.

Michael Novak's language is more explicit but his attitudes no less hidebound. The homosexual way of life, in his view, has "two basic deficiencies." The first is "the narcissism of one's own sex." Is Novak here defining narcissism in some special way that would not also force him to deplore deep friendships between people of the same gender? Is he aware that a statement such as his can only be based on the sexist assumption that male and female are polar opposites? We don't know. Like George Will—and most successful moralists—Novak has learned that one garners attention in direct proportion to the firmness, not the subtlety, of one's assertions.

The second deficiency Novak finds in homosexual relationships is that they are transient—"far more so than among married men and women." Perhaps. Given the latest divorce figures and the absence of research on long-standing gay relationships, one can't be sure. But even if Novak is right, he fails to ask any of the questions that could provoke a genuinely searching inquiry into the meaning of "transient." For example: Is it possible serial relationships might provide more optimal conditions for human happiness than lifetime pair-bonding? How many of those lifetime bondings are based on emotional insecu-

rity, lack of options, financial necessity and ingrained cultural imperatives ("the welfare of the children," etc.)—and at what cost in terms of
lost affiliation with a larger community, erotic dessication, and the per-
petuation of female dependence?

Novak never considers the possibility that sexual fidelity may not be
the most significant gauge, let alone the equivalent, of emotional commitment. Many gay people reject the common assumption that a variety of sexual partners is incompatible with a lasting and loving primary
relationship. Because gay people are less prone to overinvest in the
magical expectation that one other person can fulfill all their needs,
the partnerships they do form are often marked by an impressive
amount of egalitarian independence.

Novak concludes with this statement: "Only a decadent society
would grant them [gay people] equal status." Apparently, Novak
doesn't realize that "decadence" has many definitions and is perhaps
most appropriately appended to knee-jerk defenders of the status quo,
rather than to those outsiders who throughout history have been responsible for initiating innovation and change. The concluding words
in George Will's column, comparable to Novak's, make the point for
me: ". . . people want a few rocks to cling to in the riptide that washes
away old moral moorings. Opposition to [Dade County's pro-gay] ordinance is a way of saying 'Enough!' And it is eminently defensible."

In short: Right on, Anita! We intellectuals may differ with you on
particular points, we may not speak in the same tone, use the same vocabulary or invoke the same authorities—we have, after all, different
constituencies and must adjust our voices accordingly. But we *are*
united on fundamentals: we view gay people as a threat to the body
politic, the enemy outside the gates. They shall not pass.

Robert Hillsborough. Gentle gardener. Stabbed fifteen times in the
chest and face. Dead in a parking lot, age thirty-three. "Faggot!
Faggot!"

—This article was solicited in 1977 for the
"Great Debate Series" of *Skeptic* magazine, to
be juxtaposed alongside a piece by Jerry
Falwell. Without my consent or knowledge,
it appeared instead with a piece by Mike
Thompson, Anita Bryant's braintruster.

POSTSCRIPT 1999

The Dade County battle did damage Anita Bryant's career. A number
of her singing engagements were canceled and she was dropped from
a lucrative contract as the spokeswoman for the Florida Citrus
Commission.

Yet it took *twenty-one years* for the gay civil rights ordinance to surface again in Dade. This time, the ordinance was passed, but by the nar-
rowest of margins: in 1998, the Miami-Dade County commissioners, by
a 7 to 6 vote, banned discrimination based on sexual orientation. But
having been passed by elected officials rather than the public itself, this
ordinance, like the earlier one, could be rescinded through a referendum.

Though homophobia has lessened over the past twenty years, a recent survey showed that 80 percent of gay men and lesbians have at
some point in their lives been verbally harassed, nearly half have been
threatened with violence, 25 percent have had various objects thrown
at them, 13 percent have been spat upon and 9 percent have been assaulted with a weapon. The brutal murder of Matthew Shepard in
1998 led the American Psychoanalytic Association to hold its very
first forum on homophobia (there had been countless ones on the
"causes" and "cures" of homosexuality). For a useful summary of the
theoretical work to date on the nature of homophobia, see Barry D.
Adam, "Theorizing Homophobia," *Sexualities*, Vol. 1, No. (4), 1998.

PART THREE

Old Saws/New Refrains

I

The Tenacity of Race

The Black Response to William Styron's *The Confessions of Nat Turner*

W illiam Styron's Nat Turner: Ten Black Writers Respond is a depressing volume—for those who believe the past can and should be protected from the propagandists, for those with the lingering hope that the races in America can be reconciled, for those who have regarded blacks as the saving remnant that might help our country become something better than what it has been.

The book is a commentary—perhaps "assault" would be the more appropriate word—by ten black writers on William Styron's novel *The Confessions of Nat Turner*. There are legitimate complaints, historical and literary, to be made against Styron's book, and as presented by two of the ten essayists, Vincent Harding and Mike Thelwell, those complaints are cogently, even poignantly, set forth. Harding and Thelwell recognize that Styron, as a novelist, is entitled to certain prerogatives of invention and fantasy, but they point out that he has not been content to advertise his work as "fiction": In the preface to the novel (and in a number of public comments and debates since its publication)

Styron has insisted that he "rarely departed from the *known* facts about Nat Turner and the revolt of which he was the leader."

By inviting critics to treat his book as a work of history as well as one of fiction. Styron has increased his vulnerability to attack. Even had he not, the attack would have come, for as Thelwell points out, the acclaim given the novel by white critics and the terms in which that acclaim has been formulated (for example, Styron reveals "the agonizing essence of Negro slavery") have turned the book into a cultural phenomenon about which extraliterary questions become inescapable.

My own feelings about Styron's book are that, although seriously flawed as a novel, it is at the same time superlative history. By this, I do not mean that Styron cannot be faulted for the occasional omission or distortion of detail (an inescapable by-product of *any* work of history, no matter how rigorous and scrupulous the historian), but that *Confessions* provides the most subtle, multifaceted view of antebellum Virginia, its institution of slavery and the effects of that institution on both slaves and masters available in any single volume.

This opinion is furiously rebutted by the ten black writers in this collection. Three sets of "distortions" in the *"Confessions"* particularly outrage them. The first has to do with Turner's family background. By failing to credit the role played in Nat's upbringing by a black grandmother and father, and by de-emphasizing the influence of his mother, Styron has, it is charged, written a kind of early-day adjunct to the Moynihan Report, whereby the instability of black family life carries the inevitable corollary that the "significant others" in Nat's life had to be whites.

The second set of distortions concerns Nat Turner's sex life. Styron, it is said, has dropped Nat's black slave wife from history, has focused his desires instead on a young white girl and, by throwing a homosexual episode into the mix, has ended by creating a Nat Turner who is all at once impotent, queer, sexually repressed and full of secret lusts for white flesh.

The third indictment against Styron centers on his description of the revolt itself and the part Nat Turner played in it. Nat's vacillation at the moment of crisis, his refusal or inability to kill any white other than the young girl who had been the focus of his repressed desire, the inanity of his few black allies and the indifference or hostility of the other slaves create the impression, Styron's critics argue, that Nat was a coward, a fool, an incompetent or all three and imply, moreover, that blacks are at all times incapable of engineering their own liberation.

These are the most detailed of the indictments made against Styron, but they by no means exhaust the grievances listed by the ten authors. Among the additional, more general charges made by individual essayists, is that Styron has exaggerated the benevolent aspects of slavery, that he has portrayed all or most Negroes in slavery as "Sambos," that he has minimized the powerful resistance blacks made to bondage, that he has misunderstood the black temper, the psychology of uprisings, the very nature of American society.

Some of the essayists insist that Styron's distortions are deliberate, the conscious design of (in Ernest Kaiser's phrase) a "vile racist imagination." Two or three of the writers are willing to entertain the notion that Styron may not have intentionally maligned the character and historical significance of Nat Turner (Alvin F. Poussaint, the Boston psychiatrist, even detects in many parts of the novel the author's "strong empathy" for Nat), though they feel that his stereotypic liberal views have prevented him, despite good intentions, from understanding the black psyche and the black experience.

In drawing their charges, the essayists imply that in regard to all these matters—Nat Turner's personality, the institution of slavery, the psychology of insurrection, etc.—the historical evidence establishes clear patterns that run counter to those presented by Styron. They are certain, for example, that the "real" Nat Turner was, in the words of John Henrik Clarke, "a virile, commanding, courageous figure." It is as unthinkable to them that Turner could have been irresolute in battle or ambivalent about committing murder as it is that he could have hankered after a white woman or not "dearly loved" his black wife.

According to their countermodel, Nat Turner was one of the world's great military geniuses and one of its most resolute white haters. (Poussaint chides Styron for suggesting that Turner could have believed in "the basic humanity of some slave-holders.") This would make Nat Turner, among other things, a dedicated killer and racist—qualities which I doubt most of the essayists would ordinarily single out for praise. In any case, they see Turner not as a human being but as an epic force, a figure immune to the usual range of error, compassion and desire.

If this is what blacks mean by "rediscovering" black history and finding historical figures with whom black youths can identify, then the prospects are grim, for in the case of Turner, at least, the figure they present for emulation is frighteningly one-dimensional, even pathological. It is a question, moreover, whether the new emphasis on black heroes really will demythologize our past (as is claimed and needed), or whether it will replace one set of myths with another. To give just one other example: We have heard much of late of Crispus Attucks, who, we are being told, was a runaway Negro slave killed in the "Boston Massacre"—the first blood to be shed in the American struggle for independence. The fact is we don't know whether Attucks was a Negro, a mulatto, an Indian, or even a runaway, and no one, of course, can assign the moment or the vein from which the "first blood" for independence spurted forth.

Blacks are entitled to their version of Turner, Attucks and others, but let them not pretend that those versions are incontestably validated by the historical evidence. As regards Turner, for example, the historical documentation is so skimpy and contradictory that only by embroidering or ignoring it (the very sins for which they denounce Styron) can the black writers in this collection establish their predetermined and dogmatic "lessons." The chief—indeed with the exception of a few scattered references in contemporary accounts—the only source on Turner is the twenty-odd-page "confessions" taken down when he was in jail by a white racist lawyer named Thomas Gray.

The full text of these original confessions is printed as an appendix to this volume, as if to suggest that it carries some kind of unarguable certification for the views of the essayists. It does present some "facts," like Turner's family lineage, which contradict Styron's version—but even on this level, the black essayists should have been the first to remind us (as they do in so many other contexts) that Turner's confessions were filtered through the eyes and words of a white man and are therefore automatically suspect.

Since, to the contrary, most of the essayists seem to believe that the original confessions are Absolute Truth and that every account which deviates from them partakes of malignant intent, it is surprising they did not chastise Styron more severely for underplaying the one character trait of Turner's that emerges most clearly from those confessions—that he was a religious fanatic of terrifying, perhaps psychotic, proportions.

For matters incidental to Turner's own career—and especially for the view that rebellions like his were not rare (as Styron states) but rather frequent occurrences—the essayists rely heavily on Herbert Aptheker's *American Negro Slave Revolts*, but do not mention that most historians consider Aptheker's evidence suspect, based as it often is on inference and rumor (nor that historians are equally leery of the "oral tradition" which some of the writers are reduced to citing).[1]

The essayists wish to believe that the "craving for freedom" was to be found in every Negro breast, and that therefore there is no "big mystery," as John Oliver Killens puts it, about the causes of Nat Turner's rebellion. But although a large number of slaves did engage in various forms of "passive resistance," very few became outright revolutionaries. Thus, the phenomenon of Nat Turner does need further explanation, as does the failure of the vast majority of Negroes to attempt outright rebellion. Nor will the evidence of *some* Negro apathy or acquiescence disappear by the mere reiteration that it never existed. Denmark Vesey's Charleston insurrection in 1822—to give but one example—is known to have been betrayed by black informers.

By insisting that all slaves "craved freedom," the essayists force themselves into a bizarre view of the institution of slavery. For slavery could not have been as barbaric as they otherwise insist if it inculcated self-love and masculine assertion in the slaves, rather than the self-hate and loss of identity more usually taken to be its products.

Only when slavery is viewed as an essentially benign institution (the position associated with the scholarship of Ulrich B. Phillips and bitterly denounced by the essayists), can it follow that it left no deep personality scars on its victims. But the weight of historical evidence and opinion suggests that American slavery was harsh enough to produce serious character disorders in many slaves. If this be "slander," then I suppose we shall now have to brand Bruno Bettelheim an anti-Semite for pointing out that some prisoners in the concentration camps tended to identify with their S.S. guards and to become infantilized.

What makes Styron a better historian than any of his critics is that he will not bury unpleasant evidence or minimize the complexities of past experience in order to serve some presumed contemporary need. It seems to me grotesque to say, as some of these writers do, that because Styron portrays an occasional master as kindly, he therefore believes slavery was benevolent; Styron recognizes that some slaves had kind masters *and* that slavery was abominable. It seems to me absurd to claim that Styron "dehumanizes every black person in the book" because he portrays some Negroes as Sambos and endows others with conflicts and uncertainties (traits which I hitherto took to be among the telltale signs of humanity); Styron recognizes that slavery produced Uncle Toms *and* rebels.

Finally, I think it is obscene to say that Styron is "an unreconstructed Southern rebel" and that his purpose in writing *Confessions* was to confirm white racists in their view that Negroes are ingrates and incompetents, and to defuse black militancy by suggesting that all rebellions are acts of futility. Styron's chief crime, it appears, is his refusal to reduce any man to caricature, whether as Hero or Oppressor. His chief disability—that is, to those who wish to exploit rather than to understand the past—is his insistence on holding contradictory views in tension, on embracing paradox.

After several hundred years of white mythmaking and polemic, it looks as if we're now in for some innings by blacks. One hoped it was going to be different this time around. But that, I suppose, was one of the more recent myths: that blacks in this country could somehow transcend the destructive racism that permeates our culture, that they, unlike whites, might somehow avoid distorting the past as a way of inciting one-half of mankind to hate the other.

—The New York Times,
Aug. 11, 1968

—— POSTSCRIPT 1969 ——

There was considerable reaction to this piece, ranging from angry letters to *The New York Times* to private admonitions from black friends (though perhaps what made me most uncomfortable were the congratulations sent by a number of white liberals whose opinions I thought I did not share). My response to both the praise and blame is best summed up, I think, in a section of the reply I wrote (and which was printed only in part) in the *Times:*

My hope [that blacks could avoid the racism that has so long characterized whites] may have been naïve (a naïveté, I might add, widely shared and actively encouraged by many blacks during the early years of the civil rights movement). I also recognize, belatedly, that it is a subtle form of dehumanization to regard anyone as a potential "hero" . . .

I would like to add here a point made by a friend in a private letter to me. Although racism is as disturbing in blacks as in whites, he wrote, it may not follow that all racisms should be treated as equal in culpability. Whites, after all, started the cycle, and the intractability of their racism may leave blacks no way of surviving or of achieving "consciousness" other than by adopting similar tactics. This friend further believes, following the arguments of Frantz Fanon, that while black racism may be "a necessary stage in the psychological development of many blacks, it is not really very satisfying for most of them, and therefore is not likely to be permanent." I hope he is right, but I am not convinced that racism is the only way blacks can achieve consciousness, nor that there is any compelling reason for believing black racism need prove less durable than white . . .

The black essayists in *William Styron's Nat Turner* challenged Styron almost exclusively on historical grounds, and I therefore joined the debate on *their* chosen terms. When evaluating interpretations of the past, the criteria are inescapably those of accuracy and objectivity: "How well does the interpretation fit the known evidence?" Had I used criteria other than these in evaluating the interpretations offered by black writers, I could rightly have been accused of condescension. I suppose I might have taken the line that the black essayists were self-deceived—that they *thought* they were engaging in serious historical debate, but in fact were motivated by purely . . . [polemical] considerations. Surely this would have been a worse form of condescension. It would have put me in the position of presuming to know better than the black writers themselves what their real intentions were. Instead I accepted their purpose as they stated it: to argue the merits of Styron's novel as a work of history.

The reaction to the article that most troubled me was raised privately by a black friend. He did not, he said, dispute the details of my review; indeed, he thought my points were well taken. But the piece, he added, should have been something more than a cold "taking to task," a scholar's hard insistence on the demands of "objectivity." What was also needed, he said, was some sympathy for the psychological need forcing blacks into inventing usable myths, some sensitivity to their feeling that Styron, in denigrating Turner's virility, had assaulted their own, even some recognition of the natural resentment black writers would feel, after years of struggling to make a living, at the prospect of a white author's earning a million dollars from a book about a black hero.

I agree with my friend. It is not that I regret saying the things I did in this review, for Styron had been ruthlessly and unfairly assaulted, and, moreover, as a professional historian I did have the responsibility to take issue with the manipulation of evidence. But I regret that I did not say other things as well, did not make clear that although I was disquieted as an historian, I did sympathize as a man.

Racism in the Gay Male World (1982)

In the dozen years since Stonewall, most of the radical goals set by the early gay liberation movement have been diluted or discarded. As our movement has grown in numbers, its initial values have atrophied. Originally, the gay movement strove to speak and act boldly against entrenched privilege based on gender, racial, ethnic and class discrimination. That commitment has been largely displaced by "liberal" goals and strategies that emphasize the need to work within the established system to secure social tolerance and legal redress.

Worthy goals, to be sure. And ones which we have made some notable progress in advancing in recent years. We have gained greater visibility and protection. We are more "tolerable" to the general public. But at no small cost: the cost of making ourselves over in order better to conform to an acceptable public image, the cost of bending our energies toward adjusting to mainstream mores, to becoming Good Americans. The inevitable concomitant has been to downplay differences we once proudly affirmed, to discard radical social analysis, soft-pedal our distinctiveness, discourage and deny the very diversity of behavior and lifestyle our conformist society stands in need of most.

This quest for respectability reached an apogee of sorts just two weeks ago [Sept. 1982] when we filled the Grand Ballroom of the Waldorf-Astoria—1,000 strong and paying $150 a plate—to celebrate the first annual Human Rights dinner. Resplendent in our finery, we gave Walter Mondale, chief speaker of the evening, a standing ovation—roared our enthusiasm for what in fact was a standard (and tedious) anti-Reagan stump speech that never once directly addressed the reason for the occasion: the cause of gay rights. Nor was any resentment apparent when Mondale, the instant he finished his speech, quickly left the platform—missing the subsequent presentations and resolutely refusing any comment to the crowd of reporters that awaited him at the Waldorf's exit.

It's no coincidence that the dinner crowd, which so lustily cheered Mondale's near-shameful performance, was composed almost entirely of dinner-jacketed white males (along with a handful of women, and almost no blacks or Hispanics). Surely the nature of Mondale's audience goes far toward accounting for their grateful, even enthusiastic, response to him. A leading member of the ruling patriarchy had—at last!—graced a gay white male event with his actual presence, given it at least token legitimacy. What matter how minimal the gesture; the symbol was what counted. With Mondale appearing at an openly gay affair, surely the time was not distant when the ruling elite would grant full admission to the inner sanctum of white male privilege.

We can take some hope in the fact that at least some gay men have banded together to form an organization, Black and White Men Together, devoted to confronting rather than evading the endemic racism in our community. The ultimate impact the organization will have is unforeseeable. But what can and should be said already, is that it has punctured the reigning complacency, insisting we face up to serious problems dividing and disfiguring our community, encouraging us to reclaim our radical roots, to rechart our course.

The gay movement's evolution from radicalism to reform is typical, alas, of how protest movements in this country have always (and, usually, quickly) shifted their priorities. Originating in fierce anger and initially marked by broad-gauged demands for social change, they rapidly evolve into well-behaved, self-protective associations, and in the process abandon demands for challenging the vast inequities in our social system, substituting (at best) token liberalism.

Some thirty years ago, the philosopher Herbert Marcuse predicted that the new "sexual liberation movements" would become a powerful force, *the* agency for producing significant social transformation. As prosperous white males have come increasingly to dominate the national gay movement, Marcuse's once plausible prediction has become pathetically remote. No movement born to protest inequality can hope to accomplish contradictory purposes. In its current guise, the gay movement may well succeed in gaining broader access to the preexisting clubhouses of power, but it can not pretend that it is centrally devoted to a struggle for improving the lot of the many. The gay movement cannot opt for putting its primary energy toward winning mainstream America's approval and simultaneously pretend not to have jettisoned its earlier determination to address the plight of *all* gay people: the invisibility of lesbians, the discrimination against non-whites, the scornful disregard of the rural poor.

Which of the national gay organizations is currently directing its efforts on behalf of those nonaffluent, nonprivileged gays who constitute our actual majority, who everywhere dot the land, doing its dirty work, unacknowledged and unorganized, self-esteem disfigured, future hopes dim? Who among the leaders of our burgeoning gay officialdom speaks to those needs, acknowledges their existence? When has *one* of the proliferating week-long strategy conferences that our national organizations proudly sponsor included such concerns in its agenda or issued in its imposing concluding statements of purpose any awareness of the terrible daily burdens that weigh down the lives of so many of our people? Having at one period attended many such gatherings, I bear my share of responsibility for this callousness, now endemic.

As the black-tied diners at the Waldorf demonstrated, the gay movement has finally managed to secure the allegiance of—by surrendering control over its priorities to—prosperous white male recruits who had previously disdained association with a movement they regarded as controlled by "impractical," noisome visionaries. The more those who earlier eschewed the gay movement have now joined it, the more their bland deportment and narrow social perspectives have come to dominate: they have "upgraded" our image while diluting demands for substantive social change, shifting organizational policies into comfortable conformity with their own reformist goals.

The gay movement, radical at its inception, has today lost courage. Its national organizations are currently dominated by skilled lobbyists pressing for narrow assimilationist goals through traditional political channels. Its chief priority is to win acceptance for the most conformist, most conservative, mostly privileged, mostly male few.

It is a perilous path. The drive to establish our credentials as mainstream Americans is inextricably yoked to deemphasizing our "differentness"—and that, in turn, is tantamount to falsifying our unique historical experience and the subculture it has generated. The result is not only to rob gay people of their heritage but also to negate the potential contribution our "off-center" lifestyle(s) held out for challenging reigning assumptions—for contributing our special perspectives on the nature of "partnership," "family," gender, and friendship.

The "official"—organized, national—gay movement's current emphasis on winning short-term gains for the few *has* produced its notable successes and *has* increased "tolerance." But it may have done so at the expense of producing any substantive long-range impact on the nation's institutionalized inequalities. The more we press for limited gains, the more we twist our identity to conform with mainstream values, the more we jeopardize our chance to offer new perspectives to a nation desperately in need of moral regeneration.

—The New York Native,
June 20/July 3, 1983

POSTSCRIPT 1999

In its original form, this piece was a presentation speech awarding a "certificate of merit" to the gay organization Black and White Men Together (its name since changed to Men of All Colors Together). The speech was delivered at the seventh annual Lambda Legal Defense Fund dinner in October 1982 and, as if in confirmation of my remarks, a number of gay white men angrily walked out in the middle of it; others later expressed their strong disapproval of what one called my "inappropriate and offensive remarks." I subsequently converted the speech into two articles for *The New York Native* (June 20/July 3, 1983), which are here excerpted and combined.

As regards the overall subject of this essay—the gay movement's shift from radicalism to reformism—the birth of ACT-UP in the early eighties went a long way toward restoring *some* hope that the movement might yet return to its roots. Indeed, when I dedicated a plaque at an outdoor ceremony in June 1989, renaming a portion of Christopher Street as "Stonewall Place," I devoted most of my speech to hailing ACT-UP as a potential reincarnation of the radical, broad-gauged Gay Liberation Front of the early seventies: "what we are seeing are gay men and lesbians acting in concert, welcoming and appreciating each other's differentness, and also welcoming minority people."

In regard to the specific issue of racism within the gay world, the twenty-five years since these articles appeared have seen some, but not nearly enough progress. For a sample of the anger many nonwhite gay, lesbian, bisexual and transgender people feel about the issue, see Reginald Shepherd, "On Not Being White," and Daniel Garret, "Creating Ourselves," in the collection *In the Life*, Joseph Beam, ed. [Alyson: 1986]; and (among many others), Charles Fernandez, "Undocumented Aliens in the Queer Nation," in *Out/Look* (Spring 1991). Some radical gay black men have even become hostile to Men of All Colors Together, seeing in its concentration on *inter*racial couples the embodiment of self-hate [e.g.: Revon Kyle Banneker, "Marlon Riggs Untied," *Out/Look* (Fall 1990)].

A cogent recent summary of the issues at stake is John Gallagher's "Blacks and Gays: The Unexpected Divide," *The Advocate*, Dec. 9, 1997. Gallagher quotes Mark Johnson of the National Gay and Lesbian Task Force as saying that the mainstream white gay movement *has* made real progress regarding racism ("There's a certain respect, often distant, but still respect"), but black gay men and lesbians remain woefully underrepresented in leadership positions. Some gay African-Americans have in fact written off the larger gay community. Gallagher quotes Keith Boykin of the National Black Gay and Lesbian Leadership Forum as saying, "'Gay is considered a white, Eurocentric, culturally imperialistic term that doesn't represent the values of African-Americans'." Or as Mark Johnson puts it, "To hear a white gay man say 'I've been discriminated against' is hard for some people of color to fathom because he looks like the people who discriminated against *them*."

Recently, there has also been considerable discussion about the amount of homophobia that exists within the straight black world. Martin Luther King, Jr.'s niece, Alveda King, for example, has denounced the struggle for gay rights as an affront to the black civil rights movement. Coretta Scott King, on the other hand, has endorsed federal nondiscrimination legislation for gays as well as same-sex marriage. African-American churches—still the central institutions in black life—have dealt with homosexuality (as well as with AIDS) largely through silence, though there are recent signs that that is changing. For more on these issues, see Eric Washington, "Freedom Rings!" *The Village Voice,* June 29, 1993; and "Blacks Rejecting Gay Rights as a Battle Equal to Theirs," *The New York Times,* June 28, 1993.

Writing Robeson

It was Paul Robeson, Jr., who invited me, back in 1981, to be his father's biographer. He had offered me exclusive access for seven years to the vast family archives long closed to scholars, and had stressed at our very first meeting that he wasn't looking for a "Saint Robeson" but rather a tell-it-like-it-was account that would make his father an accessible human being rather than a pedestalized god.

Impressed, flattered and eager as I was to accept Paul Jr.'s offer, it also puzzled me. "You can see that I'm white," I said to him during that first meeting, "but do you also know that I'm gay, and that I've been actively involved in the gay political movement for years?" He casually replied that he did, that he had had me "thoroughly checked out." He had become convinced that I was the right biographer for his father because (as I recorded his words in my diary) of my "nuanced prose," my "complex understanding of personality," my left-wing politics and my experience in the theater.

Since I was not the only historian with left-wing views who wrote "nuanced" prose, I remained skeptical that Paul Jr.'s stated reasons for inviting a white gay activist to become his father's biographer exhausted the range of his motives. But wanting to believe him, I kept my skepticism to myself and accepted his invitation.

I did set one condition. I told him that I could comfortably undertake the biography only if we drew up a legal agreement in which he formally gave up all control over what I might ultimately choose to write. No self-respecting scholar, I explained, could work with someone looking over his shoulder—and especially not a son, deeply invested emotionally, and with his own pronounced views and agenda. Paul Jr. said he had expected me to set those conditions and was willing to sign such an agreement. "As we move ahead," he added with a sly grin, "I'll doubtless backslide." (Oh Lord, would he backslide!)

And so we were launched. Paul Robeson, Jr., had given me the necessary assurances, had insisted he wanted a wholly truthful—not a plaster cast—portrait, and was soon, moreover, introducing me to some of his father's closest friends. But as I set to work on the mountainous source materials, a sense of unease lingered. *Was* this, I asked myself, a case of bizarre miscasting, a grotesque mismatch of author and subject—as some were quick to charge as soon as the project was publicly announced?

To quiet my discomfort, I tried putting the issue in a larger context: What, after all, *are* the essential qualities in a given biographer that heighten the chances for understanding a given life? Who is best qualified to write about whom, and why? Are there certain unbreachable guidelines that must be followed, certain fundamental boundaries that must not be crossed? Do we want to argue, for example, that no man should attempt to write about a woman, no younger person about an older, no adult about a child, no straight person about a gay one, no white person about a person of color (or vice versa)?

Even the most committed essentialists, I feel sure, would balk at strictures this severe: We have become too aware of how reductive the standard identity categories of gender, class, race and ethnicity are when trying to capture the actual complexities of a given personality. (Paul Robeson cannot simply be summarized as "a black man," nor Martin Duberman as "a gay man.") Besides, many people have overlapping identities that compete for attention; how we rank their importance in shaping our personalities can shift over time, which in turn can lead to a re-allocation of political energies.

But why is the assumption so widespread in the first place that a match-up between author and subject in regard to standard identity categories *is* the best guarantor of understanding? Indeed, why do we lazily assume that these categories are, in every case, the critical ones, while ignoring any number of other commonalities between biographer and subject that might provide critical insights—matters such as having been raised in comparable family or regional cultures or sharing similar psychologies of self, professional experience or religious affiliation.

Which of the links, standard or otherwise, between biographer and subject are likely to prove the most trenchant pathways to understanding? Perhaps—heresy!—the answer is *none,* or none that can be presumed in advance to guarantee access into the furthest recesses of personality. Perhaps what will turn out to matter most is that which is least visible and hardest to define: something to do with an elusive empathy of the spirit between biographer and subject, a shared if shadowy sense of how one should best navigate through life, treat other people, leave a mark and make a contribution without succumbing to self-importance—or self-destruction. How one positions oneself in the world will always reflect to some degree the seminal experiences and indoctrinations of class, race and gender, but may also, perhaps even to a greater degree, float above them, wondrously unanchored in categorical imperatives, mysteriously untraceable in derivation.

The simplifications currently employed are easily enumerated. In regard to class, for example, whether one defines it in terms of income, job status or educational level, it should be obvious that not all working-class people have had an interchangeable set of experiences; being on an assembly line cannot be equated with cooking hamburgers at McDonald's, nor illiteracy with a high school education, nor life in a trailer park with life in a slum. A historian with a "working-class" background cannot assume that that fact alone will open the gates of understanding to his or her working-class subject.

As for race, surely whites now realize that there is no homogeneity of lifestyle or opinion among members of a minority group. African-Americans, for example, vary widely in their views on everything from parenting to education to politics to white people. As for gender, the mere fact of being a woman would not in itself prepare a university-trained Ph.D. doing the biography of, say, Grandma Moses, for understanding a rudimentary rural life, the techniques of primitive painting, the process of aging or the morass of celebrityhood.

To take as a given that no white person is able (or morally entitled) to write about someone black can itself be seen as a form of racism—a particularly simplistic form, for it is based on the insidious assumption that fellow-feeling hinges on the color of one's skin and that an individual's character can be accurately prejudged on the basis of their membership in a particular group.

Since no biographer can duplicate in his or her person the full range of their subject's experience—or *exactly* duplicate any of it—every biographer will be found wanting in some areas. And, yes, the disability can sometimes be directly linked to racial (or class or gender) dissonance. I do not doubt, for example, that as a white person I failed to capture some of the nuances of what it meant for Robeson to grow up in the black church (his father was a minister). Yet, oppositely, my own second career in the theater gave me a background few if any scholars could bring to bear in evaluating Robeson's stage experience.

Which brings us to the "gay issue." Soon after my biography of Robeson had been published, in February 1989, I was in San Francisco on the final leg of the book tour. Between the usual signings and readings, I made time to pay a return visit to Lee and Revels Cayton. Both had been helpful during the seven years I spent on the biography, and

Revels, a radical veteran of the trade union wars and one of Robeson's closest friends, had at several points given me crucial information and advice.

I had sent the Caytons an early copy of the book, and Revels greeted me with a bear hug, effusive with congratulations for having "gotten it right." Later, over coffee, he made a comment that startled me: "You know, I've been thinking about it and I believe that only a gay man could have understood Paul's sex life."

I had been thinking about that too—for a long time—and thought I knew what Revels meant: Most heterosexual scholars, a conservative breed not known for their erotic capers, would be likely to share the mainstream view that lifetime, monogamous pair-bonding is the optimal path to human happiness—not to say moral decency. That assumption, in turn, would incline them, when confronted with the unconventional erotic history of someone like Robeson to evade, minimize, condemn or apologize for his robust sexuality.

A legion of heterosexual scholars strenuously believe in their hearts, not merely in their public pronouncements, that sexual "restraint" is one of the admirable moral cornerstones of our national character. (It took DNA, remember, finally to break down their adamant denial of a sexual liaison between Thomas Jefferson and Sally Hemings.)

Confronted with Robeson's many sexual adventures, such scholars would most likely characterize them as "womanizing" or "Don Juanism." Additionally, they would probably "explain" the fact that Robeson's most intense, long-lasting affairs were nearly all with white women by regurgitating hoary, simplistic formulas about his need to prove himself to the white world—or to work out his anger toward it.

By the time I visited the Caytons, Revels's view that most heterosexual scholars would react uneasily to Robeson's sexuality had already been borne out in some of the early reviews. The critic in the *San Francisco Chronicle* had referred to Robeson's "compulsive womanizing." The *Village Voice* reviewer had wondered about "the unquenchable need that lay behind his behavior." Ishmael Reed, while praising my "fine" biography, had taken me to task for the book's "excessive and voyeuristic detail" about Robeson's romantic and sexual encounters. And Paul Robeson, Jr., would soon issue a formal statement, printed in the *Amsterdam News*, characterizing my biography as "prurient." When I later told Revels about *that*, he shook his head in disbelief, chuckling over what he called my "restrained" account of Robeson's sexual activities.

Was Revels Cayton right in seeing my homosexuality as an *asset* in writing Robeson's biography, or was it—as many more have asserted—an offensive liability? Lloyd Brown, who collaborated with Robeson in the fifties on his autobiographical manifesto, *Here I Stand*, has been among the more publicly outraged. When my editor at Knopf sent Brown an early copy of the biography, he wrote back that I was "a sick writer" whose "homosexual values" were asserted throughout the book. Down to the present day, Brown continues to denounce my "preoccupation with the bedroom aspects of Robeson's life."

One of the ironies in all this is that my biography is, if anything, a rather truncated—one might even say chaste—rendering of Robeson's highly charged erotic life. Only Robeson's half-dozen significant romantic attachments are discussed in any detail, and his many short-term erotic encounters are barely mentioned. Nor do I ever describe, let alone itemize, his actual sexual behavior—his preferences and performances in bed.

Moreover, as I made clear in the biography, Robeson's wife, Essie, had early on understood that her husband was not cut out for monogamy and domesticity; wanting to remain Mrs. Robeson she had made her peace with his extramarital pleasures. That Essie was knowledgeable about Paul's sexual adventures would not, of course, make them more palatable to traditional moralists—including many churchgoing African-American adherents of mainstream sexual mores.

White conservatives, long since enraged at Robeson's political militancy, gleefully latch on to his erotic history as an additional weapon in portraying him as a "moral transgressor." For white racists, moreover, Robeson's exuberant sexuality can usefully be made to play into the long-standing, vicious stereotype of the black man as a "rampaging lustful beast." That almost all of Robeson's major affairs were with white women, finally, can be used to diminish his stature even among those who otherwise deeply admire his unyielding struggle against racism and colonialism. (After my biography was published, Paul Robeson, Jr., claimed that I had deliberately omitted a "list" he had given me of his father's black female lovers. If there is such a list, I was never shown it. Besides, the evidence of Paul Sr.'s preference for white lovers is overwhelming and incontestable.)

The biographer's job is to tell the truth—to the extent that inevitable gaps in the evidence and subjective distortion will allow for it. The biographer is not responsible for how others manipulate that truth to serve agendas of their own. Those who despise Robeson's socialism will always manage to find grounds for justifying their hostility; neither the inclusion nor the omission of evidence about his sexual life will dislodge their underlying animus toward his politics.

Yet even some who feel deeply sympathetic to Robeson's socialism experience discomfort over his troubled marriage and his frequent extramarital affairs—especially socialists of the older generation, for whom economic, not sexual or gender liberation, remains the one legitimate issue of abiding importance. This discomfort needs to be directly addressed, along with the underlying assumption that feeds it: namely, that monogamous, lifetime pair-bonding is, for everyone, the only defensible, natural, moral path.

But how much sex *is* too much sex? Does the answer hinge on the number of different partners involved, the number of encounters with the same partner, particular configurations (three-way or group sex, say) or particular sexual acts (anal intercourse, say, or sadomasochism)?

The answers will hinge on individual assumptions about what is "normal," "healthy" or "moral." In this country numbers alone are likely to settle the argument: The higher the figure, the more brows start to furrow—even though we are talking about consenting adults.

We need to take a closer look as well at what most people in our culture mean when using the designation "womanizer"—the charge Robeson's detractors most often level at him (that is, when they are not denouncing his "Stalinism"). Three definitions currently predominate: A "womanizer" is someone whose self-regard hinges on frequent conquests; is someone incapable of love and, to disguise that fact (not least from himself), pursues multiple sexual encounters; and, finally, is someone who treats his partners as exploitable objects, to be used disdainfully and discarded cavalierly.

None of those definitions, I would submit, apply to Paul Robeson. That is the overwhelming testimony of his lovers, as well as his psychiatrists. Every woman I spoke to who had been involved with Robeson for an extended period emphasized that he treated her as an equal, not a mere convenience or appendage. He could be difficult, neglectful and secretive, but was much more often tender, considerate and loving. As if in confirmation, one of Robeson's psychiatrists described him to me as a man whose "motivational spring was compassion, not ego."

And so when I hear Robeson described as a "womanizer," I've learned to take it as a rule of thumb that I'm listening to someone who despises the man politically and wishes to discredit him—as nothing can do more powerfully in our sex-negative culture than the accusation of "philanderer."

Unless it be, of course, to spread rumors that he was to some degree erotically involved with men. Such rumors, as I learned to my astonishment, were already in circulation when I began Robeson's biography. In a 1981 issue of the left-wing magazine *WIN* (now defunct), an article on Robeson had referred to his bisexuality as if it were a well-established fact. Some years later *The Advocate* (a national gay magazine) printed the claim that Robeson had "recently [been] revealed to have been gay." I protested both pieces and in the biography wrote that "I had found absolutely no evidence of Robeson's erotic interest in men."

While I was working on the book, the candidate most often urged on me as Robeson's male lover was the Russian filmmaker Sergei Eisenstein. When I discussed that possibility with, among others, Zina Voynow, Eisenstein's sister-in-law, she scoffed at the notion of such an affair—though she did not, as some of his biographers have, deny Eisenstein's homosexuality.

Nevertheless, even after my biography was published, the rumor surfaced yet again in a 1990 article by one Hugh Murray that insisted—at length, and based on a fatuous twisting of suspect scraps of "evidence"—that the matter of Robeson's bisexuality remained "an open question." It does not. Barring the (almost unimaginable) surfacing of new evidence to the contrary, Robeson was—as I wrote in the biography and as I have repeatedly said in response to ongoing queries—singularly, rigorously, contentedly heterosexual.

For merely insisting on scholarly standards of evidence, I expected no medal for Meritorious Resistance to Political Correctness. But I *was* surprised that among the several critics who denounced Robeson as "oversexed" and my biography of him as "prurient," only one—in *Commentary,* no less—so much as mentioned that my book had put to rest the long-standing rumors of Robeson's bisexuality. Not even the *Commentary* reviewer thought to mention that I had done so as a gay man who might have been expected to maximize every remote innuendo or shard of evidence that could have left open the opportunity to claim Robeson for Our Side.

When nongays credit anything of value in the gay perspective—and only a few leftists ever do—they usually cite its iconoclasm, its insistent challenge to "regimes of the normal," especially in regard to gender and sexuality. In writing Robeson's biography, iconoclasm stood me in good stead. Yet ultimately I came to feel that it was less important in helping me get beneath the layers of his personality than what I would call our shared status as outsiders—outsiders who to a significant degree had been "let in," had been treated by the mainstream as an acceptable representative of an otherwise despised group.

Years into researching the book, I continued to mull over the question of whether I was an appropriate biographer for Robeson. I finally came to the conclusion that a strong argument could be made—just as Revels Cayton would later suggest—that far from disqualifying me as an effective interpreter of Robeson's life, my being gay had in fact given me some important advantages. Here is how I ultimately summed it up for myself in a diary entry:

Like Robeson I know about the double-bind of being accepted and not accepted.

I know about the outsider's need to role-play (the uses of theater off-stage).

I know about the double-vision of the outsider who is let inside: about being a "spy" in the culture.

I know some of the strategies for concealing pain, including from oneself.

I know about the exuberant investment of hope in a "liberation" movement—and the attendant despair when it falls short.

I know about the seductive double-talk employed, when considered serviceable, by the white male power structure.

I know about the tensions of trying to be a "good" role model.

I know about the conflict between the yearnings of lust and the demands of a public image.

I know about the tug-of-war between the attractions of career and of doing "good works."

I know about the disjunction between the desire to be liked (and know-ing one has the necessary social skills to accomplish that) and feeling dis-gust at the neediness of the desire.

I know about stubbornness—and about the need to sometimes play the supplicant.

I know about the counterpulls of feeling gregarious and longing for—re-quiring—solitude.

I know about concealment.

I know about buried anger.

I know about politeness substituting for anger, about anger eating up one's vitals, distorting one's judgment.

I know about loneliness.

Once the biography was published, it came as an enormous relief to me that many African-American intellectuals—including Herb Boyd, Nathan Huggins, David Levering Lewis, Nell Irvin Painter and Arnold Rampersad—hailed it. The review that perhaps pleased me most was Painter's. Some years earlier, she had rather sharply attacked me and other white historians (during an American Historical Society panel on "Black Biography") for "wrongheadedly" undertaking biographies of African-Americans. Yet reviewing my biography in the *Boston Globe,* she reversed fields, writing that the book especially "rates high marks for hav-ing seen much that white biographers of African-American subjects fre-quently disregard, notably anger and strategies for its management. . . ."

Nell Painter did not suggest that my being gay might have been im-portantly connected to my ability to see "much that white biographers . . . frequently disregard." But after years of inner debate, I have come to hold that view decisively. To whatever extent my biography of Robeson does represent an empathy of the spirit, I believe the sensi-tizing factor of critical importance was precisely my homosexuality.

—The Nation, *December 28, 1998*

LETTERS PRINTED IN *The Nation* (FEB. I, 1999) IN RESPONSE TO "WRITING ROBESON"

Paul Robeson would never have agreed with Martin Duberman's cockeyed idea that he as a white homosexual was particularly qualified to write a definitive Robeson biography. As I relate in my own biography of the man, he selected me to write his life story because I was an African-American writer with a working-class background and a socialist outlook. When, after his father's death, Robeson, Jr., dumped me in favor of Duberman, he was well aware that Duberman would focus on the bedroom aspects of his father's life. Indeed, as Duberman informed interviewees, he had been strongly urged by Robeson's son to fully explore his parents' sexuality.

I formed the opinion that Duberman was a sick writer when he asked people if my close relationship with Robeson might have been more than collegial—me, a lifelong one-woman man, openly heterosexual! Not even the many investigations made of me by J. Edgar Hoover, whose concern about the class struggle was equaled by his fixation on the ass struggle, did such probing. Paul Robeson, Jr., might reflect upon some prophetic words of an appropriate authority. "Every great man nowadays has his disciples," said Oscar Wilde, "but it is always Judas who writes the biography."

—Lloyd L. Brown

Martin Duberman's article is self-serving and inaccurate. When he signed a collaboration agreement with me to write a comprehensive biography of my father, he agreed that his sexual orientation was irrelevant to his suitability as a Robeson biographer and formally consented to suspend his gay activism for the duration of his work on the book. True to his word, he withdrew from the public gay scene for seven years. His recent revelation that he decided to filter the Robeson story through his experiences as a gay man explains the sharp and sustained conflict that arose between us during our collaboration.

I always viewed the project as an attempt to present Paul Robeson as an unfiltered historical figure in his full dimensions. In this context, I chose Duberman solely on the basis of his previous historical and biographical works, in which he had demonstrated a vision far beyond his personal experiences. Nevertheless, I told him at the outset that I was uneasy about his lack of sensitivity to African-American cultural traditions, since a broad and deep understanding of black life during my father's time was the most important (but certainly not the sole) prerequisite for a Robeson biographer. My public criticism of Duberman's biography rested primarily on its presentation of a black subject through a restrictive white lens.

Duberman is misleading when he quotes only one word—"prurient"—from my public comment on his biography. The core of my criticism reads as follows: "The chief shortcomings of the book lie in its failure to offer analysis and judgements of Robeson's historical role, and its flawed presentation of his personality. Apparently, the author's remoteness from his subject reduced his sensitivity to important aspects of Robeson's cultural and emotional makeup. The result is especially disquieting in Duberman's occasionally prurient exploration of Robeson's personal life."

Duberman claims credit for omitting descriptions or itemizations of Robeson's "actual sexual behavior." In reality, his attempts to include such material were rejected both by me and by his publisher. Then he claims, incorrectly, that "Robeson's most intense, long-lasting affairs were nearly all with white women," and adds his invention that "Paul Robeson, Jr., claimed that I had deliberately omitted a 'list' he had given me of his father's black female lovers." The fact is that I refused to give him the names of four black women with whom my father had major affairs but who chose to remain anonymous.

It is interesting that in this article Duberman, being concerned primarily with Robeson's sex life, says little about the artistic life of one of the great performing artists of the century. His unseemly boast that "my own second career in the theater gave me a background few if any scholars could bring to bear in evaluating Robeson's stage experience" belies his inadequate treatment of Robeson's acting career. For example, he fails to mention, even in a footnote, that Robeson was the only African-American to be inducted into the National Theater Hall of Fame as a charter member.

The most insightful point Duberman makes in his article serves to underscore his misreading of Robeson's legacy. Raising an issue that lies at the heart of the culture wars, Duberman suggests that "perhaps none [of the standard links between biographer and subject] are likely to prove the most trenchant pathways to understanding. . . . Perhaps what will turn out to matter most is that which is least visible and hardest to define: . . . an elusive empathy of the spirit. . . . How one positions oneself in the world will always reflect to some degree the seminal experiences and indoctrinations of class, race and gender, but may also . . . float above them, wondrously unanchored in categorical imperatives, mysteriously untraceable in derivation."

The irony is that no one was more capable than Robeson of "floating above" his class, race and gender; yet no one rejected this possibility more forcefully than he. This is why I placed my father's classic 1937 quotation on his gravestone: "The artist must elect to fight for freedom or slavery. I have made my choice; I had no alternative."

—Paul Robeson, Jr.

My Reply:

Lloyd L. Brown's addlepated letter displays his homophobia with such stupefying vulgarity that any response would be sheets to the wind. However, several outright fabrications must be corrected. Paul Robeson, Jr., never urged me to "fully explore his parents' sexuality"; nor did I ever tell an interviewee that Robeson, Jr., had; nor did I ever attempt a full exploration in my biography.

Until Brown's letter, it never crossed my mind—let alone did I probe during interviews—that Brown and Robeson might have had a romantic/sexual relationship. Which brings us to "the ass struggle." The bigotry and coarseness of mind at work here—so foreign to Robeson—lends credence to the insistence of several Robeson intimates that he did not "select" Brown as his biographer. Brown badgered Robeson so relentlessly for the post that Robeson finally, wearily, gave in and consented—anything to get Brown off his back. What we have here is the real Judas, running amok.

For more than a dozen years I've refrained from publicly responding to Paul Robeson, Jr.'s unconscionable assaults. But enough is enough. I never agreed—I never would have *considered* agreeing—to the preposterous, homophobic notion that I suspend my gay activism for the duration of preparing the biography. I decided to postpone a book I had been working on (excerpted diary entries) in order to focus full time on the biography.

As is easily demonstrated—and as Robeson, Jr., was well aware at the time—my active involvement in the gay movement continued throughout the eighties: I wrote a regular column on gay and lesbian history for the *New York Native* and began work on establishing a university-affiliated research center on gay and lesbian life. After an arduous organizing effort of five years, the Center for Lesbian and Gay Studies was formally established at the CUNY Graduate School.

There were no attempts by me to include descriptions of Paul Robeson's "actual sexual behavior—his preferences and performances in bed." Robeson, Jr.'s grandiose claim that he (and my publisher) "rejected" my efforts to include such material is false. In a formal legal agreement he had surrendered early on all control over what I might say in the biography—he had zero power either to reject or include material.

To claim that my book is primarily concerned with Robeson's sex life and says little about his artistic life is bizarre. Robeson's artistic and political lives are far and away the dominant topics—as a glance at the index will prove.

It is no less bizarre—given the overwhelming historical evidence to the contrary—for Robeson, Jr., to deny that his father's "most intense, long-lasting affairs were nearly all with white women." I'm amazed that the same Paul Robeson, Jr., who told me that Sergei Eisenstein and Marc Blitzstein had been his father's lovers (in neither case true) would, out of a newly discovered respect for privacy, withhold the names of Robeson, Sr.'s four black female lovers.

In a February 15, 1987, diary entry, I wrote the following: "Helen [Rosen, one of Robeson, Sr.'s most devoted and intimate friends] called today to report an hour-long conversation with Paul Jr., . . . He ranted on at considerable length, according to Helen, about my refusal to acknowledge his father's black lovers—'Duberman has that list and is suppressing it.' I do? The only black lovers Paul Jr., ever tried to persuade me were 'significant' were Nina Mae McKinney and Ethel Waters. McKinney *possibly* (the evidence is minuscule) had a brief, passing affair with Robeson, Sr.; there is no evidence at all that Waters had so much as a single sexual encounter with him."

Note that a dozen years ago Robeson, Jr., was accusing *me* of suppressing the "list"; now he insists that *he* had never offered it. Note, too, that he felt no compunction about naming McKinney and Waters—despite his sanctimonious insistence today that he had refused to invade the privacy of his father's black female lovers.

I couldn't agree more that Robeson, Sr. floated above his class, race and gender. But the paragraph his son quotes discussed the relationship between biographers and subjects—and had nothing to do with Robeson, Sr.'s personal qualities.

There is more, much more, I could reveal—any number of shockingly defamatory (and false) tidbits and clues that Robeson, Jr., tried to plant in my path while I was writing the biography (the most vicious ones being about his own mother). But for now I refrain. Put simply, I don't want Paul Robeson, Jr., back in my life. Once was quite enough.

—Martin Duberman

The "New" (1997) Scholarship on Race Relations

White and Black. The categories are epistemologically absurd, but as historical constructs they have centrally formed our national identity. Racial interaction has, over the centuries, been at the heart of the American story, shaping its institutions, dictating its policies, poisoning its promises. These days, there seems to be a widespread assumption among whites that a great deal of progress has been made in race relations and, as a corollary (for we are a fatuously—sorry, famously—optimistic people), that further progress will now inevitably proceed.

For many whites, this is another way of saying, "We're sick of the whole issue" ("race fatigue" is the term some social scientists use to describe this widespread feeling). Mostly in private, more and more whites are saying they are fed up with hearing about black grievances, that everything within reason has been done to improve the lot of African-Americans, that it *has* improved (even if damned few blacks seem willing to admit it), that the improvement has often come at the expense of white *dis*advantage, and that if anything more is to be done, it is up to blacks themselves to do it—to get the needed education and job skills, to rid their communities of drugs, crime, teenage pregnancy and lazy welfare loafers.

Paralleling this mounting white disengagement has come an avalanche of new books attempting to justify it; among them are Alan Wolfe's *One Nation, After All,* Jim Sleeper's *Liberal Racism,* Shelby Steele's *A Dream Deferred* and, most widely touted of all, Stephan and Abigail Thernstrom's massive *America in Black and White.*

The views advanced in these books, a number of them funded by right-wing think tanks and foundations (the Manhattan Institute, the Hoover Institute, the John M. Olin Foundation, etc.) have not gone unchallenged nor swept the field. A significant number of recent works have emphasized the ongoing plight of many black Americans, and have outlined, with varying degrees of pessimism, future prospects. Among the more widely discussed have been: Andrew Hacker's *Two Nations,* William Julius Wilson's *When Work Disappears,* Derek Bok and William G. Bowen's *The Shape of the River,* Patricia Williams's *The Alchemy of Race and Rights,* Derrick Bell's *Faces at the Bottom of the Well,* Stephen Steinberg's *Turning Back* and David Shipler's *A Country of Strangers.*

And this hardly exhausts the list. Perhaps the best way, given limitations of space, to begin to get a handle on the ideological chasm that has opened up in the debate on race is to focus on the Thernstroms' much-discussed *America in Black and White,* using Shipler's *A Country of Strangers* as the primary counterpoint.

The Thernstroms' book is already being treated as something of a bible for those suffering from burnout on the "race question." Learned, sophisticated, filled with impressive charts and statistics, announcedly antiracist, *America in Black and White* has provided an encyclopedic rationale for being all at once optimistic and inactive about racial divisions. A legion of "fatigued" white hearts have sighed in grateful relief.

America in Black and White opens with six historical chapters about race relations in the twentieth century that contain no fresh scholarship and make for dull reading. The remaining two-thirds of the book, which is focused on assorted public policy issues (poverty, crime, voting rights, education, etc.), is both livelier and more deeply suspect. Containing useful data and scattered insights, the policy discussions are compromised by a not-so-subtle partisanship masquerading as "objective" social science, and by a chilly tone of dispassion, bordering on disdain, for the purported subject of concern—the ongoing plight of African-Americans.

The Thernstroms rightly reject any easy equation of today's difficulties with those of the rigid, servile caste system in the Jim Crow South of yesteryear, when blacks were excluded from the political process (and in the North, from most labor unions, restaurants, educational and employment opportunities) and lived in constant fear for their personal safety. The Thernstroms emphasize how much has changed in all those regards, and although they also recognize that much less has changed (or changed for the worse) for the black rural poor and urban underclass, the Thernstroms nonetheless insist that the *good* news has been "too little acknowledged or even understood."

For those who are unappreciative of how much has been accomplished or who are impatient for additional advance, the Thernstroms hold up Huey Newton and the Black Panthers as a dire warning. They dismiss Newton as "a man who both played at black power politics and led a life of serious crime." They seize on recent books by Panther insiders David Hilliard (*This Side of Glory*) and Elaine Brown (*A Taste of Power*) that reveal the extent of brutality and sexism within the organization, and contentedly leave the part to stand for the whole.

The Panthers are all lumped together as "young, impatient urban black men"—as if impatience (*and* anger) could not themselves be seen as legitimate reactions to three hundred years of oppression and of unfulfilled paper promises. (It all reminds me of how historians used to commonly talk about the abolitionist William Lloyd Garrison as a "disturbed, misguided fanatic" and never credit him with a scintilla of genuine distress over the plight of the slave.)

The Thernstroms offer not a positive word about the Panthers' concern for the conditions under which black children in the ghetto live, nor their idealistic efforts to set up food, health and educational programs for them. They might also have mentioned that the Panthers were nearly alone among left-wing groups in the late sixties and early seventies in keeping open lines of communication with white activists.

Cynical media commentators—typified by the color-coordinated (all white) Tom Wolfe—had a field day making fun of drawing room gatherings between working-class blacks and monied whites like Felicia and Leonard Bernstein. But sardonic jokes about "radical chic" called attention to one element in a complicated mix in order to devalue others—like feeling actual concern for the less fortunate. Such concern is never "pure" or "selfless"—any *adult* knows that—and it thus presents an easy target for the jaded, narcissistic Tom Wolfes of the world. Because Wolfe is apparently immune to feelings of compassion does not automatically make them inauthentic or self-aggrandizing in others.

In a comparably smug spirit, the Thernstroms settle for a total of three words in disposing of left-wing Congressman John Conyers: "sarcastic and abrasive." Similarly, when they describe the 1965 Watts riot, they show no sympathy or understanding of the long bottled-up rage among blacks at the brutality of the LAPD, whose history of intimidations, false arrests and gratuitous beatings the Thernstroms wholly ignore. Instead, they announce that "whites were not the aggressors" in the rioting—it was "an ordinary police action"—and they accuse the rioters of failing to approach their problems in a "rational" way, their real aim being "to appropriate or destroy property."

If blacks had really wanted to challenge police practices, the Thernstroms write, "looting stores and burning them down was a circuitous way of going about it." All of which manages simultaneously to reduce the LAPD's long-standing history of brutality to the equivalent of a feather duster, and black rage to a "seemingly gleeful" mob.

More complex judgments would compromise the Thernstroms' eagerness to equate moral urgency with civil disorder. Militancy, they warn, leads to riots, riots mark "the end of hope."

That is, the hope of winning white sympathy—to the Thernstroms, the *summa bonum*. And they offer multiple instances of how winning white sympathy has proven possible when blacks "properly" engage the political system. They insist, for example, that when black candidates for office present themselves as acceptably mainstream in lifestyle, values and policy positions, whites vote for them and welcome them to their neighborhoods. By implication, there should be no more emphasis on the specialness of black culture or, heaven forfend, the need to respect and protect it.

And there should certainly be no further calls for preferential treatment. Good riddance, according to the Thernstroms, since affirmative action policies assume blacks are "too crippled to be judged on their individual merit." But if blacks had historically placed their hopes on convincing whites of their "individual merit," rather than on a collective struggle against a racism that stigmatizes on the basis of *group* membership, there would never have been a civil rights movement.

The Thernstroms do acknowledge, grudgingly, that preferential policies "possibly" account for the accelerated numbers of African-Americans now in law, medicine, college teaching and engineering, or employed by government. Still, the Thernstroms insist, affirmative action policies have done far more harm than good. "When students are given a preference in admission because of their race or some other extraneous characteristic," the Thernstroms write, "it means that they are jumping into a competition for which their academic achievements do not qualify them and many find it hard to keep up."

True, blacks are admitted to elite universities (about a quarter of the whole; many of the rest are required to accept all or almost all students who apply) with lower test scores and grades. It is also true that on average they continue to receive lower grades throughout their undergraduate years, and graduate at a lower rate. Conservative commentators pretty much rest their case there, leaving unremarked that wretched secondary schooling (not genes or "cultural pathology") accounts for the fact that many blacks are less-well-prepared for test-taking than their white counterparts.

They also fail to note that grades and test scores are not (as is commonly assumed) the sole gauge of "merit" and, as well, have little effect on postcollege and professional performance. The Thernstroms begrudgingly acknowledge the *possibility* that preferential policies account for the increasing number of qualified blacks in graduate schools, but give no hint of the magnitude of their success: black students earn advanced degrees at rates identical to or, in some institutions and some fields (law, business, medicine), higher than that of their white classmates. They also become more active than their white classmates in civic activities.[1]

The Thernstroms and their fellow conservatives hold as a rock-bottom assumption that preferential policies for blacks unfairly come at the expense of whites. As one example, they offer the "set-aside," a policy that has "failed miserably." Why? Because bribes, kickbacks and assorted other corrupt practices have become part of the process. My, my, how shocking—in an economic system based on greed, and endemic with corruption. If the presence of periodic bribery and dishonesty are sufficient grounds for dismantling a policy or a system, then the Thernstroms might better expend their energies on warring against market capitalism.

In Atlanta, a city that is half black, only 0.5 percent of city contracts went to black contractors before the 1974 election of an African-American mayor, Maynard Jackson. *That* is the problem: the systematic exclusion of black bids by racist power brokers when policies like set-asides are not legally in place. The Thernstroms themselves provide the Atlanta statistic, and have the grace to note that it suggests a racism so systemic and subtle as to "require a certain amount of race consciousness"—though they never say *what* amount they consider appropriate; instead, they periodically (and paradoxically) deny throughout their study that race consciousness is useful or necessary.

The Thernstroms' emphasis is elsewhere: on persuading us that white racism has declined to the point where it is no longer a significant factor in accounting for the ongoing plight of many African-Americans.

But David Shipler, in *A Country of Strangers,* disagrees. In some areas, he argues, things *are* getting better, just as the Thernstroms say, but in other areas, they are getting worse. Yes, many more blacks hold office and are in college, but (to quote Shipler) "overall, the income distribution of black families has not changed much" and the asset-ownership gap between blacks and whites is much greater than the income gap. Twenty-six percent of all blacks still lack even a high school diploma, and in nine of the 19 states that once operated racially separate colleges, there has been a *decline* from 1991 to 1996 in the proportion of blacks entering the freshman class (*The New York Times,* Aug. 26, 1998). One-third of black men in their twenties are currently in jail, on probation or parole. Even those blacks who make it into the middle class often have very little financial cushion and rightly feel that their status is insecure.

Moreover, what whites *say* and what they in practice *do* are not equivalents; public rhetoric has become more civil, but public speech should never be equated with private conviction. If, Shipler warns, "blatant bigotry has grown unfashionable in most quarters," if the United States is unquestionably less overtly racist today than earlier, and if the laws that once mandated segregation have been struck down, segregation nonetheless "remains, sustained by economic disparities and the resulting residential patterns, [as well as by] white indifference and aversion . . . "

The Thernstroms insist that racial residential segregation has notably declined in urban America, but that conclusion arises from a highly selective reading of the evidence. As Douglas S. Massey and Mary J. Fisher recently (Dec. 14, 1998) reported in *The Nation*, almost all of the decline has come in metropolitan areas with small black populations—places like Albuquerque, Tucson and Phoenix. Which leaves three-quarters of all African-Americans still living under highly segregated conditions.

The New York Times recently (Feb. 13, 1999) reported that in the city of Chicago, to take one example, an increase in black home-buying has hastened segregation not integration. New black home-owners have been *routinely* funneled into a few neighborhoods only. At the beginning of the 1990s, some 110 of Chicago's 1,169 neighborhoods could be described as integrated (that is, 10% to 50% black). By the mid-1990s, only 27 of the 110 neighborhoods remained integrated.

Moreover, the levels of white antagonism to having black neighbors remains high. The Thernstroms themselves acknowledge that to most whites "a properly integrated" neighborhood means not one roughly balanced between the races but rather "a balance much like that prevailing in American society as a whole," that is, not more than 12% black. When a neighborhood becomes as much as one-third black, 57% of whites say they would feel uncomfortable, and 40% would immediately move out. In short, the residential welcome mat is out to blacks *if* they apply in limited numbers *and* seem (or are able to act) much like their middle-class white counterparts. We are supposed to equate this with the triumph of social justice.

In challenging the Thernstoms general view that white racism is no longer a significant factor, David Shipler cites the sophisticated survey done in 1990 by the National Opinion Research Center at the University of Chicago. It found that a full 57% of nonblacks rated blacks as "less intelligent than whites"—and that just 1.9% believed blacks would rather be self-supporting than live on welfare.

These are shocking statistics. "They are measurements," as Shipler puts it, "of a cruel wind that whips across America." The consequence of nearly two out of three nonblack Americans seeing (for the most part they nurse these attitudes in private) blacks as less intelligent and lazier, is to create "a corrosive chemistry of low expectations, closed opportunities and ultimate defeat. The judgments that spring from the stereotypes become self-fulfilling prophecies, creating a reality of failure that is then taken to justify the sterotypes themselves."

The Thernstroms acknowledge the gap between white rhetoric and practice, but then construct a twisted argument that makes a mockery of the acknowledgement. They announce that "naked discrimination" among real estate agents is a thing of the past, and insist that what bias remains is far less important in accounting for residential segregation than is the unwillingness of African-Americans "to live in areas that have no more than a handful of black residents." But if some blacks wish to avoid being isolated among disapproving white neighbors, that is a commentary on white, not black, insularity.

But the Thernstroms prefer to blame the victim and exonerate the victimizer. They refuse to understand, among much else, why some African-Americans *do* prefer voluntary segregation: they know that "acceptance" and "assimilation" hinge on the degree of their willingness (and success) in "blending in," in acculturating to white values and tastes.

And there is less and less willingness to do so. As white resistance to school and housing desegregation and to affirmative action policies has increased, black interest in "melting pot" integration has decreased. Even the middle-of-the-road NAACP has been forced into a profound internal debate about whether to rethink the primary importance of its historic commitment to public school integration. They could hardly do otherwise given recent developments. The nation's schools are becoming *re*segregated at the fastest rate since the 1954

Brown v. *Board of Education* ruling. In several court decisions in the 1990's (*City* v. *Dowell*, 1991; *Freeman* v. *Pitts*, 1992), the Supreme Court has made it increasingly easy for schools to end desegregation. And they have done so in mounting numbers—a process fully documented in Gary Orfield and John T. Yun's 1999 study, "Resegregation in American Schools." What this in turn has done (yet again) is to consign low-income minorities to schools with inferior resources. And as a recent Harvard University study, *Deepening Segregation in American Public Schools,* puts it: "There is no evidence that separate but equal today works any better than it did a century ago."

The emphasis for many blacks these days—unlike in the 1960s—is on gaining equality of treatment, not assimilation; they emphasize the importance of maintaining, not diluting a black cultural identity. Black radicals are creating new organizations (Agenda 2000, the Black Radical Congress, the Ida B. Wells Collective, etc.) dedicated to developing collective strategies for fundamental social changes that have nothing to do with making "the melting pot" more effective and everything to do with destroying ingrained institutional barriers that have up to now prevented the development of a truly democratic and egalitarian society.

If we turn to the plight of the black working poor and nonworking underclass, we find that nearly a third of African-Americans still have incomes below the poverty level; the rate has not fallen since 1970—and is nearly triple that for white Americans. The absolute numbers of poor blacks have increased by nearly 700,000 in the past thirty years, while the numbers of poor whites have declined by 4 million.[2]

The Thernstroms find all this "depressing." But they are quick to add that "the black urban underclass does not define black America," and that "a majority of blacks are not poor"—a shakey statement once one learns (the Thernstroms do not tell us) that in 1992, 42.7% of all African-American households earned less than $15,000, compared to 21.6% of whites.

As for those blacks living below the poverty level, the Thernstroms argue that black poverty is not due to curtailed opportunities, but to the disintegration of "intact, two-parent families" in the black community. The news that single parents, supplemented by a kinship network, can successfully raise children and is a viable cultural pattern has not made it through the Thernstroms' radar screen. Nor has the finding that black families lovingly care for their elderly *at home* at double the rate that whites do—surely one measure of the strength of family ties.

Along with blaming the black family, the Thernstroms patronizingly explain that "there is work available—even in inner city neighborhoods"—and recent immigrants, unlike "unmotivated" (a word choice unnervingly close to "shiftless") blacks, avail themselves of it. But we hear nothing from the Thernstroms about the wretched, dead-end nature of the work, nor of the fact, now well-established, that (except for the small numbers of truly "estranged poor" who *have* rejected the larger society, and employ their entrepreneurial talents in the drug and numbers games) unemployed blacks will, against all odds, line up for long blocks and endless hours for even a chance at one of those dead-end jobs.[3]

The fundamental problem *is* jobs—as William Julius Wilson, in *The Truly Disadvantaged*, stressed more than a decade ago. The disappearance over the last quarter-century of thousands of low-skill jobs is the main reason the ghetto underclass endures. As Wilson puts it, since 1970 "all the major Northern cities had consistent job losses in industries where employee education averaged less than a high school degree, and consistent employment growth in industries where workers on the average acquired some higher education."

At a time when the economy is rapidly becoming global, and low-paying jobs are migrating out of the country, our best chance at avoiding a permanent underclass sunk in poverty and despair is (since we have been unable to loosen the stranglehold of market capitalism) to improve the nation's schools and widen opportunities for learning technological and computer skills.

If we *really* care about the extent of black poverty, we should be concentrating (as we are decidedly *not*) on creating better educational opportunities instead of attacking the affirmative action policies that have made it possible for *some* blacks to find promising work and hopeful futures.

The Thernstroms never discuss the culture of low expectations bred into some blacks by centuries of demoralizing oppression; nor acknowledge the accumulated rage among the poor over forever starting, and remaining, at the bottom-line entry level; nor the anger among middle-class black lawyers, brokers and corporate managers who still hit "glass-ceilings," whose careers stall, who are denied advancement to the highest levels of their profession.

Expect no soft-minded (or -hearted) empathy from the Thernstroms and their ilk (whose ranks include a few black intellectuals: Shelby Steele, for example, argued in his book, *The Content of Our Character,* that blacks were their own worst enemies). The Thernstroms prefer the Calvinist lecture: blacks must learn basic literacy skills and good diction, "how to dress appropriately, wake up to an alarm, arrive at work on time, and listen to direction and criticism once there." The Thernstroms, mind you, self-describe as nonracists (and objective social scientists to boot). Is it any wonder that the number of blacks who believe whites want them to "get a better break" was down to 25% by 1994?

The Thernstroms, busy trumpeting black gains and denying white racism, profess to regard such pessimism as "something of a puzzle." It is—for people who don't see or won't discuss the multitude of everyday slights that African-Americans suffer (yes, even those successful black doctors and lawyers), and the angry distrust that such disdain generates. Ellis Cose has documented that anger in *The Rage of a Privileged Class,* but the Thernstroms dismiss him as "totally credulous"—a characterization better reserved for their own obdurate forms of denial.

Much of what the Thernstroms willfully ignore or distort, David Shipler, in *A Country of Strangers,* compassionately embraces; where they arrogantly pronounce, he subtly questions, troubling to catch innuendos of style (and oppression), attuned to and appreciative of cultural differences. His emphasis is not on statistics (though he has mastered them) but on people—the images whites and blacks have of each other and what happens when their paths cross: "the physical body we see, the mental qualities we imagine, the moral character we attribute to the other and ourselves, the violence we fear, the power we seek or are loath to relinquish . . . "

Shipler agrees that real racial progress has been made, but, he argues, *true* integration—genuine power sharing—has largely failed. In most institutions (the armed forces are the chief exception), power is still reserved for whites, and a belief in black *cultural* inferiority has subtly substituted for the earlier belief in black *genetic* inferiority.

Shipler contends that whites and blacks in essential ways "remain strangers to each other." What blacks see as pride and solidarity, whites read as touchiness and hostility. Some blacks, Shipler believes, *do* "mean their behavior to be antagonistic," but he also believes that the white threshold of resentment is often low, and also that whites have an exaggerated view of black power and a growing sense of *white* victimhood. When blacks seek a comfort zone in separation, whites see a stubborn refusal to join mainstream society (and act as if such an invitation has long been on the table and is now unconditional—which is far from the truth).

The end result, in any case, is that the luster is gone from the idealistic sixties goal of integration: "It seems," Shipler writes, "an idea from a naïve time, a goal unattainable and perhaps undesirable . . ." A growing number of blacks seem to agree. "Integration," when defined to mean "assimilation" has lost ideological currency. Like other minorities—gays and lesbians, for example—the point of pressure has shifted from "let us in, we're just like you" to "we demand all the rights and privileges of first-class citizens, but in the struggle to get them, have no intention of surrendering our own hard-won, unique identity." We are marching for our rights, not for the erasure of our culture. We want economic inequities addressed; we want all the opportunities that whites have (though of course many whites *don't* have them—like most women, like the rural poor), but we certainly don't want to *be* whites.

David Shipler underscores, with the acute psychological antennae and the needed empathy so lacking in the Thernstroms and their kind, how difficult and limited are the choices available to many African-Americans. Some can travel back and forth between black and white worlds with what Shipler calls remarkable "fluidity of spirit"; they establish an easy, bicultural equilibrium between racial identity and mainstream assimilation. But many African-Americans cannot, and Shipler is at his most compassionate when describing their excruciating plight: those who take the path that "leads out of the all-black comfort of family, neighborhood and culture into the alien landscape of mostly white America" find life lonely, find a world where "whites, mostly, hire and fire and make the rules and determine the styles of interaction."

The effort to maintain their cultural roots while making it in the wider world, means an inner balancing act that "tears at black souls." Shipler suggests that if more whites—perhaps the Thernstroms—understood this, "they would be gentler." They might also be better able to value the richness of black cultural forms—which Shipler in part characterizes as "the inventiveness of humor . . . the spontaneity of feeling, the dignity of struggle, the sexuality of love, the rootedness in reality and the suffering of the street . . . a warm interactive style . . . sensitive to relational issues."

Not only do many whites fail to understand how difficult it is for some blacks to enter a corporate setting, but they also do not understand why some African-Americans get angry when whites—like the Thernstroms—proudly announce their allegiance to the ideal of "color blindness." The call for "color blindness" is often seen by blacks as a form of insult, a willful refusal to acknowledge the genuine different-ness of black experience, of black pride in their heritage, of their abil-ity to have created, against all odds, innovative religious, literary and artistic forms that have been both oppositional and revelatory to main-stream white culture.

To announce, with a pat on one's own "liberal" back, that the social goal is color blindness is tantamount to declaring that African-American culture is devoid of any real content—other than the stan-dard symptomatology of victimhood—and is therefore not worth preserving. This is the equivalent of asking African-Americans to per-form self-lobotomies, to destroy their memories of struggle and ac-complishment, to deny the legitimacy of their own life-sustaining culture. But many blacks are uninterested in "transcending" race—which in practice has meant assimilating to white values without get-ting more than token access to white power.

Whites like the Thernstroms deplore any insistence on the impor-tance of minority identity as the equivalent of having a chip on one's shoulder, as being negligent of a civic duty wholeheartedly to embrace what are being widely championed as "universal" values (which turn out to be, when defined at all, of mostly Eurocentric manufacture). They do not seem to understand that race (or class or gender or sex-ual) consciousness is a prerequisite for organizing against what is still an entrenched institutionalized bigotry that *itself* judges individuals on the basis of membership in a particular group. The paradoxes are multiple: we do not want to reify identities that are too rigidly defined or grossly constructed. But we do not dare to demobilize, to redefine established identity categories with greater subtlety and precision, until we can first feel more secure than would currently be realistic that the country has rid itself of its multiple exclusions and prejudices.[4]

None of which should be taken as sanctioning the way some black nationalists invent and distort history as a consciousness-raising tactic. But we do need to understand what lies behind such inventions. As David Shipler had put it, "[B]eliefs are windows into people's deepest pain." Besides, nationalist distortions can be viewed as no more or less pernicious than white silences.

The kind of silence that until recently had guides at Monticello referring to Jefferson's slaves as his "servants." The kind of silence that makes no reference in high school history texts to the black cowhands who drove cattle up the Chisholm Trail or fought in World Wars I and II, or to the ingenious black colleagues of Alexander Graham Bell and Thomas Alva Edison.

If one believed the noisy antagonists of a multicultural curriculum, our textbooks are already dangerously overloaded with minority materials. But in fact the representation of black achievement and experience continues to be minimal in the standard school curriculum. The Thernstroms contemptuously dismiss efforts to better represent black history and culture as "therapeutic strategies," and they insist that "black children do not need" them. Nor do they need a larger number of culturally empathic black teachers: "what helps students to perform well is not the race of their teachers," the Thernstroms simplistically insist, "but their intellectual competence."

Psychologically tone-deaf, the Thernstroms wholly reject the view that a lack of minority representation in textbooks makes any contribution to the lowered self-esteem (and test scores) of African-American students. According to the Thernstroms, black academic achievement would be most likely to improve if the discipline that characterizes Catholic schools were mandated everywhere. And they are right—if the goals of education are defined as safety, order, the rote learning of authoritarian dogma and the creation of dutiful robots.

Rather than deal with the lying silences of the textbooks, the corrosive history of stereotyping, the stultifying assumptions about black intellectual inferiority, the Thernstroms settle for platitudinous harangue: "nothing under the sun except hard work" (on the part of blacks, that is) can ever bring about racial parity. After all, they insist, "Hard-core white racism is largely a thing of the past . . . the haters have become a tiny remnant with no influence in any important sphere of American life . . . the serious inequality that remains is less a function of white racism than of the racial gap in levels of educational attainment, the structure of the black family, and the rise in black crime." In other words, blacks should place the blame for lagging behind where it belongs: on themselves.

David Shipler opts for a very different set of emphases. "The real quagmires of blacks' impotence," he believes, lie in "their tightly circumscribed political influence and their hollow economic stature." He deplores the way white anxiety and anger boil up not about black powerlessness but about attempts—like redistricting and affirmative action—to redress the imbalance of power.

Contrary to the Thernstroms' claim that white racism is essentially dead, and without denying that it *has* diminished, we need to recognize its terrifying agility, the many ways it has deftly adapted to changing circumstances, inventing new rationales for resisting every new remedy for achieving racial parity. Many whites, agreeing with the Thernstroms, would deny that they harbor any racist feelings. But, as David Shipler suggests, many are self-deceived: "Whites who discriminate subtly may not even be aware of what they are doing . . . Suitably disguised, prejudice can operate without being noticed, unseen even by those who hold the biases."

The bias is not always subtle. These days, more doors seem to be closing than opening for African-Americans. In 1996, for example, Californians voted to ban the consideration of race in all government institutions, including race-conscious admissions policies throughout the University of California system (Washington State and Texas adopted similar measures in 1998). Several important court decisions

(*Podberesky* v. *Kirwan,* 1994; *Hopwood,* 1996) have legitimized the trend in rulings that cover some eight states.

Conservative whites have long been pushing the argument that under affirmative action policies, qualified whites have been losing out to unqualified blacks. Now they have been joined in that assumption by more and more of the white citizenry and the white-dominated court system. In defending what amounts to a retreat, many have resorted to the "high-minded" argument that the new trend toward "race-neutral" policies is fairer to all concerned.

But it is in fact proving a disaster—for minorities, that is. Professors Bowen and Bok, in *The Shape of the River,* have estimated that the percentage of blacks at top-ranked universities will fall overall from 7% to less than 2%. They further estimate that this will increase the chances of whites gaining admission to those elite institutions by only 2%— from 25% to 27%. In sum, eliminating race-conscious admission policies will have a major impact on minority applicants, while only marginally helping majority ones. The accuracy of their predictions have, in just a few years, already been confirmed in the University of California system: the admission of blacks on all eight UC campuses has fallen by 29% from 1997 to 1998; by 16% for Hispanics; by 10% for whites; and have for Asians increased 1%—though in 1999 there is some evidence of a reversal in the negative percentages.

Among a growing number of *progressive* opponents of race-conscious affirmative action, there is a call to substitute instead a *class*-based policy; that is, preference would be given to low-income applicants in general, whether black, Latino, Asian or white. This sounds plausible, a way of simultaneously helping *all* low-income people while eliminating the grounds for white resentment.

But according to the analysis of Harvard public policy expert Thomas Kane, what sounds plausible turns out not to be. Blacks and Latinos, according to Kane, are three times as likely as whites to come from families with incomes below $20,000. But taking the general population as a whole, their numbers are small; blacks and Latinos account for less than half of low-income high school students and only 17% of low-income students with high test scores. The overwhelming majority of low-income/high test scores students are white and Asian. It is they who would benefit most from class-based affirmative action—not blacks and Latinos. In other words, class-based affirmative action, unlike race-conscious affirmative action, will not produce greater racial diversity on our campuses—nor even be able to sustain the amount of diversity that currently exists.

The University of Maryland sociologist Fred L. Pincus has argued that the only remaining tactic for producing racial diversity in our universities "is to de-emphasize grades and test scores and to incorporate other factors that are relevant to educational success. This gets to the whole question of what a 'qualified' student really is."

Exactly. But the nineties are not the sixties. Thirty-five years ago, the campuses were alive with challenges to traditional models of what an "education" means and by what gauges we decide who is "deserving" or "qualified" to receive it. Today, what vitality remains on campus is, among students, largely centered on sports, entertainment and, above all, career building; and, among faculty, on jostling for position and hoarding time for research (or watching television). Airing out and opening up the campuses are not high on anyone's agenda.

Meantime, black Americans watch and wait. Watch closely, for they have long since known that the country's commitment to their welfare is tenuous and subject to rapid reversal. At the moment, their highly attuned antennae are picking up mostly negative signals. With white conservatives touting "color blindness," and with increasing numbers of white progressives arguing that the primary issue is class, not race, there is ample reason for distrust and disillusion. Again.

*—this is a revised and expanded version of a piece I did
for* The Los Angeles Times, *Oct. 12, 1997.*

II

Reconfiguring the Gay Struggle

The (Contested) New History of Gays and Lesbians[1]

Virginia Woolf slept with Vita Sackville-West. Does that make her "lesbian"? Cary Grant had a long-standing affair with Randolph Scott. Does that make him "gay"? And what do we do with Colette, the lover of young men, once we learn of her involvement with the film star Marguerite Moreno? And is there a category for Lord Byron, notorious for his many affairs with women *and,* at one point, madly in love with the choirboy John Edleston?

Queer theory has tried to teach us to distrust categories as needless calcifications of what is (purportedly) our fluid, meandering erotic natures. We are told to move beyond Freud's notions of inherent bisexuality to posit a pliable sexuality that, if allowed to run free, would create all sorts of trisexual permutations. Most of us, alas, however attracted to the theory of infinite malleability, have been trained in a culture that regards sexual appetite as consisting of two, and only two, contrasting variations—gay or straight. And most of us have internalized that dichotomy to such a degree that it has become as deeply imprinted in us, as immutable, as any genetically mandated trait.

Many gays and lesbians have themselves little patience with the implicit injunction of queer theorists constantly to reinvent ourselves, and tend to dismiss such a view as utopian. Yet it is difficult to blink away the ambiguities about human sexuality that have arisen in the wake of the burgeoning new scholarship on the gay and lesbian past.[2]

A mere twenty years ago, the notion of a formal, scholarly, institutionalized inquiry into lesbian and gay history would have been unthinkable, literally not nameable. Yet there are now enough serious-minded scholars devoting their full-time efforts to its reclamation to fill conference rooms. Some are engaged in documenting the history of genital sex between members of the same gender. Others pursue evidence of passionate, romantic, *non*-genital friendships. Yet another group of scholars is at work detailing the history of gender nonconformity and of cross-gender identifications in dress, speech, mannerisms and attitudes—studies that center on the phenomena of transvestism and transsexualism or, cross-culturally, on "third gender" figures like the Native American *berdache,* the Indian *hijra* and the Polynesian *mahu.* Finally, there are scholars whose primary inquiry is describing how and why cultural definitions of sexual and gender unorthodoxy shift over time; their interest is less on the nonconforming behavior itself than on understanding the changing ways it has been regarded over time through history and across cultures.

Though all these enterprises, and more, have swiftly accelerated in the past few years, their interconnections are not always clear, and the complex nature of the evidence being unearthed has often been difficult to interpret. To take just one example—the history of passionate friendship—scholars continue to earnestly yet inconclusively debate the connection of that phenomenon to the history of erotic arousal.[3] Are they one and the same? Is passionate friendship best seen as an instance of erotic sublimation? Is overt sexuality a natural extension of emotional closeness and should we therefore view its absence as an instance of cultural repression? Further, some would argue that the pursuit of evidence of genital sex between two people of the same gender is itself a misguided enterprise, the "true" history of "gays" and "lesbians" residing not in the record of same-gender erotic arousal but in the story of gender nonconformity.

There is no question—to stay with the example of passionate friendship—but that many pairs of women in the United States and England lived together during the latter part of the nineteenth and the early part of the twentieth centuries in devoted partnerships, sharing all aspects of their lives. Well, nearly all. Emotional intimacy—yes. Frequent hand-holding, touching, even kissing—yes. But genital sexuality—apparently no. Should we therefore refrain from calling them "lesbians"?

Perhaps the answer lies not in their (apparently) celibate behavior but in their fantasy lives; perhaps these women secretly admitted to themselves what they were loath to act upon. Perhaps—but it is unlikely we will ever know. We almost never have enough information about the inner lives of people in the past to talk confidently about the content of their subjective desires. Maps to the psychological interior (in the form, say, of elaborate, unbridled diaries and letters) are almost always lacking for historical figures, especially before the twentieth century. In their absence, we form judgments from *behavioral* evidence alone—itself not easy to come by, gauge or interpret.

And what of the additionally complicating factor of *self*-definition? Should we reserve the label "lesbian" (or "gay") for those who are subjectively conscious of having a different sexuality, which they in turn reify into a different "identity"? In regard to those pair-bonded women involved in "Boston marriages" (as they were sometimes called in this country), the historian Leila Rupp has concluded that they would most probably have rejected the label "lesbian" for themselves.

Indeed some of those women lived on into a more self-conscious era when the terminology and categories "gay" and "lesbian," not earlier available, had come into common usage, and they often reacted with anger and disgust to the suggestion that *their* relationships could be so characterized. True, their very vehemence can be taken as a classic instance of denial. But if we insist on that interpretation, we have placed ourselves in the position of claiming to know the "truth" of a relationship better than the participants in it—to say nothing of placing ourselves in danger (one to which historians commonly succumb) of projecting *our* descriptive categories backward in time onto those who might have neither understood nor approved of them.

The problem of interpreting "Boston marriages" is but one example of the conundrums facing those engaged in trying to unearth a usable past for today's lesbian, gay, bisexual and transgendered communities, trying to somehow lay claim to an extended history that can provide needed nourishment and legitimacy. The large majority of gay people share the mainstream American view, common to most cultures, that legitimacy is predicated on the ability to lay claim to "roots"—to antecedents; to hoist the counter banner of being "something new under the sun" is tantamount to inviting ridicule. Again, like other mainstream Americans, most gay men and lesbians hanker after and rhetorically hallow the past even as they insistently ignore it as irrelevant.

In the case of gay people, the hankering takes on particular poignancy. Having been excluded from the textbooks, having been denied the kind of alternate, family-centered oral tradition available to other minorities, gay people long for some proof—some legitimizing evidence—that we have always existed, and in pretty much the same form that we currently do, and that we are therefore automatically entitled to the same status and rights other "official" minorities lay claim to.

Alas, we can never find *exact* precursors, and any search for them is always doomed to disappointment. This is no less true for heterosexuals than for homosexuals (as we have quaintly learned to call ourselves). Heterosexuality, too, has a history,[4] a record of shifting definitions of what has been considered "healthy" or "authentic"—and therefore allowable—behavior. Women in this country and in England in the mid-nineteenth century, for example, were commonly viewed as "passionless." Any woman who exhibited "undue" interest in sex was likely to be labeled disturbed—"neurasthetic." She would be sent away for a rest cure and, should that fail, would become a candidate for a clitorectomy. Yet a mere hundred years later a common feminist view is that women are innately *more* sexual than men, capable of that indefinite number of orgasms and ever-heightened pleasure that the low-performing male can only fantasize about (and envy so furiously in the female that he invents the domestic lockup to curtail her).

Neither gays nor straights, in short, can hope to lay claim to any kind of history other than an endlessly changing one. We can never confirm our present images by citing lengthy lineages in the past. What the past *can* be said to confirm is that "human nature," far from being a constant, has taken on, under varying cultural imperatives, a wide range of shapes—a view that is at the very heart of queer theory.

One example, a brilliant one, of how the history of same-gender attraction can be reclaimed in "usable" form—that is, as a solvent to parochialism—is Michael Rocke's recent (1996) *Forbidden Friendships: Homosexuality and Male Culture in Renaissance Florence.*

Americans, caring little and knowing less about the past, assume that contemporary behavior is the equivalent of human behavior, that the way society currently organizes desire, structures love and defines pleasure is the way societies, across time and culture, *always* have. And where they haven't—some rumors have surfaced about grown men and adolescent boys getting it on in ancient Athens—we moderns feel justified in our disgust at such a falling away from what "everyone knows" are universally valid standards of healthy sexual behavior.

Forbidden Friendships is a marvelous corrective to such insularity, but is hardly likely to find the popular audience that needs it most. Not even many gay readers will pick up the book—milestone though it is in the twenty-year rise of gay and lesbian studies. It is too densely argued, too challenging, too unlike those usual favorites in our (in every American) community: How to Find a Lifetime Mate, Secure Your Financial Future, Guarantee a Seat in Heaven. Well, perhaps scholars, at least, will recognize the book's enormous merit and importance, and its findings will slowly disseminate.

Rocke has spent some dozen years digging in the Florentine archives and his vast, mostly unsubsidized labor has yielded remarkable results. Renaissance Florence had a population of only 40,000, yet in the seventy years from 1432 to 1502 some seventeen thousand men were investigated for sodomy and about a fifth of them convicted. Same-sex acts, it seems, were so commonplace as to be integral to male culture, a normal aspect of male development.

At the same time, most Florentines had been taught to believe that sodomy was a serious sin, and in 1432 the government created a magistracy, the Office of the Night, specifically to suppress it. They failed, and the actual (as opposed to official) attitude toward homosexuality continued to be, paradoxically, one of tolerant disapproval, with punishment generally sporadic and mild. This was especially true for teenagers adhering to the "passive" role traditionally assigned them; for adult males who had sex with each other or who allowed themselves to be penetrated, penalties were often far more harsh.

What did these sexual acts *mean* to those engaging in them? The voices of "sodomites" themselves, alas, rarely make it into the historical record. We can enumerate the number of sexual acts performed far better than we can characterize the subjective feelings they generated or what "meaning" they had for the participants. Rocke has, remarkably, managed to rescue at least a few personal stories, enough to suggest a surprising range of affect—including tenderness, infatuation and love.

Though homosexual activity flourished at all levels of Florentine society, Rocke scrupulously warns against assuming a genealogy, against conflating fifteenth-century patterns with our own notions (quite foreign to the Renaissance) of a fixed and exclusive sexuality that centrally defines the self. A plethora of homosexual activity, moreover, does not denote a distinctive homosexual subculture. As Rocke puts it, for Florence "there was only a single male sexual culture with a prominent homoerotic character."

Rocke provides rich material with which to speculate on a host of large, if elusive, issues: the origin of the "sodomite" as a distinctive personality type; the predominance of the adult/adolescent sexual model in the history of male homosexuality; the symbolic importance for gender certification of "active" versus "passive" roles; the relationship between male bonding and homoeroticism; the difference between networks of shared activities (or even an established sexual "underground") and an articulated subculture; and the endlessly thorny question of self-identification.

—The Nation, *July 5, 1993/*
The Advocate, *Dec. 24, 1996*

Breaking the Codes:
Biography and Art

T wenty years ago, at the time of his first major retrospective, a reporter asked Robert Rauschenberg what it felt like to see so much of his old work brought together? "The pain and the pleasure," he answered, "come in about equal doses. A retrospective is a real obstacle. A retrospective can kill you."

It didn't. In the years since, Rauschenberg has gone on being a one-man laboratory of leapfrogging, showy creativity: a painter, sculptor, photographer, print and silk screen maker, set designer and conceptual artist. Now [1997] seventy-two, and still working in the fevered, effervescent spirit of the newest boy in town, Rauschenberg is again the subject of a major show, this time of some four hundred works of such dizzying versatility and spendthrift ambition that it will take both of New York City's Guggenheim Museums to display it.

At this moment of coronation, some long-smoldering issues relating to autobiographical readings of Rauschenberg's work—and that of his once-close associates Cy Twombly and Jasper Johns—have risen to the surface. A handful of mostly young art critics, in defiance of the curatorial/museum establishment, and in the face of the (sometimes passive) discouragement of the artists themselves, have entered the scholarly lists with new or oppositional icongraphic readings of the visual imagery at play.

Predictably, the art world establishment has ignored these mavericks: their curatorial services have not been sought, their scholarly articles have gone uncited—both in the catalogue for the new Rauschenberg show and in that of its 1993 predecessor, "Robert Rauschenberg: The Early 1950s" (organized by The Menil Collection). Some view this as censorship through silence; others, the justifiable bypassing of a polemical scholarship that invades personal privacy.

I enter this controversy as a historian and biographer, not as an art critic, impelled into it by my sense of the large issues at stake: What are we morally and legally entitled to say about the private lives of well-known artists or, for that matter, of public figures in general? Who is empowered to give that permission, and from where does that power derive? Does newly uncovered biographical information and do newly minted iconographic readings contribute to our understanding of the artworks in question, or is this merely another instance—a high-flown one—of the culture's already overwrought penchant for scandal and gossip?

Let me begin by stepping backward, back to Black Mountain College, whose history I have written, the place where Rauschenberg's artistic practice was, by his own account, centrally shaped in the late forties and early fifties. The primary influence over Rauschenberg at Black Mountain was Josef Albers. Austere, dogmatic *and* enthusiastic about the passionate response, Albers was simultaneously iconoclastic and Prussian, against art school formulas and art fashions yet insistent on "*disciplined* freedom." He inculcated in his students the prime importance of "a personal sense of looking," of staying "in a state of awareness," and of heeding the specific properties of the raw materials being used, of respecting their essences, changing surfaces, and intricate correspondences and combinations.

Rauschenberg has called Albers "the most important teacher I've had" and has added (in a 1969 film about Albers), "his criticism was so devastating that I wouldn't ask for it. But twenty-one years later, I'm still learning what he taught me." Yet in 1967, when I interviewed Albers at length for my book on Black Mountain, he claimed to have no clear memory of Rauschenberg; "a student," he said, waving his arm in vague dismissal, "has a stronger memory of his teacher than the teacher usually has of one of his many students." One of many; not one preferred.

Rauschenberg's formative work with Albers has become a commonplace of the literature. But only a few additional biographical notes have ever been included in the numerous published accounts of Rauschenberg's time at Black Mountain: namely, that he had initially followed a student friend and fellow painter, Susan Weil, there in 1948; that he subsequently married and had a son with her; that the marriage collapsed in less than two years; that he returned to Black Mountain in 1951 in the company of a young artist he had recently met named Cy Twombly; that he and Twombly became such good friends that they took off for Italy and an extended period of travel together.

Enter the new critics, dissatisfied with this truncated mapping of Rauschenberg's formative years, convinced that their own iconographic insights, in combination with newly available (though still unpublished) correspondence, allow for a far more detailed, compelling—and truthful—account. They take for granted the relevance, indeed the necessity, of biographical materials for a full appreciation of the meaning and impact of a given work of art—an assumption hardly unique to them. Mary Lynn Kotz, Rauschenberg's official biographer, as well as Walter Hopps, chief curator of both the 1993 and the 1997 retrospectives, have frequently used biographical materials to analyze the iconography of a given art piece.

Hopps has even written (in the catalogue to the 1993 show) that a knowledge of Rauschenberg's youthful experiences "is essential to an understanding of many aspects of his art in maturity." But in practice only *some* aspects of his experience have been deemed relevant. Critics have zestfully decoded the Christian symbolism in Rauschenberg's early work, while wholly ignoring its homoerotic imagery. Said another way, identification with mainstream religion brings honor; with homosexuality, disgrace.

Not that there haven't been some earlier hints. (And in the art world itself, all this has been an open secret for decades.) Calvin Tomkins, in his 1980 book, *Off the Wall*, discreetly referred to Rauschenberg's six-year love affair with Jasper Johns in the mid-fifties, and a few critics—pre-eminently Andrew Forge, Roni Feinstein and Kenneth Bendiner—referenced homoerotic imagery in Rauschensberg's art some time ago. Still, the 1963 dictum of art historian Alan Solomon has for the most part held iron sway: "There are no secret messages in Rauschenberg."

Oh, but there are, as a group of less canonical critics have been arguing since the mid-1980s. The key launching pad for this new criticism was a panel, "Homosexuality in the Arts," organized by James M. Saslow for the 1986 annual meeting of the College Art Association. And the key presentation on that panel was Kenneth E. Silver's brilliant "Belated 'Notes on Camp': Homosexuality, Representation, and the Decline of Abstract Expressionism." Silver argued (among much else) that Johns's *Target with Plaster Casts* ought to be read in tandem with Rauschenberg's *Bed*; created in the same year (1955), under the same roof, the two works offered "some approximation—maybe an inchoate and impulsive bodying forth—of the power of their then-new relationship."

Silver's speech, and the panel, caused a sensation. The silence had been broken, a door opened for iconoclastic rereadings that, since 1986, have uncovered a significant amount of autobiographical imagery, sexual and otherwise. And in Rauschenberg's case, it has proven relatively transparent—certainly when compared to comparable attempts to decode Twombly or Johns. Recently, the leading figures in this ongoing reassessment have been Jill Johnston (a contemporary and sometime friend of the Rauschenberg crowd, and herself a legendary maverick) and Jonathan Katz, the young art critic at The City College of San Francisco.

"Few artists," Jill Johnston wrote in a 1992 article ("The World Outside His Window") in *Art in America,* "have done as much intensely personal, autobiographical work as Rauschenberg has." In proof of her assertion, she proceeds persuasively to reinterpret some of his work from the late fifties, like *Rebus* and *Small Rebus,* as subversive "meditations on received ideas of gender" and as reflections on his own sense of ambivalent sexuality and uncertain "manliness." Following the earlier hints from Forge and Bendiner, Johnston also analyzes the encoded Ganymede references in Rauschenberg's famed combine, *Canyon,* as not merely illustrative of same-sex desire but more concretely, still, of homosexual abduction and rape.

In a 1993 essay, "The Art of Code," Jonathan Katz has extended Johnston's (and Silver's) analysis to include other signature Rauschenberg works. He reads Rauschenberg's inclusion in *Bantam* (1954) of the image of Judy Garland—at the time "the high priestess of gay culture"—along with various other gay cultural tropes in *Photograph* (1959) and *Wager* (1957–59), as the equivalent, for those who were willing to see, of a personal "coming out"—indeed, as daringly explicit, given the oppressive, homophobic climate of those years.

Additionally, Katz notes that in Rauschenberg's 1959–60 series, *Thirty-four Drawings for Dante's Inferno,* he has included—when illustrating the canto in which Dante describes sodomites as sentenced to the eternal fate of running barefoot over hot sands—his own foot, outlined in red, at the top of the drawing. Another young scholar, Laura Auricchio, in her essay "Lifting the Veil," has provided a detailed, careful look at the *Thirty-four Drawings* and has firmly concluded that the illustrations, in their coded visual vocabulary, "simultaneously create and conceal a subtext of male homosexual desire."

Which brings us to the toughest question: whether and to what degree it is "permissible" to discuss an artist's personal life (in distinction to reading possible—and controvertible—"facts" about the life from the art). Perhaps I should note at the top that as someone more or less of the same generation as Rauschenberg and Johns, I, too, grew up with the deeply ingrained habits of the closet, and am not merely sympathetic to the problematics of emergence but aware, too, of the underappreciated psychological compensations and pleasures that secrecy, especially when inconsistently employed, can provide.

More than ten years ago, Kenneth E. Silver (as well as the critics Roberta Bernstein, Charles Harrison and Fred Orton) began directly to explore the biographical connections of Rauschenberg and Johns to the gay subculture of their day. More recently, both Jill Johnston and Jonathan Katz have explicitly said in print that Cy Twombly and Robert Rauschenberg, and later and for a longer period, Rauschenberg and Jasper Johns, were "lovers."

Both critics have been punished for their audacity. Jonathan Katz, published often in Europe, cannot gain entree into the established art journals in this country. And when Jill Johnston published her book, *Jasper Johns: Privileged Information* (1996), the artist obdurately refused permission to allow any reproduction of his work. The book's publisher, Thames and Hudson, appended a frontispiece—a "Note To The Reader"—declaring Johns's decision "an obstacle to the free exchange of ideas, interpretation, and critical response."

That sounds like a deserved rebuke. But then what about the equally hallowed right to privacy? Is it not Johns's right, at least while alive (many famous folk are inclined to extend their reach beyond the grave, but guardians of the culture are less inclined to go along) to control what is publicly said about his personal life? Is this not one of the cornerstones of our liberties? Well . . . yes and no.

In a culture that sanctions the relentless airing of the private life of the President of the United States, on what conceivable grounds do we then exempt from discussion biographical details about any other public figure? That Robert Rauschenberg is a famous personage is beyond dispute. But he is "public" in several other senses as well. He insists on displaying his products for the public's gaze, response, critical commentary—and sale. And they are often displayed, moreover, in museum venues reliant (to varying degrees) on public support.

Since all aspects of the artist's experience goes (in unmeasurable amounts) into creating art, why are only some aspects of that experience considered mentionable? In Rauschenberg's case, the matter is further complicated by his own equivocal candor. He has loaded his early work with same-sex iconography. He has always (so Jill Johnston tells us) been "a very upfront and open guy" with friends, freely discussing his sexuality (this in distinct contrast to the obsessively hermetic Twombly and Johns). He has even edged close to doing so publicly, telling *Interview* magazine in 1990, "I'm not frightened of the affection that Jasper and I had, both personally and as working artists. I don't see any sin or conflict in those days when each of us was the most important person in the other's life." He then added, astonishingly, this comment: "It was sort of new to the art world that the two most well-known, up-and-coming studs were affectionately involved."

No clear boundaries any longer exist between the "public" and the "private"—as witness any showing of Oprah or any gossip column in the print media. Moreover, those who strive for and achieve celebrity status surely now recognize that in the process they surrender a portion of their privacy. Let us not even bring up the historic mission of scholarship to "tell the truth." But do let us remember that discussing a public figure's sexual orientation is not the equivalent of revealing the details of their intimate acts.

Michel Foucault opened up the strategic high road on these matters: "There is no binary division to be made," he wrote, "between what one says and what one does not say; we must try the different ways of not saying such things." This, one can argue, is precisely the strategy Rauschenberg himself has long adopted: overtly to affirm nothing while implying everything, of being *resonantly* silent.

In this regard, Rauschenberg is in *advance* of a curatorial/museum establishment that is merely silent. In shows, and in catalogues of shows, that establishment not only blocks out all mention of sexuality, but develops an ideology around its reticence: direct biographical discussion, its high priests announce, is the most retrograde sort of intervention in critical inquiry—a vulgar and sentimental concretization of what "we all" know is an unstable, shifting, multivariant reality.

Susan Sontag long ago tried to argue that to reduce art to its content was to tame it, to make its magical, mysterious depths somehow manageable. Well, that very much depends on the content. Discussions of same-sex imagery is likely to *explode* the manageable. Encoded messages, once revealed, serve as depth-charges: they affront the prescribed formulas that have tyrannized our understanding, rip off the masks, let all sorts of alive things breathe at last.

—*in somewhat shorter form,*
this piece was published in
The New York Times, *Sept. 7, 1997*

—— Epidemic Arguments ——

Gabriel Rotello's *Sexual Ecology: AIDS and the Destiny of Gay Men* is the most important book about the epidemic since Randy Shilts's *And The Band Played On.* And it is far better. Rotello's research is deeper, his approach less sensationalistic (and self-aggrandizing), and his grave, muted prose perfectly attuned to his somber message. *Sexual Ecology* is at once closely argued and profoundly troubling. Rotello has bravely challenged some of the central dogmas of gay male "liberation," and he is surely right in predicting that the challenge will provoke sharp controversy and angry rebuttal.

Rotello's essential argument is that the gay sexual revolution of the seventies was "anti-ecological." Though it has long been unpopular (and in hip circles impossible) to say so, the prevalence of anal sex with a multiplicity of partners that characterized the behavior of a small percentage of gay men in bathhouses and sex clubs made a decided contribution to the outbreak and spread of the AIDS epidemic. Yes, the government's failure to issue warnings or to fund research, the scientific and pharmaceutical establishment's refusal to investigate, the media's avoidance, and the public's homophobic indifference have all made their large contributions. But those have long been cited and deplored. Because of Rotello's analysis, we must consider the additional factor of "the brotherhood of promiscuity." Even now, despite the educational campaigns and the resurgence in research and awareness, gay male culture, in Rotello's view, continues "to shy away from analyzing . . . our own ecology, including our desire to preserve what appear to be toxic aspects of our hard-won sexual freedoms."

This ostrich attitude, Rotello argues, has led to unwarranted optimism about the nearing end of the epidemic and mounting evidence of a relapse in following safe sex practices—thus heightening the likelihood of additional and worsening pandemics.* Moreover, Rotello descries the recent logic of many leaders in the prevention struggle which ascribes "relapse" to the inhuman strictness of the condom code and the homophobic assumption at its core: that gay men could or should accomplish a degree of behavioral change that no self-respecting heterosexual man would ever think of imposing on himself. (Forget sex; think of all the people who are unable to quit smoking, sustain a diet or pursue an exercise routine.)

To state Rotello's argument is immediately to recognize that it provides dangerous ammunition for those on the right who have long argued that gay men are out-of-control compulsives unable or unwilling to restrain their "diseased" promiscuity. Rotello is well aware of the negative uses to which his analysis can and will be put. And he knows, too, that his call for a changed gay male sexual ecology—limiting partners, restricting the variety of sexual acts—will be angrily denounced in "liberationist" circles as a betrayal of the cherished ideals of sexual adventurism.

Rotello's call for "a more balanced" style will be denounced as reflecting precisely that squeamish, uptight middle-class value set gay men have devoted their transgressive lives to testifying *against*. And many will characterize his willingness to invoke "direct intervention and regulation by the gay community or, as a last resort, the government," as an invitation further to stigmatize gay male life—and drive it underground.

---

*Some counterevidence has recently emerged to the effect that gay men in New York City—but not everywhere— "have significantly reduced their levels of risky sexual behavior" (*The New York Times,* June 28, 1999).

Sexual Ecology, in short, will most assuredly produce an explosive and protracted debate. My own reaction to the book's argument is conflicted. Rotello's facts, and the arguments he builds from them, seem to me mostly persuasive. But not entirely so. Now and then his distortion of historical evidence to point a present-day moral seems to me dubious. And some of his recommendations give me more than momentary pause. This is as it should be in a book of immense complexity, ambition and consequence; indeed, my ambivalence (where once there was certitude) is a tribute to Rotello's brilliant provocations.

To begin with history, Rotello insists that gay male sexual behavior has shifted radically since the sixties. Previously, he tells us, anal sex was unusual and analingus all but unknown. Few gay men had multiple partners, and few sought each other out for sex; rather, they pursued aggressively masculine straight men. But I believe Rotello is conflating the limited "fairy" culture of the 1890s to 1930s (its distinguishing features themselves under debate among historians) with *all* gay male sexuality—and then unwarrantedly extending it far beyond its time frame.

The fact is, as Rotello acknowledges, data on gay male sexual behavior are scarce and for recent decades often anecdotal. I can only say, as someone who became sexually active in the early fifties, that in my own circles (and I checked my memory against a few others) plenty of gay men slept with each other, pursued gay romance not straight "trade," and frequently enjoyed anal sex.

What has changed, I believe, are not acts (with the probable exception of fist fucking), but their frequence. Rotello is surely right that the multiplicity of partners among a significant minority of gay men has skyrocketed beyond the wildest fantasies most of us once indulged. It has been a matter of new opportunities creating a new (and still defensible) morality of pleasure; disastrous viral and microbial consequences could not have been foreseen, nor factored into a more cautionary equation. Some day, hopefully, they can once again be factored out.

Rotello also expresses such a hope, but he clearly thinks it faint. And possibly immoral—though he never uses the word. He never overtly preaches the inherent superiority of monogamy and lifetime pairbonding; yet at bottom, that seems to be where his heart is: gay men are here *not* to challenge heterosexist hypocrisy and repression; their touted "revolutionary" promiscuity, he implies (he needed to argue it through more thoroughly—we all need to), really represents the internalization of a hostile caricature. What we should be doing with our lives instead, is putting them in service to what Rotello calls "the ageless lessons of social cohesion." Every society, he insists (on the basis of a skewed reading of the evidence about sexuality in the ancient world), "has attempted to channel the sexual drive in ways that promote stability . . . "

The rhetoric here—in contrast to Rotello's characteristically lean and concrete prose—gets a little sonorous: "living openly and with dignity and health in a supportive world." And in fashioning it, Rotello is similarly vague in referencing sources; he frequently cites "thinkers," "theorists," "leaders," and "researchers," but often omits specific names or texts. This is altogether strange in a writer who is usually a precise and careful guide.

Similarly, Rotello walks you through the most intricate epidemiological details with caution and skill, and yet he unaccountably accepts as a *biological* given the much-debated, still unproven assertation that the male sex drive is stronger than the female (if anything, primatology seems to be piling up evidence to the contrary). As a necessary corollary, Rotello praises lesbians for "honor[ing] fidelity in relationships as the ideal"—as if that, too, was factual and uncontested.

And so, as veracious and honorable as Rotello generally is, it is fair to feel uneasy about some very large matters. *Is* sexual fidelity the ideal that best suits human needs and promotes human happiness? Doesn't erotic zest hinge to a significant degree on mystery, tension, even anonymity—and if so, how do we introduce and sustain them in a monogamous relationship? (Eroticism and romantic love, are not, after all, interchangeable—despite the tenets of our official culture.) Isn't much of what is deplorably shallow or indulgent about a *segment* of gay male culture in fact characteristic of American culture in general—even if heterosexual consumption is less centered on the sexual? What precise form should the social regulation of sexual behavior take? Would not many or even most forms end by unconscionably interfering with individual rights? Who will regulate the regulators? And if regulation or self-reformation is in the name of something more than biological survival (hardly a small thing), than in the name of what else, beyond "social cohesion," will such a transformation, even assuming it possible, be undertaken?

Rotello makes it clear that he expects such questions and welcomes an expansive debate; "no one," he writes, "has easy answers." *Sexual Ecology* is an immensely conscientious, caring effort to think about what has for too long been unthinkable: an unending, escalating series of epidemiological disasters, and the potential destruction (at its own hands or those of its enemies) of gay male life. It hardly matters whether one agrees with all aspects of Rotello's analysis. He has outlined the current situation with strenuous courage and insight. He's going to catch hell. But then hell is already here.

—The Nation, *May 5, 1997*

─────── POSTSCRIPT 1999 ───────

Soon after this piece appeared, a debate erupted in gay male circles about the growing phenomenon known as "bare-backing" (having unprotected sex). The underpinnings of the debate had earlier been laid out by Jesse Green, "Flirting with Suicide," *The New York Times*

Magazine (Sept. 15, 1996) and by Walt Odets, a psychotherapist, in his book *In the Shadow of the Epidemic,* and elaborated further in his "On the Need for a Gay Reconstruction of Public Health" (in Duberman, ed., *A Queer World:* 1997). Odets outlined many of the emotions that were drawing gay men toward "raw" or "skin-to-skin" sex: survivor guilt, a feeling that seroconversion was inevitable anyway, and a longing for the deep intimacy of semen sharing. Other analyses and defenses of barebacking include a 1995 editorial, "Exit the Rubberman," in *Steam,* by the writer and porn star Scott O'Hara; Tony Valenzuela's impromptu speech about his sex life at the November 1997 Creating Change Conference; two articles by Stephen Gendin (*POZ:* June 1997, Feb. 1999); and the four discussions of barebacking by David Kirby, Chris Bull, Ingrid Ricks and Michaelangelo Signorile in *The Advocate* (April 13, 1999). The gap between public HIV prevention messages (the "condom code") and the refusal in some gay male circles to abide by it, seems to be widening. A number of websites (XtremeSex, et al.) have sprung up, and as of early 1999 there were more than eighty different bareback electronic mailing lists. As well, it was revealed early in 1999 that nationally there had been a large increase in the number of gay men who had become infected with HIV in the previous two years (*The New York Times,* Feb. 16, 1999). The figures vary, however, from place to place: where New York City has shown a decline in HIV infection and a rise in the number of gay men using condoms, the opposite trends are true of San Francisco (*The New York Times,* June 28, 30, 1999).

III

In Conclusion
The Divided Left:
Identity Politics Versus Class

In Conclusion
The Divided Left: Identity Politics Versus Class

In recent years there has been a mounting attack on "identity politics," on political groupings that push agendas based on race, ethnicity, gender and sexual orientation. Such a politics, it is being argued, hardens boundaries between oppressed groups and, further, prevents them from mobilizing collectively around the transcendent issues of class division and economic inequity.

The attack is being spearheaded by what the historian Jesse Lemisch has called "Angry Straight White Men on the Left" (a few of whom are women). Among the more prominent are Eric Hobsbawm, Arthur Schlesinger, Jr., Ralph Nader, Richard Rorty, Michael Lerner, Todd Gitlin, Michael Tomasky, Jack Newfield, Bogdan Denitch—and Betty Friedan.

In his 1995 book, *The Twilight of Common Dreams,* the influential activist/sociologist Todd Gitlin characterized "identity politics" as "groups overly concerned with protecting and purifying what they imagine to be their identities." Not only are these groups self-deluded, but according to Gitlin they have produced "a cacophony without much listening or the sympathy needed to keep up a common conversation . . . the result is . . . aggression and deafness, an obsession with purifications . . . Identity politics is an American tragedy . . . a very bad turn, a detour into quicksand."

In 1996, Michael Tomasky, the political columnist, published *Left for Dead: The Life, Death, and Possible Resurrection of Progressive Politics in America,* which detailed, sharpened and extended Gitlin's critique. The floodgates were open. Through them poured a horde of disgruntled, righteous straight Leftists, eager to join with others who deplored the derailing of class struggle (and their own leadership) for the trivial self-therapies of "imagined" identity politics. (At the fourteenth annual Socialist Scholars Conference in April 1996, its chair, the sociologist Bogdan Denitch, announced, "[W]e don't care if you are gay; we want to know whether you're a Left gay!")[1]

Tomasky's seminal *Left for Dead* addresses basic issues regarding the history, agendas and prospects of the Left in the United States and, speaking as it does for so many others, warrants close analysis. The heart of this inquiry must be the considerable mystery of why people like Tomasky, Gitlin, Hobsbawm et al., themselves unquestionably committed to creating a more just society and to figuring out a politics that can get us there, can be so enraged at fellow Leftists working toward the same ends.

The basic argument in *Left for Dead* runs along these lines: No substantial or unified Left exists today. Instead there are "several small Lefts," disconnected shards "sometimes agreeing on things, sometimes not." (No quarrel yet.) Among these fragments, are remnants of the 1960s civil rights movement, some segments of organized labor (much reduced in power and influence), some environmentalists, and various activists for the disabled, the aged and the homeless.

But towering above all these—"the vanguard, without question," in Tomasky's view—are the ideologically riven "identity movements" based on race, ethnicity, gender and sexual orientation. It is a vanguard he, and other straight white male Leftists, greatly deplore; as Eric

Hobsbawm has angrily put it: "The political project of the Left is . . . for *all* human beings. However we interpret the words, it isn't liberty for shareholders or blacks, but for everybody. It isn't equality for all members of the Garrick Club or the handicapped, but for everybody. It is not fraternity only for old Etonians or gays, but for everybody. And identity politics is essentially not for everybody but for the members of a specific group only."[2]

The anger and the accuracy alike of such statements needs close scrutiny. But let me first acknowledge that Tomasky/Hobsbawm et al. are right in deploring the Left's insufficient attention in recent years to class-based oppression and the mounting insecurities and resentments of blue-collar life (though not right in failing to see how inextricably that oppression is tied to those based on race, gender and sexual orientation).

We have no disagreement about the danger to democracy from the growing disparity of income between the richest and the poorest. The overclass (Michael Lind's now popular term) has succeeded in siphoning off more and more of the country's wealth, leaving the working poor fighting each other for the crumbs, and the jobless underclass sinking ever deeper into immiseration. From 1968 to 1994, the share of the nation's aggregate income that went to the top 20 percent of its households increased from 40.5 percent to 46.9 percent. Even as the richest nation on earth permits widespread poverty to persist, it manages to provide the Pentagon with an annual budget of $240 billion (and going up). Even as it scales down welfare and social services, welfare for the rich continues to rise; the capital gains tax has largely become academic to the wealthy, who rely on a growing arsenal of Wall Street loopholes and shelters to avoid paying taxes on their investment gains.[3]

Matters may well get worse—welfare substantially scaled back, immigration curtailed, benefits to undocumented (and possibly even documented) people reduced, affirmative action further assailed, and health care left in limbo. In addition, as Tomasky himself predicts and deplores, there is the likelihood that many federal programs will devolve, in the form of block grants to the states (where business elites have even more control than in Washington), further reducing social services for the poor. Yet resistance is likely, too, since many Americans *like* specific government programs and the safety nets they provide, and do *not* trust the workings of a "free market" economy.

In *Left for Dead*, Tomasky analyses many of these matters with lucidity and skill. But the analysis is not accompanied by any promising program for change. He advocates a thirty-hour work week as a solution for continuing layoffs, an end to government subsidies to corporations (some $85 billion a year), increasing the share of the tax burden (it has been steadily falling) that corporations and rich people contribute, putting limits on the cash contributions individuals can make to political parties, providing free television time for candidates, and ending government intrusion into people's private spaces.

A banal wish list perhaps, but we'd certainly take it if we could get it. But we won't, not in the current climate. Besides, the enactment of such reforms would not prove remotely sufficient to deal with the structural causes of poverty, racism and class exploitation. Only a determination to give the highest priority to the needs of the least fortunate—that classic socialist goal—could make the needed headway. No such determination exists.

The inadequacies of Tomasky's "solutions" are exemplified in his treatment of affirmative action. He is against it. He worries that the policy, which he sees as giving "unfair advantage" to African Americans, offends and alienates working-class white voters. He initially states the high ground ("Nothing should be supported or opposed simply on the basis of popular opinion") and then, in regard to affirmative action policies, promptly ignores his own advice. His implicit argument throughout is that it is more important to play to the majority than to support policies that, albeit unpopular, could (as in the case of affirmative action) foster social justice.[4]

Yet as Ellen Willis has argued, "It's not necessary, as many Leftists imagine, to round up popular support before anything can be done . . . The history of movements is crowded with acts of defiance by individuals and small groups—from the 1937 sit-in of workers in a Flint, Michigan auto plant, to Rosa Parks's refusal to get up, to radical feminists' disrupting an expert hearing on abortion reform—that inspired a wave of similar actions and a broader revolt." Barbara Ehrenreich has added another telling point: "The American Left, throughout history, has taken stands that seemed bizarre or extreme to large numbers of their fellow citizens: in favor of abolishing slavery, or giving women the right to vote, or keeping the United States out of various wars . . . standing on principle, including deeply unpopular principle, is the business of the Left."[5]

True, every time you push an antiracist, profeminist or gay agenda you are likely to harden the opposition. But necessarily so; polarization is *how* social progress takes place. Until the abolitionists attacked slavery, for example, the white South hadn't bothered to develop a formal ideological defense of the institution. The polarization of public opinion around a given issue signals that a heightened level of social dialogue has begun. The alternative (sometimes glamorized as "pragmatic politics") is to avoid giving offense by avoiding any full-scale discussion of a controversial public issue—which all but guarantees the preservation of the status quo. We know a social justice movement is making headway when it *does* disrupt civic culture, does spur a significant backlash. Think the 1950s sit-ins. Think ACT-UP. A nondisrupted civic culture is one where the outs have failed to make their grievances known, or have been successfully silenced. Putting primary emphasis on the placation of anger and the avoidance of offense is a prescription for social stagnation.

Tomasky deplores "a corporate world ruled by dishonesty and cupidity, whose aims are fundamentally at odds with the needs of most working people." When he goes on to argue the importance of "redefining society in a deeply moral sense," we expect him to follow through with a trenchant critique of the ruling class. Not at all. Tomasky trains his guns not on a corporate structure whose immorality and malfeasance he has himself highlighted, but, astonishingly, on the Left itself, and on its multicultural "vanguard" in particular.

Tomasky acknowledges that "the Left has faced an uphill battle in this country, fundamentally because it opposes the agenda of corporate America, which has the influence and money to safeguard its domination." But having made that crucial point, Tomasky blandly declares it too obvious to dwell on: "Moaning about the fact is roughly as useful as complaining about the weather." "No-one today," he adds, "can talk seriously about dismantling capitalism." But can't we at least talk about how to make it more humane? That was the main project of the Left in America from the 1870s to the 1930s, but capitalism, as Tomasky puts it, "has shown a resiliency and fluidity that old Leftists did not anticipate, and it looks like it's here to stay."

And so—as if power confers immunity—Tomasky turns his prime attention instead to itemizing the failures of the Left. His list is long. He excoriates us for a host of "badly conceived or executed programs" (like the war on poverty) or for particular policy "missteps"—like the "disastrously wrongheaded" attempt at court-mandated busing ("disastrous" because it "put working-class whites and poor blacks at war"), and for the "misguided" attempt to introduce "rainbow curricula" into the schools.

Tomasky sees in these efforts a mistaken overall reliance by the Left on "litigating social change . . . forging ahead through the legal byways without attempting to establish anything approaching popular consensus; and the reliance on finely wrought legalistic arguments that will do nothing at all in practical terms to change the world—except, possibly, to harden and strengthen the opposition."

Whoa! Haven't federal legislation and judicial opinions been essential tools in past struggles for social justice like school integration and the right to form unions? If these "victories" have not proven tantamount to permanent solutions, they have surely been worth having. And just as surely, it is a case of the chicken before the egg when Tomasky blames policy "missteps" like busing for an antagonism between working-class whites and blacks that had been long since in place.

The working class has been racially riven for centuries; until the CIO came along in the 1930s, black workers were essentially bared from union membership, and down to the present day are still not fully welcome in some industries, like construction. Many working-class whites have long since chosen to identify with their skin color rather than with "alien others" (and especially blacks) who share their class oppression; it has been more important to declare their superiority to blacks—and their primary bond with fellow whites of all classes—than to collaborate with "inferiors" in a protest movement based on class. In other words, long before the Left's "missteps" purportedly *pushed* the white working class to the right, its own conservative cultural views had long since solidly planted it there.[6]

Tomasky does not doubt that identity politics has had "a salutary effect on the broader culture"—has, for example, opened up opportunities for women and for racial, ethnic and sexual minorities. But in his view these partial gains have come at the gigantic costs of abandoning class politics and "civic community."

Tomasky wants the Left to focus on economics. He emphasizes the need to get people off welfare and into salaried work, and he quotes Marx (no less) on "productive activity [being] the life of the species." But he avoids any hard look at what "salaried work" and "productive activity" tend to mean these days, and whether "life" is being given to the workers or their employers.

Flipping hamburgers and cleaning toilets full-time and forever (not as temporary ways of piecing out college tuition) isn't the equivalent of "real jobs at good wages"—which Tomasky himself calls "the ultimate answer" (under current conditions, "ultimate" can only mean "nowhere on the horizon"). But he doesn't talk much about the tedious, humiliating conditions that surround the minimal-pay job scene. Some 30 million poor Americans, the majority of them white, do have jobs, that is, jobs nobody else wants. As Katherine Newman points out in *No Shame in My Game: The Working Poor in the Inner City,* vacation pay, health insurance, sick leave and so forth, are all unknown to the working poor. To survive, they form "family units" with those on welfare (for whom Aid to Dependent Children rarely pays enough to cover even basics like rent).

These are not "real jobs at good wages," though they are often all that is available to poor people who want to work (and, contrary to stereotypes of the "shiftless" poor, they *do:* for every job announced in the low-wage fast-food industry, there are fourteen applications). But the "lucky" poor person who lands the one job is hardly gaining entry into the life-affirming world of "productive activity."

Having a job is not the equivalent for most poor people of having satisfying work (let alone livable incomes and safety-net benefits). *Satisfying* work means work connected to some kind of creative challenge, in conditions conducive to self-esteem and allowing for enough security, leisure time and leftover energy to pursue outside interests. The notion that "work," any kind of work, is somehow an intrinsic good, serves bosses, not workers. It is part and parcel of a productive system that urges workers to be content with their lot and allows employers to go on reaping most of the fruits of their workers' labor—as socialists and anarchists have been saying for more than a century.

Tomasky recognizes all this only parenthetically. He writes with eloquence and empathy of the befouled air and rising rates of asthma in the poor Mott Haven neighborhood of the Bronx. And he describes those conditions as "not the result of the moral and ethical deficiencies of poor people, but of decision makers." He even adds, "The Left has argued this for years, to sadly little avail, but it has been right to do so."

Exactly. But then why does Tomasky devote the bulk of *Left for Dead* to blaming the Left for ongoing inequities that he himself (at least sporadically) recognizes are due to the amorality of our dominant business, social and religious elites? After his eloquent words on Mott Haven, it is mystifying when, within three pages, Tomasky returns to his harsh threnody of blaming the Left for conditions he has just finished ascribing to the indifference of the "decision makers." Instead of excoriating the powers-that-be, he excoriates the Left: it "watches from the bleachers, failing to match either right or center with ideas of its own . . . failing to come up with substantive programs to solve the country's ills."

What he means by this, he tells us, is that the Left has "no analysis of what unites people." Tomasky thinks he knows what does: "Enlightenment universalism," what he calls "the philosophical bedrock of advanced Western society as a whole." What this purported "bedrock" consists of goes unspecified (to say nothing of whether these "advanced" Western views can speak to the conditions of *global* poverty). Tomasky simply settles for the abstract statement that "the ideas of Locke and Hume and Voltaire and Jefferson and Paine remain the ideas that bind these countries together and that animate their sense of mission and progress." This is not very helpful; a list of names, a quite arbitrary list, is hardly the equivalent of an analysis of the precise content or relevance of "Enlightenment universalism."

Whatever these vague, undefined Enlightenment "ideas" are, Tomasky is sure that the Left has abandoned them. And especially those on the Left who are involved in identity politics, who have mistakenly elevated their own particular histories and involuntary affiliations based on race, ethnicity, gender or sexuality into primary values. He quotes approvingly Arthur Schlesinger, Jr.'s view that "the ideal of the universal melting pot is put at grave risk by a politics of difference." You bet it is—since the "melting pot" has been revealed as a considerable fiction, a convenient rationale employed by the powers-that-be to justify current monopolies of wealth and power.

Tomasky and his cohorts insist that people on the Left must "stretch beyond" their cultures and identities, beyond a "shriveling coalition of out-groups," beyond demands that have "nothing to do with a larger concern for our common humanity and everything to do with a narrow concern for fragmented and supposedly oppositional cultures." Others who inveigh against identity politics usually do so in comparably patronizing terms. Ralph Nader has told us, for example, that "gonadal politics" are a trivializing distraction from the genuinely important agenda of economic issues. Richard Rorty and Betty Friedan (during a 1996 teach-in at Columbia) both urged that the time had come to graduate from the "narrow" politics of identity to the "bigger" picture of class inequalities. And Todd Gitlin wants us to consider "what changes matter most, and get to work on them."

In all these indictments "class" is simply assumed to be the transcendent category, and issues relating to gender, race and sexuality are marginalized as comparatively insignificant. Among the many confusions in attempting to establish a hierarchy of what is the "most" or "least" important social issue is a bottom-line unawareness of how these struggles intersect; racism, sexism and homophobia in the workplace inescapably inflect how and whether workers will see their grievances as ones held in common. "Class," in other words, is inherently a cultural issue; solidarity based on economic issues can never come about until divisions based on gender, race and sexuality are recognized (even if not resolved) as central to achieving such a goal.

Instead of such recognition, we have the white, male, heterosexual Tomaskys lecturing the rest of us about the relative unimportance of *our* issues and chastising us for our "narrow" concern with our "supposedly oppositional cultures." That word "supposedly" says a lot. Tomasky and friends continually refer to identity politics as a "distraction," not among the issues that matter most. Tomasky himself refers to "faux-radical multiculturalism" and its "superficially transgressive ideas."

But declaring certain ideas superficial does not make them so—especially since it is far from clear that the Tomaskys or Schlesingers or Friedans have remotely understood and absorbed them. They need to draw their chairs in closer and listen harder to the intricate conversations taking place on the multicultural Left. The radical redefinitions of gender and sexuality that are under discussion (and contention) in feminist and queer circles contain a potentially transformative challenge to what has been called "regimes of the normal."

Tomasky and friends give no sign that they have actually read, let alone absorbed, the work of queer scholars like Eve Kosofsky Sedgwick, Jeffrey Weeks, Michael Warner, Majorie Garber, Wayne Koestenbaum or Judith Butler—to name only a few of the more prominent. There has accumulated a large body of theoretical work that collectively presents a startling set of postulates about such matters of *universal* importance as the historicity and fluidity of sexual desire, the performative nature of gender, and the complex multiplicity of attractions, fantasies, impulses and narratives that lie within us all—and that argues against any notion of a fixed, stable self.

These are no small, narrow, superficial matters, of concern only to the self-absorbed few—ignorance alone allows them to be so characterized. Were the Tomaskys to open their ears and refuse to settle for *Reader's Digest* versions of feminist and gay analysis, they would have to come to grips with any number of discomforting notions and challenges.

To understand how and why sexual and gender identities get socially constructed is to open up a new way of talking about politics, about how relations of power get established, about the role of the state in reinforcing and policing that set of relations in the name of maintaining the stakes of the already privileged. Try to imagine the consequences of reconsidering, as feminist and queer theorists have been asking us to do, traditional definitions of gender. Is it fair to *men* (we know it isn't fair to anyone else) to be viewed as inflexible, driven engines of action, accumulation and domination? A freer definition of the male self, the heightened ability of men to embrace the *varied* impulses within, could loosen their iron drive for control, their overrepresentation in positions of power, their unmodulated resort to means of violence in order to resolve conflict. These are *emancipatory* possibilities—for everyone. And they could lead us back to that unfinished dialogue from the 1960s about the nature of "human nature," about the need for personal transformation to precede or accompany any lasting social transformation.

Hardly an ersatz sideshow. Hardly—in the flip, dismissive words of Todd Gitlin—mere "rhetorical fillips." Far from being devoid of ideas, or ideas of more than parochial interest, as Tomasky and friends claim, it is a matter instead of the nonfeminist, nonqueer Left not bothering to listen, not taking seriously the foundational work being done on gender and sexuality. If the Tomaskys were listening, they would find potent tools at hand for informing the struggle against entrenched class (and race, and gender) hierarchies of privilege and power about which they claim to care so much.

The ideas being generated on the multicultural Left are not "supposedly" oppositional; they are fundamentally so. They have *everything* to do with that "larger concern for our common humanity" that the Tomaskys and Gitlins so loudly insist is absent from identity politics. Perhaps henceforth, when we talk about "reenvisioning the Left," we need to put high on the agenda (it is now nowhere in sight) the patronizing inability or unwillingness of heterosexual white males (and some women like Betty Friedan and some blacks like Shelby Steele) to take seriously the far-reaching work being done in feminist and queer circles.

Moreover—though you would never know it from the antimulticulturalists' charges of nullity and irrelevance—a long-standing debate has been going on *among multiculturalists themselves* about the inadequacy, incompleteness or possible transience of identity labels like "black" or "gay" or "Latino."

It is a charged and conflicted debate because many minority intellectuals are well aware that in order to join with others in fighting for a common cause, they must surrender the expectation that that cause can or should represent and express all aspects of their own special, unique selves. When one organizes collectively to gain attention and to pressure for change, one must (at least publicly) downplay individual variations. It is the bargain one makes, and the price one pays, for being political.

Still, many remain troubled about the inability of overarching categories or labels ("black," "gay," etc.) to represent accurately the complexities and sometimes overlapping identities of individual lives. They are uncomfortable about referring to "communities" as if they were homogenous units rather than hothouses of contradiction. They are concerned about the inadequacy of efforts to create bridges between marginalized people and then extensions outward to broader constituencies.

Yet one holds on to a group identity, despite its insufficiencies, because for most nonmainstream people it's the closest they have ever gotten to having a political home—and voice. Yes, identity politics reduces and simplifies. Yes, it is a kind of prison. But it is also, paradoxically, a haven. It is at once confining *and* empowering. And in the absence of alternative havens, group identity will for many continue to be the appropriate site of resistance and the main source of comfort.

The anti-multiculturalists' highflown, hectoring rhetoric about the need to transcend these allegiances and unite behind Enlightenment "rationalism," to become "universal human beings with universal rights," rings hollow and hypocritical. It is difficult to march into the sunset as a "civic community" with a "common culture" when the legitimacy of our differentness as minorities has not yet been more than superficially acknowledged—let alone safeguarded. You cannot link arms under a universalist banner when you can't find your own name on it. A minority identity may be contingent or incomplete, but that does not make it fabricated or needless. And cultural unity cannot be purchased at the cost of cultural erasure.

The appeal of a Michael Tomasky "to connect with those unlike one-self" is unimpeachable, but he's addressed it to the wrong crowd. Many of us involved in identity politics *have* been looking for ways to "reason" with opponents over issues relating to race, gender and sexuality. Tomasky claims we have "simply written off" many potential allies.

In the case of the gay movement, this is standing truth on its head. Our efforts at dialogue might well stand improving, but they have hardly been as nothing. Yet we've mostly been met with patronization and hostility from straight Leftists (particularly the males). That multitude of (in Tomasky's words) "working-class whites, housewives, churchgoers" purportedly eager to link arms with us have been notable by their absence: they do not attend our open discussions and conferences, they rarely appear at our rallies or marches, they almost never contribute time or money to the understaffed, underfinanced offices of the few national gay organizations that exist.

But neither have self-proclaimed Leftists, whether Old or New. Their energy goes to writing patronizing screeds about the triviality or irrelevance of our grievances and insights alike. They have shown little interest in lending support to our struggle or in listening sympathetically to the story of our lives—that is, when we *really* try to talk about them, rather than pretend that we are "just folks." It is not our identity politics that turn off the Tomaskys, and the purported legions of the well disposed—it is our lives.

None of which is to say that those of us involved in identity politics who self-identify as "radical" (and we are far outnumbered by the assimilationist liberals in our movements) have paid sufficient attention to class; we are, after all, Americans, and, like the rest of the citizenry, we have imbibed with our pabulum the notion that ours is *not* (unlike nasty old Europe) a class-riven society. Nor does it mean that the organized gay political movement has not far too often been single issue–minded (based on the gut feeling that since no one else is dealing with our issues, *we* have to focus on them). To be exclusively concerned with one's own group, and to succumb to the fantasy that we can solve our problems in isolation, is foolish and self-defeating.

But none of this is the equivalent of arguing, as Tomasky does, that the multicultural Left has "cashiered" class-based analysis. When the gay movement is operating at its best, its goal is to add to the story of class-based oppression an awareness of discriminatory attitudes and practices based on other forms of differentness. At our best, we are also able to emphasize that the labor movement itself can quite reasonably be described as historically based on identity politics: for a long period it exclusively defended "its own," and class solidarity was reduced to protecting union members *against* the great unwashed, unorganized mass of female and nonwhite workers.

A common tactic the anti-multiculturalists use to discredit identity politics is to select one extreme set of views as characteristic of the whole. Thus Tomasky skewers Molefi Kete Asanti's "proofs" that all inventions ascribed to the Greeks were stolen from black Egyptians, but fails to note that many African-American intellectuals have also scoffed at Asanti's claims. Unlike Tomasky, however, they do not use the exaggerations of one man to discredit the need for racially based group political action.

Tomasky and his cohorts do not want to appear, of course, as being remotely akin to racists, sexists and homophobes. "Genuine diversity," Tomasky magnanimously suggests, "is by no means a bad thing," and he announces himself "a firm supporter of black, female and gay rights." But apparently diversity is not much of a good thing either, that is, *real* diversity, for Tomasky insists that "it is absolutely crucial that Black people and Latinos and gays and others be assimilated, and assimilate themselves, fully into society."

Not surprisingly, therefore, it turns out that the full rights of citizenship should only be extended to a certain kind of gay person. Sounding to the *right* of gay conservatives like Bruce Bawer and Andrew Sullivan, Tomasky wants to reserve the legal benefits of marriage, for example, for those "gay couples who can reasonably demonstrate that they are committed to spending their lives together." In thus emphasizing conformity to middle-class norms, Tomasky is rejecting a proposition widely held on the Left: it is *non*conformity that opens up the path to social change.

The only form of gay activism that wins Tomasky's approval is the Bawer-Sullivan strain "that has been able to show straight America that 'we're just like you'." (So much for diversity, and its value.) Tomasky finds in-your-face tactics like "kiss-ins" offensive, and he characterizes ACT-UP's militant demonstration inside St. Patrick's Cathedral in New York City in the early nineties "deeply misguided." Does that mean, by analogy, that confrontational tactics—like the defiant march from Selma to Montgomery in behalf of black rights—are also to be deplored, or only when shaded in lavender or deployed against "holy" institutions?

In excoriating ACT-UP's demonstration inside St. Patrick's, Tomasky manages to omit entirely from discussion the provocation for that action—namely, the Catholic hierarchy's resolute refusal of dialogue with or about homosexuals, a blanket refusal that all but forced the adoption of tactics that at least had the chance of gaining the media's (if not the hierarchy's) attention.

To say nothing of seizing a well-earned opportunity to vent some rage against the Catholic church's centuries-long vilification and abuse of homosexuals, and against a pope who has carried that tradition forward in the present-day by declaring homosexuality an "objective disorder." (The same pope who, on his visit to Mexico in January 1999, called saintly attention to the plight of the poor—while having done his best to dismantle, through earlier words and actions, the liberation theology movement within the church that had focused on that very plight.)

Forgetting that real injustice fuels real outrage, Tomasky is quick to denounce the ACT-UP protestors as "intolerant, unreasonable, and against the spirit of critical inquiry," while managing never to even entertain the notion that it may well be the Catholic hierarchy that has most consistently embodied those attributes—their only rivals being orthodox Judaism and fundamentalist Protestantism. Surely it is not multicultural Leftists but the Cardinal O'Connors and Jerry Falwells of the world, with their blithe ignorance of biblical scholarship and their hate-filled sermons on "woman's place" and the "abomination of homosexuality," who personify "intolerant, unreasonable" attitudes. Tomasky claims that gay militants are up to nothing more than trying to achieve "the illusion of saintliness." Well, someone has to produce saints, since the church isn't.

Similarly, one wonders about Tomasky's choice of emphasis when, on the subject of race, he asserts that "most people, confronted with hard evidence and compelling moral arguments, could overcome racism and think and act in a better way." But haven't "most people" already heard a mountain of "compelling moral arguments" and converted them into proofs that blacks are congenitally lazy, stupid and ungrateful? Tomasky accuses the Left of lacking "faith in the mass of people to be fair," with the result that "people have no faith in us." Oh, is *that* why the Left is unpopular—people are angry with us for not properly crediting their high moral purpose? Give me a break!

Tomasky and his anti-multiculturalist friends package the decline of the Left as an act of self-combustion: "we got here, in no small part, through our own doing. The particularism and intolerance, the miserly spirit, the self-righteousness and sniping, the plain lack of great and unifying ideas—and ideals—have brought a once great movement to its knees." "Inflexible and intolerant" adherents of identity politics have no ideals or values other than "vague and pietistic" ones.

As pietistic as the religious right's call for "a return to traditional family values," even as it cultivates hate? As vague as Bob Dole's "we are deeply concerned about the working people of America," even as he remains negligent and obtuse about their needs? Tomasky never does more than parenthetically indict the religious and corporate right in accounting for the Left's—the country's—plight. His *Left for Dead*, and the many other works that have made a cottage industry of assaulting multiculturalism, make it sound as if the globalization of capital, massive corporate downsizing and the fanatic intolerance of the religious right of nontraditional sexual and gender roles, are mere incidental players in the current riot of social discord.

Ironically, bizarrely, Tomasky freely acknowledges that the corporate world has aims "fundamentally at odds with the needs of most working people." Yet he, and so many others on the Left, insist on directing their fire primarily at defenders of identity politics as the chief villains of the piece—as if *they* were the ones callously cutting jobs, employing poverty-stricken children as laborers, destroying the environment, fighting against health insurance and other social benefits.

The business, social and religious elites that rule this country are neither heeding working-class grievances nor leading the nation toward a goal of, to quote Tomasky, "a politics that transcends fixed group interests." They are doing precisely what they have always done: feathering their own nests, ruthlessly cutting down any threat to their "birthright" wealth. The ideal of "civic empathy" being touted by left-wing anti-multiculturalists is as surely desirable as it is just as surely a joke, given the refusal of the country's ruling elites to pay it (at most) more than lip service.

In the sixties, we used to talk a lot about "the patriarchy," and about the need to destroy its monopoly of power. The term, and the attack, need to be resurrected. But this time with the proper prefixes attached to patriarchy: white and heterosexual—and with the sad recognition that some of its members actually call themselves Leftists.

— *this is a revised and expanded version
of a piece that first appeared
in* The Nation, *July 1, 1996*

NOTES

INTRODUCTION

1. Amos Oz, "Social Democracy & the Kibbutz," *Dissent* (Summer 1997).

THE NORTHERN RESPONSE TO SLAVERY

1. Arresting slavery's further spread, Lincoln said, would "place it where the public mind shall rest in the belief that it is in course of ultimate extinction . . ." ["House Divided" speech, June 16, 1858, Roy P. Basler, ed., *The Collected Works of Abraham Lincoln*, II (New Brunswick, 1953), p. 461].

2. For a sample pamphlet exchange, see Lysander Spooner, *Unconstitutionality of Slavery* (Boston, 1845), and Wendell Phillips, *Review of Lysander Spooner's Essays on the Unconstitutionality of Slavery* (Boston, 1845).

3. On this point, see W. S. Jenkins, *Pro-Slavery Thought in the Old South* (Chapel Hill, 1935), and William Stanton, *The Leopard's Spots* (Chicago, 1960).

4. See, for example, L. Maria Child, *The Right Way, the Safe Way* (New York, 1860). After the Civil War began, the abolitionists modified their stand on compensation—thus showing that "pragmatic flexibility" of which they were supposedly devoid. In the winter of 1861, Garrison got up a petition to compensate loyal slaveholders, and in 1862 most abolitionists gave enthusiastic approval to plans for compensated emancipation in the District of Columbia.

5. For sample abolitionist writings advocating gradual freedom, after apprenticeship, see L. Maria Child, *Anti-Slavery Catechism* (Newburyport, 1836), pp. 18–19; J. A. Thome and J. W. Alvord to T. Weld, February 9, 1836, *Letters of Theodore Dwight Weld, Angelina Grimke Weld, and Sarah Grimke, 1822–1844*, G. H. Barnes and D. L. Dumond, eds. (New York, 1934), I, 257; C. K. Whipple, "The Abolitionists' Plan," *The Liberty Bell* (1845). Even Garrison was at first willing to hold newly freed slaves in "the benevolent restraint of guardianship" (*Thoughts on African Colonization* [Boston, 1832], pp. 79–80). Donald Mathews has pointed out to me that Benjamin Lundy, in *The Genius of Universal Emancipation*, printed many

plans for gradual freedom (e.g., in the issues Sept. 5, 12, 15, 1825), but discouraged by the lack of response, Lundy finally discontinued doing so.

6. See, for example, James A. Thorne and J. Horace Kimball, *Emancipation in the West Indies* (New York, 1838), pp. 83, 85, 108.

7. For sample awareness of the dilemma inherent in "plans," see William Jay, *An Inquiry into . . . the American Colonization and Anti-Slavery Societies* (New York, 1835), p. 197; "Instructions of the American Anti-Slavery Society to Theodore Weld," February 20, 1834, in Barnes and Dumond, *Weld-Grimke Letters,* I, p. 126. For Wendell Phillips, see his speech "Daniel O'Connell" in Wendell Phillips, *Speeches, Lectures, and Letters* (Boston, 1891), Second Series, pp. 384–420.

8. I am not suggesting that all those who opposed immediatism were necessarily opposed to emancipation; no doubt some in opposition objected only to the means, not the end. I know of no way, though, to measure accurately the proportionate strength of the two groups, nor, more complicated still, the degree to which each actually understood its position.

9. See R. S. Peters, *The Concept of Motivation* (London, 1958); Gardner Lindzey, ed., *Assessment of Human Motives* (New York, 1958); Robert C. Birney and Richard C. Teevan, eds., *Measuring Human Motivation* (New York, 1962); Erich Fromm, "The Revolutionary Character" in *The Dogma of Christ* (New York, 1963).

Postscript 1999: Among the later works that speak to the same points, see Alfie Kohn, *The Brighter Side of Human Nature: Altruism and Empathy in Everyday Life* (BasicBooks: 1990); Matt Ridley, *The Origins of Virtue* (Penguin: 1997); Robert M. Sapolsky, *The Trouble with Testosterone* (Scribner: 1997); Eliott Sober and David Sloan Wilson, *Unto Others: The Evolution and Psychology of Unselfish Behavior* (Harvard Univ. Press: 1997); and Jonathan Lear, *Open Minded: Working Out the Logic of the Soul* (Harvard Univ. Press: 1998).

HISTORICAL INTERPRETATION AND THE POLITICS OF EVIDENCE

1. This essay, entitled "'Writhing Bedfellows' in Antebellum South Carolina: Historical Interpretation and the Politics of Evidence," was first published, in somewhat different form than it appears here, in the *Journal of Homosexuality* (Fall/Winter 1980–81).

2. Most of what is known about Withers can be found in two studies: William H. Freehling, *Prelude to Civil War: The Nullification Controversy in South Carolina, 1816–1836* (Harper & Row: 1965); and Charles Robert Lee, Jr., *The Confederate Constitutions* (Univ. of North Carolina Press: 1963).

3. See, for example, Clement Eaton, *The Mind of the Old South* (Louisiana State Univ. Press: 1964), p. 21. For more on Hammond, see: Charles S. Sydnor, *The Development of Southern Sectionalism* (Louisiana State Univ. Press: 1948); Allan Nevins, *The Ordeal of the Union* and *The Emergence of Lincoln* (Scribners: 1947; 1950); Avery Craven, *The Growth of Southern Nationalism* (Louisiana State Univ. Press: 1953); Holman Hamilton, *Prologue to Conflict* (Univ. Press of Kentucky: 1964); Steven A. Channing, *Crisis of Fear* (Simon & Schuster: 1970).

4. For reasons explained in the article, I've excerpted and published here only the erotic portions of the two letters. The remaining material is at any rate of little historical interest, dealing as it does with various mundane matters—news of friends, complaints about the Boredom of Life, youthful pontifications on public events.

5. If Hammond's letter is extant, its whereabouts is unknown.

6. Freehling contains the best description of South Carolina in this period and the life-style of its ruling class (see op. cit., especially pp. 11–24). Eaton is most helpful for biographical detail on Hammond himself. I've relied heavily on both books for the factual material in this section.

7. For additional details on Hammond's severity as a slave owner, see Gutman, op. cit., pp. 221–2; Freehling, op. cit., pp. 68–71; and Genovese, *Roll*, p. 455, 561. For more on Hammond's skills as a planter, see Nevins, *Ordeal*, pp. 482–3.

8. Wade, op. cit., p. 122; Gutman, op. cit., pp. 62, 572.

9. Eaton's account (op. cit., pp. 30 ff.), is blurred on the central question of whether (and to what degree) Hammond's seduction succeeded. In a book published after the appearance of this essay, Drew Faust has argued that the seduction consisted of Hammond repeatedly fondling his four teenage nieces in their "most secret and sacred regions" over a two-year period, until one of his nieces finally told her father, Wade Hampton, about it [Drew Faust, *James Henry Hammond and the Old South: A Design for Mastery*, Louisiana State Univ. Press: 1982]. Two other books on Hammond have appeared since I wrote this essay, both by Carol Bleser: *The Hammonds of Redcliffe* (Oxford: 1981), and *Secret and Sacred: The Diaries of James Henry Hammond, A Southerner Slaveowner* (Oxford: 1988). In the latter (p. 5), Bleser dismisses my essay as "a rather tortured reading," and denies any homoerotic implications in Hammond's and Withers's behavior.

10. Eaton, op. cit., pp. 31–32.

11. The importance of regional variations in sexual mores is marginally confirmed in the linkage Walt Whitman made (in a letter to John Addington

Symonds, Aug. 19, 1890): "My life, young manhood, mid-age, *times South* [italics mine], etc., have been jolly bodily. . . ".

12. Orlando Paterson [in his review of Bertram Wyatt Brown's *Southern Honor: Ethics and Behavior in the Old South*, in *Reviews in American History* (March 1984)] makes this provocative comment: "There is not a single reference to homosexuality in the work. I draw attention to this not out of intellectual fashion, but simply because anyone acquainted with the comparative ethnohistory of honorific cultures will be immediately struck by it. Homosexuality is pronounced in such systems, both ancient and modern. Southern domestic life most closely resembles that of the Mediterranean in precisely those areas which are most highly conducive to homosexuality. Does the author's silence imply its absence in the pronounced male bonding of the Old South?"

13. This seems the appropriate point to thank several other people whose advice or expertise proved of critical importance: Jesse Lemisch, Joan Warnow, Jonathan Weiss, Eric Foner, Martin Garbus and Ann Morgan Campbell. To prevent any one of them from being held accountable for actions and decisions for which I alone am ultimately responsible, I deliberately refrain from specifying which individual gave what advice or recommended which line of strategy.

MASTERS AND JOHNSON

1. For a detailed and comprehensive treatment of the reparative therapy movement, see Jack Drescher, *Psychoanalytic Therapy and the Gay Man* (The Analytic Press: 1998).

VIETNAM AND AMERICAN FOREIGN POLICY (1967)

1. Ernest R. May's "American Imperialism: A Reinterpretation," *Perspectives in American History*, vol. 1 (Charles Warren Center for Studies in American History at Harvard University: 1967), pp. 123–183.

THE HAVANA INQUIRY (1974)

1. This is a condensed and slightly revised version of my introduction to Hans Enzenberger's *The Havana Inquiry* (Holt, Rinehart and Winston: 1974). I'd like to thank several people for help in gathering material and formulating views. Their widely differing perspectives on Castro's Cuba should itself be a sufficient

way of saying that none of them is to be held responsible for the opinions of this essay: David Barkin, Meg Crahan, Rosalyn Higgins, Sandra Levinson, Kalman Silvert, Thomas C. Wallace and José Yglesias.

2. Samuel Flagg Bemis, *A Diplomatic History of the United States,* 3rd ed. (Henry Holt & Co.: 1950), p. 506.

3. The fullest treatment is Philip S. Foner's *History of Cuba and Its Relations with the United States,* 2 vols. (International Publishers: 1962–1963). A brief, useful summary is "Cuba: 100 Years of Struggle," a resource packet produced by The Center for Cuban Studies, 186 West 4th Street, New York, NY.

4. For more details on the episode, see Allan Nevins, *Ordeal of the Union,* vol. II, (Charles Scribner's Sons: 1947), pp. 347–363.

5. See Paul A. Baran and Paul M. Sweezy, *Monopoly Capitalism* (Monthly Review Press: 1966), and David Wise and Thomas B. Ross, *The Invisible Government* (Bantam Books: 1964).

6. See Richard R. Fagen, Richard A. Brody and Thomas J. O'Leary, *Cubans in Exile: Disaffection and the Revolution* (Stanford University Press: 1968).

7. Of the four working papers by Fox in the files of the Center for Cuban Studies (New York City), I found of particular value, "Honor, Shame and Women's Liberation in Cuba: Views of Working Class Emigré Men."

8. Hugh Thomas, *Cuba: The Pursuit of Freedom* (Harper & Row: 1971), p. 1360. The International Rescue Committee of New York estimated at the end of 1960 that as many as 30 percent of those who had left Cuba were laborers (Thomas, *Cuba,* p. 1354).

9. Desnoes's novel (New American Library: 1967) is the source of the profoundly moving Cuban movie "Memories of Underdevelopment," released in the United States in 1973.

10. K. S. Karol, *Guerrillas in Power* (Hill & Wang: 1970); René Dumont, *Cuba: Socialism and Development* (Grove: 1970); Allan Young, "The Cuban Revolution and Gay Liberation," in Allen Young and Karla Jay, eds., *Out of the Closets* (Douglas: 1972).

11. Thomas, *Cuba,* p. 1292. See also Frank McDonald's "Report from a Cuban Prison," a series of letters (1972–1973) printed by the Institute of Current World Affairs.

12. A friend who read a draft of this essay suggested it shows insufficient understanding of the role that such mass organizations as the "People's Tribunals" and the "Committees of Defense of the Revolution" have played in formulating policy. But "*ratifying* policy" still seems to me the more accurate phrase. The friend further suggested that since the failure of the 10-million-ton harvest in

1970 (and having taken seriously the criticism of such left-wing friends of the Revolution as K. S. Karol), Castro has made new efforts at democratization—though they do not seem apparent.

13. Thomas, *Cuba*, p. 1484.

Black Power and
the American Radical Tradition (1968)

1. "The Lair of the Black Panther," *The New Republic* (August 13, 1966).

2. I have not seen a clear assessment of the causes for defeat. The "Newsletter" from the New York Office of SNCC of November 1966 makes two points regarding the election: that according to a November report from the Southern Regional Council, 2,823 whites and 2,758 Negroes had registered in Lowndes County, though the white population eligible to vote was approximately 1,900; and that "the influential Baptist Alliance told Negroes throughout Alabama to vote the straight Democratic ticket."

3. On this point, see what to me are the persuasive arguments made by Pat Watters, "The Negroes Enter Southern Politics," *Dissent* (July–August 1966), and Bayard Rustin, "Black Power and Coalition Politics," *Commentary* (September 1966).

4. See, on this point, David Danzig, "In Defense of 'Black Power,'" *Commentary* (September 1966).

5. SNCC's "position paper" was printed in *The New York Times*, August 5, 1966. It is important to point out, however, that SNCC staffers have since denied the official nature of this paper; see, for example, Elizabeth Sutherland's letter to the editors of *Liberation* (November 1966), in which she insists that it was "not a SNCC position paper but a document prepared by a group of workers on one SNCC project." (She goes on to note that the *Times* refused to print a SNCC letter to this effect.) For other denials of the "racist" overtones in "Black Power," see Stokely Carmichael, "What We Want," *The New York Review of Books* (September 22, 1966), and C. E. Wilson, "Black Power and the Myth of Black Racism," *Liberation* (September 1966). But Andrew Kopkind's report on SNCC staff conferences ["The Future of Black Power," *The New Republic* (January 7, 1967)] makes me believe that the dangers of black racism are real and not merely the invention of frightened white liberals [see also James Peck, "Black Racism," *Liberation* (October 1966)].

6. For a discussion of "extremism" and the confused uses to which the word can be and has been put, see Howard Zinn, "Abolitionists, Freedom Riders, and the

Tactics of Agitation," *The Antislavery Vanguard,* Martin Duberman, ed. (Princeton, 1965), especially pp. 421–426.

7. For the shifting nature of SNCC see Howard Zinn, *SNCC: The New Abolitionists* (Boston, 1964); and Gene Roberts, "From 'Freedom High' to 'Black Power,'" *The New York Times,* September 25, 1966.

8. See Art Goldberg, "Negro Self-Help," *The New Republic* (June 10, 1967), and Abbie Hoffman, "Liberty House/Poor People's Corporation," *Liberation* (April 1967).

9. For more detailed discussions of the way in which the rhetoric of the New Left and the traditional Right have begun to merge, see Ronald Hamowy, "Left and Right Meet," *The New Republic* (March 12, 1966); Martin Duberman, "Anarchism Left and Right," *Partisan Review* (Fall 1966); Paul Feldman, "The Pathos of 'Black Power'," *Dissent* (Jan.–Feb. 1967); and Carl Oglesby and Richard Schaull, *Containment and Change* (Macmillan: 1967). Oglesby (on p. 167) seems actually to call for a merger between the two groups, arguing that both are "in the grain of American humanist individualism and voluntaristic associational action." He confuses, it seems to me, a similarity of rhetoric and means with a similarity of goals.

10. The only overall study of American anarchism is Eunice M. Schuster, *Native American Anarchism* (Northampton: 1932), but some useful biographies exist of individual figures in the movement; see especially Richard Drinnon, *Rebel in Paradise: A Biography of Emma Goldman* (Chicago: 1961). [Since this essay was published, the number of sources has expanded considerably; see, for example, Candace Falk, et al. *Love, Anarchy, and Emma Goldman* (Holt, Rinehart and Winston: 1984).]

11. Richard J. Barber, "The New Partnership: Big Government and Big Business," *The New Republic* (Aug. 13, 1966). But see, too, Alexander Bickel's article in the same journal for May 20, 1967.

12. Kay Boyle, "On Black Power," *Liberation* (January 1967).

YOUNG RADICALS: POLITICS OR CULTURE?

1. *Postscript 1999*: This essay (and others in this section) were written some thirty years ago, and there has since been a huge outpouring of commentary on the issues central to the decade of the '60s. I have cited elsewhere in the Notes to this volume a significant number of major recent works, but it's worth adding here a few others of general interest: Terry H. Anderson, *The Movement and the Sixties* (Oxford: 1995); David Farber, ed., *The Sixties* (Univ. of North Carolina Press: 1994); and Doug Rossinow, *The Politics of Authenticity* (Columbia Univ. Press: 1998).

FEMINISM AND GAY MEN

1. *Postscript 1999:* Over the past twenty years, the numbers have risen significantly: 10 states have banned sexual orientation discrimination (though some of the bans, especially those issued through executive order, apply only to the public sector); and 21 states plus the District of Columbia include sexual orientation in hate crime statutes. As well, there are some 165 city ordinances supporting gay rights, and as of late 1998, 5 state courts had rejected anti-sodomy laws. On the other hand, a number of "pro-gay" state, county and city laws have been repealed through referendum ballots. [See, Arthur S. Leonard, "Sexual Orientation Discrimination: A Growing Issue in State and Local Law," in *Contemporary Issues in Labor and Employment Law*, B. Stein, ed., Proceedings of the New York University 46th Annual National Conference on Labor (Little, Brown: 1994.)]

In the 1970s, when the first antigay ballot battles took place, a mere 29% of the voters reacted positively to gay civil rights legislation. In the early nineties, the percentage had risen to 39%. By 1998 it was at 47%. For a subtle analysis of mainstream public opinion on gay and lesbian Americans, see Alan S. Yang, *From Rights to Wrongs*, a 1998 publication of the Policy Institute of the National and Lesbian Task Force.

However, the glass is still decidedly half-empty. The continuing high levels of opposition to homosexuality among middle-class Americans is spelled out in Alan Wolfe's *One Nation, After All* (Viking: 1998), though given its small sample, the book has been much-controverted. A 1996 Gallup Poll revealed that nearly half of the Americans surveyed believed that the traditional family structure (a breadwinner father and a homemaker mother) remained the ideal family unit. (See the summary of the study in *The New York Times*, March 27, 1996.)

2. *Postscript 1999:* Over the past twenty years antagonism between lesbian-feminists and gay men seems to have abated. Part of the story is the compassionate way lesbians reached out to their afflicted brother from the earliest days of the AIDS crisis. Another part of the story is that among the younger generation, lifestyle divisions are less sharp. From the early '80s onwards, there's been a greater celebration among lesbians of depoliticized lust, as well as the public emergence of S/M dykes and other forms of sexual expression once thought confined to gay males. One could say that as lust became a more central attribute of lesbianism (the heralding of "bad girls"), the '70s lifestyle of gay men became more like a role model than an anathema. And all this at a time when gay male sexuality itself, due to AIDS, was in retreat from erotic adventuring. Thus younger gay men and lesbians have come to more closely resemble each other in lifestyle than had earlier been the case.

At the same time, it remains true, and is rightly resented. That so many gay white men continue to act as it race and gender are not important variables in defining gayness: and have not affected political formation priorities. Moreover, issues relating to bisexuality and transgenderism have increasingly surfaced, providing grounds aplenty for ongoing tension and hostility within the varied gender and sexual communities that constitute "the gay movement."

For a sense of both of the historical shifts that have taken place and the current content of debate, see, especially, the writing of Michael Bronski, Judith Butler, Leslie Feinberg, Wayne Koestenbaum, John Preston, Michael Warner and Ricki Ann Wilchens. Other work of particular relevance to these issues includes: Clausen, *Apples and Oranges* (Houghton Mifflin: 1999); Joshua Gamson, "Messages of Exclusion: Gender, Movements, and Symbolic Boundaries," *Gender & Society* (April 1997); Natasha Gray, "Bored with the Boys: Cracks in the Queer Coalition," *NYQ* (April 26, 1992); Donald E. Hall and Maria Pramaggiore, *RePresenting Bisexualitites* (NYU Press: 1996); Eric Rofes, "Roots of 'Horizontal Hostitilty' in the Lesbian & Gay Community," *Gay Community News* (June 1994); Matt Rottnek, *Sissies and Tomboys* (NYU Press: 1999); Ruth L. Schwarz, "New Alliances, Strange Bedfellows: Lesbians, Gay Men, and AIDs," in Arlene Stein, ed., *Sisters, Sexperts, Queers* (Plume: 1993); Susan Stryker, ed., *The Transexual Issue, Journal of Lesbian and Gay Studies* 4, No. 2, (1998).

SEX AND THE MILITARY: THE MATLOVICH CASE

1. *Postscript 1999* In the years since this essay was written, Money's work is no longer considered as authoritative as it then was, or even persuasive. Indeed, as regards the "famous example" I cite below, it has recently been revealed (*The New York Times,* March 14, 1997) that the accidentally castrated male baby was *not* successfully reassigned as a female. Two researchers, Dr. Milton Diamond and Dr. H. Keith Signundeson did an in-depth follow-up and found anything but a success story. It turns out that the boy renounced his female identity at age fourteen, is today living as a man, and underwent extensive surgery in an attempt to reconstruct his genitals. A mounting debate has also been underway about the nature and treatment of intersexuality. For more details, see "Gender Limbo," *Newsweek,* May 19, 1997; Cheryl Chase, "Hermaphrodites with Attitude: Mapping the Emergence of Intersex Political Activism," *GLQ* 4, No. 2 (1998); and the pioneering work of Suzanne Kessler ("Creating Good-Looking Genitals in the Service of Gender"), in *A Queer World,* Martin Duberman, ed. (NYU Press: 1997).

2. *Postscript 1999*: The resurgence of biological "explanations" for human behavior in general, and sexual orientation in particular, has greatly accelerated in the past twenty years and has produced a large, hotly contested literature. For a sample of those arguing for the persuasiveness of a biological explanation, see, Simon LeVay, *Queer Science* (MIT Press: 1996); Dean Hamer and Peter Copeland, *The Science of Desire* (Simon & Schuster: 1994); William Wright, *Born That Way* (Knopf: 1998). For a sample of those challenging the biological argument, see Janice M. Irvine, *Disorders of Desire* (Temple: 1990); Vernon A. Rosario, ed., *Science and Homosexualities* (Routledge: 1997); the four essays in "Part Three: Genes, Hormones, and the Brain," in *A Queer World*, Martin Duberman, ed. (NYU Press: 1997); and Bruce Bagemihl, *Biological Exuberance: Animal Homosexuality and Natural Diversity* (St. Martin's Press: 1999). For further discussion, see the introduction to this volume.

3. *Postscript 1999*: The shift in attitude within the churches has accelerated over the past twenty years, but the degree of change varies widely from denomination to denomination. Among Reform Jews, both the Reconstructionist Movement and the Central Conference of American Rabbis now admit openly acknowledged, sexually active homosexuals into its rabbinate. And the Episcopal church has for some time been welcoming of openly gay or lesbian congregants. However, when Episcopal Bishop Walter C. Righter ordained a gay man as a deacon in 1995, ten of his fellow bishops formally accused him of heresy and he had to face trial in a church court; it ruled he had *not* violated the church's "core doctrine" (*The New York Times*, Aug. 28, 1996). On the other hand, under the current Pope (who has declared homosexuality "an objective disorder"), the Roman Catholic church no longer allows chapters of DIGNITY—an organization that works for a reconciliation of Catholic gays with the church—to meet in church buildings. Yet even within Catholicism, there is a progressive counter-movement exemplified by "liberation theology."

Speaking more generally still, the last few decades have seen the rise of feminist theology, with its refusal automatically to view the Bible as a source of divine revelation, and its spirited characterization of both Old and New Testaments as works centrally shaped to sacralize patriarchy. (See, for example, the many books by Elaine H. Pagels, Mary Daly, Rosemary Radford Reuther and Elisabeth Schussler Fiorenza.)

As of 1996, only two Protestant denominations—the 1.5-million-member United Church of Christ, and the much smaller Unitarian-Universalist Association—have allowed noncelibate homosexuals to be ordained. Nonetheless, most Protestant denominations are, at a cautious pace, at least openly debating the issue of homosexuality for the first time—even if the outcome of those debates has thus far led to little or no change in official attitudes. Among Presbyterians there has been some growth in the progay More Light Churches, but in June 1999 the General Assembly, the top policy-making body of the Presbyterian church (USA) defeated by a vote of 319 to 198 an effort to repeal the law that bars the ordination of gay men and lesbians. In 1996 the second largest (after the Baptists) Protestant denomination, the United Methodist church, decisively upheld its traditional doctrine that homosexuality is "incompatible with Christian teaching." In March 1998, the Rev. Jimmy Creech, who had blessed the union of two men at his Methodist church in Omaha, was narrowly acquitted in a church trial. But the following year, the Rev. Greg Dell, who had blessed the union of two men in his church in Chicago was not only convicted in a church trial, but lost his pulpit. Four Baptist and two Lutheran congregations have been (as of 1999) formally expelled for announcing that they would welcome homosexuals as members and would no longer teach that homosexual activity was a sin.

The Black Response to
William Styron's *The Confessions of Nat Turner*

1.*Postscript 1999*: Though Aptheker's work has remained controversial, it has found some new respect among historians in the thirty years since this essay was written. Eugene D. Genovese, for example, while noting Aptheker's "exaggerations and doubtful evaluations," believes that he unearthed enough new evidence of "physical resistance" on the part of the slaves to compel "a new departure in the historiography." Yet Genovese nonetheless concludes that slave insurrections in the Old South "did not compare in size, frequency, intensity, or general historical significance with those of the Caribbean or South America" [*Roll, Jordan, Roll,* (Pantheon: 1974), pp. 587–588]. Similarly, "oral tradition" is today held in far greater esteem, and is considered far more valuable, than was earlier the case. [See, for example, Ira Berlin et al., *Remembering Slavery,* (The New Press: 1998).]

As for the seeming "apathy or acquiescence" mentioned in the next paragraph, John Hope Franklin and Loren Schweninger's recent *Runaway Slaves: Rebels on the Plantation* (Oxford Univ. Press: 1999) finally dispels that once-common notion. The authors' many years of research in civil court records, divorce petitions and newspaper advertisements make it clear that brutal punishment was commonplace on the plantation and that slaves responded with routine insubordination (deliberately slowing down work, breaking farm tools and so forth) if not often through open insurrection. Moreover, attempts at escape were frequent; Franklin and Schweninger estimate that *each year* some 50,000 of the 2 million adult slaves tried to run away, though few (perhaps 5 percent) succeeded.

This searing and persuasive indictment of the slave system is further corroborated by another recent volume, Philip D. Morgan's *Slave Counterpoint: Black Culture in the Eighteenth-Century Chesapeake and Lowcountry* (Univ. of North Carolina Press: 1998). Morgan makes a number of needed distinctions between Chesapeake and Lowcountry and between eighteenth- and nineteenth-century slavery, but draws the general conclusion—contra Fogel and Engerman [see "The Latest Word on Slavery in the United States (1974)," this volume]—that slaves had insubstantial diet and housing and limited clothing or material goods. Morgan further suggests that if the "austere patriarchialism" of the eighteenth century gave way in some areas to a more "mellow paternalism" in the nineteenth, that shift was accompanied by an "extreme" deprivation of freedom of movement *and* a "matter-of-fact" attitude toward the infliction of violent punishment on slaves—even though slavery *could* "encompass within it warm and caring human relationships" between masters and slaves.

The New (1997) Scholarship on Race Relations

1. For more information and discussion, see "Reclaiming Integration," a special section of articles in *The Nation* (Dec. 14, 1998), and William G. Bowen and Derek Bok's *The Shape of the River: Long-term Consequences of Considering Race in College and University Admissions*—a superb work, deeply researched, calmly argued, and to my mind unanswerable in its defense of affirmative action.

2. For these figures—and a great deal more—see Jennifer L. Hochschild's important book, *Facing Up to the American Dream: Race, Class, and the Soul of the Nation* (Princeton Univ. Press: 1996).

3. See Richard B. Freeman's summary of the many studies that have concluded (even as early as 1986) that "young black men from the inner city are as willing to work . . . as are white youth . . . at jobs and with wages that are comparable to those received by their white counterparts"; there is no doubt that "black youth clearly want to work . . ." (*The New York Times,* July 20, 1986). See also, Katherine Newman, *No Shame in My Game: The Working Poor in the Inner City* (Knopf: 1999).

4. For a more detailed discussion of these issues, see "The Divided Left: Identity Politics Versus Class," the concluding essay in this volume.

The (Contested) New History of Gays and Lesbians

1. Portions of this piece have been taken from two speeches I gave, a week apart, at the Museum of Natural History in New York City in February 1991. In those speeches I sometimes quoted directly from my article, "Reclaiming the Gay Past," *Reviews in American History* (Dec. 1988), as supplemented by the Introduction I coauthored with Martha Vicinus and George Chauncey, Jr., to our anthology, *Hidden From History: Reclaiming the Gay and Lesbian Past* (Dutton: 1989). The larger part of this essay consists of combined excerpts from two articles of mine: *The Nation* (July 5, 1993); *The Advocate* (December 24, 1996).

2. For recent samples of this new scholarship, see Martin Duberman, ed., *A Queer World* and *Queer Representations* (both published by NYU Press: 1997); Roger N. Lancaster and Micaela di Leonardo, *The Gender/Sexuality Reader* (Routledge: 1997); and Robert A. Nye, *Sexuality* (Oxford: 1999). For the difficulties many gays and lesbians have with the concept of "fluid" sexuality, see Tim Edwards, "Queer Fears: Against the Cultural Turn," *Sexualities* (Sage: 1998).

3. See, for example, Carroll Smith-Rosenberg, "The Female World of Love and Ritual: Relations Between Women in Nineteenth-Century America," SIGNS (Autumn 1975); Leila Rupp, "Imagine My Surprise: Women's Relationships in Historical Perspective," *Frontiers* (Fall 1981), reprinted in revised form in Duberman et al., *Hidden from History,* (Dutton: 1989); Martha Vincinus, "Distance and Desire: English Boarding School Friendships, 1870–1920," SIGNS 9 (1984), reprinted in revised form in *Hidden from History;* and Nancy Sahli, "Smashing: Women's Relationships Before the Fall," *Chrysalis* (Summer 1979).

4. See Jonathan Ned Katz, *The Invention of Heterosexuality* (Dutton: 1995).

In Conclusion
The Divided Left: Identity Politics vs. Class

1. Jesse Lemisch, "Angry White Men On the Left," *Radical Historians Newsletter,* No. 74 (June 1996).

2. Eric Hobsbawn, "Identity Politics and the Left," *New Left Review,* No. 217 (May/June 1996).

3. *The New York Times,* Dec. 1, 1996. For one of the more cogent recent books in a long list of works revealing the tax evading practices of the rich, see Russell Mokhiber and Robert Weissman, *Corporate Predators* (Common Courage: 1999).

4. For a more detailed argument on affirmative action, see, in this volume, "The 'New' Scholarship (1997) on Race Relations."

5. For Ellen Willis's comments, see *The Nation* (June 29, 1998), and for Barbara Ehrenreich's, see *The Progressive* (July 1996).

6. In a provocative new book [*From the Ashes of the Old: American Labor and America's Future* (Houghton Mifflin: 1998)], Stanley Aronowitz excoriates organized labor for having long since ceased to be a progressive force. In the seventies, Aronowitz points out, many unions had still made no significant efforts to integrate, and were as well, scornful of both the feminist and gay movements. The election of John Sweeney to the presidency of the AFL-CIO in 1996, and the organization's announcement of new progressive policies, has recently raised hopes among some that organized labor is on the verge of regaining a social conscience—especially since a new generation of labor activists has emerged on some campuses (See "Postscript 1999," this volume, pp. 253–54). On Oct. 3, 1996, there was a labor/academic teach-in at Columbia University that drew an unexpected 2,500 people; for reports on the event, see *Radical Historians Newsletter*, No. 75 (Dec. 1996).Yet we have also had indications and warnings that "the Sweeney years" may not prove as notable a break with the past as many hope. Steve Early, for example, has pointed to the discrepancy between the new AFL's rhetoric and some of its practices: to the fact that the federation's programs are "still top-down and staff-driven" and to the continuing gap between "union strength and internal democracy." The lack of a greater rank-and-file role in AFL decision-making, Early warns, "will prevent it from becoming an instrument of fundamental social change"—despite the larger number of new, diverse faces in the front office. If the membership itself does not have "any effective control over the functioning of the organization, particularly its finances, that's a formula for decay and decline—sooner or later." For a counter, more sanguine, argument about labor's prospects, see Michael Kazin, "Don't Mourn for Labor," *The Nation* (March 1, 1999), in which Kazin emphasizes the AFL-CIO's promising focus on signing up new members (400,000 in 1998 alone) and the resurgent grass-roots energy that has led to hundreds of localized networks.

INDEX